Cracking the LSAT

with Practice Tests on CD-ROM

ADAM ROBINSON AND
KEVIN BLEMEL

2005 EDITION

RANDOM HOUSE, INC.
NEW YORK

www.PrincetonReview.com

Princeton Review Publishing, L.L.C.
2315 Broadway
New York, NY 10024
E-mail: booksupport@review.com

Originally published by Villard Books, a division of Random House, Inc., 1989.

ISBN: 0-375-76412-7
ISSN: 1549-6910

Editor: Ellen Mendlow
Production Editor: Patricia Dublin
Production Coordinator: Jennifer Arias

Manufactured in the United States of America.

10 9 8 7 6 5 4 3 2 1

2005 Edition

ACKNOWLEDGMENTS

A successful LSAT program is a collaborative effort. We'd especially like to thank Tricia McCloskey, Jeff Rubenstein, Dan Edmonds, John Sheehan, Lindsey van Wagenen, Mark Sawula, Dave Schaller, Timothy Wheeler, Jim Reynolds, Omar Goodleg, Adam Frank, and Adam Landis for their suggestions and contributions. An extra thanks to contributing author Kevin Blemel, to Fritz Stewart and to Bob Spruill for their expertise, and to Production Editor Patricia Dublin and Production Coordinator Jennifer Arias.

A very special thanks to Oliver Hart, professor of economics at M.I.T., and to Debora Davies and the folks at *Columbia Law Review* for their generous permission to quote an excerpt from an article by Professor Hart.

Finally, we'd like to thank all those who have taught us everything we know about taking tests—our students.

Special thanks to Adam Robinson, who conceived of and perfected the Joe Bloggs approach to standardized tests and many of the other successful techniques used by The Princeton Review.

CONTENTS

Dear Prospective Law Student:

Congratulations on your decision to purchase The Princeton Review's *Cracking the LSAT*. This self-study guide will help you achieve your highest possible score on the LSAT—arguably the most significant single factor in law school admissions decisions.

While most applicants understand the importance that the LSAT plays in their law school applications many are unaware that the score they receive can have far-reaching consequences—often determining much more than just which law school they will attend. For example, many law schools consider LSAT scores when awarding merit scholarships and grants. Given that the average full-time *juris doctor* degree costs more than $125,000, a high score on the LSAT may well translate into tens of thousands of dollars in financial aid that can significantly reduce your law school debt upon graduation.

The LSAT purports to gauge your reading comprehension, reasoning, and analytical skills in an effort to predict your ability to survive a demanding law school curriculum. Those who hone their LSAT test-taking skills usually score the highest. Indeed, a strong LSAT score can be as much an indication of a strong work ethic as it is of intellect.

So invest the time and master The Princeton Review's proven test-taking strategies. While that investment begins with *Cracking the LSAT*, it should not end there. In order to truly benefit from this book, you should also visit The Princeton Review's website, (www.PrincetonReview.com/cracking), to take advantage of the online resources available to purchasers of this book. There you will be able to supplement your self-study with free online exercises and tutorials, including additional practice questions and score reports based upon the practice tests you will take.

The Princeton Review's master instructors are devoted to sharing their wisdom and inspiration so that you can conquer the LSAT. *Cracking the LSAT* and its online supplement are the fruits of their efforts. I firmly believe that The Princeton Review, with its personalized instruction and test-taking techniques, is the very best way for you to prepare comprehensively for the LSAT.

Good Luck!

Sincerely,

Donald W. Macaulay, Esq.
President & Founder, Law Preview

GET MORE FROM *CRACKING THE LSAT* BY USING OUR FREE ONLINE TOOLS

Buyers of this book receive access to the latest in interactive test-preparation tools. The **CD-ROM** included at the back of the book allows you to take four full-length LSAT tests at your computer. Upon completion of each test, you'll receive a personalized score report that will show you your strengths and weaknesses. Afterward, you'll know exactly where you should be concentrating your preparation efforts.

Furthermore, by buying this book you'll also get a subscription to *Cracking the LSAT's* **online companion course**. Go to www.PrincetonReview.com/cracking to register for all the free online services we offer to help you improve your test score and find the right law school. Once you've logged on, you'll be able to:

- **Learn Key Test-Taking Skills Through Our Distance Learning Tools.** Some of the key lessons of *Cracking the LSAT* will be even clearer after you've spent a few hours seeing and hearing them presented online. You'll also have online access to full-length LSAT practice tests.
- **Analyze Your Performance on the Tests in this Book.** By logging on to our site and submitting your answers to the diagnostic tests in this book, you can get personalized score reports that will help you focus your energy on specific areas of weakness.
- **Research and Apply to the Best Colleges for You.** Through www.PrincetonReview.com, our award-winning school search site, you can access our complete library of information about U.S. law schools, manage your application process, and even apply electronically.

You're in Complete Control

Here's what you'll see once you've registered:

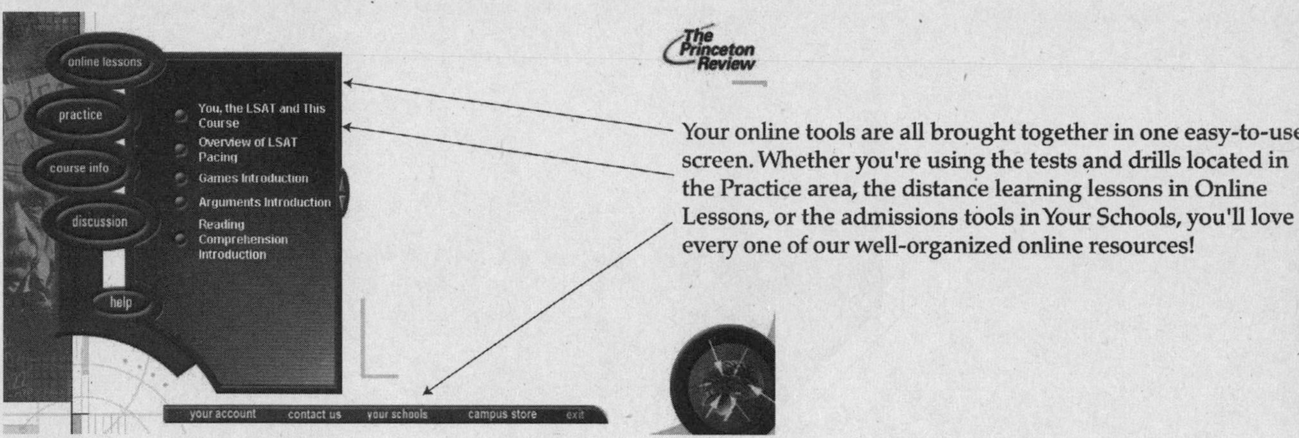

Your online tools are all brought together in one easy-to-use screen. Whether you're using the tests and drills located in the Practice area, the distance learning lessons in Online Lessons, or the admissions tools in Your Schools, you'll love every one of our well-organized online resources!

Reading Your Score Report

After you take your extra diagnostic exams, here's how to use your score report:

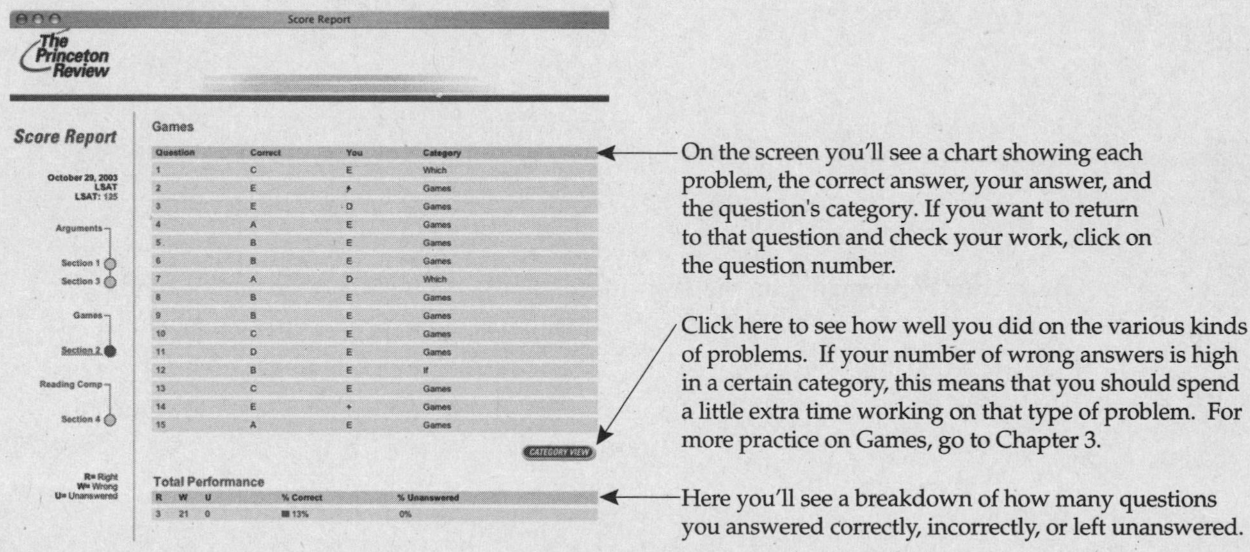

Games

Question	Correct	You	Category
1	C	E	Which
2	E	*	Games
3	E	D	Games
4	A	E	Games
5.	B	E	Games
6	B	E	Games
7	A	D	Which
8	B	E	Games
9	B	E	Games
10	C	E	Games
11	D	E	Games
12	B	E	If
13	C	E	Games
14	E	*	Games
15	A	E	Games

Total Performance

R	W	U	% Correct	% Unanswered
3	21	0	13%	0%

On the screen you'll see a chart showing each problem, the correct answer, your answer, and the question's category. If you want to return to that question and check your work, click on the question number.

Click here to see how well you did on the various kinds of problems. If your number of wrong answers is high in a certain category, this means that you should spend a little extra time working on that type of problem. For more practice on Games, go to Chapter 3.

Here you'll see a breakdown of how many questions you answered correctly, incorrectly, or left unanswered.

ONLINE TOOLS

1

General Information and Strategies

"CRACKING" THE LAW SCHOOL ADMISSION TEST

In this chapter, we're going to give you an overall preparation plan for the LSAT. We hope you've bought this book at least a few months before the date of the LSAT you plan to take, so you'll have time to (a) actually follow the suggestions we make below, including working on actual LSAT tests released by the Law School Admission Council (LSAC); (b) work through (at least twice) the specific problems in Chapters 2, 3, and 4; and (c) complete both practice tests at the end of this book.

If you've bought this book only a few weeks before the LSAT, read through this chapter and absorb the test-taking tips that we give you, then work through Chapters 2, 3, and 4. Finally, try to take at least one of the tests in the back of the book.

If you've bought (or are merely opening) this book for the first time only a few *days* before the LSAT, well, we admire your bravado. Take a complete test to see approximately what you would score on a real LSAT. If it's more than five or six points below where you want to be, consider skipping the test and taking it at a later date. The best way to improve your score dramatically is to work steadily on hundreds of problems throughout the course of a few months. Remember, the title of this book is *Cracking the LSAT,* not Crashing the LSAT.

The Structure of This Chapter

Before we hit you with some general test-taking techniques, we want to make sure that you know all that we know about the LSAT itself. We'll start with a few pages' worth of information on the test—make sure you read all this info carefully so you'll know exactly what you're up against.

REMINDER: Order the *LSAT Registration Bulletin* from LSAC—you can download a copy or get one mailed to you by going to their website (www.lsac.org) or by calling them at 215-968-1001.

In addition, you'll want a copy of the *LSAT Registration Bulletin* from the Law School Admissions Council (LSAC)—you can get one mailed to you by calling them at 215-968-1001, or by going to their website (www.lsac.org) where you can also simply download it. The *Bulletin* has much more information than we give you here, such as order forms for signing up for the LSAT and for the Law School Data Assembly Service (LSDAS), forms for obtaining previously released LSATs, and a full-length, previously administered LSAT.

WHAT IS THE LSAT?

The LSAT is a 100- or 101-question, tightly timed multiple-choice test. By *tightly timed*, we mean that the test is designed so that the "average" test taker (someone scoring around the fiftieth percentile) should not be able to comfortably complete all the questions in the time allotted. The LSAT also includes a 30-minute essay. The LSAT is required by every single American Bar Association (ABA)–certified law school in the United States—if you want to go to a U.S. law school, you not only have to take the LSAT, but you also have to do pretty well on it.

When Is the LSAT Given?

The LSAT is administered four times a year—February, June, September/October, and December. Typically, students applying for regular fall admission to a law program take the test either the previous June or October. You can take the test in December, but many schools will have filled at least a portion of their seats by the time your scores hit the admissions office. See Chapter 7 on Law School Admissions for more information about when and how to apply to law school.

HOW IMPORTANT IS THE LSAT?

Not only is the LSAT required by every single ABA-approved U.S. law school, but it is also weighted very heavily in the admissions process. For many schools, it is weighted just as heavily as (or even more heavily than) your undergraduate grade point average (UGPA). That's the number that you worked very hard on in college, remember? The fact that a four-hour, multiple-choice test—one that is a questionable indicator of how well you'll do in law school—is considered as important as your undergraduate performance seems unjust. We wouldn't be surprised if you feel the same way.

HOW IS THE LSAT SCORED?

The LSAT is scored on a scale of 120 to 180, with the mean score being a 151. You need to get about 56 questions right (out of 101) to get that mean score of 151, which means you need to bat about 55 percent. Very few people get a perfect score, mainly because the test is designed so that very few people can answer all the questions, let alone do so in the time allotted.

Along with your LSAT score, you will receive a percentile ranking. This ranking compares your performance with that of everyone else who has taken the LSAT for the previous five years. Because a 151 is the average LSAT score, it would give you a percentile ranking of approximately 50. A score of 156 moves you up to a ranking of 70. A 161 pulls you up to a ranking of 85. And any score over 166 puts you above 95 percent of all the LSAT takers.

As you can see, small numerical jumps (five points or so) can lead to a difference of as much as 20 percentile points. That means you're jumping over 20 percent of all test takers if, on your first practice test, you score a 150, but on the real test, you score a 155. Small gains net big results.

The following table summarizes how many questions you can skip or miss and still reach your LSAT goal. Notice that 93 percent of those taking the test make *more* than nineteen errors. Take this into consideration if you're one of those testers who believes it's necessary to try to answer each and every question.

Approximate Number of Errors (out of 101)	LSAT Score	Percentile Rank
2	180	approx. 99^{++}
6	175	approx. 99^{+}
11	170	approx. 98^{+}
19	165	approx. 93^{+}
28	160	approx. 82^{+}
36	155	approx. 66^{+}
45	150	approx. 46^{+}
54	145	approx. 27^{+}
62	140	approx. 14^{+}
69	135	approx. 5^{+}

WHAT IS A GOOD SCORE?

A good score on the LSAT is one that gets you into the law school you want to attend.

Many people feel that you have to score at least a 160 to get into a "good" law school. That's pure myth. Remember, any ABA-approved law school has to meet very strict standards in terms of its teaching staff, library, and facilities. Most schools use the Socratic method to teach students basic law. Therefore, a student's fundamental law school experiences can be very similar no matter where he or she went to school—be it NYU or Quinnipiac Law School. Read through Chapter 7 for a much more comprehensive discussion of "good" scores and where to go to law school.

WHO'S RESPONSIBLE FOR THIS, ANYWAY?

The LSAT is brought to you by the wonderful folks at the LSAC, based in Newtown, PA. They work with the law schools and the ABA on many facets of the admissions process. You will register for the Law School Data Assembly Service (LSDAS), and that too is run by the LSAC. See Chapter 7 for a full discussion of this alphabet soup.

WHAT EXACTLY IS ON THE LSAT?

The LSAT is composed of five 35-minute multiple-choice sections and one 30-minute essay. Two of the five multiple-choice sections will be Arguments, one will be Games, and one will be Reading Comprehension. The remaining section (which is usually one of the first three to be administered) will be an experimental section, which will not count toward your score. During this section you will do 35 minutes of unpaid work for LSAC, allowing them to test out new types of questions on a representative audience (you can send them a bill after you've passed the Bar). This experimental section can be Arguments, Games, or Reading Comprehension.

A SAMPLE LSAT

For instance, your LSAT could look like this:

Section 1: Games (35 minutes)

Section 2: Experimental Reading Comprehension (35 minutes)

Section 3: Arguments (35 minutes)

10-minute break

Section 4: Reading Comprehension (35 minutes)

Section 5: Arguments (35 minutes)

30-minute Essay

As you can see, it's four hours of pure, unbridled joy. And because they fingerprint you and check your ID before the test begins, you can add another hour's worth of administrative mumbo-jumbo to that number. That's why we say that you should prepare very well for this test—so you only have to take it once. Then you can celebrate by burning all your LSAT prep materials in the nearest incinerator.

Make your preparation for the LSAT a priority so you'll only have to take it once.

The structure of an Arguments section

There will be two scored Arguments sections, each lasting 35 minutes, on your LSAT. Each section has between 24 and 26 questions. Sometimes, there will be two questions attached to one argument, so a section may contain 20 passages and still have 25 questions. Typically, the argument passages are no more than three or four sentences in length, but they can still be very dense and every word is potentially important. The arguments are not arranged in order of difficulty.

The structure of a Games section

You will be given four "logic games" in a 35-minute section. Each game will have a setup and a set of conditions or clues that are attached to it. Then five to seven questions will ask you about various possible arrangements of the elements in the game. The four games are not arranged in order of difficulty.

The structure of a Reading Comprehension section

You will be given four reading comprehension passages, of about 60 to 80 lines each, in a 35-minute section. Between five and eight questions will be attached to each passage. This is probably something you're familiar with from the SAT, the ACT, the CATs, and the other myriad standardized tests you might have taken over the years. Just like Games and Arguments, these passages are not arranged in any order of difficulty.

WHAT DOES ALL THIS TEST?

The LSAT tests a few different things; the most obvious is your ability to read a passage or argument very closely and figure out what the author is and is not saying. On some questions, you'll have to figure out what the author is *implying*, and on others, what the author is *assuming to be true*. You'll find that the ability to read efficiently and identify the salient parts of a passage will be very useful on the test. Games are a test of your ability to work with certain types of logical reasoning, including conditional logic and logical deduction. But the real question is whether or not what the LSAT tests is relevant to law school—and there is no solid evidence that it is. All the LSAT appears to test is a narrow range of logical thinking and a certain approach to reading.

The schools all have access to your complete undergraduate transcript, your academic and professional recommendations, and your essays. They could also ask for some of your undergraduate papers if they wanted to. However, all this reading would take too much time and cost admissions offices too much money—hence they've got a neat little shortcut in the form of the LSAT. When they combine this with your undergraduate grade point average, or UGPA, they generate your index, a number that allows them to quickly sort your application into one of a few preliminary piles to make the process of evaluating the increasing number of applications more efficient.

The overriding point is that it doesn't matter what it's testing—your goal is to do as well as possible on the LSAT and take it only once. That's just what we're going to show you how to do.

GENERAL STRATEGIES

Following are several key things you should do when taking any multiple-choice test, especially the LSAT. Make sure you follow all of these mantras—they are the sum of 20 years' worth of our experience in the rather surreal world of the standardized test.

TECHNIQUE #1: SLOW DOWN

Most LSAT takers see, for instance, that there are 27 reading comprehension questions attached to four fairly long passages. They figure that the best way to attack the section is to make sure that they "get a look at" every one of the questions. That's not necessarily the best approach. You'll need to do some detailed analysis to determine your best approach (something we'll work on a bit later). If you attempt to work all the questions, but get only half of them right because you couldn't work that quickly and still be accurate, you would have done better to answer only half the questions correctly and then guess the rest—simply playing the odds and guessing should give you one correct answer in every five to add points to your score.

If you've been scoring quite well on a given section (say 85 percent), you still might benefit by slowing down on tricky questions. By skipping a few questions that are difficult for you or time consuming, and by looking back to see if you've made any careless errors that could have been avoided if you had worked more deliberately, you ultimately will get more raw points, which equals a higher score.

Still others may find that they have time left over in a section to go back and check their work. If you fall into this camp, you will almost inevitably find that you made a couple of careless errors that could have been avoided. Even if you only get one or two more questions correct in a section, and guess randomly on any remaining questions, you'll get three or four more raw points per section. Multiply by four sections and you've gained twelve to sixteen more raw points, which will translate into five or six more points on your LSAT, depending on where you fall on the scale. And without having done any work! Any way you slice it, the vast majority of testers can benefit by fighting the urge to rush.

Your mantra here is: *I will fight the urge to rush. I will work more deliberately, making choices about where to concentrate my energies so I can answer questions more accurately and end up with a higher score.*

Technique #2: Fill in Every Bubble

Unlike the SAT, for instance, there is no penalty for guessing on the LSAT, meaning that no points are subtracted for wrong answers. Therefore, even if you don't get to work on every question in a section, you want to make sure to fill in the rest of the bubbles before time is called. Even if you do only 75 percent of the test, you'll get an average of five more questions correct by picking a "letter of the day" and bubbling it in on the remaining 25 questions. Make sure you watch the time carefully. Just to be safe, assume the proctor will cut you off two minutes early, and stop when ten minutes remain to bubble in every remaining blank space in the section. Then, during the last five minutes, you can change your answer on any questions you have time to work through individually.

This is a key concept that you should remember when you're taking the practice tests in the back of this book and when you're taking previously administered LSATs for practice. Some people want to wait until test day to bubble in questions they don't get to, thinking that they should see what their "real" score will be on practice tests. However, if you bubble in questions you didn't get to on your practice tests, *you are finding out what your "real" score would be.* And this will ensure that you won't forget to do it on test day—bubbling in randomly could be the difference between a 159 and a 161, for instance.

Your mantra here is: *I will always remember to bubble in answers for any questions I don't get to, thereby getting a higher score.*

Technique #3: Use Process of Elimination

One solace (perhaps) on multiple-choice tests is the fact that all the correct answers (*credited responses* in test-speak) will be in front of you. Naturally, they will each be camouflaged by four incorrect answers, some of which will look just as good as, and often better than, the credited response. But the fact remains that if you can clear away some of that jungle foliage, you'll be left staring at the credited response. Your goal is to clear away the underbrush and not to expect that the correct answers will just leap off the page at you. They won't. In fact, those choices that leap off the page at you are often very attractive *wrong* answers. Remember that the test writers have to be sure that they end up with a normal, or bell, curve when they administer the test. Making a wrong answer look very appealing (with a small and camouflaged flaw) is a great way to accomplish the goal of making sure that not everyone gets all the questions right.

You may find yourself saying "so what?" to this. The point is that using Process of Elimination may be a very different test-taking mindset from what you are used to. If you look first at the answer choices critically, with an eye toward trying to see what's wrong with them, you'll do better on almost any standardized test than by always trying to find the right answer. This is because, given enough time and creativity, you can justify the correctness of any answer choice that you find appealing. That skill may be useful in certain situations, but on the LSAT, creativity of that sort is worse than dangerous.

Using Process of Elimination will also give you better odds on every question. Every time you cross out an incorrect choice, your chances of answering the question correctly go up. If you eliminate even two of the choices, your chances have jumped from 20 percent to 33 percent. You'd much rather have 33 percent odds on a section of questions that perplex you than 20 percent odds on those same questions. Eliminating two choices on each will likely get you seven questions right; eliminating none and getting frustrated will likely only get you four. And remember that when you don't read carefully, and keep a flawed answer because you like it, your odds basically become zero.

Your mantra here is: *I will always try to eliminate answer choices using Process of Elimination, thereby increasing my chances on each question and getting a higher score.*

Technique #4: Be Prepared for Anything

You will be. Honest. You might not always feel that way, but you will be. True, you'll be nervous on test day, but a little nervousness is good because it can keep you focused. Just don't let this test psych you out. Remember that when you go into the test, you'll have worked through reams of LSAT problems and be a lot more prepared than all the other people who didn't put in the same amount of good work you did. You'll have absorbed all the techniques we've given you, and you'll be wise to all the tricks and traps that the LSAT can throw at you.

Therefore, don't let anything get to you. If the room is too cold for you, you've brought along a heavy shirt. If the room gets too warm, you've layered your clothing and can get comfortable. If the person sitting next to you is scratching away loudly or coughing nervously, you've practiced working in an environment with similar distractions and know how to tune them out and stay focused on the task at hand. If the proctor cuts your time short by a minute on one of the sections, you've already bubbled in the remaining choices with ten minutes left and aren't caught with your pants down, so to speak. Relax and stay focused; you're prepared for anything.

No matter how prepared you are, it may happen that you lose focus temporarily. If you find yourself getting distracted or anxious, take a moment to focus and move on with confidence.

Your mantra here is: *I'm fully prepared to succeed. Nothing will distract me on test day. Nothing.*

Technique #5: Practice Consistently, on Real LSATs

We've given you two full sample tests, plus explanations, to work through in the back of this book. Unfortunately, that's just the tip of the iceberg. You should be ordering *at least* four to six recent real tests from LSAC (www.lsac.org or 215-968-1001), if not more. Here's a rough study plan for you, over a two-month period:

Week 1: Order at least four to six real LSATs (the most recent ones) from LSAC. Take one of the LSATs timed. Have a friend proctor the test for you so it's as legitimate as possible.

Week 2: Work through the arguments chapter in this book; redo the arguments questions from the test you took in week 1.

Week 3: Work through the games chapter in this book; redo the games from the test you took in week 1. Take one of the the two practice LSATs in the back of this book.

Week 4:	Work through the reading comprehension chapter in this book; redo the reading comprehension passages from the test you took in week 1, and from the practice LSAT you took in week 3.
Week 5:	Work untimed through one of the real LSATs you've ordered from LSAC; time yourself on another one.
Week 6:	Review your mistakes in the work you did in week 5 and review the arguments, games, and reading comprehension chapters in this book. Work the specific problems again. Take the second test in this book.
Week 7:	Work untimed through another real LSAT you've ordered from LSAC; time yourself on another one (this should be the fifth real LSAT you've looked at).
Week 8:	Review all the general techniques in this book, and review any specific problems you might be having in arguments, games, and reading comprehension. Take one more real LSAT timed (using a friend as a proctor again) and analyze the hell out of it.

If you follow the plan above, you'll be extremely well prepared for the LSAT when it comes around. Don't worry too much about your scores on any of these practice tests, though. Your performance on the real LSAT should be a bit higher than any of your practice tests if you've been working steadily—you should be taking the LSAT at the culmination of your studies, and if you follow the plan above, you will be. Never let more than one, or at most two, days pass without looking at LSAT problems once you've started this workout. You'll waste valuable study time relearning techniques that you would have remembered if you had been practicing steadily. The best athletes and musicians are the ones who practice all the time—follow their example and you'll be totally prepared for the LSAT on test day.

Your mantra here is: *I will work steadily and consistently to master the techniques in this manual by practicing them with real LSATs that I've ordered from LSAC.*

Technique #6: Choose Your Battles

Not all questions on the LSAT are created equal, yet each is worth one raw point. Also, most test takers won't have enough time to finish all the questions and still maintain a high level of accuracy. Clearly it is in your best interest to choose carefully which questions to work through and, even more important, which questions to skip if you don't have time for them all. It is a matter of being able to *predict* which ones are good and which ones are bad *before* you've worked through them. By knowing the test and by knowing yourself, you will be able to make good *predictions* about which questions are your friends and which are your enemies before you start working on them; this will save you time, prevent frustration, and ultimately get you more points.

Your mantra here is: *I will fight my urge to work aimlessly through all of the questions in the order they're presented. Instead, I will make good decisions based on sound reasoning that will ultimately get me the most points.*

Technique #7: Keep Your Pencil Moving

During almost any standardized test, you can find people who have just completely lost their concentration. Losing concentration can take different forms, but we've all experienced it—staring at the same question for too long, reading and re-reading without really having anything sink in. Needless to say, you don't want to join this group of test zombies.

Using your pencil is a surprisingly easy way to stay focused and on task, and it can help to ensure that you're sticking with the method, visualizing information.

You should constantly be crossing out incorrect answers, circling the right answer before transferring the information to your bubble sheet, underlining and jotting down key pieces of information, taking notes, drawing diagrams, etc. Don't let the test take you—take the test on your own terms; attack the test. Keeping your pencil involved in the process prevents you from getting passive and losing touch. Stay engaged, stay aggressive, and stay confident.

Your mantra here is: *I will use my pencil to stay engaged with the test and maximize my performance.*

GENERAL STRATEGIES: SUMMARY

Take these mantras, learn them well and—most important—use them. They are the distilled wisdom of much test-taking expertise. Here they are again.

- I will fight the urge to rush and will work more deliberately, making choices about where to concentrate my energies so I can answer questions more accurately and end up with a higher score.
- I will always remember to bubble in answers for all the questions I don't get to, thereby getting a higher score.
- I will always look to eliminate answer choices using Process of Elimination, thereby increasing my chances on each question and getting a higher score.
- I'm fully prepared to succeed. Nothing will distract me on test day. Nothing.
- I will work steadily and consistently to master the techniques in this manual by practicing them on real LSATs that I've ordered from LSAC.
- I will fight my urge to work aimlessly through all of the questions in the order they are presented. Instead, I will make good decisions based on sound reasoning that will ultimately get me the most points.
- I will use my pencil to stay engaged with the test and maximize my performance.

Got 'em? Good. Now let's break the test down section by section.

2

Arguments

ARGUMENTS: HALF OF THE EXAM

That's right, for better or for worse, arguments (*logical reasoning* in LSAT-speak) questions make up half of the LSAT. For the past six years, there have either been 50 or 51 arguments questions on the LSAT. The good news is that if you can substantially increase your Arguments performance, you've taken a major step toward achieving the LSAT score that you need. How do you go about improving your Arguments score? Well, let's get right to it.

WHAT DOES THIS SECTION TEST?

Arguments test your ability to read closely and critically.

The Arguments section of the LSAT tests a very useful skill: the ability to read closely. Whether it tests your ability to read closely in the same way that law school will is something that no one knows the answer to (especially not the LSAT writers!). It also tests your ability to break an argument into parts, to identify flaws and methods of reasoning, and to find assumptions. Each argument is packed with issues that you have to identify to be able to get the correct answer. It's a minefield.

WHY IS THIS SECTION ON THE LSAT?

As we said above, it is testing a skill, or at least part of a skill, that will be useful in law school. Whether this is the best way to test the skill of reading closely is questionable—but here it is.

THE SECTION ITSELF

There are two Arguments sections on the LSAT. Each one will have between 24 and 26 questions, for a total of 50 arguments questions. Some arguments passages are followed by two questions, and although the test writers could probably generate several questions for each passage, most arguments passages are followed by a single question. The fact that you are presented with 25 or so arguments to do in a 35-minute period indicates that the Arguments section is just as time intensive as the Games or Reading Comprehension sections. If you took the advice in Chapter 1, you've already completed a real LSAT (preferably one from the last year or two), and you're familiar with the directions that appear at the start of each Arguments section. Here they are again:

> Directions: The questions in this section are based on the reasoning contained in brief statements or passages. For some questions, more than one of the choices could conceivably answer the question. However, you are to choose the best answer; that is, the response that most accurately and completely answers the question. You should not make assumptions that are by commonsense standards implausible, superfluous, or incompatible with the passage. After you have chosen the best answer, blacken the corresponding space on your answer sheet.

When you're ready to take the real LSAT you'll no longer need to read these directions—in fact, doing so would be a waste of time—but we can learn something from them. First, they tell us that the tasks we will be asked to perform will revolve around the reasoning used in each argument. They also indirectly tell us how important it is to stick to only the information presented on the page and not to consider any outside information. As for the part about picking the best answer, we'll get to that a little later on—first let's see how to simply and efficiently understand the reasoning of an LSAT argument.

ARGUMENTS: STRATEGIES

In the next few pages we'll look at the general strategies you need to use during the Arguments sections of the LSAT. These pages contain a few simple rules that you must take to heart. We've taught hundreds of thousands of students how to work through arguments, and these strategies reflect some of the wisdom we have gained in the process.

Always read the question first

Why should you read the question first? Because often the question will tell you what you should be looking for when you read the argument, whether it be the conclusion of the argument, a weak spot in the argument, how to diagram the argument, or something else. If you don't read the question until after the argument, you'll often find that you need to read the argument *again*—wasting valuable time—after you find out what your task is. The question is a tip-off, so use it.

Your mantra: *I will always remember to read the question first.*

Pay close attention

Reading arguments too quickly is a recipe for disaster. They look simple, right? Usually the arguments are merely three sentences, and the answer choices are just a sentence each. But their brevity can be deceptive, because very often complex ideas are presented in these sentences. The answers often hinge on whether you've read each word correctly—especially words like *not*, *but*, or *some*. You should be reading as closely as if you were deconstructing Shakespeare, not as if you were reading the latest thriller on the beach. So slow down, and pay attention!

Your mantra: *I will slow down and read the arguments carefully the first time.*

Choose your battles

What should you do if you read the first sentence of the argument and you don't understand what it's saying? Should you read sentence two? The answer is NO. Sentence two is not there to help you understand sentence one. Neither is sentence three. Neither are the answer choices—the answer choices exist to generate a bell curve, not to get you a 180. If you start reading an argument and you are confused, make sure you're focused and read the first sentence again—more slowly. If this still doesn't help, skip it. You've got other fish to fry. There are 24 to 26 arguments in the section—go do another one! It doesn't matter which argument questions you work on, just that you do good work on those that you choose to do. Don't waste time pounding your head against a frustrating argument if you don't understand what it's saying—you'll be less able to do any good work on that question. Also, you can jeopardize your performance on subsequent questions when you lose focus fighting with a frustrating question. The LSAT rewards confidence, so it's important to maintain a confident mindset. Working through difficult questions when there are other more manageable ones still available is not good form. Yes, you will feel as if you should finish the argument once you've invested the time to read part of it. But trust us, you'll benefit by leaving it. Remember, you can always come back to it later when there are no better opportunities to get points. Just mark the argument so you can find it if you have time later. It's not going anywhere. Come back to it when it won't affect other questions that are more likely to yield points. After all, that's what you're after—points.

Your mantra: *If I don't understand the first sentence of an argument, I will move on to another argument I do understand.*

Transfer your answers in groups

A classic question about standardized tests: Should I transfer my answers to the bubble sheet in groups, or transfer each answer after I've solved it? Our response: This section will have two or three arguments on the left-hand page and another two or three arguments on the right-hand page; work on all those questions, and then transfer your answers before you turn the page. If you've left one blank, circle the argument you left blank on your test page, but bubble in an answer on your answer sheet anyway (remember: there's no guessing penalty). Why should you do this? Because if you don't have time to come back to it, you've still remembered to put an answer on your sheet (most Princeton Review students favor either (B) or (C)—pick your favorite, your "letter of the day" if you will, and stick with it; there's no best letter, so just be consistent). And if you do have time to go back and work on arguments you skipped the first time around, you've got them handily marked in your test booklet. Then go back and change the answer (if necessary) on the answer sheet for that question.

Your mantra: *I will transfer my answers in groups, even bubbling in answers to questions that I'm skipping for the time being.*

With ten minutes left, transfer answers one at a time

When there are ten minutes left, begin to transfer your answers one at a time. You can even skip ahead for a moment and bubble in (B) or (C) (or whatever you've chosen) for all the remaining questions. That way, if the proctor erroneously calls time before he or she is supposed to, or if you simply know you aren't going to finish in time (these things can happen, you know), you've still got an answer on your sheet for every question.

Your mantra: *When ten minutes are left, I will transfer answers singly and make sure I have bubbled in an answer to every question.*

Breathe

Please remember to do this! You will of course feel some tension—some tension is good because it keeps your adrenaline pumping and can help keep you focused. But don't get so stressed out that you lose the thread of reality. So, after finishing each two-page spread of arguments and transferring your answers, take ten seconds, close your eyes, and inhale deeply three times. You'll invest only about a minute over the course of the entire section for these short breaks, but the payback will be enormous because they will help you to stay focused and to avoid careless errors. Trust us on this one.

Your mantra: *I will take a ten-second break after every five or six arguments.*

YOUR MANTRAS AND YOU

Here are your arguments mantras. Feel free to discard them after the LSAT is over.

I will always remember to read the question first.

I will slow down and read the arguments carefully the first time.

If I don't understand the first sentence of an argument, I will move on to another argument I do understand.

I will transfer my answers in groups, even bubbling in answers to questions that I'm skipping for the time being.

When ten minutes are left, I will transfer answers singly and make sure I have bubbled in an answer to every question.

I will take a ten-second break after every five or six arguments.

ARGUMENTS: HOW TO READ THEM

The first step in doing arguments is to make sure you're thinking critically when you read. Maybe you've had a lot of practice reading critically (philosophy and literature majors, please stand up) or maybe you haven't. And if you were a philosophy major in college but your favorite pastime has been watching "The Simpsons" for the past five years, you're probably out of practice. The next few pages show you on what level you need to be reading arguments to be able to answer questions correctly.

ARGUMENT BASICS

So, what is an argument? When people hear the term *argument* they often think of a debate between two people, with each party trying to advance his or her own view. People are often emotionally invested in an "argument," and thus arguments can become heated quickly. On the LSAT it's crucial that you don't develop such an emotional response to the information.

Here's a definition of arguments that applies in LSAT-land: "An argument is the *reasoned presentation of an idea* that is *supported by evidence* that is *assumed to be true.*" Notice that we've italicized certain words for emphasis.

Let's examine each of these in turn:

Reasoned presentation: By this we mean that the author of an LSAT argument has organized the information presented according to some kind of logical structure, however flawed the end result may be.

An idea: The point of the author's argument is really nothing more than an idea. Just because it's on the LSAT doesn't mean it's valid. In fact, the only way to evaluate the validity of an author's point is to examine the evidence in support of it and decide whether or not the author makes any leaps of logic between the evidence and his or her point.

Supported by evidence: All of the arguments on the test in which an author is advancing a point—there are a few exceptions to this, which we'll refer to as "passages" rather than "arguments"—have some kind of evidence presented in support of the author's point. That's just the way it works.

Assumed to be true: On the LSAT we are not allowed to question the validity of the *evidence* presented in support of a claim. In other words, we have to assume that whatever information the author presents as evidence is, in fact, true, even when the evidence includes arguable statements. We can question the validity of the *argument* by evaluating whether the evidence alone is able to support the point without making too big a leap.

Keep in mind that it is generally difficult to make an airtight case for a point of view if you only have three or four sentences in which to get that point across. Yet that's exactly the format of an argument on the LSAT. What can we take from that? The vast majority of the arguments you run across on this test are flawed in some way. That's a valuable thing to know because it reminds you to maintain a critical stance when evaluating these arguments. As you read an argument, always pay attention to *what* the author is trying to persuade you of, *how* the author is making the case, and *where* the author has lapsed in that attempt.

Your goal: point and reasons

TIP: If you can understand the reasoning of the person who wrote the argument, you've won half the battle, because most of the questions in Arguments revolve around the hows and whys of the arguer's reasoning.

Remember that arguments are constructed to persuade you of the author's idea. So, you should always get a firm grasp on the argument's main point (whether or not you think it's valid) and how the arguer structured the evidence to reach that point. If you understand the point and the reasoning behind it, you've won half the battle, because most of the questions in Arguments revolve around the "hows" and "whys" of the arguer's reasoning.

Sample argument #1

Let's start with something fairly simple. Even though this argument is simple, its structure is similar to that of many of the "real" LSAT arguments that you will see. Here it is:

> I have to move to Kentucky. I lost the lease on my New York apartment and my company is moving to Kentucky.

Okay, now what? We've got to make sure we understand the following things about this argument:

- the point that the author is trying to make
- the reason or reasons the author presents in support of his or her argument

> I have to move to Kentucky. I lost the lease on my New York apartment and my company is moving to Kentucky.

If we are able to identify the point and reasons, we are well on our way to being able to tackle an LSAT question about the argument. After reading the argument again, try to identify the following elements:

- author's point
- author's reasons

What's the author's point?
When looking for the author's point, try to figure out what it is that the author is attempting to persuade us of. Ultimately, he is trying to persuade us that he has to move to Kentucky. The rest of the information (about the lease and his company's move) is given in support of that conclusion. Often, the author's point includes signal words such as "thus," "therefore," or "so," or is a recommendation, a prediction, or an explanation of the evidence presented.

What are the author's reasons?
So, why does this guy think that he has to move to Kentucky? (1) He tells us that he lost the lease on his apartment in New York, and (2) his company is relocating to Kentucky. Each of these is one of the author's reasons to support his point. Now you know the author's point and the reasons behind it. This should be the first step you take in analyzing almost every argument on the LSAT. After taking a look at this argument, though, you might be thinking that this guy may not have thought this whole thing through. After all, couldn't he get another apartment in New York? And does he really have to stick with his company just because it's moving halfway across the country? If you're asking these kinds of questions, GOOD! Hold onto those thoughts for another few minutes—we'll come back to these questions soon.

What if I didn't properly identify the author's point?
Getting the author's point and understanding the reasoning behind it is crucial to effectively tackling an argument and performing whatever task the question demands of you. But let's face it: Not every argument will be as simplistic as this one. It would be a good idea to have a technique to use when you aren't sure of an argument's point. This test is called the "Why Test."

The Why Test

The Why Test should be applied every time you state the author's point or conclusion. Let's take the example above and see how it works. If you had said that the author's point was that he had lost his lease, the next step is to ask: *Why did the author lose his lease?* Well, we have no idea why the author lost his lease.

The Why Test:
A great way to make sure you've properly identified the author's main point.

There is absolutely no evidence in the argument to answer that question. Therefore, we can't have found the author's point. Every LSAT argument that has a point has at least one reason given in support of the point or conclusion. If you can't find one, you don't have the author's point.

Now, let's say that you had chosen the fact that the author's company was moving to Kentucky as the author's point. Once again, you would then ask: *Why is the author's company moving to Kentucky?* Once again, we have no idea. But notice what happens when we use the Why Test on the author's point: that he has to move to Kentucky. *Why does he have to move to Kentucky?* Now we have some answers: because his company is moving to Kentucky, and because he lost the lease on his New York apartment. In this case, the Why Test works perfectly. You have identified the author's point.

Sample Argument #2

Now let's take a look at another argument that deals with a slightly more complicated subject, one that's closer to what you'll see on the LSAT.

> The mayor of the town of Shasta sent a letter to the townspeople instructing them to burn less wood. A few weeks after the letter was delivered, there was a noticeable decrease in the amount of wood the townspeople of Shasta were burning on a daily basis. Therefore, it is obvious that the letter was successful in helping the mayor achieve his goal.

Okay, now let's identify the point and reasons in this argument:

What's the author's point?

The author is trying to persuade us that the letter was, in fact, the cause of the townspeople's burning less wood. Notice the phrase "it is obvious that," which indicates that a point is being made and that the point is debatable. Is there enough information preceding this statement to possibly back it up? Can two short sentences persuade us that there is an "obvious" conclusion that we should come to when evaluating this information? Not if we're thinking about the issue critically and thinking about some of the other possible causes for this effect.

What are the author's reasons?

Let's use the Why Test here, shall we? If we've chosen the right conclusion, asking "why" will give us the author's reasons. *Why did the author conclude that the letter was successful in getting the townspeople of Shasta to burn less wood?* The author's reasons are that the mayor sent a letter, and that the people started burning less wood a few weeks later.

What's missing?

Remember how we said that you need to be critical and ask questions? Well, here's your chance. Arguments on the LSAT are full of holes. Remember—it's difficult to make a solid, airtight case in just three sentences. So let's be skeptical and poke holes in this author's reasoning.

What do you think about the author's conclusion that the letter was responsible for helping the mayor achieve his goal? In evaluating the author's argument, we'll start with her reasons—they're the only facts that we have to go on. The mayor sends a letter to the townspeople, urging them to burn less wood, and a few weeks later, the townspeople start to burn less wood. (Remember that you have to accept these facts at face value. So we have to accept that, for instance, there was in fact a noticeable decrease in the amount of wood being burned in Shasta.) Now, do we know *for certain* that the mayor's letter is what caused the decline in burning? Couldn't it have been something else? This author evidently doesn't think so—she thinks it's the letter, and nothing else. We could come up with a hundred possible reasons that might explain why the residents of Shasta started to burn less wood, other than the mayor's letter.

For all we know, the price of firewood could have doubled right before the decline in burning. But by asking these questions, we know the important thing—that this author *assumes* that there wasn't any other cause.

What is an assumption?

An assumption, both in life and on the LSAT, is a leap of logic that we make to get from one piece of information to another. For instance, if you see a friend of yours wearing a yellow shirt and you conclude that your friend likes yellow, you would be making the following assumptions:

> Your friend is not color-blind and does not actually think he's wearing purple.
>
> Your friend was not threatened by a madman who said that unless he wore a yellow shirt for one month straight, his house would be burned to the ground.
>
> Your friend was not down to his last clean shirt, the one that he only wears when everything else needs to be washed.
>
> Your friend . . .

You get the point. You make these assumptions because you've seen a particular effect (in this case, your friend wearing a yellow shirt), and you think you've identified the proper cause (in this case, that your friend likes yellow, and not that he is color-blind or needs to do some laundry). Then, for better or for worse, you *assume a connection* between the cause and the effect. You've made a leap of logic.

Assumptions on the LSAT

The assumptions made in the arguments on the LSAT are also leaps of logic. Sometimes, it's logic so simple that it looks as if the author has actually stated it but really hasn't. The author's assumption is never explicitly stated in the passage. By definition, it is always unstated.

Let's go back to the wood-burning argument. Here, we have an observed effect—the townspeople of Shasta burning less wood. We have a possible cause—the mayor's letter. In LSAT-land, the arguer will often try to make a direct connection between these two pieces of information—in this case, that the letter *caused* the wood-burning decrease.

However, as we've seen from the above example, we're also assuming the following:

> That the decrease in the burning of wood was not due to an increase in the price of wood.
>
> That the town didn't experience unexpectedly warm temperatures, lessening the demand for wood as a heat source.
>
> That the townspeople actually received and read the letters the mayor sent out.
>
> That . . .

Once again, you get the point. The author actually made many assumptions when she made the leap of logic from the letter being sent to the townspeople burning less wood, and they all revolve around making the assumption that the letter was the cause of the observed effect.

This Is All Really Exciting, But...

You want to get to the answer choices, don't you? Well, we will—soon. But what has been the point of the last several pages? To show you how to read the argument itself in a critical way. This will help you immensely in evaluating the answer choices, because you will have already identified the parts of the argument: the author's point, reasons, and any underlying assumptions. This means that many times you'll have the answer to the question in mind before you read any answer choices, and you can simply eliminate any that don't match.

The reason we want you to stop and think before going to the answer choices is that the answer choices are not there to help you get a good score on the LSAT. Four of the answer choices are going to be wrong, and their purpose is to distract you from the "best" answer choice. True, many times this "best" choice will merely be the least sketchy of five sketchy answer choices. Nonetheless, the more work you put into analyzing the argument before reading the choices, the better your chance of eliminating the four distracters and choosing the "credited response."

Four of the answer choices are going to be wrong, and their purpose is to distract you from the "best" answer choice.

So why do we hammer this at you? Because you may or may not have had a lot of practice reading critically. You're not simply reading for pleasure, or reading the newspaper or a menu at a restaurant—here, you've got to focus your attention on these short paragraphs. Read LSAT arguments critically, as if you're reading a contract you're about to sign. Don't just casually glance over them so you can quickly get to the answer choices. You'll end up spending more time with the answer choices trying to determine the credited response if you don't have a solid understanding of the author's point and how she got there. The most important single thing to read super-carefully is the author's point, whenever it is explicitly stated. Take the time to think critically about the argument, to break it down, and to be sure that you can paraphrase what the author is saying and articulate any flaws in her reasoning. Doing this will actually save you time by enabling you to evaluate the answer choices more quickly and efficiently.

WORKING ARGUMENTS: A STEP-BY-STEP PROCESS

We have developed a four-step process for working LSAT Arguments. It is a very simple process that will keep you on task and increase your odds of success if you follow it for every argument that you do. Here are the steps:

Step 1: Read the question and identify your task

Sound familiar? This is one of your mantras. Reading the question first will tip you off about what you need to look for in the argument. You won't waste time reading the argument before you know how you will need to evaluate it for that particular question. If you don't know what your task is, you have no hope of ever being able to perform it effectively.

Step 2: Work the argument

This is what we've been practicing for the last few pages. You've got to read the argument *critically*, looking for the author's point and the evidence used to support it. For now, you should write these down in the margin. You only have to jot down a thumbnail sketch of the argument; short paraphrases of the information are sufficient. But remember that you're trying to learn how to apply a new technique effectively and you'll want to be sure that you don't start off with bad habits. By forcing yourself to write things out in the beginning you'll build the process into your approach. Later, after you've set up the good habits, you'll actually only need to write down little notes to yourself for arguments that are particularly confusing.

For many of the questions on the LSAT you will also want to identify any big assumptions that the author has made in reaching his point. In order to find these, you should keep your eyes open for any shifts in the author's language or gaps in the argument. Remember that the author's point is reached using *only* the information on the page in front of you, so any gaps need to be filled in by assumptions. But you'll always want to be sure that you're reading critically and articulating the parts of the argument (both stated and unstated) in your own words. This will take a few extra seconds, but the investment will more than pay off by saving you loads of time in dealing with the answer choices.

Step 3: Answer the question in your own words as best you can

The test writers rely on the fact that the people who are taking the LSAT feel pressured to get through all the questions quickly. Many answer choices will seem appealing if you don't have a clear idea of what you're looking for before you start reading through them. The best way to keep yourself from falling into this trap is to approach the answer choices with a clear idea of what it is that you'll look for.

Step 4: Use Process of Elimination

We first mentioned Process of Elimination (POE) in Chapter 1. It's a key to success on every section of the LSAT, especially Arguments and Reading Comprehension.

Why? Here are the directions for Arguments again:

> Directions: The questions in this section are based on the reasoning contained in brief statements or passages. For some questions, more than one of the choices could conceivably answer the question. However, you are to choose the best answer; that is, the response that most accurately and completely answers the question. You should not make assumptions that are by commonsense standards implausible, superfluous, or incompatible with the passage. After you have chosen the best answer, blacken the corresponding space on your answer sheet.

As you can see, the point here is that there is no one right answer (as there is in logic games, for instance). Your goal is to pick the "best" answer, which sometimes means that you pick the strongest answer out of five pretty weak answer choices. So it's important to always use POE when you get to the answer choices. What does this mean? It means that your goal should be to *eliminate the four answer choices that have clear flaws*.

Most people look for the best answer, and, in the process, end up falling for answer choices that are designed to look appealing but actually contain artfully concealed flaws. The part that looks good looks *really* good and the little bit that's wrong blends right into the background if you're not reading carefully and critically. The "best" answer on a tricky question won't necessarily sound very good at all. That's why the question is hard. But if you're keenly attuned to crossing out those choices with identifiable flaws, you'll be left with that one that wasn't appealing, but *didn't have anything wrong with it*. And that's the winner because it's the "best" one of a group of flawed answers. If you can find a reason to cross off a choice, you've just improved your chances of getting the question right. So be aggressive about finding the flaws in answer choices that will allow you to eliminate them.

The Ten Types of Arguments Questions

Almost every question in the Arguments section of the exam will fit into one of the following ten categories: main point, assumption, weaken, strengthen, resolve/explain, inference, reasoning, flaw, principle, and parallel-the-reasoning. Each of these types of questions has its own unique characteristics, which we'll cover in the following pages. At the end of each question type you'll find a chart summarizing the most important things to remember. The chart will be repeated in full at the end of the chapter for all ten categories.

So Are You Ready?

Yep. We're finally going to give you an entire LSAT argument. First, we'll give you the whole argument, and you can attack it using the process we just outlined. Then, you can compare your results against ours. Finally, after each argument "lesson," we'll explain some extra techniques that you'll want to absorb. That way, by the end of Lesson 10, you'll know everything you need to attack any argument question the LSAT might throw at you. This first lesson is about main point questions. Good luck!

LESSON 1: MAIN POINT QUESTIONS

These questions are relatively rare, but because finding the main point is essential in order to correctly answer most other argument questions, it's a good place to start.

THE ARGUMENT

1. A growing number of ecologists have begun to recommend lifting the ban on the hunting of leopards, which are not an endangered species, and on the international trade of leopard skins. Why, then, do I continue to support the protection of leopards? For the same reason that I oppose the hunting of people. Admittedly, there are far too many human beings on this planet to qualify us for inclusion on the list of endangered species. Still, I doubt the same ecologists endorsing the resumption of leopard hunting would use that fact to recommend the hunting of human beings.

   Which of the following is the main point of the argument above?

   (A) The ban on leopard hunting should not be lifted.
   (B) Human beings are a species like any other animal, and should be placed on the endangered species list in view of the threat of nuclear annihilation.
   (C) Hunting of animals, whether or not they are an endangered species, should not be permitted.
   (D) Ecologists do not consider human beings a species, much less an endangered species.
   (E) Ecologists cannot be trusted when emotional issues such as hunting are involved.

CRACKING MAIN POINT QUESTIONS

Step 1: Read the question and identify your task

Did you remember to read the question before you started reading the argument? Here it is again:

1. Which of the following is the main point of the argument above?

This question is asking for the main point, or conclusion, of the argument. Now you're going to work the argument, and your goal is to identify the author's main point.

Always read the question first. Always.

Step 2: Work the argument

Read the argument. Read it slowly enough that you maintain a critical stance and identify the author's main point and reasons. Here it is again:

> A growing number of ecologists have begun to recommend lifting the ban on the hunting of leopards, which are not an endangered species, and on the international trade of leopard skins. Why, then, do I continue to support the protection of leopards? For the same reason that I oppose the hunting of people. Admittedly, there are far too many human beings on this planet to qualify us for inclusion on the list of endangered species. Still, I doubt the same ecologists endorsing the resumption of leopard hunting would use that fact to recommend the hunting of human beings.

So here is an argument about hunting leopards. Keep in mind that we only need to find the main point and reasons when we're working on a main point question. Finding any assumptions won't help us, so don't waste precious time trying to figure them out. Here's what we got for the author's point and reasons:

- Author's point: *We should not lift the ban on hunting leopards.*
- Author's reasons: *One, because it would be like hunting human beings, and two, just because a species is not endangered is not a good reason to hunt it.*

Remember, you can use the Why Test to check the author's point if you're not sure. Let's go to Step 3.

Step 3: Answer the question in your own words as best you can

Now that you've broken down the argument and have all the pieces clear in your mind, it's time to make sure that you approach the answer choices knowing what it is that you've been asked to find. If you're not sure about exactly what you're supposed to be looking for, you will be much more likely to fall for one of the appealing answer choices designed to distract you from the credited response. So, just to be sure you're ready for the next step, we said that the author's main point was that we shouldn't lift the ban on hunting leopards.

Step 4: Use Process of Elimination

Okay, now let's look at each of the answer choices. Your goal is to eliminate four of the choices by crossing out anything that doesn't match the paraphrase of the author's main point. If any part of it doesn't fit, get rid of it.

> (A) The ban on leopard hunting should not be lifted.

Does this sound like what you wrote for the author's point? Yes. Let's leave it.

> (B) Human beings are a species like any other animal, and should be placed on the endangered species list in view of the threat of nuclear annihilation.

Is this the author's point? No, he never mentions anything about putting human beings on the endangered species list. In fact, he says that human beings are NOT an endangered species. Also, what's this stuff about nuclear annihilation? Was that ever mentioned in the argument? No. Let's cross it off.

(C) Hunting of animals, whether or not they are an endangered species, should not be permitted.

This looks pretty good, except that it's too general. The argument is talking about leopards only. This might be a politically correct thought, but it's not relevant to the argument. Let's cross it off.

(D) Ecologists do not consider human beings a species, much less an endangered species.

Do you know anything from what's written in the argument about ecologists' views on this matter? No. Furthermore, this doesn't say anything about leopards, which is what we decided the argument is about. Once again, it's not relevant to the argument. Let's cross it off.

(E) Ecologists cannot be trusted when emotional issues such as hunting are involved.

Absolutely, positively, never trust an ecologist. But seriously, it's got the same problem as (D). It doesn't talk about leopards at all, so once again it is not relevant. It's also a bit extreme, don't you think? Let's cross it off. Well, it looks like you've got (A), the right answer here. Nice job!

ARGUMENTS TECHNIQUES: PROCESS OF ELIMINATION

Let's go into a bit more depth with Process of Elimination. Answer choices (B), (C), (D), and (E) above all presented us with specific reasons for crossing them off. Below are ways in which you can analyze answer choices to see if you can eliminate them.

Relevance

LSAT arguments have very specific limits; the author of an argument stays within these limits in reaching his point. Anything else is not relevant. When you read an argument, you must pretend that you only know what is written on the page in front of you. Never assume anything else. So, any answer choice that is outside the scope of the argument can be eliminated. We did this for answer choices (B), (C), (D), and (E) above. Many times, answer choices will be so general that they are no longer relevant. Arguments are usually about specific things—like leopards, as opposed to just "animals." Also, when a specific phrase such as "nuclear annihilation" appears in an answer choice, but has no bearing on the author's argument, it's a pretty safe bet that this answer choice is ripe for elimination. The ultimate deciding factor about what is or is not within the scope of the argument is the *exact wording* of the main point.

Extreme language

Pay attention to the wording of the answer choices. For some question types (most notably main point and inference), extreme, absolute language (*never, must, exactly, cannot, always, only*) tends to be wrong, and choices with extreme language can usually be eliminated. Keep in mind, however, that an argument that uses strong language can support an *equally* strong answer choice. Extreme language is another reason that we eliminated answer choice (E). You should always note extreme language anywhere—in the passage, the question, or the answer choices, as it will frequently play an important role.

Opposites

Make sure that you are not choosing the exact *opposite* of the viewpoint asked for. Many times, this type of answer choice will look good because it's talking about the same subject matter as the correct answer; the trouble is that this answer choice presents an opposite viewpoint. For some question types, such as weaken, strengthen, main point, and parallel-the-reasoning, one of the answer choices will almost always be an "opposite."

Arguments Techniques: Use of the Word "Conclusion"

You'll notice that we've labeled these first questions "main point" questions. We saw that our task on these questions is to determine the author's conclusion. You might be wondering why we don't just call them "conclusion" questions. Well, there is a method to our madness. You'll find that when the word "conclusions" shows up in a question on the LSAT, it doesn't refer to the main point at all. You'll see this when we get to the chapter on inference questions. Keep your eyes open for this.

Cracking Main Point Questions: Summary

Check out the chart below for some quick tips on main point questions. The left column of the chart shows some of the ways in which the LSAT folks will ask you to find the conclusion. The right column is a brief summary of the techniques you should use when attacking main point questions.

Sample Question Phrasings	Attack! Attack! Attack!
What is the author's main point? *The main conclusion drawn in the author's argument is that* *The argument is structured to lead to which one of the following conclusions?*	• Identify the main point and reasons. • Use the Why Test, and then match your point against the five answer choices. • Be careful not to fall for the opposite. • When down to two choices, use extreme wording and relevance to eliminate one choice.

LESSON 2: ASSUMPTION QUESTIONS

Assumption questions prompt you to analyze an argument and look for holes in the author's proof or reasoning.

THE ARGUMENT

2a. Some people fear that our first extraterrestrial visitors will not be the friendly aliens envisaged in popular science fiction movies, but rather hostile invaders bent on global domination. This fear is groundless. Any alien civilization that makes it to our planet must have acquired the wisdom to control war, or it would have destroyed itself long before contacting us.

The author bases the argument above on which of the following assumptions?

(A) Our planet will have contact with extraterrestrial visitors at some time in the future.
(B) Interstellar travel is unworkable except in a society much more technologically advanced than ours.
(C) A civilization that has learned to control war on its own planet will not wage war on another.
(D) Alien civilizations are more morally advanced than those on Earth.
(E) Most people are afraid that if extraterrestrials do visit the earth, it will be for the purpose of invasion.

CRACKING ASSUMPTION QUESTIONS

Step 1: Read the question and identify your task
Good, so you've read the question. Here it is again:

2a. The author bases the argument above on which of the following assumptions?

As you can see, it's an assumption question. With this argument, you need to identify not only the main point and reasons, but also the underlying assumptions that the author makes to get to her point.

Step 2: Work the argument
Read the argument. Read it slowly enough that you can identify the author's main point and her reasons. Here it is again:

Some people fear that our first extraterrestrial visitors will not be the friendly aliens envisaged in popular science fiction movies, but rather hostile invaders bent on global domination. This fear is groundless. Any alien civilization that makes it to our planet must have acquired the wisdom to control war, or it would have destroyed itself long before contacting us.

Always read the argument critically, looking for the author's main point and reasons.

So, aliens and global domination. Cool stuff, but you never thought you'd read about it on the LSAT, eh? The topic shouldn't faze us though because we're only out to evaluate the structure of the argument and stay within the boundaries of the author's language. Doesn't there seem to be a little break in the logic toward the end of the argument? Hmmm. Now let's break it down:

- Author's main point: *We shouldn't fear aliens.*
- Author's reasons: *Any alien civilization that can make it to Earth must have acquired the wisdom to control war, or else it would have destroyed itself long ago.*
- Author's assumption: *It's some connection between having developed the ability to travel through outer space and being wise enough to control war, right? Start by looking at the reasons. If the aliens make it to Earth, we know they haven't destroyed themselves, but is it really safe to say that they haven't destroyed other civilizations at some point? Aha! The author certainly assumes that they haven't.*

The author makes a pretty impressive leap of logic there! But she doesn't close the gap. She doesn't convince us that just because the aliens haven't destroyed themselves that they couldn't (and haven't) destroyed others.

The key thing here is to understand the leap of logic. Here's this argument about the aliens traveling to Earth, and then WHAM! In the last sentence, the author talks about acquiring wisdom. That's a gap in the argument that we have to fill. We're going to bridge it with something that can connect the author's reasons to her point.

Step 3: Answer the question in your own words as best you can
Now let's make sure that we have a good paraphrase of the author's assumption in mind so we don't get tripped up in the answers.

We said that in order to get from the evidence she presented to the point she made, the author would have to assume that knowing that the aliens hadn't destroyed their own civilization is enough for us to believe that they are not invaders bent on the domination of other civilizations, including our own.

Step 4: Use Process of Elimination
Let's go to the answer choices. We know that the credited response is going to have to say something that will link a civilization's not having destroyed itself with the idea that we can trust that the same civilization has no intention of destroying us.

(A) Our planet will have contact with extraterrestrial visitors at some time in the future.

Does this close the gap? We can be pretty sure that the credited response will probably have something to do with the author's assumption that the aliens haven't and won't destroy others. Also, be careful of the words in the future tense here—very rarely will an author assume something that hasn't happened yet.

(B) Interstellar travel is unworkable except in a society much more technologically advanced than ours.

This one sounds somewhat reasonable. If interstellar travel isn't an option unless you're highly advanced, we don't need to worry, right? Let's hold on to it.

(C) A civilization that has learned to control war on its own planet will not wage war on another.

This language is pretty close to what we said was the assumption of this argument. It looks good. Hold onto it.

(D) Alien civilizations are more morally advanced than those on Earth.

Huh? Where did the author ever talk about morals? And even if they were more morally advanced than our civilizations, does that guarantee that they won't want to destroy us? Notice that we had to make *another* assumption to get to the author's point. This one alone doesn't fill the gap, so we can get rid of it.

(E) Most people are afraid that if extraterrestrials do visit the earth, it will be for the purpose of invasion.

This is a slightly stronger way of saying something that the author used as evidence in her argument. But remember that the author believes that these fears are groundless. She doesn't have to believe that "most people" are afraid in order to prove that they shouldn't be. You can cross it off.

We're down to two choices—now what?

Well, welcome to the real deal. This is what is going to happen more often than you'd like. You're going to get down to two answer choices on many arguments, especially on arguments that have assumption questions attached. And it's possible that neither of the answer choices will look all that much like the assumption that you came up with in your working of the argument. However, you still know what the argument is about and can determine which of the two choices that are left does the best job of filling the gap between the author's reasons and main point. Both answer choices will seem to strengthen the author's argument, but only one of them will be *necessary*.

Now it's time to learn some more techniques.

ARGUMENTS TECHNIQUES: HOW TO SPOT AN ASSUMPTION

Finding the assumption can be one of the most difficult things to do on the LSAT. But as we said before, sometimes looking for a gap between the main point and the reasons will help you spot it. Let's look at an example of how this works. Consider the following argument:

Ronald Reagan ate too many jellybeans. Therefore, he was a bad president.

All right. You probably already think you know the assumption here; it's pretty obvious. After all, how do you get from "too many jellybeans" to "bad president?" This argument just doesn't make any sense, and the reason it doesn't make sense is that it's ridiculous.

But now consider this argument:

> Ronald Reagan was responsible for a huge national debt. Therefore, he was a bad president.

Suppose you were a staunch Reagan supporter, and someone came up to you and made this argument. How would you respond? You'd probably say that the debt wasn't his fault, that it was caused by Congress, Jimmy Carter, or the policies of a previous administration. You would attack the premise of the argument (the author's reason) rather than its assumption. But why? Well, because the assumption here might seem reasonable to you. Consider the parts of the argument:

Main point: *Ronald Reagan was a bad president.*

Reason: *Ronald Reagan was responsible for a huge debt.*

So where's the gap? According to the statements, the fact that Ronald Reagan was responsible for a huge national debt means that he was a bad president, so that's the assumption. Really, it's almost the same assumption we saw in the first argument—statement A (too many jellybeans, or huge debt) is sufficient to establish statement B (bad president). But the assumption is easier to spot in the first argument than in the second, because the connection between jellybeans and presidential performance is harder to justify than the one between economic factors and presidential performance. The bottom line is that both assumptions were easily identified in the same way: by finding the gap in the language of the argument. Something new was mentioned in the main point (the idea that Ronald Reagan was a bad president) that wasn't mentioned anywhere else in the argument. But in order for the new information to follow from the reason offered, some sort of bridge must have been built over the gap—and the information that bridges the gap is the assumption.

So that's how you find assumptions on the LSAT: Look for the gap and think of how to bridge it. Most of the gaps that exist fall between the main point and one of the reasons supporting that point, but sometimes a gap will exist between two reasons.

Don't forget that the hardest assumptions to spot are the ones that make sense to you—if you find yourself agreeing with an argument, you'll have to work twice as hard to find the assumption. And even if you can't quite put the assumption into words, once you've identified the gap you simply have to decide which answer choice is sufficient to fill the gap.

Arguments Techniques: Negating Assumption Answer Choices

One of the most important things to remember about any assumption is the fact that, when making an argument, assumptions are *necessary* for the main point to be valid, *using only the evidence offered by the author*. Remember the guy who thought he had to move to Kentucky? Yeah, that guy again. Well, if you take his assumptions and show him that they're false, what would happen? The whole argument would fall apart. So here's the technique: To see if any answer choice on assumption questions is really necessary (and therefore the correct answer), make that statement false. Simply negate the language of the choice, and see if the argument falls apart in the process. Let's make (B) from our previous argument about aliens false.

> (B) Interstellar travel is unworkable except in a society much more technologically advanced than ours.

What if it were *not* true that interstellar travel were impossible unless you were highly advanced? What if aliens who weren't much more technologically advanced than us could, in fact, make it to our planet?

Does this information now destroy the author's argument? No. The argument could still stand because we are told by the author that regardless of their *technological* savvy, they would have acquired the wisdom to control war. So we can cross this one off. Now let's check out what happens when we negate our only other choice, (C):

> (C) Civilization that has learned to control war on its own planet will not wage war on another.

What if it were not true that civilization that has learned to control war on its own planet will not wage war on another? You have to be careful here because of the double negative. Let's paraphrase what this means. What if at least some of the civilizations that have learned to control war on their own planet would wage war on another civilization? Then her argument falls apart. We're no longer safe from visiting aliens. And, you've found your answer.

As you can see, you've got a lot of techniques to use when dealing with assumption questions. You can sometimes use *relevance* to knock out answers—as in answer choice (D)—because the correct answer will many times link two ideas from the argument. You can watch out for *extreme wording*—as in answer choices (B) and (D)—though sometimes it may in fact be present in the correct answer choice. You should also cross out anything that says the *opposite* of what the author thinks and actually weakens the argument. And you've learned how to *negate* an answer choice to see if, when negated, the argument falls apart. Remember, the negation test *only* works for assumption questions.

Now let's try another.

2b. Car owner: My mechanic believes that my car's wheels must be out of alignment, because the fact the tires are underinflated cannot by itself account for the steering problems I've been having for the past several months. But because my gas mileage has been steady during the same time period, the alignment of my car's wheels must be normal.

Which one of the following is an assumption required by the car owner's argument?

(A) A drop in gas mileage occurs only if a car's wheels are out of alignment.
(B) Underinflated tires can cause a car's mileage to drop.
(C) A car's mileage varies less under test conditions than it does on the open road.
(D) Misaligned wheels can sometimes cause a car's mileage to drop.
(E) Underinflated tires and misaligned wheels cannot both cause steering problems.

Step 1: Read the question and identify your task

As always, read the question first. Here it is again:

2b. Which one of the following is an assumption required by the car owner's argument?

The words "assumption" and "required" tell you that this is an assumption question. You know that you'll need to identify the main point and the reasons, and that you'll need to think about the gap in the author's logic.

Step 2: Work the Argument

Read the argument. Identify the important components. Here it is again:

2b. Car owner: My mechanic believes that my car's wheels must be out of alignment, because the fact the tires are underinflated cannot by itself account for the steering problems I've been having for the past several months. But because my gas mileage has been steady during the same time period, the alignment of my car's wheels must be normal.

One common way that you'll see the main point phrased on the LSAT is as the opposite of someone else's opinion. We're told that the mechanic believes that the car's wheels are out of alignment. Notice, though, the word "But" at the beginning of the second sentence. This tells us that the author is about to disagree with the mechanic, and you can quickly identify the main point as the last line of the argument, "the alignment of my car's wheels must be normal."

What information is given to support this? Well, the author has been having steering problems, underinflated tires by themselves can't be the reason for those problems, and his gas mileage has been holding steady. If you notice that none of these reasons mentions wheel alignment, you're on your way to finding the right answer.

- Author's main point: *The car's wheels aren't misaligned.*
- Author's reasons: *Careful—don't confuse the car owner's reasons with the mechanic's reasons. The only reason the car owner (author) gives for the impossibility of misalignment is that his gas mileage hasn't changed.*
- Author's assumption: *Well, it has to link the reasons to the point, but you might be having a hard time articulating the idea clearly. Don't worry. That will happen frequently, especially on harder arguments. For now, let's just say it's an idea that relates gas mileage to alignment.*

Step 3: Answer the question in your own words as best you can
So, this one is a little rougher. All we know for sure is that the right answer will have to link the point and the reason together somehow. Let's use that as our first POE criterion and move to the answer choices.

Step 4: Use Process of Elimination
Here we go:

(A) A drop in gas mileage occurs only if a car's wheels are out of alignment.

Does this suggest a link between alignment and the reason? Yes, it does. We'll hold onto it.

(B) Underinflated tires can cause a car's mileage to drop.

Does this suggest a link between alignment and mileage? No, it doesn't. In fact, alignment isn't mentioned at all. This links the car owner's reason with the reason from the mechanic's argument. Let's cross it off.

(C) A car's mileage varies less under test conditions than it does on the open road.

This seems completely irrelevant, and doesn't mention the point at all. Let's cross it off.

(D) Misaligned wheels can sometimes cause a car's mileage to drop.

This seems a lot like (A). It mentions both the reason and the main point. We'll hold onto it.

(E) Underinflated tires and misaligned wheels cannot both cause steering problems.

This mentions the main topic of the argument, steering problems, and also mentions the misaligned wheels. Let's keep it, just in case.

We're down to three this time—now what?

This will happen from time to time. It looks like we'll have to do some thinking. Always reread the main point and reread the question before you compare the answer choices. Here they are again:

Author's main point: *The car's wheels aren't misaligned.*

Question: *Which one of the following is an assumption required by the car owner's argument?*

Let's start with (E), only because it's unlike the other two. Don't forget about negating answer choices—it's a useful technique. If you negate (E), it will read, "Underinflated tires and misaligned wheels *can* both cause steering problems." Remember that when you negate the correct answer, it should make the argument fall apart. Just because misaligned wheels (and underinflated tires) can both cause steering problems doesn't mean that they absolutely are causing the steering problems in this case. It weakens the argument a little, but not a lot. It's probably not right, but let's see if something else is better.

How about (A)? Let's look at it more closely.

(A) A drop in gas mileage occurs only if a car's wheels are out of alignment.

This says that if my mileage drops, then I know for sure that my wheels aren't aligned (because according to the answer choice, misaligned wheels are necessary in order for a drop in gas mileage to occur). Does this say anything about what I know if I *don't* get a drop in gas mileage? No, it doesn't. Because we only care about what's true if I don't get a drop in gas mileage (because that's the reason in the argument), we can eliminate this choice.

That leaves us with (D):

(D) Misaligned wheels can sometimes cause a car's mileage to drop.

Try negating that one: Misaligned wheels can *never* cause a car's mileage to drop. If it were true that misaligned wheels could never be the cause of a decrease in mileage, then how could the author cite steady mileage as proof that the wheels were aligned? He couldn't. The negated version of answer choice (D) destroys the argument and is therefore the credited response to the argument.

ARGUMENTS TECHNIQUES: TYPES OF ASSUMPTIONS

There are many types of assumptions that one can make. However, there are a few classic ones that show up repeatedly on the LSAT. You've already learned one, in fact—the wood-burning argument was an example of a *causal* (i.e., cause-and-effect) assumption. Let's examine that type first.

Causal assumptions

"Causal" is shorthand for cause and effect. It means making an assumption by linking an observed effect (people burning less wood, for instance) with a possible cause for that effect (the mayor's letter). A causal assumption presumes that the stated possible cause was *the* cause. When you make such an assumption, you're also saying that there was no other cause.

Here's another causal argument:

> Every time I walk my dog, it rains. Therefore, walking my dog must be the cause of the rain.

Silly, right? However, this is classic causality. We see the observed effect (it's raining), we see a possible cause (walking the dog), and then the author connects the two by saying that walking his dog caused the rain, thereby implying that nothing else caused it. Got it? So why are causal assumptions so popular on the LSAT? Because people often confuse correlation with causality. If we use shorthand for the possible cause (A) and the effect (B), we can see what the common assumptions are when working with a causal argument:

1. *A* caused *B*.
2. Nothing else could have caused *B*. (There are no possible alternate causes.)

Causal assumptions:

The stated possible cause is the ONLY cause.

Of course, causal arguments on the LSAT won't be that silly, but they'll have the same basic structure. The great thing about being able to identify causal arguments is that once you know the assumption it becomes a breeze to identify the credited response for assumption, weaken, and strengthen questions.

On assumption questions, the credited response will be a paraphrase of the assumption you've identified, as you saw above. For weaken questions, the credited response will suggest an alternate cause for the observed effect. And for strengthen questions, the credited response will eliminate a possible alternate cause or give more evidence linking the stated possible cause with the stated effect. Eliminating answer choices to get to the credited response becomes purely mechanical.

Sampling assumptions

Another popular type of assumption on the LSAT is the *sampling* or *statistical* assumption. This assumes that a given statistic or sample is sufficient to justify a given conclusion, or that an individual is representative of a group. Here's an example:

Sampling assumptions:

A given statistic or sample is representative of the whole.

> In a group of 50 college students chosen from among those who receive athletic scholarships, more than 80 percent said in a recent survey that they read magazines daily. So it follows that advertisers who wish to reach a college-age audience should place ads in magazines.

What is being assumed here? That the students who were chosen are a representative sample of the college-age population. In this case, the students who are used as evidence are (a) college students and (b) recipients of athletic scholarships. That's a small subset of the population. The population the advertisers wish to reach is a "college-age" audience, a much broader group. Here the sample is non-representative in two ways. Those surveyed are college students while the target audience is "college-age." Can we assume that college students are representative of everyone who is college-age? If not, the argument has a problem. Further, even if we could accept college students as representative of college-age people in general, we would still have to believe that those college students who receive athletic scholarships are representative of all college students.

Whenever you see something about a group being used as evidence to conclude something about a larger population, you'll know the author made a sampling assumption.

Analogy assumptions

A third type of assumption on the LSAT is the analogy assumption. In this case the author assumes that a given group, idea, or action is logically similar to another group, idea, or action. Read the argument below.

> Overcrowding of rats in laboratory experiments has been shown to lead to aberrant behavior. So it follows that if people are placed in overcrowded situations they will begin to exhibit aberrant behavior as well.

Analogy assumptions:
One group, idea, or action is the same as another, with respect to the terms of the argument.

What is being assumed here? That, with respect to the conditions of the argument—here, overcrowding and aberrant behavior—people and rats are *analogous*. If they are, the argument stands up. But if there is no connection between rats and people when it comes to overcrowding and aberrant behavior, what happens to the argument? It falls apart. And just as with causal and statistical assumptions, the LSAT writers can ask assumption, weaken, and strengthen questions based on analogy assumptions.

Arguments Techniques: A Note on Tasks

We've been talking about common assumptions that appear in LSAT arguments. These are not the only types of assumptions that you'll find on the test, but if you learn to recognize these common assumptions, you'll be one step ahead on a lot of questions. Because the gaps in arguments—assumptions—are important on a number of different question types, if you can identify them quickly you'll know just what to look for in the answer choices. You'll notice that we don't say that there are causal questions; rather, that there are causal arguments and these can have any type of question attached to them. Questions might ask you to carry out any of a variety of tasks: find the assumption, or weaken the argument, or identify the flaw in reasoning, or whatever. Once the test writer puts together an argument, he can attach just about any of the question types to it. We'll look at a couple of special situations later on, but for now just know that if you have identified one of the common assumption types above, you'll be well on your way to identifying the best answer choice.

Cracking Assumption Questions: Summary

Whew! We've just covered a ton of information surrounding assumption questions. You learned more Process of Elimination techniques (specifically, how to negate answer choices to find the most powerful assumption), and then you learned three very popular types of assumptions—causal, sampling, and analogy—and how to tackle assumption, weaken, and strengthen questions that might be attached to them.

Below is a chart that summarizes assumption questions.

Sample Question Phrasings	Attack! Attack! Attack!
Which of the following is an assumption on which the argument relies? *The argument above assumes which of the following?* *The writer's argument depends upon assuming which of the following?*	• Identify the main point, reasons, and assumptions of the author. • If you're having trouble finding the assumption, look for a gap between two different ideas in the argument. • The assumption will always strengthen the author's point and is NECESSARY for the point to follow from the information provided. • When down to two choices, negate each statement to see if the argument falls apart. If it does, that's your answer.

LESSON 3: WEAKEN QUESTIONS

Weaken questions ask you to find logic that goes *against* the given argument. This means you will have to find a flaw in the author's reasoning—in other words, to attack her assumptions.

The Argument

3a. A growing number of ecologists have begun to recommend lifting the ban on the hunting of leopards, which are not an endangered species, and on the international trade of leopard skins. Why, then, do I continue to support the protection of leopards? For the same reason that I oppose the hunting of people. Admittedly, there are far too many human beings on this planet to qualify us for inclusion on the list of endangered species. Still, I doubt the same ecologists endorsing the resumption of leopard hunting would use that fact to recommend the hunting of human beings.

Which of the following, if true, would most weaken the author's argument?

(A) Human beings might, in fact, be placed on the list of endangered species.
(B) It is impossible to ensure complete compliance with any international hunting ban.
(C) Leopards, now dangerously overpopulated, cannot be supported by their ecosystems.
(D) Despite the growing number of ecologists supporting a repeal of the ban on leopard hunting, most still support it.
(E) The international ban on leopard hunting was instituted before leopards became an endangered species.

CRACKING WEAKEN QUESTIONS

Step 1: Read the question and identify your task

Good, you've read the question. Here it is again:

> 3a. Which of the following, if true, would most weaken the author's argument?

Remember that we'll keep our task in mind as we work the argument. Because we're asked to weaken the author's argument, we'll want to pay close attention to any gaps in the author's reasoning that we might be able to exploit. Read critically and look for any areas of vulnerability.

Step 2: Work the argument

Hey! You've read this argument already, right? It's the one about the leopards. The first time around all you had to do was identify the main point, but now you'll have to go one step further.

Let's stay focused and maintain a critical stance so that we'll be able to tell which answer choice does a good job of weakening the author's underlying assumption. Here it is again:

> A growing number of ecologists have begun to recommend lifting the ban on the hunting of leopards, which are not an endangered species, and on the international trade of leopard skins. Why, then, do I continue to support the protection of leopards? For the same reason that I oppose the hunting of people. Admittedly, there are far too many human beings on this planet to qualify us for inclusion on the list of endangered species. Still, I doubt the same ecologists endorsing the resumption of leopard hunting would use that fact to recommend the hunting of human beings.

Here's what we've got as our point, reasons, and assumption:

- Author's point: *We should not lift the ban on hunting leopards.*
- Author's reasons: *One, because hunting leopards is like hunting human beings, and two, just because a species is not endangered is not a legitimate reason to hunt it.*
- Author's assumption: *That with respect to the conditions of this argument, leopards and humans are analogous.*

We just talked about analogy assumptions, and this author certainly makes one. The author says that in terms of hunting bans and endangered species, leopards and humans are similar, so we shouldn't hunt leopards for the same reason that we shouldn't hunt humans.

Step 3: Answer the question in your own words as best you can
Keep your task in mind: You need to find something that will weaken the author's argument by showing that the relationship between leopards and humans with respect to endangered species and hunting bans is not, in fact, analogous. We could come up with any number of specific pieces of information that would hurt this argument. If we come up with something too specific, we may not find something like it in the answer choices, so it's best not to narrow things down too much at this point. And be careful not to be lured in by an answer choice that has some of the same topical information but isn't relevant to the argument.

Instead, we'll carry the assumption—or at least an understanding of where the gap in the argument lies—with us to the answer choices and then we'll be able to recognize the answer choice that weakens it.

Step 4: Use Process of Elimination
Let's go to the answer choices. In order to weaken this argument, the credited response is going to have to show that leopards and humans are *dissimilar* in terms of this argument.

(A) Human beings might, in fact, be placed on the list of endangered species.

This might sound ridiculous at first, but note that according to our question we have to take each answer choice as though it were true and *then* see what impact it might have on the argument. So let's pretend that (A) is, in fact, true. Does it weaken the argument? No, it still doesn't. It's not relevant to the argument because what "might" happen to human beings doesn't impact the argument. The goal here is to find ways in which humans are *not* like leopards.

(B) It is impossible to ensure complete compliance with any international hunting ban.

Is the author worried about whether or not we can ensure compliance with any ban? No, that goes beyond what the argument discusses. Even if this were true, it doesn't really address the analogy between humans and leopards. Let's get rid of it.

(C) Leopards, now dangerously overpopulated, cannot be supported by their ecosystems.

Interesting. This seems to be saying that if we *don't* kill some leopards, they might die out because they "cannot be supported by their ecosystems." Would this call into question the fact that leopards and humans are similar? Maybe. Let's leave it.

(D) Despite the growing number of ecologists supporting a repeal of the ban on leopard hunting, most still support it.

We're looking for some way to weaken the author's reasoning here; other people's viewpoints on the issue won't affect the analogy the author has drawn between leopards and humans. Whether the number of ecologists supporting the ban is a majority or a minority isn't relevant. Let's cross it off.

(E) The international ban on leopard hunting was instituted before leopards became an endangered species.

Again, we are looking for something that will broaden the gap in the argument. When the ban was originally instituted doesn't affect the author's contention that it should remain in place currently. And there's nothing to show how they're a different case from humans. We'll cross it off.

Nice job. You stayed focused on the fact that only one piece of information, answer choice (C), somehow showed that humans and leopards aren't all that analogous. It said that leopards are overpopulated, which would weaken the author's argument that we should not hunt them. Now let's take a look at some weaken question techniques.

Arguments Techniques: Looking for Impact and Opinions

The answer to a weaken question will not be the opposite of what the point of the argument is—it's going to be a bit more subtle than that. On the LSAT, we weaken the argument by attacking one of the author's assumptions. Rather than simply refuting the point, the credited response will come in from the side and widen the gap between the reasons and the point.

The correct answer on a weaken question demonstrates that the author's point isn't necessarily true, even if all the reasons are.

The key thing to look for in weaken answer choices, then, is direct impact. Remember how weaken questions are phrased? The question always contains the phrase, "which of the following, if true, would . . ." What this is telling us to do is treat each answer choice *as if it were hypothetically true*. The five answer choices represent five facts we have to take at face value and apply to the argument. One of them, when added to the information in the passage, will have the most negative direct impact on the point of the argument. Answer choices (A), (B), and (E) in the previous argument had no impact on the fact that we should not lift the ban on hunting leopards. They are all pieces of information that, when applied to the information in the argument, have no relevance to the author's point. Finally, remember answer choice (D), the one about the opinions of the ecologists? Unless the argument is about people's opinions of one thing or another, this type of answer choice is almost always wrong. So what if the ecologists, or the head of the World Wildlife Fund, or anyone else for that matter, has an opinion about what is discussed? Even the opinions of supposed "experts" don't weaken arguments—facts that destroy the arguer's chain of reasoning weaken arguments.

Let's try another example.

The Argument

3b. A study was conducted to determine what impact, if any, last year's aggressive shark-fishing campaign had on the local seal population. Since the campaign began, the seal population has increased by 25 percent. Thus, the removal of large numbers of sharks from the ecosystem allowed the population of seals to increase.

Which of the following, if true, most seriously weakens the argument?

(A) A previously unidentified virus was responsible for the deaths of a large number of sharks in the same area in the last year.
(B) Sharks prey on many species of fish as well as seals.
(C) Excess bait used to lure the sharks provided the seals with a plentiful source of nutrition.
(D) The shark-fishing campaign included many different shark species.
(E) Reducing the shark population has a number of negative side effects on the ecosystem as a whole.

Step 1: Read the question and identify your task
This should be familiar. Here's the question again:

3b. Which of the following, if true, most seriously weakens the argument?

Clearly, we're out to weaken the argument.

Step 2: Work the argument
Read the argument carefully. Identify the main point, the reasons the author offers as evidence, and any assumptions he makes. Here's the body of the argument:

3b. A study was conducted to determine what impact, if any, last year's aggressive shark-fishing campaign had on the local seal population. Since the campaign began, the seal population has increased by 25 percent. Thus, the removal of large numbers of sharks from the ecosystem allowed the population of seals to increase.

Did you recognize this as a causal argument? The main point suggests that the decrease in the shark population caused the increase in the seal population. What evidence did the author use to back this up? Apparently nothing more than the increase in population itself since the time the fishing began. This is a classic causal argument. The author wants you to believe that just because two things happened at the same time, one of them must have caused the other.

What are the automatic assumptions that an author makes in a causal argument? One is that the cause-and-effect relationship isn't reversed. In this case, that doesn't make much sense: how could an increase in the seal population cause the shark population to go down? The second assumption is that nothing else caused the observed effect. In this case, that means the author is assuming that nothing else besides the decrease in the shark population caused the increase in the seal population.

Let's summarize:

- Author's point: *Fewer sharks caused more seals.*
- Author's reasons: *The seal population increased at the same time that the shark population decreased.*
- Author's assumption: *Nothing else caused the seal population to increase.*

Step 3: Answer the question in your own words as best you can

Okay. We're looking for an alternate cause, and there could be many of them. In fact, it's highly unlikely that we'll be able to predict the "right" one. In general, we're looking for a choice that suggests another reason why the seal population increased.

Step 4: Use Process of Elimination

Be careful here. Because we're looking for an alternate cause, the right answer might seem out of scope because it doesn't necessarily have to refer to something in the body of the argument. Let's look at them one by one:

(A) A previously unidentified virus was responsible for the deaths of a large number of sharks in the same area in the last year.

This seems to giving an alternate cause for the decrease in the number of sharks, not the increase in the number of seals. It's not what we're looking for, but let's leave it in for now.

(B) Sharks prey on many species of fish as well as seals.

This is completely out of the scope of our argument, and it doesn't give a reason why the seal population might have increased other than the removal of the sharks. Let's get rid of it.

(C) Excess bait used to lure the sharks provided the seals with a plentiful source of nutrition.

Who cares what the bait....Oh...wait. This is what we need to be careful of. The choice seems irrelevant at first glance, but it does give another reason why the seal population went up. If we accept this information as true, then we can conclude that it wasn't necessarily the absence of the sharks that caused the increase in the seal population. It could have been that the seals were getting more food. This effectively weakens the argument.

(D) The shark-fishing campaign included many different shark species.

This is out of the scope of our argument. Get rid of it.

(E) Reducing the shark population has a number of negative side effects on the ecosystem as a whole.

This weakens the idea of the shark-fishing campaign in general, but that's not what our argument is about. Our argument is about the link between the campaign and the seal population. Let's get rid of it.

We did leave (A) in the first time, but compared with (C), it's a bad answer, since it provides an alternate cause for the reason, not for the main point.

CRACKING WEAKEN QUESTIONS: SUMMARY

Remember these two key ideas when doing weaken questions: The correct answer will probably destroy one of the author's assumptions, and you should treat each answer choice as hypothetically true, looking for its direct negative impact on the point. On more difficult weaken questions there will often be an appealing answer that, with just a little interpretation, looks right. The key is to avoid making any new assumptions when you try to determine the impact of an answer: Look for the *most direct* impact.

Sample Question Phrasings	Attack! Attack! Attack!
Which one of the following, if true, would most weaken the author's point? *Which of the following statements, if true, would most call into question the results achieved by the scientists?*	• Identify the main point, reasons, and assumptions of the author. • Read critically, looking for where the author made too big a leap in logic. • Then, when you go to the answer choices, look for a choice that has the most negative impact on that leap in logic. • Assume all choices to be hypothetically true.

LESSON 4: STRENGTHEN QUESTIONS

Stregthen questions ask you to find a way to make the argument stronger, or in other words, to *support* the author's assumptions.

THE ARGUMENT

4. Most major retail electronics chains experienced a dramatic increase in the amount of merchandise lost to shoplifting during the early 1980s. By 1986, however, all large chains had installed new anti-theft devices in their stores. Since this time, there has been a sharp decline in the number of shoplifting incidents taking place in those stores annually.

   Which one of the following, if true, would most strengthen the claim that the anti-theft devices were responsible for the decrease in shoplifting?

   (A) The average size of electronic merchandise is now small enough to fit into a person's pocket.
   (B) The average cost of electronic merchandise decreased since 1986.
   (C) Each item in the store was clearly marked with a permanently attached security number.
   (D) Shoplifting has increased at single outlet retail electronics operations since 1986.
   (E) Shoplifting has increased in the retail industry overall since 1986.

CRACKING STRENGTHEN QUESTIONS

Step 1: Read the question and identify your task

Good, you've read the question. Here it is again:

4. Which one of the following, if true, would most strengthen the claim that the anti-theft devices were responsible for the decrease in shoplifting?

This is a strengthen question. It asks us to find a hypothetically true answer that will help the author make his conclusion. Also, it tells us that the argument isn't all that great, or why would the author need help?

Step 2: Work the argument
Remember to keep a critical eye open for the author's main point and reasons. Jot down any notes you need to keep them straight. Here it is again:

> Most major retail electronics chains experienced a dramatic increase in the amount of merchandise lost to shoplifting during the early 1980s. By 1986, however, all large chains had installed new anti-theft devices in their stores. Since this time, there has been a sharp decline in the number of shoplifting incidents taking place in those stores annually.

You'll notice something a bit different as you read through this argument. The author doesn't really support a claim here. But, in the question we're presented with a claim. In this case we'll use the pieces of evidence provided by the author to support the claim offered in the question. If we hadn't read the question first, we'd be at a loss for what the author was claiming. Now we know how to look for the necessary pieces. You might also recognize that we're looking at an argument that deals with causality here. A possible cause is offered and assumed to be the only one.

- Main point (from the question): *There has been a decrease in shoplifting due to anti-theft devices.*
- Author's reasons: *The number of thefts went down after devices were installed.*
- Author's assumption: *The devices were the cause for the decrease, and there could have been no alternate cause.*

You're getting the hang of this causal assumption thing, aren't you?

Step 3: Answer the question in your own words as best you can
Remember what we said about this step in weaken questions? We don't want to carry a particular idea in our heads, but rather bring along the assumption—or at least the gap—so that we can evaluate the impact that each answer choice would have on it. We'll do the same thing here in strengthen questions. So here we need to strengthen the assumption that it was the installation of the anti-theft devices—and nothing else—that was, in fact, responsible for the decrease in shoplifting.

Step 4: Use Process of Elimination
Let's go to the answer choices. We know that the credited response is probably going to strengthen the causality of the argument in some way, perhaps by showing us that another possible cause wasn't responsible.

> (A) The average size of electronic merchandise is now small enough to fit into a person's pocket.

This looks pretty good. Stuff is smaller (therefore probably easier to shoplift), yet the number of crimes has decreased over the same period. Maybe it is the anti-theft devices, after all. Let's leave it.

(B) The average cost of electronic merchandise decreased since 1986.

Prices of the merchandise have gone down. Perhaps this means that, therefore, people have less incentive to steal it. If this were true, then the anti-theft devices would *not* be the cause of the decrease in shoplifting. This choice actually weakens the argument and is therefore not the right answer. Cross it off.

(C) Each item in the store was clearly marked with a permanently attached security number.

This would represent another possible cause for the decrease. It might act as a deterrent independent of the anti-theft devices. Again, a possible alternate cause *weakens* a causal argument. It's just the opposite of what we're looking for, so let's get rid of it.

(D) Shoplifting has increased at single outlet retail electronics operations since 1986.

Too bad for the little guy. However, do these folks have the anti-theft devices or not? Because we don't know, this answer choice doesn't have any direct impact. Let's cross it off.

(E) Shoplifting has increased in the retail industry overall since 1986.

If shoplifting in the retail industry overall is up, then what is causing the retail electronics chains to be different? Let's leave this one—we're down to two.

Let's see how far we can legitimately apply our logic to justify an answer choice.

Consider answer choice (A), which says that average electronics goods are now small enough to fit in one's pocket. It says (by valid inference), that before now, things weren't small enough to fit in one's pocket. So if the goods are smaller it would seem that it would be easier to shoplift them. But do we have any information to *directly* support the claim that the anti-theft devices were responsible? We could probably find a way to make it fit if we were trying to make the answer choice work, but remember that's a very dangerous way to evaluate. All we need to do here is to show that the answer choice doesn't directly support the point and we can get rid of it. We're trying to get rid of answers, not to find ways to make them stick around.

So we're left with answer choice (E), which tells us that the industry overall has been victimized to a greater degree since 1986. We know from the argument that shoplifting was on the rise in the early 1980s. And we know that there has been a decrease in shoplifting in a specific sector (major retail electronics chains) since then. We had to assume before that the decrease in those stores was *not* due to some factor other than the anti-theft devices, like a decrease in shoplifting overall. This answer choice eliminates the possibility of this alternate cause and directly supports the claim put forth in the question. Notice that the argument isn't airtight at this point; we could still come up with yet another alternate cause. But we've directly supported the argument by providing a piece of information that helps to fill in a gap in the reasoning.

Arguments Techniques: Direct Impact

As you saw from answer choice (A) in the previous argument, you can justify almost any answer choice as long as you have enough time and creativity. And because most people look for the right answer, that's often what they do. They find answer choices that are appealing and start to make them fit into the argument. They tell themselves, "Well, that *could* be the answer, because if we looked at the argument *this* way...." Because there are always four incorrect answers and at least a couple of them will be pretty appealing if you're not careful, that kind of thinking can waste a lot of your time.

Instead, we want to get you into the habit of looking for the flaws. On the LSAT, the correct answers for assumption, weaken, and strengthen questions will have a *direct impact* on the argument. As soon as you find yourself having to add anything else to the argument or draw on information that wasn't explicitly mentioned in order for the answer to have an impact on the point, get rid of that choice.

What If I Can't Find the Assumption?

We've been talking about what an important role the assumption plays in weakening or strengthening arguments on the LSAT. So you may be asking yourself, "What am I supposed to do if I can't find the assumption?" Well, there's still hope. Finding assumptions is one of the trickier skills for many students to develop. Here are two ideas to keep in mind.

First, look for any shifts in the author's language. Anytime the author makes a point, we'll evaluate that point *only* on the basis of the evidence we're given in support of that point. So if there are any changes in language between the reasons and the point, these changes key you into the assumption. This shift can be blatant, as when something that was never mentioned before suddenly shows up in the conclusion. Or it can be more subtle, such as if the author makes a statement that is more strongly qualified than the evidence. For instance, if we had evidence about what "almost always" is the case and concluded something that "will" happen, that would require a leap in logic.

Remember also that many arguments have multiple assumptions. Even if you identify an assumption correctly, it might not be the "right" one.

So what if you can't articulate an assumption, or you find the "wrong" one? Don't worry, there's *still* hope. You'll remember that we've been saying that you should approach the answer choices armed with the assumption or at least an understanding of the gap between main point and reasons. This is because it's not necessary for you to be able to *generate* the assumption in order to find the best answer. You can also be prepared to *recognize* the assumption (or an answer that will impact it, in the case of weaken and strengthen questions). Sure, you might find that you can get through POE more quickly if you have the assumption neatly paraphrased in your head, but if you've at least identified any gaps in the argument you'll be able to evaluate the answer choices and recognize the one that has the proper impact.

ARGUMENTS TECHNIQUES: WHAT TO DO WHEN YOU'RE DOWN TO TWO

As you do more LSAT arguments, you may find yourself falling into a predictable pattern in which you find it easy to eliminate three of the answer choices but then have no clear idea of which one of the two remaining choices is correct. There's the first problem. You should know that it isn't your job to determine which is the *correct* answer. The trickiest incorrect answers on LSAT arguments are usually mostly right—they contain just a word or two that makes them wrong.

Oftentimes these wrong answers will even sound better than the "credited" response. The writers of the LSAT are experts at writing answers that are *almost* all correct, so if you spot anything that makes the choice wrong, eliminate it.

So what do you do when you get down to two choices? Well, you focus on finding something that makes one of them incorrect. There must be something appealing about each of them, or you would have eliminated one of them by now.

Here are a few steps to follow:

1. Identify how the answer choices are different.
2. Go back to the argument and re-read, keeping the difference in mind. Use the difference that you've spotted to help you read the argument from a new, critical perspective. Try to find something in the language of the argument that points out a problem with one of the remaining two choices. Focus on the statement of the main point; this is very often what makes the final decision, especially if you didn't read it closely enough the first time.
3. Eliminate the choice with the flaw. Now that you've found the problem, cross off that choice and move on.

This process will work on any type of argument question—and, for that matter, on Games and Reading Comprehension. Be critical and methodical and you'll get results.

CRACKING STRENGTHEN QUESTIONS: SUMMARY

With strengthen questions, we once again looked for what impact each of the answer choices had on the argument—only this time, a favorable impact. We also learned that we can justify almost any answer choice if we want to, but that requires making additional assumptions that take us further away from the information provided. Instead, we must focus on finding the flaws that allow us to eliminate the attractive distracters and leave us with the only choice that has a direct impact on the author's assumption. Here is the chart:

Sample Question Phrasings	Attack! Attack! Attack!
Which one of the following statements, if true, would most support the author's conclusion? *Which one of the following statements, if true, would strengthen the author's point?*	• Identify the main point, reasons, and assumptions of the author. • Read critically, looking for where the author made too big a leap in logic. • Then, when you go to the answer choices, look for a choice that has the most positive impact on that gap. • Assume all choices to be hypothetically true.

LESSON 5: RESOLVE/EXPLAIN QUESTIONS

So far, we've been working with arguments in which the author has presented reasons to support a main point. And with the exception of main point questions, we've been paying attention to any gaps in the argument that might help us to pinpoint the assumptions the author has made. The process for working the arguments (Step 2) has been almost identical for conclusion, assumption, weaken, and strengthen question types.

We're going to do something a bit different for Step 2 in answering resolve/explain questions. That's because the "argument" attached to these questions is more like a passage. With these types of questions, the author will present a couple of pieces of information that don't seem to fit together. Our task will be to find the answer choice that will do the best job of *resolving* the apparent discrepancy between these two pieces of information, and that will *explain* how both pieces of information could be true at once. The other steps remain the same; we just don't have the same pieces to break down that we've seen so far.

Let's look at a typical passage that would be used when asking a resolve/explain question:

> The ancient Dirdirs used water power for various purposes in the outlying cities and towns in their empire. However, they did not use this technology in their capital city of Avallone.

Notice that there's no evidence provided to support a particular claim; just two pieces of information that don't really seem to fit with one another. Here we've got this ancient culture that has this great technology but doesn't use it in the capital city. That's the discrepancy or paradox, right? Good. Your goal

Your goal will be to spot an answer choice that resolves or explains the discrepancy or paradox.

then will be to spot an answer choice that in some way resolves or explains that discrepancy or paradox. You might be able to think up a few reasons why the Dirdirs had this technology and didn't use it, such as:

- There were no rivers or other bodies of water in or near Avallone.
- It was cheaper or more efficient to use another source of power in the capital, such as abundant labor.
- There was not enough space for the equipment in Avallone.

That's good for a start. You could actually come up with a multitude of theoretical reasons why they didn't use this technology (the actual historical reason has something to do with the fact that it would have caused social unrest because this technology would have put too many people out of work), but the nice thing is that you don't have to! All you have to do is identify the discrepancy and be able to recognize the answer choice that allows both parts of the discrepancy to be true. That'll save you a lot of work and keep you from generating ideas that are far away from what the test writers were thinking when they wrote the question. Now let's put this idea to work on a full question.

The Argument

5. A psychologist once performed the following experiment. Subjects were divided into two groups: excellent chess players and beginning chess players. Each group was exposed to a position arising from an actual game. Not surprisingly, when asked to reconstruct the position from memory an hour later, the expert chess players did much better than the beginners. On a board where the pieces were placed in a position at random, however, the expert players were no better able to reconstruct the position from memory than were the beginners.

   Which of the following explains the result of the psychologist's experiment above?

(A) Memory is an important part of chess-playing ability.
(B) The beginning chess players as well as the experts were less able to memorize the random position than the "actual" position.
(C) The ability to memorize varies with experience and ability.
(D) Memory is a skill that can be improved with practice.
(E) Being able to infer the causes of a situation plays an important role in memorization.

Cracking Resolve/Explain Questions

Step 1: Read the question and identify your task

Good, you're in the habit of reading the question first. Here it is again:

> Which of the following explains the result of the psychologist's experiment above?

This question is once again tipping your hand—it's telling you that there is something you need to *explain*. That means that somewhere in the "argument" is a *discrepancy* or *paradox* and you're going to have to find an answer choice that resolves these seemingly opposing facts.

Step 2: Work the argument

Read through the argument, looking for any situations or facts that seem contrary to one another. Here it is again:

> 5. A psychologist once performed the following experiment. Subjects were divided into two groups: excellent chess players and beginning chess players. Each group was exposed to a position arising from an actual game. Not surprisingly, when asked to reconstruct the position from memory an hour later, the expert chess players did much better than the beginners. On a board where the pieces were placed in a position at random, however, the expert players were no better able to reconstruct the position from memory than were the beginners.

What is the apparent paradox? On the one hand, when the pieces were arranged in a position that was part of a real game, the experts were much better at reconstructing the board. But in another scenario, where the pieces were randomly arranged, the beginners were just as good as the experts. How come the experts lost their edge when the pieces were randomly arranged?

Step 3: Answer the question in your own words as best you can

Remember that there are probably a number of specific theories we could come up with to explain this discrepency, and if one possible explanation jumps into your head, that's fine—it may turn out to be an answer choice. But fundamentally, we just need to be aware of the discrepancy and see what impact, if any, each of the answer choices will have on it.

In resolve/explain questions, the answer choices are all hypothetically true.

Step 4: Use Process of Elimination

Just as with weaken and strengthen answer choices, you have to accept each of the answer choices here as facts first, and then apply them to the "argument." One of these facts, when added to the argument, will resolve the apparent paradox, or explain the supposed discrepancy.

Let's see which one of the following choices does this.

(A) Memory is an important part of chess-playing ability.

That's right, it is. That's why the expert players were able to memorize the first situation better than the beginners were. However, it doesn't explain the second situation. The correct answer will have to help both parts of the argument make sense. So let's cross it out.

(B) The beginning chess players as well as the experts were less able to memorize the random position than the "actual" position.

This is interesting information, but it doesn't explain why the experts did just as poorly as the beginners did. So let's get rid of it.

(C) The ability to memorize varies with experience and ability.

This is like answer choice (A) in that it explains the first situation well, but fails to provide an explanation for the second situation—where the experts did just as poorly as the beginners. Let's toss it.

(D) Memory is a skill that can be improved with practice.

Again, this is like answer choices (A) and (C). Certainly the experts have practiced more, which is why they're experts to begin with. However, it still doesn't provide an explanation for the second scenario. Let's cross it out.

(E) Being able to infer the causes of a situation plays an important role in memorization.

Aha! There is a link between memory and familiarity, i.e., "inferring the cause of a situation." The expert chess players were able to make sense of the position of the pieces in the first scenario, so they could memorize it more easily. However, there was nothing to make sense of in the second scenario. This is why, when presented with a random pattern of chess pieces, the experts didn't do any better than the beginners did.

Argument Techniques: Process of Elimination with Resolve/Explain Questions

In using Process of Elimination with resolve/explain questions it is important to remember that the correct answer will be some explanation that will allow *both* of the facts from the argument to be true. In the Dirdir argument, the two facts were (a) they had water power and (b) they did not use this technology in their capital city. In the chess argument, the facts were (a) that the experts did better than the beginners at memorizing the positions of chess pieces from a previously played position and (b) that the experts did not do any better at memorizing a set of pieces randomly placed on the board. The correct answer in each case allowed each of these facts to be true independently of the other and allowed both to make sense together.

Additionally, note that the phrasing of most resolve/explain questions contains the clause "if true." Your methodology should be exactly the same here as it is with weaken and strengthen questions—you assume each of the five answer choices to be hypothetically true and look for impact on the argument. In the case of resolve/explain questions, the impact will be about how it will resolve an apparent discrepancy.

Cracking Resolve/Explain Questions: Summary

With resolve/explain questions, the only thing you must find before going to the answer choices is the apparent discrepancy or paradox. Remember that you have to work under the belief that the answers are true, regardless of how unreasonable they may seem. Evaluate what impact the answer choice would have on the argument *if it were true*. Finally, look to see which one of the answer choices allows both of the facts or sides of the argument to be true at the same time. Only one of them will do this.

Sample Question Phrasings	Attack! Attack! Attack!
Which of the following provides the best resolution to the apparent paradox described by the committee member? *Which of the following statements, if true, would explain the discrepancy found by the scientists?*	• Identify the apparent discrepancy or paradox. • Go to the answer choices and look for a piece of information that, when added to the argument, allows both facts from the argument to be true. • Assume all choices to be hypothetically true.

LESSON 6: INFERENCE QUESTIONS

Like the arguments attached to resolve/explain questions, many inference "arguments" are not written in the familiar *main point supported by reasons* format. Instead, they will ask passages that may or may not seem to be headed somewhere. And the test writers will ask you to find a piece of information that either must be true, based on the information provided in the argument, or will be best supported by the argument. That something can come from anywhere in the argument and doesn't have to come from anything important.

So here are a few tips right off the bat. You can't go beyond the boundaries of the argument, you don't have to find the main point, and you have to pay very close attention to any qualifying language (e.g., *most, always, each, few, might*) that is used. Ready to put this information to work? Then let's get to it.

THE ARGUMENT

6a. Many scientists and researchers equate addiction with physical dependence. This interpretation is fallacious. It fails to account for the most problematic aspect of addiction: drug-seeking behavior. Physical dependence is nothing more than the adaptive result of taking certain chemicals repeatedly. The distinction between dependence and addiction can clearly be seen in the usual failure of detoxification—the supervised gradual withdrawal of the drug—to cure addicted human beings.

Which of the following can be properly inferred from the statements above?

(A) Detoxification is usually able to cure human beings of a physical dependence on drugs.
(B) Addiction is not an adaptive result.
(C) Addiction, while not completely understood, has nothing to do with physical dependence.
(D) Drug-seeking behavior is a consequence of physical dependence as well as of addiction.
(E) It is impossible to completely and permanently cure addicted human beings.

CRACKING INFERENCE QUESTIONS

Step 1: Read the question and identify your task
Good, you've read the question. Here it is again:

6a. Which of the following can be properly inferred from the statements above?

This question is asking you to *infer* some piece of information from the argument. However, the word *inference* does not mean the same thing on the LSAT as it means in real life. On the LSAT, an inference is something that can be drawn using *only* the information presented in the passage. You can't go any further than what is on the page. In life, we make inferences all the time based on common sense, life experiences, etc. This is not allowed on the LSAT. The answer to this question must be provably true according to the information in the passage.

Step 2: Work the argument
Read carefully, paying special attention to any qualifying language. Make sure you have a good understanding of what the issue is that is discussed. Here it is again:

> Many scientists and researchers equate addiction with physical dependence. This interpretation is fallacious. It fails to account for the most problematic aspect of addiction: drug-seeking behavior. Physical dependence is nothing more than the adaptive result of taking certain chemicals repeatedly. The distinction between dependence and addiction can clearly be seen in the usual failure of detoxification—the supervised gradual withdrawal of the drug—to cure addicted human beings.

This argument is about drug addiction, physical dependence, and the failure of detoxification. Be sure to pay special attention to those qualifying words like "*many* scientists and researchers," "*most* problematic aspect," and "*usual* failure." Because you're going to be asked to identify something that *must be true* based only on the information presented in the argument, those details will be crucial to your task.

Step 3: Answer the question in your own words as best you can

The credited response could come from anywhere in the argument, and by definition we can make any number of inferences based on the information presented. Rather than getting caught up in trying to predict where the test writers are going to be taking the inference from, we're just going to head right to the answer choices—armed with a close reading of the argument, of course—and compare each of the answer choices with the argument to see whether or not the answer choice is a valid inference. Off we go.

Step 4: Use Process of Elimination

We're looking to eliminate any answers that are not consistent with the information in the argument. Remember that we must have solid evidence to support each part of an answer choice. Find one flaw and it's gone. Let's give it a shot:

> (A) Detoxification is usually able to cure human beings of a physical dependence on drugs.

There don't appear to be any flaws in this one. Note the word *usually* in this case, which is a pretty weak word. The passage states that the difference between dependence and addiction is revealed by the fact that detox usually fails to cure addiction. What does this tell you? That it probably *can* cure dependence. So let's leave it.

> (B) Addiction is not an adaptive result.

Two things wrong with this one, right? First, all the argument said was that physical dependence is an adaptive result, not that addiction isn't. There was no contrast made with addiction, so, unlike (A), we can't infer that addiction is the opposite of physical dependence in this area. Second, notice how strong the word *not* is. That kind of unequivocal language requires equally strong language in the passage for support. We don't have it in this case. Let's cross it out.

> (C) Addiction, while not completely understood, has nothing to do with physical dependence.

As in choice (B), note the extreme language. Addiction has "nothing to do" with dependence. What evidence do we have in the argument to support that? None. Let's cross it off.

(D) Drug-seeking behavior is a consequence of physical dependence as well as of addiction.

Well, this certainly hits all the issues mentioned in the argument, right? Drug-seeking behavior, physical dependence, addiction. And it might seem to make sense to someone based on what they know from outside the LSAT. So it sounds pretty good, but we're going to have to go back and re-read the argument to see if it actually said that drug-seeking behavior is a result (that's what *consequence* means here) of both dependence and addiction. Go back and read the argument now. Got it? As you can see, the argument only talked about drug-seeking behavior being a result of addiction. We don't know anything about the consequences of physical dependence based on the information given to us. No doubt there are consequences of physical dependence, but the argument does not provide us with this information. Let's cross it out.

(E) It is impossible to completely and permanently cure addicted human beings.

That's an awfully strong statement. "It is *impossible* to *completely* and *permanently...*" There are some really extreme words here that we'll have to find support for in the passage. If any of them fail, we can eliminate it. Notice that the author says the detoxification *usually* fails to cure addicted human beings. That means that at least sometimes it must succeed. That's enough to get rid of this answer.

Well, we got the credited response, but only after going back and really checking to make sure answer choice (D) was not necessarily true given the information in the passage. So, (A) is a good and typical answer to an inference question. It is based on a specific sentence and *explicitly* states something that is *implicitly* stated in the sentence.

Now let's spend some more time with our good friend Process of Elimination.

Arguments Techniques: Extreme Language Revisited

Do you remember the Process of Elimination techniques we used to cross off wrong answer choices in main point questions? They included relevance, opposites, and extreme language. Relevance is still certainly an issue with inference questions, because if there is something in an answer choice that wasn't mentioned in the argument, there's no way you could have inferred it from the information presented. However, when it comes to inference questions, extreme wording (as you saw in the above example) plays a key role. It is much easier to say that something is *usually* true than to say that something is *always* true. You have to spend a lot more time backing up the second phrase. Let's take a look at another example:

1. Most Rhodes scholars enjoy reading.
2. All Rhodes scholars enjoy reading.

There's only one difference between these two sentences: One has the word *most*, the other has the word *all*. Yet there is a vast difference between these two statements. Certainly, anyone who becomes nominated for such a prestigious academic award has done more than his fair share of reading. Very rigorous standards must be met and outstanding academic performance must be demonstrated. This requires a ton of reading. It's reasonable to think that if someone's doing that much reading, she probably enjoys reading. But if we were asked which of those statements *must be true*, we would have to eliminate the second statement. It would be incredibly difficult to prove that *all* Rhodes scholars enjoy reading. It would only take *one* person who never really liked to read, but was driven to this level of success for other reasons, to disprove the second statement. It would be much easier to prove the first statement because it leaves a lot more room for a few exceptions to the general rule. Both statements involve strong wording, but the second is *too* strong.

It's much easier to show that something is usually true than it is to show that something is always true.

Take a look at the chart below:

Nice and Vague	Dangerously Extreme
might	always
could	never
may	at no time
can	must
some	will
possible	all
usually	not
sometimes	positively
at least once	absolutely
frequently	unequivocally
	each

The sample inference question we just worked through asked us to find the answer choice that could be "properly inferred," in other words, the one that *must be true* based on the information in the argument. Other inference questions will require a slightly different task. Rather than finding the answer that must be true, you will be asked to find the one that would be best supported by the information in the argument. This may seem like a subtle difference, but it is important to pay attention to nuances in language such as this on the LSAT. Let's take a look at how these work on the following page.

6b. Chinchillas raised in captivity who have not yet learned to feed on their own often stop squawking from hunger when the bottle used to feed them is brought into their view. Bringing in the bottles of other sizes or colors has no similar effect.

Which one of the following is most reasonably supported by the information above?

(A) Chinchillas raised in captivity learn to recognize the bottle used to feed them before they recognize any other objects.
(B) Chinchillas more easily learn to recognize the bottle used to feed them than any bottles of other sizes or colors.
(C) Chinchillas raised in captivity are able to connect the presence of their feeding bottle with a release from hunger.
(D) The best way to stop chinchillas raised in captivity from squawking is to bring their feeding bottle into their visual field.
(E) Chinchillas raised in captivity will only feed from the bottle that has been used to feed them in the past.

Step 1: Read the question and identify your task
Let's make sure that we're clear about our task. This question asks us to find the answer that is "most reasonably supported" by the information in the passage. We don't have to be able to show that the answer *must be true* according to the information we have from the author. We still need evidence from the author's language, but it doesn't *have to be* true.

Step 2: Work the argument
We still need to read the argument carefully. This step will be the same as it was with our first inference question. We'll still pay close attention to qualifying language, underlining key words and jotting down any notes we need to keep things straight. Here's the passage again:

> Chinchillas raised in captivity who have not yet learned to feed on their own often stop squawking from hunger when the bottle used to feed them is brought into their view. Bringing in the bottles of other sizes or colors has no similar effect.

We've been told that for a particular group one action causes a given response, but other similar actions don't yield the same response.

Step 3: Answer the question in your own words as best you can
Remember that on inference questions, you can't predict with any assurance what the test writers will look for. We'll head right to the answer choices and start Step 4.

Step 4: Use Process of Elimination

Let's check out each answer choice in turn and see which ones we can eliminate. We'll be on the lookout for answers such as those that fall outside of the scope of the information that we're given or are inconsistent with what we were told; answers that include extreme language; and answers that make unwarranted comparisons. If any part of an answer choice isn't supported we'll get rid of it. Here we go:

> (A) Chinchillas raised in captivity learn to recognize the bottle used to feed them before they recognize any other objects.

We have pretty good evidence that these chinchillas learn to recognize the bottle used to feed them, but do we have support for the idea that they recognize that bottle "before they recognize *any* other objects"? That's more than the blurb can support, so we'll get rid of it.

> (B) Chinchillas more easily learn to recognize the bottle used to feed them than any bottles of other sizes or colors.

Again, we have evidence that chinchillas learn to recognize at least some bottles, but can we say that they learn to recognize some "more easily" than others? We don't have any evidence about how easy it is for them to learn recognition, so that's an unwarranted comparison. Cross it off.

> (C) Chinchillas raised in captivity are able to connect the presence of their feeding bottle with a release from hunger.

The language in this one seems reasonable. When the hungry chinchillas see their feeding bottle, they temporarily stop squawking. It seems to support the idea that they make some connection between seeing this bottle and not being hungry anymore. This might be a bit of a stretch to prove beyond the shadow of a doubt from the argument, but because we only have to find the answer choice that is most reasonably supported, we'll keep it for now.

> (D) The best way to stop chinchillas raised in captivity from squawking is to bring their feeding bottle into their visual field.

We know that bringing the feeding bottle into sight leads to a temporary stop in the chinchillas' squawking, but is there any evidence to suggest that this is the "best" way to stop them from squawking? There could be a number of other ways to stop them from squawking, but we're not given any information about them, so we can't say that this is *the best* way to do it. Let's get rid of it.

> (E) Chinchillas raised in captivity will only feed from the bottle that has been used to feed them in the past.

In this answer choice we have another one of those really strong words. Did you notice the word *only* here? So we have another choice that goes further than the information we have to support it. We're not given any information, one way or the other, about what sources these chinchillas will feed from. This one's a goner, too.

So there we have it. We found (C), which is the credited response. Notice that we can't say *for sure* that the chinchilla can connect the presence of the feeding bottle with a release from hunger. Although there could be other explanations, this is a reasonable inference.

Basically, when we have this kind of weaker inference, we have a little bit more latitude. We still need evidence to support the choice, but we don't have to be able to show that an answer *must be true.*

Arguments Techniques: The Word *Support*

The word *support* shows up in two different types of arguments questions and you'll need to be able to keep them straight if you hope to attack the questions effectively. Let's take a look at a couple of sample questions:

> Which one of the following, if true, provides the most support for the argument?

> The passage provides the most support for which one of the following?

If you're not careful, you might mistakenly think that these two questions ask you to perform the same task. After all, they both talk about support, right? Actually, we have two different tasks here, and if we get them mixed up we're going to have a heck of time with POE. Let's examine the first question more closely. Here it is again:

> Which one of the following, if true, provides the most support for the argument?

This should look familiar. Care to guess what your task is here? If you identified this as a strengthen question, bravo! There are two indicators that will help us to properly identify it. First, notice the phrase "if true" and recall that the answers on strengthen questions are hypothetically true. Second, notice that you are being asked to find the answer choice that *provides the most support for* the argument. In other words, you're being asked to evaluate the impact that each answer choice has on the author's point. Sound familiar? We hope so.

Here's the second question again:

> The passage provides the most support for which one of the following?

Notice the difference here. Aside from the obvious lack of the words "if true," this question also asks for the support to happen, but *in the other direction.* Here you are asked to find the answer choice that *is best supported by* the argument. That's what you were just doing in the argument you worked on a minute ago, so this is an inference question.

Here we'll eliminate answers that aren't relevant because the passage doesn't offer enough evidence to support them, a pretty different mode of elimination from that used with strengthen questions. So, two things to look for: The words "if true" indicate hypotheticals in the answers, so it won't be an inference question.

If the *answer choices* are being used to support the *argument*, we have a strengthen question. If the *argument* is being used to support one of the *answer choices*, we have an inference question.

ARGUMENTS TECHNIQUES: CONDITIONAL STATEMENTS AND THE CONTRAPOSITIVE

Do you know what an "if . . . then" statement is? If you've taken any classes in logic you might know it as a "conditional statement." Actually, it's very simple. Read this sentence:

> If you hit a glass with a hammer, the glass will break.

When you run across a statement like this, you can diagram it. A common way to diagram conditional statements is to use a symbol for each element in the statement—here we'll use "H" for hitting the glass with a hammer and "B" for breaking—and use an arrow to connect them, showing that the action leads directly to the effect. So $H \rightarrow B$ would represent the original statement.

This statement would seem reasonable to most people because it's what we would expect to happen in the real world. On the LSAT we would have to take this statement as true if it were part of an argument because, as we stated earlier, we have to accept all of the evidence presented in arguments at face value. This is true even when they aren't things that necessarily make reasonable sense to us.

With inference questions you are often asked to identify another statement—in the form of an answer choice—that also *must be true* if the statements in the argument are accepted as true.

Here's our original statement:

> If you hit a glass with a hammer, the glass will break.

We can come up with a few other statements that we think would also have to be true.

For example, we could say:

> If the glass is broken, it was hit with a hammer.

We would symbolize this as $B \rightarrow H$. That seems like a reasonable outcome, but can we say that it *must be true* given our original statement?

Not *necessarily*. The glass could have been thrown out the window, stepped on by a giraffe, shot up with a Red Rider BB gun, etc. If this were an answer choice on an inference question in which the argument contained our original statement, what would you do? Hopefully, you would cross it out, because it doesn't have to be true. We could also suppose that:

> If you don't hit a glass with a hammer, the glass won't break.

In this case, our symbolization would become $-H \rightarrow -B$. Once again this seems reasonable in many cases, but does it *have to be true*? Again, not necessarily. It could have been thrown out the window, run over by a car, shattered by an opera singer's high C note, etc. If this were an answer choice on an inference question in which the argument contained our original statement, what would you do? Hopefully, you would cross it out too, because just like the last one, it doesn't have to be true.

So how about this statement:

If the glass isn't broken, it wasn't hit with a hammer.

This would by symbolized as –B → –H. This *must* be true. It makes sense if you think about it because we know for sure that if you hit the glass with a hammer, you're definitely going to break the glass. So if you come across an unbroken glass, there's no way it could have been hit with a hammer, at least not if you accept the truth of the original statement the way we have to on the LSAT. The only way that you could argue the truth of the above statement is by arguing the truth of the original. And while you can do that in real life, you can't do it on the LSAT.

To get the contrapositive, flip the order of the original statements and negate each of them.

This statement, which must always be true given that the original statement is true, is known as the *contrapositive*. To create the contrapositive of a statement all you have to do is take the original statement (or its symbolization, which is easier to work with) and perform the following two steps: Flip the order of the statements and then negate each of them.

Here's how it works with our original:

H → B

Flip the order of the statements and we get:

B → H

Then remember to negate each of them and we have our contrapositive:

–B → –H

So what do you do if you have to negate something that's already negative? Let's take a look at an example:

If Pablo attends the dance, Christina won't attend the dance.

We can symbolize this as follows:

P → –C

When we flip the order of the statements we will get:

–C → P

And now we have to negate. How do we negate –C? Well, here two negatives make a positive. When we negate a statement like "Christina won't attend the dance," it becomes "Christina will attend the dance." From our statement above, the last step—negating each of the original statements—will yield:

C → –P

With these examples, which are tied to real life and make reasonable sense, it might seem like it's more work to learn how to apply this process than it would be to just reason out what the only other true statement would be. And it would be pretty reasonable to do that if you understand the way conditionals and contrapositives work, and if the original statement makes sense. If only the LSAT were always that straightforward....

Instead, what will often happen is the original statement will be some abstract and complicated notion that's hard to get a handle on. For instance, you might see a conditional statement like "Copper will not be added to the alloy only if aluminum is also not added to the alloy." Not nearly as intuitive, is it? Add to that the pressure of taking a timed, standardized exam and you'll wish you had memorized the simple steps above. These steps always work so it's worth having them at your disposal, don't you think? We're telling you all this because sometimes arguments contain "if . . . then" statements like the ones above. Usually the LSAT writers then ask an inference question that requires you to find the answer that *must be true*. And then what happens is that a couple of the answer choices will seem like reasonable things to believe. Another one or two will be variations on the original conditional statement, but won't be valid contrapositives. As always, there will only be one right answer—it'll be the one where the statements have been reversed and negated!

Arguments Techniques: Because Little Things Can Mean a Lot

Another key to cracking inference questions is to pay close attention to detail. Inferences are often made around seemingly innocuous words or phrases. For instance, any time you see a term of quantity, comparison, or frequency, odds are it contains an inference:

Statement: *Most people like Picasso.*

Inference: *Some people do not like Picasso.*

Statement: *Unlike her jacket, mine is real leather.*

Inference: *Her jacket is not real leather.*

Statement: *Russ almost never shows up on time.*

Inference: *Russ rarely (or occasionally) does show up on time.*

So keep an eye out for details and you'll stand a better chance of getting inference questions right.

Cracking Inference Questions: Summary

With inference questions, first read the argument closely and pay close attention to details like qualifying language. Once you're at the answer choices, your goal is to eliminate the four answer choices that don't have to be true or are not wholly supported by evidence provided in the argument. You're also going to look out for relevance and, especially, issues of extreme language.

The way that inference questions are phrased can be very tricky. See the "Sample Question Phrasings" column in the chart below for some examples.

"Conclusions" means that it's an inference question, not a main point.

Sample Question Phrasings	Attack! Attack! Attack!
Which one of the following statements can be validly inferred from the information above? *If the statements above are true, then which of the following must also be true?* **Which one of the following conclusions can be validly drawn from the passage above?* **Which one of the following conclusions is best supported by the passage above?*	• Read carefully, paying close attention to qualifying language, then go to the answer choices. • Once there, cross off any answer choices that are not *directly* supported by evidence in the passage. • Use relevance and extreme language to eliminate answer choices. • Use the contrapositive if there are "if . . . then" statements contained in the passage and in the answer choices.

*Note the fact that this example says "conclusions" and not "conclusion."

LESSON 7: REASONING QUESTIONS

So far, the questions we've seen in the Arguments section have been concerned with the literal contents: What's the conclusion, how do you attack or support it, or what does it assume? What piece of information will resolve two seemingly inconsistent pieces of information or what else do we know to be true if the statements in the argument are true? Now we're going to look at some questions that deal with the arguments on a more abstract or descriptive level.

The first of these is the reasoning question, which asks you to determine not what the argument is about, but how the argument is made. This sounds pretty straightforward, doesn't it? Well, sometimes it will be, but sometimes it'll be pretty difficult, due to very attractive incorrect answers and deliberately impenetrable vocabulary. The answers to reasoning questions will fall into one of two categories: general answers that don't actually mention the subject matter of the argument, and specific answers that do address the subject matter of the argument. Occasionally, the answer choices will be a mix of both.

So how do you attack questions such as these? Well, first you have to be able to identify the task. Then your goal is to describe what's happening in the argument—in other words, how the author made his or her point. Got it? Let's try one.

The Argument

7. Fortunately for the development of astronomy, observations of Mars were not exact in Kepler's timc. If they had been, Kepler might not have "discovered" that the planets move in elliptical rather than circular orbits, and he would not have formulated his three laws of planetary motion. There are those who complain that the science of economics is inexact, and that economic theories neglect certain details. That is their merit. Theories in economics, like those in astronomy, must be allowed some imprecision.

   In the passage above, the author reaches his conclusion by

   (A) finding an exception to a general rule
   (B) drawing an analogy
   (C) appealing to an authority
   (D) attributing an unknown cause to a known effect
   (E) using the word "theory" ambiguously

Cracking Reasoning Questions

Step 1: Read the question and identify your task

So you've read the question. Here it is again:

7. In the passage above, the author reaches his conclusion by

This asks us to describe the author's method of reasoning. So let's read the argument and see how he gets from the evidence to his main point.

Step 2: Work the argument

Read the argument closely, paying attention to the author's reasoning. In order to do this, you'll have to identify the main point and the reasons because this will allow you to understand the structure of the argument; in other words, how the author used the evidence to support his point. Here it is again:

> Fortunately for the development of astronomy, observations of Mars were not exact in Kepler's time. If they had been, Kepler might not have "discovered" that the planets move in elliptical rather than circular orbits, and he would not have formulated his three laws of planetary motion. There are those who complain that the science of economics is inexact, and that economic theories neglect certain details. That is their merit. Theories in economics, like those in astronomy, must be allowed some imprecision.

This argument is about Kepler, astronomy, and the benefits of imprecision in economic theories.

Step 3: Answer the question in your own words as best you can
Our goal here is simply to describe how the author made his argument.

Let's make sure that we understand the pieces.

Your goal on reasoning questions is to describe how the author constructed the argument.

Author's main point: *Economic theories must be allowed some imprecision.*

Author's reasons: *Look at Kepler's laws of planetary motion; they were made possible by the imprecision in the observations of Mars in Kepler's time. And other people's complaints about the inexact nature of economics are misguided.*

Notice that we didn't have to worry about identifying any assumptions for this type of question.

In this case, it looks as if the entire thing about Kepler is an analogy used to say that it's actually a good thing that economic theories are imprecise. So this author made his argument by analogy, one of our common types of arguments.

Step 4: Use Process of Elimination
Now we're going to attack the answer choices. We can eliminate any answer choices that don't have to do with the author making an analogy. Let's check them out:

(A) finding an exception to a general rule

The author doesn't make an exception to any rule, so let's cross it off.

(B) drawing an analogy

Looks pretty good. Let's leave it.

(C) appealing to an authority

Who does the term "authority" apply to in the argument? The author doesn't look to any authority to justify his conclusion. We can get rid of it.

(D) attributing an unknown cause to a known effect

Sounds impressive, but this argument isn't about cause and effect. It's about making an analogy. Let's eliminate it.

(E) using the word "theory" ambiguously

How is the word "theory" used ambiguously? It's used the same way in reference to both astronomy and economics. Let's cross it off.

That one was pretty straightforward. We were able to recognize the credited response pretty easily because we understood the author's reasoning—using an analogy—before we approached the answer choices. Note how abstract the answers were. They didn't mention any of the specifics (e.g., astronomy, theories, Kepler, etc.) but took a much broader view.

Arguments Techniques: Process of Elimination with Reasoning Questions

You may have noticed that when we discussed some of the answer choices we took each word or phrase from the answer choice and asked, "Does this correspond to anything that actually occurred in the argument?" Most of the time, the answer to this question was no. The answer choices might sound abstract and technical, but unless you can go back to the argument and say, "Ah, yes, this is where the author gives the example and this is where he gives the counterexample," then an answer choice that mentions "examples" and "counterexamples" will be wrong. This technique is the key to dealing with reasoning questions; it should allow you to eliminate two or three answer choices every time. One other nice advantage of this technique is that it works even if you can't articulate the author's reasoning in your own words.

So look through the answers on reasoning questions very slowly and make sure to match each piece of the answer choice to a piece of the argument. When you come across something in an answer choice that doesn't correspond to anything in the argument, you can get rid of that choice. If it's even a little bad, it's all bad.

On reasoning questions, try to match each piece of the answer choice to a piece of the argument.

Cracking Reasoning Questions: Summary

As you can see, in reasoning questions you'll want to come up with your own description of how the argument unfolds. If you're able to come up with a terse, exact description of the argument, you can usually match it with one of the answer choices. Even if you can't come up with a good description, you can eliminate any answers that have elements that don't correspond with what actually happens in the author's argument. The vocabulary in the answer choices will probably be more esoteric than that which you used, but as long as the meaning is the same, you're fine.

Sample Question Phrasings	Attack! Attack! Attack!
The argument proceeds by *Leah responds to Kevin by doing which one of the following?* *The method the activist uses to object to the developer's argument is to* *Dr. Jacobs does which of the following?*	• Read the argument carefully and then describe what is happening in your own words. • Take this description and rigorously apply it to all the answer choices. • Once you're at the answer choices, use the technique of comparing the actions described in the choices against those that actually occurred in the argument. • Cross out anything that didn't appear in the argument. Lather, rinse, repeat.

LESSON 8: FLAW QUESTIONS

Flaw questions are similar to reasoning questions, but they're dissimilar enough that they call for a slightly different approach. On recent LSATs, flaw questions have been far more common than have reasoning questions. So what's the difference? Well, while a reasoning question asks you to identify what the argument does, or how it's argued, a flaw question asks you what the argument does *wrong*. And as we mentioned before, if you find the assumption in an argument, you've probably found its flaw. So the approach to flaw and reasoning questions is the same, but with one important distinction: During Step 2, you'll want to break down the argument into its parts and locate the assumption. After you've spotted the assumption, you just need to state what's wrong with the argument. Let's look at the Kepler argument again:

THE ARGUMENT

8a. Fortunately for the development of astronomy, observations of Mars were not exact in Kepler's time. If they had been, Kepler might not have "discovered" that the planets move in elliptical rather than circular orbits, and he would not have formulated his three laws of planetary motion. There are those who complain that the science of economics is inexact, and that economic theories neglect certain details. That is their merit. Theories in economics, like those in astronomy, must be allowed some imprecision.

A logical critique of the argument above would most likely emphasize that the author

(A) fails to cite other authorities
(B) does not consider nonscientific theories
(C) neglects the possibility that there may have been other reasons for Kepler's success
(D) assumes the truth of the very position he is trying to prove
(E) ignores the differences between the sort of imprecision allowed in astronomy and that allowed in economics

Step 1: Read the question and identify your task

You've already read the question, but here it is again:

8a. A logical critique of the argument above would most likely emphasize that the author

So you're expected to describe why the above argument is bad. Remember that this is totally different from "weakening" an argument, in which you'd hypothesize that the five answer choices were true. All you're looking for here is the way in which the argument is bad, not something that would make it worse.

Step 2: Work the argument

Okay, so start by breaking it down into its parts.

Author's main point: *Economic theories must be allowed some imprecision.*

Author's reasons: *Look at Kepler's laws of planetary motion; they were made possible by the imprecision in the observations of Mars in Kepler's time. And other people's complaints about the inexact nature of economics are misguided.*

Author's assumption: *With respect to the terms of the argument, theories of astronomy are analogous to theories of economics.*

Step 3: Answer the question in your own words as best you can

The correct answer to a flaw question often draws attention to the assumption. So if the assumption is that astronomy and economics are in some way similar, the *flaw* is the failure of the argument to demonstrate that similarity. The correct answer should draw attention to the fact that the two fields are not necessarily similar.

Step 4: Use Process of Elimination

Now we're going to attack the answer choices. Let's see if we can find an answer choice that has something to do with the author making an analogy:

(A) fails to cite other authorities

This is almost never the correct answer in a flaw question. Usually, the argument is wrong somehow *internally*, not because the author didn't bring in some expert from the big city. Let's cross it off.

(B) does not consider nonscientific theories

True, but once again, so what? The author doesn't talk about nonscientific theories, but the analogy is either a good or a bad one on its own. Let's kill it.

(C) neglects the possibility that there may have been other reasons for Kepler's success

Aha. This means that Kepler might have been great for other reasons. However, we're not trying to weaken causality here, but show how the analogy is weak. Let's cross it off.

(D) assumes the truth of the very proposition he is trying to prove

An answer choice like this one *can* be a correct answer to a flaw question, but only when the argument is circular—when the main point just restates one of the reasons. That's not the case here; the author is drawing an analogy. Let's cross it off.

(E) ignores the differences between the sort of imprecision allowed in astronomy and that allowed in economics

Oops, right? The analogy isn't very good between astronomy and economics. Hence, this is our answer.

So you know that flaw questions usually deal with assumptions. You also know that they're pretty similar to reasoning questions, and they can exhibit similar "traps" (overly wordy or confusing answers). Finally, you can use similar techniques on flaw questions, such as trying to match each word or phrase in the answer choices with something in the argument.

ARGUMENTS TECHNIQUES: PROCESS OF ELIMINATION WITH FLAW QUESTIONS

One thing you might have noticed we did when discussing some of the answer choices was again to take each word or phrase from the answer choice and ask, "Does this correspond to anything that actually occurred in the argument?" Most of the time, the answer is no. The answer choices might sound impressive ("the author assumes what he sets out to prove," "the author appeals to authority," etc.), but unless you can go back to the argument and say, "Ah, yes, *this* is where the author gives evidence," or "*this* is where the author makes an assumption," then an answer choice that mentions "examples" or "assumptions" will be wrong. This technique is HUGE. It will eliminate two or three answer choices every time.

Therefore, take answer choices on flaw questions very slowly, and make sure to match each piece of the answer choice to a piece of the argument. Once you come across something in an answer choice that doesn't correspond to anything in the argument, you can get rid of that answer choice. Once it's a little bad, it's all bad. This process will allow you to eliminate two or three answer choices in most cases, but what about the ones that remain? You'll find that some of the answer choices on flaw questions will be consistent with the argument but won't represent a flaw in the author's reasoning.

So once you've eliminated any answer choices on flaw questions that are not consistent with what actually happened in the argument, then go back to check the rest to see if they represent a logical flaw in the structure of the author's argument.

Let's try another one:

THE ARGUMENT

8b. Expert musicologists believe that Beethoven wrote his last piano sonata in 1824, three years before his death. However, the manuscript of a piano sonata was recently discovered that bears Beethoven's name and dates from 1825. Clearly, the experts are mistaken, because not every piece that Beethoven wrote was catalogued in his lifetime, and it is known that Beethoven continued to compose until just weeks before his death.

The reasoning in the argument is most vulnerable to which of the following criticisms?

(A) A given position that is widely believed to be true is taken to show that the position in question must, in fact, be true.
(B) That either of two things could have occurred independently is taken to show that those two things could not have occurred simultaneously.
(C) Establishing that a certain event occurred is confused with having established the cause of that event.
(D) A claim that has a very general application is based entirely on evidence from a narrowly restricted range of cases.
(E) An inconsistency that, as presented, has more than one possible resolution is treated as though only one resolution is possible.

Step 1: Read the question and identify your task
Here's the question again:

8b. The reasoning in the argument is most vulnerable to which of the following criticisms?

This is a classic flaw question. You're asked to describe what's wrong with the author's reasoning.

Step 2: Work the argument
Again, we're reading for the main point and the reasons, and we should think about assumptions the author makes. Here's the argument again:

8b. Expert musicologists believe that Beethoven wrote his last piano sonata in 1824, three years before his death. However, the manuscript of a piano sonata was recently discovered that bears Beethoven's name and dates from 1825. Clearly, the experts are mistaken, because not every piece that Beethoven wrote was catalogued in his lifetime, and it is known that Beethoven continued to compose until just weeks before his death.

So, the main point is that the experts are mistaken: Beethoven wrote a piano sonata after 1824. How does the author justify this? By showing that a sonata with Beethoven's name on it was written in 1825, and giving reasons that support the idea that Beethoven wrote it.

Any idea what's wrong here? If you noticed that the author didn't prove that Beethoven actually wrote the sonata that was written in 1825, then you're on the right track. Let's summarize:

- Author's main point: *The experts are wrong about when Beethoven wrote his last piano sonata.*
- Author's reasons: *There's a sonata with Beethoven's name on it dated 1825, and it's possible the experts didn't know about it, and Beethoven could have written it.*
- Author's assumption: *Beethoven actually wrote the 1825 sonata.*

Step 3: Answer the question in your own words as best you can
Remember, this is a flaw question, so we need to describe what's wrong. You might come up with something like, "Just because he *could* have written it doesn't mean he *did* write it." Keep this in mind as we look through the answer choices.

Step 4: Use Process of Elimination

(A) A given position that is widely believed to be true is taken to show that the position in question must, in fact, be true.

This doesn't seem to match what we're looking for. The "widely held belief" (that of the experts) is what the argument is trying to disprove, not prove. Let's cross it out.

(B) That either of two things could have occurred independently is taken to show that those two things could not have occurred simultaneously.

The argument didn't talk about two things that could have occurred independently. Let's cross it out.

(C) Establishing that a certain event occurred is confused with having established the cause of that event.

Maybe. What's the "certain event?" The writing of the 1825 sonata. What's the cause of that event that it's being confused with? Beethoven writing it. Does it fit with the idea of "Just because he *could* have written it doesn't mean he *did* write it?" Sort of. It's not great, but it's the best so far. Let's keep it.

(D) A claim that has a very general application is based entirely on evidence from a narrowly restricted range of cases.

The claim in the argument is very specific: that Beethoven wrote piano sonatas after 1825. And it wasn't based on a narrow range of test cases, it was based on a single counterexample to the experts' belief. This doesn't match. Let's cross it off.

(E) An inconsistency that, as presented, has more than one possible resolution is treated as though only one resolution is possible.

What's the inconsistency? The experts' belief versus the newly-discovered manuscript. Could it have more than one possible resolution? Yes, the experts could be wrong, or the manuscript could be a fake. Is it treated as though there could be only one solution? Yes, the author concludes that the experts are wrong. Does this fit with the idea of "Just because he *could* have written it doesn't mean he *did* write it?" Yes, very closely.

So, although (C) had some good things going for it, you could easily match each general term in (E) (e.g., "inconsistency" and "one possible resolution") to a specific concept in the argument itself. With (C), the fit wasn't as close (i.e., is the "cause" of an "event" the same thing as someone writing a sonata?). (E) is a better answer.

Cracking Flaw Questions: Summary

So the key to cracking flaw questions is finding the assumption. Once you've found the assumption, everything else should fall into place. Just remember that these questions are different from weaken questions, in which new information is brought in to attack the argument, and are different from reasoning questions, in which finding the assumption won't be nearly as useful.

Sample Question Phrasings	Attack! Attack! Attack!
Which of the following indicates a flaw in the author's reasoning?	• Break down the argument into its parts; the flaw is usually related to the assumption.
A criticism of the argument would most likely emphasize that it	• State in your own words what the problem with the argument is.
The reasoning in the argument is most vulnerable to criticism on the grounds that the argument	• With each answer, try to match the actions described in the answer choices with those of the argument itself. Look for the choice that has the same problem you found.
The argument above relies on which of the following questionable techniques?	• Eliminate the answers that don't match; look for the answer that addresses the assumption.

LESSON 9: PRINCIPLE QUESTIONS

We're nearing the home stretch here on arguments. The last two question types we will cover are principle and parallel-the-reasoning.

We saved principle questions until now for two reasons. First, there are a couple of different forms of principle questions and now that we've covered the other question types, we'll be able to see the ways in which the approach for those is similar to that for principle questions. And second, most principle questions are reasonable, but the ones that get nasty can get really nasty. If you could tell just by looking at them which were straightforward and which were more complicated, it'd be easy to just bail on the nasty ones. But usually you can't tell until you're in the thick of them, so you might consider holding off on the principle questions until you've worked the majority of the other question types.

Let's dive in and see how one of these works on the following page.

9. The development of secured-funds transfer via the Internet has played an important role in legitimizing those who support the new era of Internet commerce. People can now have access to a huge variety of goods without ever leaving their homes. This allows people to cut transportation time and fuel costs, and avoid the frustration of arriving at a store only to find that the item they want is out of stock. It is not surprising then that the proponents of Internet commerce have conveniently overlooked the dangers inherent in this activity before the technology has come far enough to eliminate potential identity theft and fraud, dangers that could be serious enough to dissuade consumers from embracing the technology.

The reasoning above would most closely conform to which one of the following principles?

(A) People have a tendency to ignore possible negative consequences of actions that support their own goals.
(B) Technology often has some negative impact on society, even when the technology is largely beneficial.
(C) Even solutions that are well intentioned can, at times, do more harm than good.
(D) A negative result of an action may be outweighed by its potential positive results.
(E) Many technological advances have unanticipated consequences that turn out to be detrimental.

Step 1: Read the question and identify your task
First, as always, we have to identify our task. Here it is again:

9. The reasoning above would most closely conform to which one of the following principles?

We are asked to find a principle among the answers with which the argument would be consistent. Similarly, on a main point question we have to choose an answer that's consistent with the argument; we have to make sure that a given answer doesn't violate anything that was stated in the argument. However, in the case of principle questions we have to make sure that what is stated in the argument doesn't violate anything in the correct answer. In other words, the argument has to "fit into" the answer.

Step 2: Work the argument
We need to have a clear understanding of what's happening in the argument. Basically, we are presented with some pretty good reasons for supporting the spread of Internet commerce: It saves time, money, and frustration. But then we're told that the people who support Internet commerce tend to overlook some of the drawbacks of using such technology; we might wonder why they would still support it given its potential danger.

Step 3: Answer the question in your own words as best you can

Because we're going to be asked to identify the principle with which the argument would fit best, we'll want to be able to state in basic terms what's going on. For this example, we might come up with something like: Proponents of a cause sometimes overlook the drawbacks when there is good evidence to support their case. Let's see if we can find a match in the answers.

Step 4: Use Process of Elimination

As we evaluate the answer choices, we'll want to cross off any that are not consistent with the basic premise we just came up with or with the information presented in the argument. Let's get right to it.

(A) People have a tendency to ignore possible negative consequences of actions that support their own goals.

This sounds like a pretty close match to what we are looking for; it says that possible drawbacks don't dissuade people from promoting their cause. We'll hold onto it.

(B) Technology often has some negative impact on society, even when the technology is largely beneficial.

While this may be true, it leaves out some important elements mentioned in the argument. It never talks about *why* people would still support technology that has some negative impact. Let's get rid of it.

(C) Even solutions that are well-intentioned can, at times, do more harm than good.

Again, this addresses some possible harm, but, like (B), it doesn't help us to understand why the proponents in the argument would overlook the dangers involved. We'll cross it off.

(D) A negative result of an action may be outweighed by its potential positive results.

Once again, we have a statement that seems reasonable but doesn't match the argument. The fact that the positives outweigh the negative doesn't get at the particular agenda of the proponents in the argument. We have to find an answer choice that suggests why it's "not surprising" that the proponents would overlook the negative. Close, but no cigar. Get rid of it.

(E) Many technological advances have unanticipated consequences that turn out to be detrimental.

That's all fine and good. And we know from our own experience that this is often the case. But again, this answer falls short in addressing the element of why the proponents act in the way they do. Let's eliminate it.

That wasn't so bad. Once we understood why the people mentioned in the argument acted the way that they did, we were able to eliminate any answer that didn't match up with our paraphrase.

ARGUMENTS TECHNIQUES: PROCESS OF ELIMINATION WITH PRINCIPLE QUESTIONS

As we saw from this example, you are looking to find a principle among the answer choices that will match the conditions or actions stated in the argument. If the principle were contained in the argument you might be asked to find an answer choice that would conform to that principle. But your task would stay the same: to eliminate any answers that didn't match up with your paraphrase.

Principle questions ask you either to match or validate a decision or action.

Other principle questions will ask you to find the answer that would validate or justify someone's action or position. You'll want to evaluate whether or not the answer choice will validate the argument. So your job here will feel similar to that on a strengthen question.

The important thing to remember: You're looking for the answer that makes clear or validates *why* the action or decision in the argument took place.

CRACKING PRINCIPLE QUESTIONS: SUMMARY

Refer to the chart below on how to attack principle questions.

Sample Question Phrasings	Attack! Attack! Attack!
Which one of the following principles, if established, justifies the actions taken by Mia in the argument above? *Which of the following examples conforms most closely to the principle given in the argument above?*	• Make sure you're clear in which direction the argument is flowing—are you being asked to find something that supports or conforms? • Once you're sure, look for the answer that either justifies the action or matches the principle in the argument.

LESSON 10: PARALLEL-THE-REASONING QUESTIONS

We're at the end, finally. And there is a reason we saved parallel-the-reasoning questions for last—because you should probably avoid them until you've worked all the other questions you can tackle. These questions are not necessarily more difficult, but they are certainly more time consuming on average than most other question types. Don't forget that all of the questions are worth one point each; why spend more time for the same reward?

Save parallel questions for last or skip them altogether.

The reason that these take so long is that you have to perform Step 2 (Work the argument) for six arguments rather than just one! Each answer choice is another argument. Most arguments attached to parallel-the-reasoning questions can be diagrammed in some fashion. Your job is then to find the answer choice that has the same diagram.

The Argument

10. A full moon is known to cause strange behavior in people. People are behaving strangely today, so there is probably a full moon.

    Which of the following most closely parallels the flawed pattern of reasoning used in the argument above?

    (A) Abnormal sunspot activity causes animals to act strangely. We are experiencing abnormal sunspot activity today, so animals are probably acting strangely.
    (B) Studies have shown that the use of turn signals reduces the likelihood of highway accidents. There has been a decrease in highway accidents, so people are most likely using their turn signals.
    (C) The law of gravity has worked for as long as mankind has been able to observe it. It's working today, and it will probably continue to work tomorrow.
    (D) Increased stress has been shown to decrease the effectiveness of a person's immune system. So it follows that someone who does not have a diminished immune system is not likely to be experiencing an increased level of stress.
    (E) People with an ear for music often have an equal facility for learning languages. Bill doesn't have an ear for music, so he probably doesn't have a facility for learning languages.

Cracking Parallel-the-Reasoning Questions

Step 1: Read the question and identify your task

Good, you've read the question. Here it is again:

> Which of the following most closely parallels the flawed pattern of reasoning used in the argument above?

Okay, so it's a parallel-the-reasoning argument, and we know that we have to try to diagram the argument, if possible, and match that diagram against the diagrams for each of the answer choices. We also know that the reasoning itself is bad, because the question tips us off to that. Let's go to it.

Step 2: Work the argument

As always, read it through carefully. Here it is again:

> 10. A full moon is known to cause strange behavior in people. People are behaving strangely today, so there is probably a full moon.

This looks eminently diagrammable. It also sounds like an invalid contrapositive, doesn't it? Let's see . . .

Step 3: Answer the question in your own words as best you can
Here's what we got as our diagram:

A full moon is known to cause strange behavior in people (A → B); people are behaving strangely today, so there is probably a full moon (B → A). This looks familiar from our earlier discussion about the contrapositive, but it's not right!

The arguer messed up, didn't she? She didn't properly create a contrapositive in the second sentence. She flipped the elements, but didn't negate them! Now all we have to do is eliminate any answer choice that doesn't exhibit the same flawed logic (flipping a conditional, but not negating it).

Step 4: Use Process of Elimination
Now we're going to carry our diagram to the answer choices and eliminate anything that doesn't match.

> (A) Abnormal sunspot activity causes animals to act strangely. We are experiencing abnormal sunspot activity today, so animals are probably acting strangely.

Diagram it: Abnormal sunspot activity causes animals to act strangely (A → B); we are experiencing abnormal sunspot activity today, so animals are probably acting strangely (A → B again). This doesn't match the argument, so this isn't the answer. Cross it off.

> (B) Studies have shown that the use of turn signals reduces the likelihood of highway accidents. There has been a decrease in highway accidents, so people are most likely using their turn signals.

Diagram it: Using turn signals reduces the likelihood of accidents (A → B). There has been a decrease in highway accidents, so people are probably using their turn signals (B → A). Bingo! This is the same type of flawed reasoning, another conditional that has been flipped without being negated. Let's hold onto it.

> (C) The law of gravity has worked for as long as mankind has been able to observe it. It's working today, and it will probably continue to work tomorrow.

Can we even diagram this? It looks like the entire thing is merely saying that the law of gravity has worked in the past, it's working today, and it'll work tomorrow. So it's just (A → B → C) and nothing else. Eliminate it.

(D) Increased stress has been shown to decrease the effectiveness of a person's immune system. So it follows that someone who does not have a diminished immune system is not likely to be experiencing an increased level of stress.

This is (A → B), and then in the second sentence (–B → –A). This is actually a valid contrapositive, fixing the flaw in the original argument. This can be appealing because it fixes the flawed logic, so be careful *not* to fix the flaw in a "parallel-the-flaw" question. Find the *same* flaw. Let's get rid of this one.

(E) People with an ear for music often have an equal facility for learning languages. Bill doesn't have an ear for music, so he probably doesn't have a facility for learning languages.

Here we have (A → B) in the first sentence, and then (–A → –B) in the second sentence. So here the original was negated without being flipped. It's flawed, but not flawed in the *same* way as the original. It's out.

Nice job! We got the right answer simply by diagramming the statement in the argument, and then diagramming each of the answer choices until we found the one that matched our original diagram. However, we're sure you noticed that it took you a long time to do this question. Many times, parallel-the-reasoning questions are even longer than this one, and will take you three minutes apiece to do. If you spend your time doing these questions, you might only get through half of an Arguments section!

Arguments Techniques: Process of Elimination with Parallel-the-Reasoning Questions

It's pretty straightforward here—if you are able to diagram the argument, then you must go to the answer choices and diagram those as well. You can't tell just by "looking" either. Write it out and then you've got proof that the choice either matches or doesn't match the argument.

Whenever possible, diagram parallel arguments.

Sometimes you can't diagram parallel-the-reasoning questions. In these instances, try to describe the reasoning questions. Look for patterns that can be easily summed up (e.g., we have two things that appear to be similar, then we note a difference, or one thing is attributed to be the cause of another). Try to find an answer that could be summed up in the same way. If you find any part of an answer choice that you can't match up with part of the original argument, eliminate it.

Cracking Parallel-the-Reasoning Questions: Summary

Refer to the chart below on how to attack parallel-the-reasoning questions.

Sample Question Phrasings	Attack! Attack! Attack!
Which one of the following is most similar in reasoning to the argument above? *The flawed pattern of reasoning exhibited by the argument above is most paralleled by that in which of the following?*	• Parallel-the-reasoning questions will either contain flawed or valid reasoning, and the question will tip you off. • Try to diagram the argument and then diagram each of the answer choices, comparing each one to the diagram you came up with for the argument itself. • If the argument is flawed, be careful not to choose an answer that fixes it. • Save parallel-the-reasoning questions for *last*!!!

CRACKING ARGUMENTS: PUTTING IT ALL TOGETHER

Now you've learned how to attack every type of question they will throw at you in an Arguments section.

How do you integrate this knowledge into working a whole Arguments section?

Slow down

You know that you only have 35 minutes to tackle an entire Arguments section. But you're also faced with the fact that, in order to get the credited response, you have to invest a significant amount of time into each argument. Hopefully, you've seen that these questions are doable—with the right approach—but that you might fall for traps or miss key words if you rush through in your quest to get to all of the arguments.

So here's tip #1: *Slow down!* It makes no sense to blaze through an entire Arguments section and only get half of the questions right. If you slow down and take your time, you'll find that by doing fewer questions, your overall score will most likely go up. How does this happen?

Basically, when you take your time, you make fewer mistakes. You may end up doing fewer questions, but the number you actually get right can be much higher. And the added bonus is that even if you don't get to eight or nine questions, you'll guess on those—and you can count on getting a fifth of those right, since there's no guessing penalty!

Those of you who are already getting most of the arguments correct can also benefit from this advice. Making good decisions about which arguments to save until the end will keep you confident and aggressive as you work, two qualities that are rewarded on the LSAT. And we all know how frustrating it is to look back on our work in a timed section and find out that we missed questions because we were being careless or didn't read closely enough.

Choose wisely

You know that you have to invest a certain amount of time into each type of argument question in order to get the credited response. But you also know that some types of arguments take less time than others. For instance, compare the amount of time that a main point question takes to the amount of time that a parallel-the-reasoning question takes. You have a choice in how to spend your time with each question. Does it make sense to tackle a bunch of time-consuming questions when there are others that take a lot less time to do, but give you the same amount of points? As you do more practice problems and evaluate your performance on them you should get a pretty clear sense of where your strengths and weaknesses lie. You'll benefit by making charts of your performance on each section, broken down by question type, so that you can see your progress. To help you plan your approach here's a chart of the proportion of questions of each type that have shown up on recently administered LSATs:

	Approximate Number Per Section	% of Total Arguments
Main Point	2	7%
Assumption	4	14%
Weaken	3	13%
Strengthen	2	8%
Resolve/Explain	1	5%
Inference	4	14%
Reasoning	2	6%
Flaw	3	13%
Principle	3	10%
Parallel-the-Reasoning	2	7%
Other	1	3%

The bottom line is this: Do the questions that take you the least amount of time and that you're most comfortable with first. Open your test booklet and just take a look at what's on the page. Go after the ones that look short, sweet, and to the point, and leave the longer ones for later. Give priority to the tasks that you know play to your strengths. Likewise, if you come to an argument that really stumps you, don't worry about it—just put a mark next to it and move on. You can always come back once you've gone through all of the other arguments in the section.

Finally . . .

Practice, practice, practice. There are a number of different tasks that you'll be asked to perform in the Arguments section. As we've seen, each task will vary slightly in how you approach the argument and what you need to get out of it. There's no substitute for experience here. Use those previously administered LSATs that you've ordered from LSAC to get plenty of practice. You have ordered them already, right? Good. And remember that it's not enough to just work all the arguments questions under the sun. You'll have to go back and carefully evaluate your work. Figure out *why* you missed a question rather than simply looking at the right answer and being happy to know why that one works. Did you miss the question because you didn't understand the argument? Did you miss a key word? Did you fall for an attractive distractor? Was the credited response one that didn't look very good, but didn't have any flaw? Did you misinterpret the task presented by the question?

This kind of detailed evaluation will take time, but it is well worth it. Do it for Arguments. Do it for Games. Do it for Reading Comprehension. There are many places where errors can creep into the process. You'll only be able to improve if you know what your tendencies are and how you can go about changing those tendencies that negatively impact your performance.

Now you know what you need to do, so keep up the effort and you'll see the results.

You and Your Chart

The chart on the following page will help you on the Arguments section. You should probably retype the chart yourself (it will help you to better remember all the information in it), and then print out a copy for yourself. Put it in a prominent place. Make another copy and carry it along with you so can refer to it while you're working practice problems. You should know this chart like the back of your hand by the time you take the real LSAT.

Question Type	Sample Question Phrasings	Attack! Attack! Attack!
Main Point	*What is the author's main point?* *The main conclusion drawn in the author's argument is that* *The argument is structured to lead to which one of the following conclusions?*	Identify the main point and reasons. Use the Why Test, and then match your point against the five answer choices. Be careful not to fall for the opposite. When down to two choices, use extreme wording and relevance to eliminate one choice.
Assumption	*Which of the following is an assumption on which the argument relies?* *The argument above assumes which of the following?* *The writer's argument depends upon assuming which of the following?*	Identify the issue, point, reasons, and assumptions of the author. If you're having trouble finding the assumption, look for a gap between two different ideas in th argument. The assumption will always strengthen the author's point and is NECESSARY for the point to follow from the information provided. When down to two choices, negate each statement to see if the argument falls apart. If it does, that' s your answer.
Weaken	*Which one of the following, if true, would most weaken the author's point?* *Which of the following statements, if true, would most call into question the results achieved by the scientists?*	Identify the issue, point, reasons, and assumptions of the author. Read critically, looking for where the author made too big a leap in logic. Then, when you go to the answer choices, look for a choice that has the most negative impact on that leap in logic. Assume all choices to be hypothetically true.
Strengthen	*Which one of the following statements, if true, would support the author's conclusion?* *Which one of the following statements, if true, would strengthen the author's point?* *Which of the following statements, i.e.; if assumed, would allow the author's conclusion to be properly drawn?*	Identify the issue, point, reasons, and assumptions of the author. Read critically, looking for where the author made too big a leap in logic. Then, when you go to the answer choices, look for a choice that has the most positive impact on that gap. Assume all choices to be hypothetically true.
Resolve/ Explain	*Which one of the following provides the best resolution to the apparent paradox described by the committee member?* *Which one of the following statements, if true, would explain the discrepancy found by the scientists?*	Identify the apparent discrepancy or paradox. Go to the answer choices and look for a piece of information that, when added to the argument, allows both facts from the argument to be true. Assume all choices to be hypothetically true.

Question Type	Sample Question Phrasings	Attack! Attack! Attack!
Inference	*Which one of the following statements can be validly inferred from the information above?* *If the statements above are true, then which of the following must also be true?* *Which one of the following conclusions can be validly drawn from the passage above?* *Which one of the following conclusions is best supported by the passage above?*	Read carefully, paying close attention to qualifying language, then go to the answer choices. Once there, cross off any answer choices that are not *directly* supported by evidence in the passage. Use relevance and extreme language to eliminate answer choices. Use the contrapositive if there are "if...then" statements contained in the passage and in the answer choices.
Reasoning	*The argument proceeds by* *Leah responds to Kevin by doing which one of the following?* *The method the activist uses to object to the developer's argument is to* *Dr. Jacobs does which of the following?*	Read the argument carefully and then describe what is happening in your own words. Take this description and rigorously apply it to all the answer choices. Once you're at the answer choices, use the technique of comparing the actions described in the answer choices against those that actually occurred in the argument. Cross out anything that didn't appear in the argument.
Flaw	*Which of the following indicates a flaw in the author's reasoning?* *A criticism of the argument would most likely emphasize that it* *The reasoning in the argument is most vulnerable to criticism on the grounds that the argument* *The argument above relies on which of the following questionable techniques?*	Break down the argument into its parts; the flaw is usually related to an assumption. State in your own words what the problem with the argument is. With each answer, try to match the actions described in the answer choices with those of the argument itself. Look for the choice that has the same problem you found. Eliminate the answers that don't match; look for the answer that addresses the assumption.
Principle	*Which one of the following principles, if established, justifies the actions taken by Mia in the argument above?* *Which of the following examples conforms most closely to the principle given in the argument above?*	Make sure you're clear in which direction the argument is flowing—are you being asked to find something that supports or conforms? Once you're sure, look for the answer that either justifies the action or matches the principle in the argument.
Parallel-the-Reasoning	*Which one of the following is most similar in reasoning to the argument above?* *The flawed pattern of reasoning exhibited by the argument above is most paralleled by that in which of the following?*	Parallel-the-Reasoning questions will either contain flawed or valid reasoning, and the question will tip you off. Try to diagram the argument and then diagram each of the answer choices, trying to match one of these against the diagram you came up with for the argument itself. If the argument is flawed, be careful not to choose an answer that fixes it. Save the Parallel-the-Reasoning questions for *last*!!!

3

Games

WHAT IS A GAME?

The folks who write the test call this section the "Analytical Reasoning" section, but really the questions are just puzzles, so we call it the "Games" section. You are presented with the basic format and structure of the game in the *setup*, an initial paragraph that also provides the *elements*; you will be asked to determine the relationships between these elements. Following the setup will be a number of conditions, or *clues*, which put restrictions on how the elements can be manipulated and sometimes give you valuable information about the overall structure of the game as well. Finally, you will have a number of questions, each of which may introduce new restrictions or even occasionally change one of the original clues. Each question is independent of the others, although work completed for one question may help in eliminating answer choices on another question.

WHAT DOES THIS SECTION TEST?

Games test how well you can organize an incomplete set of spatial relations in order to extract information efficiently.

Games test how well you can organize information, understand spatial relationships, and make deductions from those relationships when presented with limitations on the arrangements allowed by the rules. They also reward you for being able to extract this information efficiently.

WHY IS THIS SECTION ON THE LSAT?

Games are designed to predict your ability to perform the kind of detailed analyses required of law students. They really just test how well you answer the games on the LSAT under strict time pressure. You won't do any of these in law school—unless, of course, they're in a puzzle book you got from your eccentric uncle for your birthday. You certainly won't do these when you become a lawyer. Or if you do, you won't be allowed to bill for them.

THE SECTION ITSELF

The Games section is made up of four games. Each game includes five to seven questions. The section has a total of 23 or 24 questions.

Before we begin, take a moment to read the instructions to this section:

> Directions: Each group of questions in this section is based on a set of conditions. In answering some of the questions, it may be useful to draw a rough diagram. Choose the response that most accurately and completely answers each question and blacken the corresponding space on your answer sheet.

These are the directions that will appear on your LSAT. As usual on the LSAT, the official directions are of little help. Review them now. They will not change. Don't waste time reading them in the test room.

THE GOOD NEWS

The good news is that with some rigorous practice diagramming games, you can radically improve your LSAT score. Many students have walked into The Princeton Review classes getting only a few games questions right, but walk out scoring 75 percent or higher on the section. You can do the same, as long as you follow our step-by-step process and practice, practice, practice.

Games: General Strategies

Following is a list of general strategies that you should use when you are working the Games section. Make sure you take these strategies to heart.

Slow and steady wins the race

As in the Arguments section, you want to maintain a high level of accuracy on the games questions in order to maximize the number of points you get. Trying to rush through the section to make sure you'll finish every question isn't a productive approach. You will achieve the highest level of accuracy by using an approach that increases efficiency—not necessarily pace—without sacrificing your ability to be effective. As with arguments, you'll need to develop an approach that is best suited to your strengths. If you find you can't finish a Games section in the allotted time, don't fret; remember, you don't need to finish to get a good score. Through consistent practice you will be able to move more quickly through the section without having to work so fast that you start to make careless errors.

Your mantra: *I will not rush through the games just so that I can finish. I will work to improve efficiency and accuracy, thereby improving my score.*

Survey the field

Remember, every correct answer on the LSAT is worth exactly one raw point toward your scaled score. It's quite possible that the two games that you should do first in a section may be the third and fourth games presented. Remember, the LSAT games and the questions attached to them are not arranged in order of difficulty. Therefore, you should look over all four games in the section, and decide which ones are most attackable. We'll spend time later outlining what characteristics make a game more attractive or less attractive.

Your mantra: *I will look over the Games section and rank the games before I begin working on them.*

Just do something

Keep working, keep moving forward, and don't ever just stare at a game in search of divine inspiration.

Your mantra: *I will keep moving forward.*

Transfer your answers after each game

As soon as you've finished working all the questions on a particular game, transfer those answers to your bubble sheet. This method has a number of advantages: it is the most efficient, it helps prevent careless errors, and it gives your brain a much needed change of task before you dive into the next game. When there are about ten minutes remaining in the section, bubble in all the remaining blanks. Then you can go back and work any remaining questions you have time for, changing the bubbles one at a time as you go.

Your mantra: *I will transfer my answers in a group after each game until ten minutes are left.*

Take short breaks

After you've completed each game, take a short break. Not a nap, just ten seconds to take three deep breaths and ready yourself for the next game. Transfer your answers from that game, and then start the next game. You've cleared your mind and you're ready to push on.

Your mantra: *I will use ten seconds after each game I complete to take some deep breaths and refocus.*

Your Mantras and You

Here they are again:

> *I will not rush through the games just so that I can finish. I will work to improve efficiency and accuracy, thereby improving my score.*
>
> *I will look over the Games section and rank the games before I begin working on them.*
>
> *I will keep moving forward.*
>
> *I will transfer my answers in a group after each game until ten minutes are left.*
>
> *I will use ten seconds after each game I complete to take some deep breaths and refocus.*

Games: Specific Strategies

The directions for the Games section misleadingly state that "it may be useful to draw a rough diagram" when working the section. That's like saying it may be useful to train before running your first marathon. Actually, it is *necessary* to draw a very *detailed* diagram. Furthermore, you want to "symbolize" all of the clues that you are given.

Make it visual

Games are a visual exercise. Games test your ability to determine how various elements can be arranged in space. Therefore, words don't help you, images do. Your goal will be to translate all the words that you are given in the setup and the clues, and sometimes in the questions themselves, into visual symbols. Once you've done this you won't need to (or want to) refer to that confusing verbal mess again.

The LSAT writers are banking on the fact that most test takers will try to organize all this information in their heads in their rush to finish. And they're right; most test takers do. But you'll also notice that when the bell curve gets played out, most test takers are lumped around the middle of the curve, getting only about half of the questions right. Coincidence? We think not. Don't be another statistic. Use your pencil and draw it out rather than trying to work it all in your head.

Be consistent

There are various ways you can symbolize and diagram the information that is presented to you in a game. We're going to show you what we've found to be the best and most efficient way to diagram and symbolize. Whatever method you choose, be consistent with your symbols and your diagram—don't mix and match. You'll get confused and wonder why you've gotten three answers that all look right for half the questions, and none that seem to work for the other half of the questions.

Be careful

Your goal is to translate all the information that you received from the setup and the clues into some sort of visual symbolization. However, if you don't read the clues carefully enough, you can wind up symbolizing something incorrectly. This will eventually lead to your diagram becoming a liability rather than an asset. So make sure you read the information slowly enough that you don't make mistakes in your symbolization.

Be flexible

The four games that you will see on the real LSAT may look slightly different from the games you have practiced with. Under the time pressure of test day, they may seem *completely* different. They won't be. Once you understand how games work and can recognize the basic structures the test writers use to build them, you can see how consistent they really are. Just stay calm and take a step back to evaluate the information. The details will change but the basic ingredients won't. Focus on the big picture. Focus on the similarities to other games you've already done. And get to work.

Don't simply stare at a game that seems confusing. Focus on the underlying similarities to games you've already seen and get to work applying the process.

GAMES: A STEP-BY-STEP PROCESS

Just as in the Arguments section, The Princeton Review has boiled down the Games section into a step-by-step process. You will follow this process for every game that you do. Learn these steps, practice them rigorously, apply them consistently, and you'll improve your score. Sound good? Then let's go to it!

Step 1: Draw your diagram

Your first step will be to determine the appropriate diagram for the game by evaluating both the setup and the clues. Remember that we want to translate all of the verbal information from the test into visual information on the page, because this is really a test of *spatial* reasoning. You will be given enough information to understand the basic structure of the game. You will eventually assign elements and perhaps their characteristics to the places available in the diagram, so your basis for the diagram will figure out the underlying structure to which you will assign these elements. You will also want to list the elements next to the diagram so that you'll have everything in one place and will be able to keep track of it easily. Don't rush through this step, because this is the core of your process. People often want to start scribbling a diagram as soon as something pops out at them from the setup. Take the time to evaluate both the setup and the clues and you'll be well equipped for the rest of the process.

Step 2: Symbolize the clues

After you've drawn the core of a diagram, move on to symbolizing the clues listed below the setup. Once again, we'll convert the written clues into visual symbols. The clues should be symbolized in a way that is consistent with the diagram you have set up. The goal is to transform the clues into pieces that will fit into your diagram visually. Remember the three Cs: Keep your symbols clear, concise, and consistent.

Step 3: Double-check your clues and make deductions

Never forget how important it is to symbolize everything correctly. Invest the few seconds it will take to be sure that your symbols match the information given in the clues. A foolproof way to accomplish this is to *work against the grain*: Articulate what each of your symbols means and then carry that back up to the clues you were given. When you find a match, check off that clue. Once you're sure they're all accounted for, you're finished. It's that simple.

Now that you're sure you've got everything properly symbolized, it's time to make sure that you've made any *deductions* that you can from the information that was given. Look for overlap between the clues and the diagram, and among the clues that share elements, and see if there's anything else that you know *for sure*. For instance, does putting two clues together give you a third piece of information? Add your deductions to the information you already have. You'll notice that many deductions give you concrete limitations about where elements are restricted—where they *can't* go—rather than where they *must* go.

While you're looking for these deductions, you'll find that you're also learning how the game is going to work. Keep your eyes open for anything that seems as if it will have a particularly large impact on the outcome of the game. The most restricted places and the most restrictive clues tend to have the most impact when you start working the questions. The more you know about how the game will work, the more efficient you'll be at working through the questions.

Step 4: Attack the questions
Not all games questions are on the same level of difficulty. We'll show you which types of questions to attack first and why. As a rule, you should always look for questions that further limit the initial conditions of the game and provide you with more information. These questions can be done much more quickly than those questions that don't provide you with any information. Plus, when you get to later questions, the work you've done on the early ones will often help you to find the right answer. A nice bonus!

Step 5: Use Process of Elimination
We know, you're sick of hearing about Process of Elimination. But get used to it. It will come in handy on Games, just as it did on Arguments. (Oh, and by the way, you'll use it in the Reading Comprehension section, too.) Of all the sections, Games is the one where the correct answer will be the most clear, and often you'll find that you know exactly what you're looking for in the answers. But don't be fooled into thinking this will always happen; you'll still find that POE will be your friend on many questions, especially when things get a bit trickier.

READY FOR SOME GAMES?

Now let's see how the five steps work on a real game. Give yourself as much time as you need to apply the method to the following game. Focus on using the proper technique (feel free to have the steps written out next to you) and pay no attention to time—that will come later. Work the game using only the space available on the page. On the day of the test you won't have any scratch paper, so you'll have to get accustomed to writing small and keeping things neat. Do the best you can, and then compare what you did to our explanation. After each game, we'll give you some extra techniques for attacking this section of the LSAT. You should work through each exercise fully before going on to the next game. By the end of the chapter, you'll know everything we do about how to tackle LSAT Games.

GAME #1: DAYS AND ENTREES

A restaurant must choose its main dinner entree for each night of one week, beginning on Sunday and ending on Saturday. The possible entrees are beef, lamb, manicotti, pork, spaghetti, trout, and veal, each of which will be used on a different night. The following conditions must be met when determining the menu:

Don't worry about time yet. Just focus on the process. Your speed will increase naturally with practice.

The lamb must be served either the night before or the night after the spaghetti is served.

The beef must be served either the night before or the night after either the pork or the trout is served.

The manicotti cannot be served the night before or the night after the veal is served.

The veal must be served on Monday.

1. Which one of the following is a possible menu in order from Sunday to Saturday?

   (A) pork, veal, trout, lamb, beef, spaghetti, manicotti
   (B) trout, veal, manicotti, beef, lamb, spaghetti, pork
   (C) spaghetti, veal, lamb, trout, manicotti, beef, pork
   (D) trout, veal, beef, pork, manicotti, lamb, spaghetti
   (E) manicotti, veal, beef, trout, lamb, spaghetti, pork

2. If lamb is served on Saturday, which one of the following must be true?

   (A) The spaghetti is served on Thursday.
   (B) The beef is served on Tuesday.
   (C) The manicotti is served on Thursday.
   (D) The pork is served on Wednesday.
   (E) The trout is served on Sunday.

3. If the trout is served on Thursday, the pork must be served on

   (A) Sunday
   (B) Tuesday
   (C) Wednesday
   (D) Friday
   (E) Saturday

4. Which one of the following is a night on which the manicotti could be served?

   (A) Sunday
   (B) Tuesday
   (C) Wednesday
   (D) Friday
   (E) Saturday

5. If beef is served on Saturday, which one of the following must be true?

   (A) The trout is served on Friday.
   (B) The pork is served on Thursday.
   (C) The spaghetti is served on Wednesday.
   (D) The lamb is served on Tuesday.
   (E) The manicotti is served on Thursday.

Cracking Game #1

Step 1: Draw your diagram

What we have here is seven days of the week and seven entrees. We learned this from the first paragraph, which is called the *setup*. We recommend using a grid in this situation to organize the information. In this case, we need to decide what goes on top of the grid—the days of the week or the entrees. We want the things that won't change order (our core) across the top of our diagram. Notice that the clues give us information about how the entrees can be organized in relation to one another. We are assigning elements (entrees) to places (days), so the days go on top of the grid. Also, we have what is called a *one-to-one correspondence* in this game—there are seven places (days) and seven elements (entrees) that correspond to each of the places. In addition, we're told that each will be used, so we have to use all of them; one-to-one correspondence isn't just a matter of the number of each, but also whether all are used, or any can be reused. This is a good thing, because it will limit the number of possible places to which the elements can be assigned. We have to use each element once and, because we only have seven nights, we can't repeat any of the elements. That answers two questions you'll want to ask for each game you work: "Can we leave out any elements?" and "Can there be any repeats?" If the answer to either of these is yes, the game becomes more complicated. We'll talk more about this when we get to ordering the games later. In this game, the answer to both questions is no, so we should be able to tackle this one as long as we follow the steps.

Don't forget to list your elements near the diagram so that you'll have everything you need in one place.

In general, factors with a natural order (days of the week, rooms numbered 1 through 4, etc.) will act as the core of the diagram. For most diagrams, place what doesn't change on top of the diagram. For example: Nine people ride to work in three cars. The three cars don't change, but who rides with whom will change, depending on the question. So the cars would go across the top of the diagram.

Take a look at our diagram for this game:

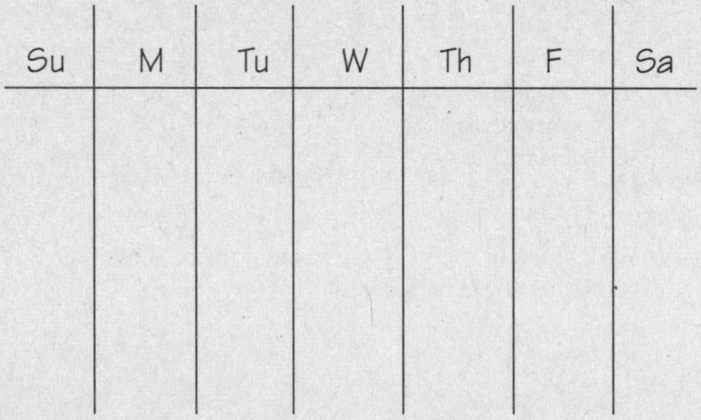

Su	M	Tu	W	Th	F	Sa

Step 2: Symbolize the clues

Draw excruciatingly exact symbols for the information given to you. Remember the three Cs for symbols: clear, concise, and consistent.

Now that we've drawn a diagram, it's important that we symbolize the clues so that they fit into our diagram. We want to get rid of the words and transform the clues into visual puzzle pieces that fit into the framework that we've already drawn. Let's take a look at the first clue:

> The lamb must be served either the night before or the night after the spaghetti is served.

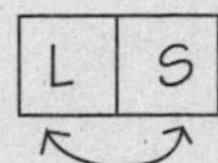

As you can see, we created a shorthand for each of the entrees, denoting them by their first letter (L = lamb and S = spaghetti). We then put these two letters next to each other to show that they must be *consecutive*. We then put a box around the two letters to show that this is a "block" of information that is fixed. Finally, we put the double-pointed arrow underneath the block to show that the order can be either the order "LS" or "SL."

The great thing about this piece of information is that it will occupy two of the seven possible spaces. Blocks are concrete, restrictive clues that limit the possible arrangements and will make your job easier, so look for them when you are reading over the clues and deciding whether to do a particular game.

The beef must be served either the night before or the night after either the pork or the trout is served.

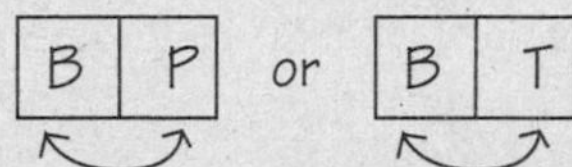

This is also good information, but not quite as good as the "LS" block. We do know that B (beef) must be next to either P (pork) or T (trout), so we drew two blocks, remembering to put the word "or" in between to show that it can be either of these two options. Note the double arrow again, indicating that it could either be "BT" or "TB" if T is next to B, or "BP" or "PB" if P is next to B. The good thing here is that B *must* be next to one or the other of these elements.

The manicotti cannot be served the night before or the night after the veal is served.

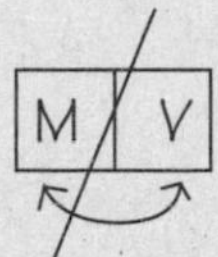

As you can see, this clue is telling us what we *can't* have. Here, we can't have the M (manicotti) next to the V (veal). So we drew another block, again with the double arrow underneath, and then we drew a slash through the block itself to indicate that this can never be true. We've just drawn our first *antiblock clue*.

The veal must be served on Monday.

Su	M	Tu	W	Th	F	Sa
	(V)					
	↓					

Not surprisingly, the best piece of information is saved until last. As you can see, this piece of information is so definitive that we were able to put it directly into the diagram. Whenever you have a clue that expresses a concrete relationship between an element and the diagram, go ahead and put it directly into the diagram. It will save time and your diagram will be better for it. Additionally, we circled the letter and ran an arrow down the appropriate column to show that veal will *always* be served on Monday, and nothing else will ever be.

Step 3: Double-check your clues and make deductions

As we mentioned, this is the time to compare your symbols to the clues and make sure nothing got mixed up in the translation from verbal to visual. This seems like a waste of time until the first time you skip it or forget and end up spending a long, frustrating time fighting with answers because you goofed up. Now, let's take a look at the clues we've drawn to see what kinds of deductions we might make.

The first thing we notice, perhaps, is that V is fixed on Monday. What else do we know about V? That M cannot be next to it. Therefore, we know that M cannot be Sunday or Tuesday, because V is always on Monday. Look at the diagram below to see how we indicated this.

Su	M	Tu	W	Th	F	Sa
-M	(V)	-M				
	↓					

Now, what is our next most definitive piece of information? It is the fact that L and S must always be next to each other. This is good information, because there is one place that neither L nor S can go, because they must be next to each other—that place is Sunday. Why? Because there's no consecutive space next to Sunday for the second letter in this block to go in—V is in Monday. Therefore, *neither* L nor S can go in Sunday.

Next, let's go to our B block. We know that one other entree (either P or T) must go next to B. Therefore, B needs a space next to it just like L and S do. Thus, B can't go in Sunday either, for the same reason that L and S can't. Now let's look at the work we did on the next page.

Su	M	Tu	W	Th	F	Sa
-M -L -S -B	(V) ↓	-M				

It looks as if Sunday is a very restricted day, right? Four of our seven letters can't go there. If you count V also (which you should), it's actually five out of seven letters that can't go in Sunday. So what can go in Sunday? Only P or T. Let's add that information to our diagram:

Pay close attention to slots that are very restricted.

Su	M	Tu	W	Th	F	Sa
-M -L -S -B P/T	(V) ↓	-M				

Clearly, we've done some good work with the left side of our diagram. We looked at each of the clues against the diagram itself, and came up with some solid restrictions to indicate on our diagram. We know that both blocks will need to go to the right of Monday. That leaves one more space to be filled after we place the blocks, which will have to be occupied by M (manicotti). Having both blocks—each with two elements—fit in five spaces leaves us with only a few possibilities. It turns out that M can only be put on one of the ends or right in the middle. So you can't place M on either Wednesday or Friday. Try it and you'll see why.

So here's your final set of deductions:

Su	M	Tu	W	Th	F	Sa
-M -L -S -B P/T	(V) ↓	-M	-M		-M	

We know that this might be the toughest concept we've thrown at you so far. Below is an illustration of what the possibilities are when you've got two blocks of two spaces each that need to go into a total of only five consecutive slots. Take a look at what happens:

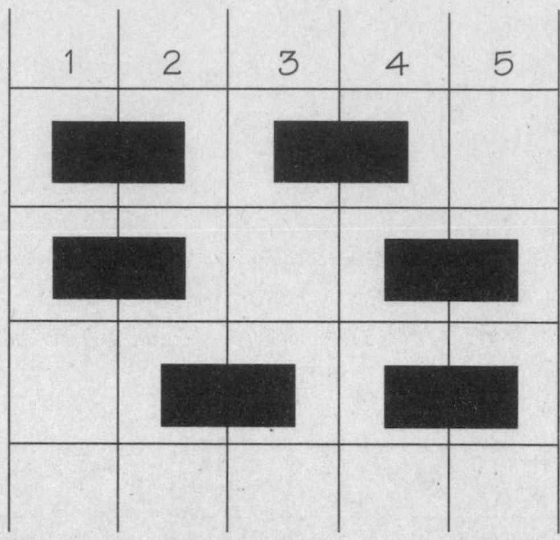

As you can see, the second and fourth spaces are always going to be needed for one half of one of the blocks. In our diagram, we're playing with five spaces—Tuesday, Wednesday, Thursday, Friday, and Saturday. Therefore, M cannot go in either the second (Wednesday) or the fourth (Friday) space, because we have two blocks that we must place in those five spaces. Make sense? M is one of the most restricted elements left, so, if we can place M—which can now only go on Thursday or Saturday—we'll know exactly where our blocks can and can't go!

At this point, we've come up with all the deductions we can and have a pretty good sense of the way this game is going to work. Things will hinge on the most restricted places (like Sunday), and the placement of restricted elements (like M and the two blocks). All the information that we've put in the diagram so far will be true for the whole game, so we'll draw a line under it to separate it off and remind ourselves to pay attention to those limitations as we work each new question. We'll call this row of restrictions that apply to the whole game our *clue shelf* and keep it separate from the other information we fill in as we work the questions so we can easily refer to the conditions that are always true.

Step 4: Attack the questions

There are basically three types of questions that you will encounter on games. Our favorite kind—the kind you'll want to search out and do first—we'll call "if" questions. You'll be able to identify them because they start with the word *if* and ask you to find the answer choice that *must be true*, *must be false*, *could be true*, or *could be false*. They will also give you an extra piece of information that will further limit the possibilities on your diagram—for that question only, of course. The more concrete the information given by an "if" question, the easier the question will be to do.

Hunt down and do all the "if" questions that have straightforward tasks FIRST.

Next come the "which" questions. Not surprisingly, these begin with the word *which* and differ from "if" questions in that they don't give you any extra limiting information. That's why we don't answer them first. If you save them until after you've done the "if" questions, you'll find that you will be able to eliminate many answer choices simply by referring back to the work that you've already done on "if" questions. How's that for efficiency?

Finally are the aptly named "weird" questions. Sometimes these will start with the word *suppose* and an established condition will be removed or, rarely, a new condition will be added. Talk about time consuming! Other times they will start with either *if* or *which* but will have a complicated task like figuring out which of the answer choices, if it were true, would completely determine the outcome of the game. Ugh. You'll see why they're last if it's not clear already.

Step 5: Use Process of Elimination

Because there are between five and seven questions for each game, Steps 4 and 5 will go hand in hand for each until it's time to move on to the next game.

You'll find that POE on games is sometimes quite straightforward and other times a more murky business, but the goal is always the same: Get to the credited response by eliminating answer choices that have a flaw. When you have a question for which the answer seems clear before you even go to the answer choices, the credited response will jump right off the page at you. With other questions you'll find you need to check each answer choice carefully and perhaps even use work from other questions to help you eliminate. And with some particularly unwieldy questions, you may find that you need to put each answer choice through the wringer by actually working it out in the diagram. We call these time-consuming chores "plug and chug" questions.

For now, just be conscious of using POE on each answer choice and you'll learn to recognize the various types as you practice more and more questions. The bottom line: POE works *every* time, but it should also be your last resort on most questions.

Let's answer the "if" questions in this game and see how we do.

2. If lamb is served on Saturday, which one of the following must be true?
   (A) The spaghetti is served on Thursday.
   (B) The beef is served on Tuesday.
   (C) The manicotti is served on Thursday.
   (D) The pork is served on Wednesday.
   (E) The trout is served on Sunday.

Here's how to crack it

First, include the extra information from this question into a row of your diagram. Next, determine what other restrictions will allow you to fill in more information by looking for any overlap with your clues. Continue to include conditions that you know must happen or can't happen until you can't fill in any more information. If you find yourself in a situation where slots have been limited to only two options, it's worth filling them in. If there are more than two options, don't bother or it will get messy fast. Let's see what happens on the following page.

Su	M	Tu	W	Th	F	Sa
-M -L -S -B P/T	(V)	-M	-M		-M	
				M	S	L (2)

As you can see, putting L into the Saturday slot forces the S into the Friday slot, because they need to be together. And because M can only go on Saturday or Thursday, we know that M is now in the Thursday slot. L in Saturday, S in Friday, and M in Thursday: These three things MUST be true. We don't know for sure where B, P, or T are so we won't try to write down all the possible options for them. Remember that our task is to find the answer choice that *must be true*, so odds are we won't need to know anything about elements that we can't place concretely anyway. We'll just head to the answer choices and see if we can find an answer. We can—it's answer choice (C). Because we were able to fill in a fair amount of information and the question was asking for something that *must be true* this was a pretty straightforward job of POE.

On to our next "if" question:

3. If the trout is served on Thursday, the pork must be served on

   (A) Sunday
   (B) Tuesday
   (C) Wednesday
   (D) Friday
   (E) Saturday

Here's how to crack it

Wait! Don't erase the information from the last question. You won't need it for another "if" question, but remember, the work you do for the "if" questions will help you with POE when you get to the more general questions. Just leave that information for now, draw a line, and start another row of information. It's useful to write the number of the question next to the row that you're working on in case you need to come back to it later for some reason.

Fill in all the information you can BEFORE looking at the answer choices.

We have another "if" question, which will give us a new set of possibilities for entree orders, so we'll fill in new information for this question first and then look for any other ramifications until we've gotten all the concrete information written down on the next page.

Su	M	Tu	W	Th	F	Sa	
-M -L -S -B P/T	(V)	-M	-M		-M		
				M	S	L	(2)
P		S/L	S/L	T	B	M	(3)
	↓						

This question tells us to put T into Thursday. This forces M into Saturday. Putting T into Thursday also forces P into Sunday, because Sunday can be only P or T. Finally, there are only three spaces left, and only two (Tuesday and Wednesday) are consecutive. Thus, the S/L block must go into Tuesday and Wednesday. Notice that we couldn't be sure of their order, but there were only two possibilities, so it was worth writing down what we knew. We indicated the possibility with a slash. Now, we've only got B left, and the only place it can go is Friday. What's the question again? P must be where? Sunday, of course. (A) is our answer.

You might be wondering why we kept filling in information after we knew that P had to go to the Sunday slot. After all, that answered the question. Keep in mind that the information we generate here can help us with POE on later questions, and because we're in the groove, it's worth taking a few extra seconds to finish the sequence of events triggered when we started the question.

We'll skip number 4 and move on to our final "if" question:

5. If beef is served on Saturday, which one of the following must be true?

   (A) The trout is served on Friday.
   (B) The pork is served on Thursday.
   (C) The spaghetti is served on Wednesday.
   (D) The lamb is served on Tuesday.
   (E) The manicotti is served on Thursday.

Here's how to crack it

Use the same process. Fill in the information the question gives you plus any other concrete information that you can. Here's what we've got:

Su	M	Tu	W	Th	F	Sa	
-M -L -S -B P/T	(V)	-M	-M		-M		
				M	S	L	(2)
P		S/L	S/L	T	B	M	(3)
P/T	↓	S/L	S/L	M	P/T	B	(5)

So we're told B is in Saturday. That only leaves Thursday for M, and P or T must be in the Friday slot next to B. This once again pushes the S/L block into Tuesday and Wednesday. That's all we can fill in so we'll head to the answers. We can eliminate any that *could be false*. Let's see how it works:

Choice (A) could be false because P could be in Friday. Cross it off.
Choice (B) *must* be false according to our diagram. Cross it off.
Choice (C) could be false because L could also be in Wednesday. Cross it off.
Choice (D) could be false because S could also be in Tuesday. Cross it off.
Choice (E) must be true from our diagram. Keep it.

It's much easier to get through the answer choices once you have that diagram filled in, isn't it? The investment was worth it.

We've got only two questions left now. Both of them begin with the word *which*, indicating that the questions will be general in nature. Typically, this means that you won't be able to fill in any information in your diagram prior to evaluating the answer choices. Just head to the answers and start POE.

Take a look at the following question:

1. Which one of the following is a possible menu in order from Sunday to Saturday?

   (A) pork, veal, trout, lamb, beef, spaghetti, manicotti
   (B) trout, veal, manicotti, beef, lamb, spaghetti, pork
   (C) spaghetti, veal, lamb, trout, manicotti, beef, pork
   (D) trout, veal, beef, pork, manicotti, lamb, spaghetti
   (E) manicotti, veal, beef, trout, lamb, spaghetti, pork

Here's how to crack it

This is a special kind of "which" question. It's called a grab-a-rule question because all you have to do is apply each rule—or clue—to the answer choices and eliminate any choice that violates the rule. These tend to be straightforward, quick questions that will give you valuable insight into how a game works (if you missed anything during the deductions step). You should do grab-a-rule questions first. They sound almost too good to be true, and, as is so often the case, there's a catch: Not all games have one. But if they do, it's the first question and you should work on it right away. A hint: If you start with the most restrictive clues, you'll eliminate most efficiently. Let's go to it. We'll start with this clue:

Grab-a-rule questions: Apply each clue to each answer choice, starting with the most concrete and restrictive.

> The veal must be served on Monday.

Drat! That doesn't get rid of any. We'll just look at the next most restrictive piece of information.

We found out from our deductions that Sunday has to have either P or T.

That eliminates answer choices (C) and (E).

We also deduced that M has to be in either Thursday or Saturday.

That eliminates answer choice (B).

Back to the clues from our diagram:

> The lamb must be served either the night before or the night after the spaghetti is served.

That eliminates answer choice (A).

Voila! We've crossed off four choices, so (D) is left and that's our answer.

Note: Your process here is to take the clues and apply them to the choices, *not* the other way around. Taking each choice and applying it to each of the clues is very cumbersome. It will take more time and could lead to careless errors. Trust us.

Here's our last "which" question. Go to it:

4. Which one of the following is a night on which the manicotti could be served?

   (A) Sunday
   (B) Tuesday
   (C) Wednesday
   (D) Friday
   (E) Saturday

Here's how to crack it

Well, we deduced that M can only go one of two places—Thursday and Saturday. Even if we hadn't come up with that deduction, we could check back to our previous work and see where M has been placed throughout the game—we'd see that Thursday and Saturday were the only possible answers. Only Saturday is listed in the choices, so (E) is our answer.

So, what did we just do? Once again, here's the step-by-step approach to all games:

Step 1: Draw your diagram

Step 2: Symbolize the clues

Step 3: Double-check your clues and make deductions

Step 4: Attack the questions

Step 5: Use Process of Elimination

Games Techniques: Good Symbolization

Good symbolization is a major step toward getting all the questions in a particular game correct. Success with symbolization comes from familiarity and practice. There are a number of common types of clues that you'll see repeatedly on the LSAT; once you become familiar with them, most of the process becomes mechanical. While you're practicing your symbolization, keep in mind the three Cs: *clear*, *concise*, and *consistent*.

Clear: You want your symbols to make quick and apparent sense. If you find yourself having to interpret a clue as you use it in the game, it's not working.

Concise: Your symbols should be terse and to the point. Part of the reason for having them is to eliminate the wasted energy of reading those long-winded, confusing clues each time you refer to them in working the questions.

Consistent: As we mentioned above, you should start to recognize distinct types of LSAT clues that you'll symbolize in the same manner each time they show up in a game. But you should also be sure that your clues are consistent with one another within a game and that they are consistent with the way that you drew your diagram. They should all fit together.

Go ahead and symbolize the clues listed on the next page. First take a sheet of scratch paper and cover up the rest of the page. Move it down as you work, keeping the material covered until you get to it. Now symbolize each clue in the margin next to where it is written out on the page. Then compare your symbol with the symbol we have. We'll explain how we got to ours, and why you should be symbolizing in much the same way.

Anna sits to the east of Bob and to the west of Carol.

This is a very common type of clue. It's testing your ability to read carefully and to recognize the fact that you are being given two separate pieces of information: the relationship between A and B and the relationship between A and C. It is possible to consolidate these pieces of information into one symbol, but be careful! Make sure you are consistent throughout the game about which way is east and which way is west—under time pressure, these basic pieces of knowledge can get twisted around.

B – A – C

As you can see, we've put A in between B and C. "To the east" here means to the right, so the first thing we did was to put A to the right of B. Then, we read that Anna sits "to the west," or to the left, of Carol, so we can place A to the left of C. We didn't put this in a box because we don't know whether or not these people are sitting right next to one another—all we know is "to the right" and "to the left." Therefore we used a line to show that there might be one or more elements in between them or that they could end up right next to one another. We'll call these *range* clues because they only tell us the range of places that one element can occupy in relation to another element. You can think of the line as a rubber band; sometimes the elements will be pulled apart from one another and one or more other elements will be placed in between them, while other times they will pull right up next to one another.

Because we were able to link these two range clues into one larger clue we actually know more than if we had symbolized them separately. For instance, we know that A must always be placed in between the other two elements. And we know that B must always have *at least* two other elements to its right. Whenever you have the chance to link two or more range clues together, do so.

The two philosophers never sit together.

Probably a good idea—they can get rowdy. This is very similar to a clue we had in the game we just did. Remember the M/V antiblock? It didn't give us information about how two elements *must be* positioned with relation to one another, but rather how they *cannot be*. Here we know that there are two Ps and that these two Ps can never be together. It's another basic antiblock:

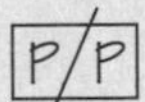

If the game ever gives us the placement of one of the philosophers, we know now that the other philosopher can't go immediately to the right or left of the first one. We also know that there are only two philosophers from the concrete language used in the clue. If we weren't sure how many philosphers there were in the game, we would want to be sure to note that fact in addition to our antiblock clue.

In a five-story building, J lives two floors above W.

This type of clue would be best symbolized by inserting it directly into the diagram. So for our example we're going to draw a rough little diagram similar to what you would have already constructed had you come across this clue in an actual game.

5
4
3
2
1

We've made this diagram vertical because that makes the most sense visually. Now let's symbolize the fact that J lives two floors above W. But be careful here—if you live two floors above your friend, for instance, there is only *one* floor that actually separates you. Take a look at our symbol:

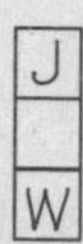

Re-read each clue to see if your visual matches the exact text of the clue!

As you can see, the wording is meant to lead you astray. If you weren't vigilant and had inserted an extra floor, your game would have swiftly degenerated into confusion. Also, notice the fact that our symbol was consistent with the diagram—we used a vertical diagram, so we need a vertical symbol.

The three boys are flanked by two girls.

This clue gives you several pieces of information. First, there are exactly three boys. Second, there are at least two girls. Third, the three boys all sit together. Fourth, one girl sits on either end of the line of boys. Let's put it all together:

GBBBG

Notice that we didn't just write "3B" and "2G." Instead, we wrote three separate Bs and two separate Gs. That's consistent with the information the clue gives. If the clue involves five engines, for instance, draw "EEEEE" and not "5E." The former is much more visual, which is your goal. And if later you are given further characteristics about the boys and girls, such as what color hats they might be wearing, you will be able to note these characteristics as subscripts.

Hannah will not attend the dance unless David attends the dance.

Here, we have another instance of a conditional statement. Remember this from arguments? This conditional statement doesn't have the words *if* and *then* as cues for us, but take note that the word *unless* is another cue for a conditional statement. And because it's a conditional statement, we can draw the contrapositive. Before we can flip and negate, we need to put the original into the same form that we used before. There's a very simple rule for how to accomplish this. Replace the word "unless" with the words "if not" and start your statement there. So for our example above, we would get the following:

If not David attends the dance, Hannah will not attend the dance.

Granted, this is a bit awkward to say, but we're just going to be using it to generate a conditional statement, and for that purpose it will work just fine. Here's what we get when we symbolize:

$$-D \rightarrow -H$$

Look familiar? Good. Now to get the contrapositive, all we have to do is flip and negate.

$$H \rightarrow D$$

So we have a nice, mechanical way to generate both the conditional statement and its contrapositive. Remember the rule and you're all set. If you're more familiar with symbolic logic, you might be able to get to the symbols without having to use our rule, but you should still learn it. What seems like a simple task right now might feel entirely different on the day of the test. Leave nothing to chance. Here's the rule once more so you won't forget:

Replace the word "unless" with the words "if not" and start your statement there.

Make a flash card if you'd like. Just make sure you know the process for the LSAT.

A, B, and C are saxophonists; D, E, and F are percussionists.

In this case, we are given elements that fall into two categories: saxophonists and percussionists. We'll want to have a way to keep these straight as we work the game. Probably the simplest way to accomplish this is by symbolizing one group with uppercase letters and the other with lowercase letters. We'll end up with:

S: A B C
p: d e f

There are games that have more than two types of elements, or elements that can have more than one characteristic associated with them. In these cases, you'll want to use subscripts to distinguish the elements. For instance, if we had those same saxophonists and percussionists, but we were also told that A and f were leads and C and e were backups, we would need some way to keep all of this straight. Furthermore, we might have to assign these elements to either the marching band or the orchestra, the two groups available in the game. We would need to make sure that we could tell what characteristics each element had so that we could assign them accordingly. Here's how we would symbolize:

S: A_L B C_B
p: d e_B f_L

You'll have to be sure to keep things neat, but now you'll be able to work with the elements effectively.

There is at least one fire drill per week.

How would you do this one? This doesn't give us very concrete information because we still don't know exactly how many fire drills there will be each week. But it is an important piece of information because we know for sure that we have to include a fire drill in each valid arrangement for the game. It's a pretty simple piece of information, so our symbol will also be pretty simple. Don't succumb to the urge to just keep it in your head; yes, it's simple, but no, that doesn't give license to skip the visualization. Here's a good way to symbolize it:

$$F^{1+}$$

We used the plus sign to indicate *at least*, which will remind us that we can have more than one of these, according to the rules. A corollary clue type is one that tells you that an element will be used *at most* a certain number of times; in that case we would use a minus sign as the superscript.

Here's a summary chart of how we symbolized each clue:

CLUE	**SYMBOL**
Anna sits to the east of Bob and to the west of Carol.	B — A — C
The two philosophers never sit together.	P/P (boxed, slashed)
In a five-story building, J lives two floors above W.	J / [ ] / W (stacked boxes)
The three boys are flanked by two girls.	GBBBG (boxed)
Hannah will not attend the dance unless David attends the dance.	–D → –H
[Contrapositive]	H → D
A, B, and C are saxophonists; D, E, and F are percussionists.	S: A B C p: d e f
There is at least one fire drill per week.	F^{1+}

Games Techniques: When Not to Symbolize

Ideally, you will symbolize every clue. Some clues, however, have no clear and concise visual equivalent, especially negative clues that do not refer to any specific element. For example, consider the following clues:

> No more than three books of any given subject are put on the shelf.
>
> Players cannot score more than three points in the first round.

A visualization of these would end up being obtuse and potentially confusing. So we need another method. Remember that we want to keep all the information in one place and not have to refer to the written information provided. Just jot down the essence of the clue in a few words among the rest of your clues. That way you can't forget about it and you won't have to wade through the original, confusing clue. Now let's try another game.

If you can't think of a quick and simple way to symbolize a clue, just jot down the essence of it and move on.

GAME #2: TENANTS AND APARTMENTS

You will be able to use a grid diagram with many types of games. However, at times you'll manage two or more sets of elements within this grid diagram. Not to worry—it's very approachable. Take time to master the process. You can worry about pacing as you work through the games from the back of this book as well as in the real LSATs you'll take for practice.

> Eight tenants—J, K, L, M, N, O, P, and Q—live in a five-story building. On each floor, there is one studio apartment and one one-bedroom apartment. From the ground floor up, the floors are numbered one through five. The following is known about the tenants' living arrangements:
>
> No tenant shares an apartment with any other tenant.
> No one lives in the fifth-floor studio.
> No one lives in the third-floor one-bedroom.
> M lives in the second-floor studio.
> P lives in the fourth-floor studio.
> M and O each live on a higher floor than Q.
> K, N, and Q live in one-bedroom apartments.

1. If K lives on a lower floor than P, then who must live in the second-floor one-bedroom?

   (A) J
   (B) K
   (C) L
   (D) N
   (E) Q

2. What is the maximum number of tenants any one of whom could be the one who lives in the fifth-floor one-bedroom?

(A) 1
(B) 2
(C) 3
(D) 4
(E) 5

3. If J lives on a lower floor than L, then which of the following statements must be false?

(A) J lives in the second-floor one-bedroom.
(B) K lives in the fourth-floor one-bedroom.
(C) L lives in the third-floor studio.
(D) N lives in the fourth-floor one-bedroom.
(E) O lives in the fifth-floor one-bedroom.

4. If P lives on the floor above O, and O lives on the floor above N, then what is the maximum number of possible living arrangements for all eight tenants?

(A) 1
(B) 2
(C) 3
(D) 4
(E) 5

5. Suppose that M moves from the second-floor studio into the second-floor one-bedroom, but all the other conditions remain the same. Which of the following statements could be false?

(A) J lives on a floor below K.
(B) K lives on a floor below N.
(C) L lives on a floor below K.
(D) O lives on a floor below N.
(E) O lives on a floor below K.

Cracking Game #2

Step 1: Draw your diagram

This looks a bit more complex than what we've seen so far. Notice here that there are more spaces (10) than elements (8). However, the clues tell us that there are two unoccupied spaces, so we will end up using all of our elements, without repeating any of them; we have another one-to-one ratio of elements to slots. In this game we have two types of apartments: studios and one-bedrooms. Here's how we drew our diagram:

	S	1B	S	1B	S	1B
5						
4						
3						
2						
1						

We have another grid here—now it's just two columns for each question.

First, we drew a vertical grid because it will mimic the same design as an apartment building. The clues include words like *above* and *below* when referring to the relationship between the elements, so a vertical diagram will keep us organized. Second, notice the fact that we really had to make two columns in the diagram for each arrangement—a studio apartment column and a one-bedroom column. We indicated the difference between the columns by making dashed lines. We used solid lines to separate the work we do for each new question. Now let's look at the clues.

Step 2: Symbolize the clues

The first clue tells us that we'll put one element in each slot. We can jot down a note like "one per slot." The next four clues are all things we can put directly into our diagram. Here they are:

No one lives in the fifth-floor studio.
No one lives in the third-floor one-bedroom.
M lives in the second-floor studio.
P lives in the fourth-floor studio.

We'll get to these clues in a minute. The fifth clue is this:

M and O each live on a higher floor than Q.

This clue is giving us two pieces of information, that both M and O live on a higher floor than Q. Here are our symbols for this clue:

As you can see, all we did was show how M and O are both "above" Q. We used a line because we don't know how far above Q each one is. This is another range clue. Here's the sixth and final clue:

K, N, and Q live in one-bedroom apartments.

Now we know that K, N, and Q all have to be in the one-bedroom column. We made a quick notation of that:

K,N,Q = 1B

However, we'll probably wind up integrating this information directly into the diagram before we go to the questions. Now, here are the first four clues again—and then our diagram that shows how we added the information.

No one lives in the fifth-floor studio.
No one lives in the third-floor one-bedroom.
M lives in the second-floor studio.
P lives in the fourth-floor studio.

	S	1B	S	1B	S	1B	S	1B
5	X							
4	P							
3		X						
2	M							
1								

So we've put Xs through the two empty apartments and then put the P and the M directly into the diagram. Now we're ready for Step 3.

Step 3: Double-check your clues and make deductions

Did you re-read the clues to make sure you symbolized correctly? Good. As for deductions, if M lives on the second floor and must live above Q, then Q must live on the first floor. Because Q must live in a one-bedroom, Q lives in the first-floor one-bedroom. That's our first major deduction. There are several more deductions that we can make. Take a look at the diagram to see how many other deductions we were able to make. Remember also that we wanted to indicate that K, N, and Q all had to be in one-bedrooms, but because we have no way of knowing which one each will be in, we'll note the places where they *cannot* be. Here is our diagram:

	S	1B	S	1B	S	1B	S	1B
5	X							
4	P							
3	-N -K	X						
2	M							
1	-O -N -K J/L	Q						

There are only two studios that remain open. Both are limited because neither N nor K can go in them. Furthermore, O cannot go in the first-floor studio, because O must be higher than Q. Therefore, the first-floor studio is an extremely limited space, and the only remaining elements that can go in it are J or L. Because there are only two elements that can occupy the space, it's worth writing this in our diagram. If we step back and evaluate things before diving right into the questions, we'll notice that the studios are much more restricted than are the one-bedrooms. Keep this in mind as you work.

Step 4: Attack the questions

Remember, go for the "if" questions first and leave the "which" and other general questions for later.

Step 5: Use Process of Elimination

Here's our first "if" question.

1. If K lives on a lower floor than P, then who must live in the second-floor one-bedroom?

   (A) J
   (B) K
   (C) L
   (D) N
   (E) Q

Here's how to crack it

This question provides us with new information about the relationship between K and P. It tells us that K must live on a lower floor than P, and there is only one open slot below P for K to fill. So take a look at our diagram:

			(1)					
	S	1B	S	1B	S	1B	S	1B
5	X		X					
4	P		P					
3	-N -K	X		X				
2	M		M	K				
1	-O -N -K J/L	Q	J/L	Q				

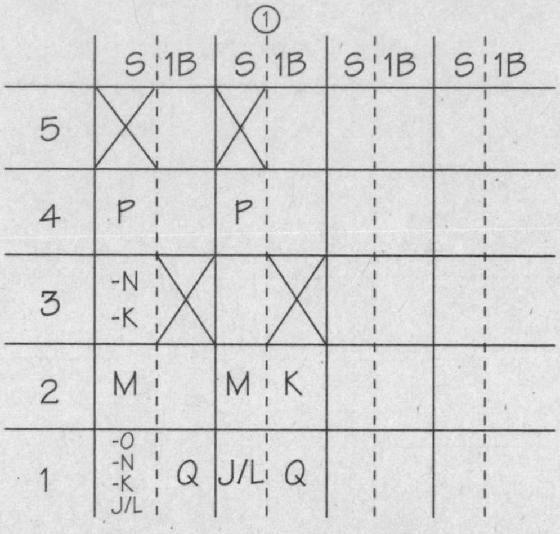

That's right! K is forced into the second-floor one-bedroom, and hence it's our answer. Circle (B). Let's hit the next "if" question.

3. If J lives on a lower floor than L, then which of the following statements must be false?
   (A) J lives in the second-floor one-bedroom.
   (B) K lives in the fourth-floor one-bedroom.
   (C) L lives in the third-floor studio.
   (D) N lives in the fourth-floor one-bedroom.
   (E) O lives in the fifth-floor one-bedroom.

Here's how to crack it

Well, this settles the question about who will occupy the first-floor studio, doesn't it? If J is lower than L, that means that J must live in the first-floor studio and L must be somewhere above the first floor. Take a look at our diagram:

			(1)		(3)			
	S	1B	S	1B	S	1B	S	1B
5	X		X		X			
4	P		P		P			
3	-N -K	X		X	-N -K	X		
2	M		M	K	M			
1	-O -N -K J/L	Q	J/L	Q	J	Q		

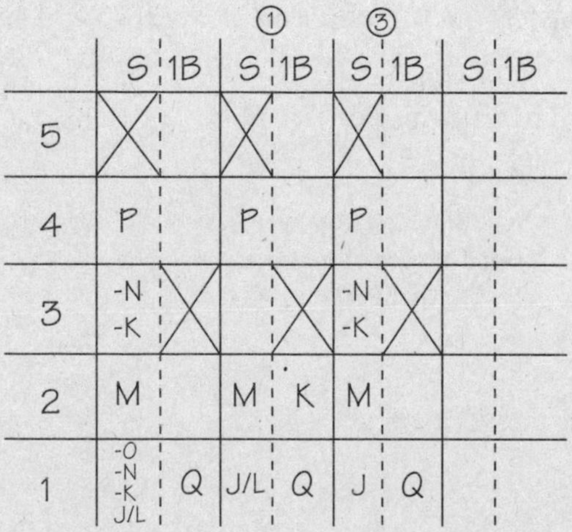

Our task here is to find the statement that must be false. So we'll head to the answer choices and cross out any choices that can be true. You do this by reading each choice and looking at your diagram. So let's do that. (A) cannot be true because we've already definitively placed J on the first floor. So it's our answer. (B), (C), (D), and (E) can all be true because those spaces are still open on the diagram. Let's move on.

4. If P lives on the floor above O, and O lives on the floor above N, then what is the maximum number of possible living arrangements for all eight tenants?

(A) 1
(B) 2
(C) 3
(D) 4
(E) 5

Here's how to crack it

This question contains two very good pieces of information. Let's put the information in first and then talk about exactly what our task is.

			①		③		④	
	S	1B	S	1B	S	1B	S	1B
5	X		X		X		X	
4	P		P		P		P	
3	-N -K	X		X	-N -K	X	O	X
2	M		M	K	M		M	N
1	-O -N -K -J/L	Q	J/L	Q	J	Q	J/L	Q

Keep everything neat so you can refer back to your previous work accurately and efficiently.

Good, we were able to definitively place two other elements. However, the question asks us about how many different ways the full diagram can look. The manner in which the question is phrased ("the maximum number of possible living arrangements for all eight tenants") might be confusing. If so, translate it to say something like, "How many different ways can we make the diagram work?" Then, write out the possibilities in your diagram. The only open spaces are the first-floor studio, the fourth-floor one-bedroom, and the fifth-floor one-bedroom. Additionally, the first-floor studio can only be one of two possible elements—J or L. So break it down as we do on the following page.

WHEN *J* IS IN 1S:

1S	41B	51B
J	K	L

OR

1S	41B	51B
J	L	K

WHEN *L* IS IN 1S:

1S	41B	51B
L	J	K

OR

1S	41B	51B
L	K	J

So we've got two possibilities for each of the two scenarios—when J is in the first-floor studio, and when L is in the first-floor studio. Hence, a total of four possibilities, so the answer is (D). Let's move on.

The final two questions in this game are "weird" questions. Let's leave the one that changes the rules for the end.

2. What is the maximum number of tenants any one of whom could be the one who lives in the fifth-floor one-bedroom?

(A) 1
(B) 2
(C) 3
(D) 4
(E) 5

Here's how to crack it

This is an overly complex way of asking how many different people can be in the fifth-floor one-bedroom. You know it can't be P, M, or Q. Now check your previous work and see who we've placed there before: On question 4, we put K, J, and L there. This leaves us with O and N. Can we put them there without breaking any rules? Try and you'll find you can. So the correct answer is (E).

Now let's knock out the last question, the "suppose" question. You can use your original diagram for this question, but you must review all the clues before you can start filling anything in. The addition of new rules can alter deductions and/or add new ones.

5. Suppose that M moves from the second-floor studio into the second-floor one-bedroom, but all the other conditions remain the same. Which of the following statements could be false?

(A) J lives on a floor below K.
(B) K lives on a floor below N.
(C) L lives on a floor below K.
(D) O lives on a floor below N.
(E) O lives on a floor below K.

Here's how to crack it

Well, we have to shift M over to the second-floor one-bedroom. Do that, and then make sure that this doesn't screw up any of your original deductions. Does it?

			①		③		④		⑤	
	S	1B	S	1B	S	1B	S	1B	S	1B
5	X		X		X		X		X	K/N
4	P		P		P		P		P	K/N
3	-N -K	X		X	-N -K	X	O	X		X
2	M		M	K	M		M	N		M
1	-O -N -K J/L	Q	J/L	Q	J	Q	J/L	Q	J/L	Q

Fortunately, it doesn't. In fact, it further limits the diagram (as we've indicated) because now K and N have only two places to go. So now let's attack the answer choices, and we'll do that by eliminating anything that must be true to isolate the one that could be false. (A) must be true, because K, N, P, and an empty apartment take up the entire fourth and fifth floors. Cross it out. (B) does not have to be true—K could also live above N. Therefore, it "could be false" and it's our answer. (C), (D), and (E) all must be true, if you feel like checking. That's another game under our belts.

Games Techniques: Making Deductions

Two ways to make deductions: Learn them and practice them.

We've worked through two games now, and hopefully you recognize how important it is to make deductions before starting to work through the questions. Think of them as unwritten clues. You can't make good deductions by glancing briefly at your diagram and clues, while hurrying to get to the questions. You have to look carefully at the diagram and your symbolizations. Some people think that making deductions is the result of some kind of epiphany, that you either see them or you don't. Actually, finding deductions is the result of a purely mechanical process. Once you understand the process and have had some time to practice it on a number of different games, you'll be able to ferret out those critical extra pieces of information that will save you valuable time down the road. Here's an overview of the process.

- First, take each symbol and apply it to the diagram. Write in any deductions. In the first game, for example, once we determined that the veal had to be served on Monday, we were able to determine that the manicotti could not be served Sunday or Tuesday, because it could not be served on the day before or after the veal was served. This is how you should apply clues to a diagram, and make deductions.

- Second, take each symbol and apply it to all the other symbols, looking for any overlapping elements. Combine them if it's appropriate, or write a new symbol for the deduction. Then check the diagram to see if your deduction points out any more restrictions in the diagram. For example, suppose we had a game in which we had to make two teams of four players each. Suppose we're told that A and B must be on the same team, and that B and C cannot be on the same team. Because A must always be with B, and B cannot be with C, we would then be able to deduce that A and C cannot be on the same team. Combining clues with common elements often leads to deductions.
- Finally, take a step back and look at the entire diagram. Notice any spaces that are extremely "limited," meaning that they have lots of minuses in them. See if there are only one or two remaining choices for that space. Write in any deductions. Limited spaces may also lead to deductions, under other circumstances. For example, suppose you had a game in which you were dividing nine children into three groups for a boating trip. You are told that Alex and Carlos are in the same boat, and that Danielle and Eleanor are in the same boat. Because only three children can be in any given boat, our two blocks can never go together in a single boat, which would allow you to make several deductions (A cannot be with D or E, C cannot be with D or E).

These three steps should take you about 30 to 45 seconds. And although this process won't guarantee that you find *all* the deductions on *every* game, it is time well spent; you won't spend as much time on the questions, because you'll be able to eliminate answer choices more easily. In some cases you'll still have some answer choices to work out, but the less you have to do, the better!

Give yourself a pat on the back. You're about halfway through the Games chapter—and things should be starting to fall into place.

GAME #3: OFFICES AND FURNISHINGS

The first two games that we worked on used one of the most common diagrams found on the LSAT: a straight grid diagram with the core across the top or on one side to which we add rows or columns as we work the questions. But sometimes the setup will describe a spatial relationship that doesn't fit into that pattern. If that happens, just be flexible and use the information given to create a visual framework that matches the description in the setup. You'll still assign elements to places according to the rules; you'll just put them into a different structure. Remember to work on the limited space of the page—or if you're using scratch paper, mark off a quarter of a page to work on—so that you won't be in for an unpleasant surprise when you get to the real thing. We're still working on cementing the games process, so don't be concerned about time right now. Be methodical and refer to the earlier parts of the chapter as necessary. After you've finished, compare your results to ours.

There are exactly ten offices arranged on either side of a hallway. The offices with windows facing north are on one side of the hallway and are numbered 1, 2, 3, 4, and 5, respectively, from the west end of the building to the east. The offices with windows facing south are on the other side of the hallway and are numbered 6, 7, 8, 9, and 10, respectively, also from west to east. The offices on the north side are directly across from the offices on the south side, facing each other in the following pairs: 1 and 6; 2 and 7; 3 and 8; 4 and 9; 5 and 10. Each office has been furnished in exactly one of the following styles: Bauhaus, Moderne, or Pop according to the following conditions:

None of the offices is furnished in the same style as the office that is located directly across the hallway from it.

None of the offices is furnished in the same style as any office adjacent to it.

Bauhaus furnishings are found in exactly one office on each side of the hallway.

Bauhaus furnishings are found in office number 3.

Moderne furnishings are found in office number 7.

1. Which one of the following could be an accurate list of the styles of furnishings found in offices 6, 7, 8, 9, and 10, respectively?

   (A) Pop, Moderne, Pop, Moderne, Pop
   (B) Pop, Moderne, Pop, Bauhaus, Moderne
   (C) Bauhaus, Pop, Moderne, Pop, Moderne
   (D) Bauhaus, Moderne, Pop, Moderne, Bauhaus
   (E) Pop, Moderne, Bauhaus, Pop, Moderne

2. If Pop furnishings are found in exactly five of the offices along the hallway, then which one of the following statements must be true?

   (A) Moderne furnishings are found in office 6.
   (B) Moderne furnishings are found in office 4.
   (C) Pop furnishings are found in office 5.
   (D) Moderne furnishings are found in office 10.
   (E) Bauhaus furnishings are found in office 9.

3. Which one of the following statements must be false?

   (A) Pop furnishings are found in office 10.
   (B) Pop furnishings are found in office 1.
   (C) Moderne furnishings are found in office 9.
   (D) Bauhaus furnishings are found in office 9.
   (E) Bauhaus furnishings are found in office 10.

4. If office 4 is furnished in Pop, then each of the following statements could be false, EXCEPT:
    (A) Pop furnishings are found in office 10.
    (B) Pop furnishings are found in office 6.
    (C) Bauhaus furnishings are found in office 6.
    (D) Moderne furnishings are found in office 5.
    (E) Moderne furnishings are found in office 9.

5. Suppose that exactly two offices are furnished in Bauhaus, rather than just one, among the offices facing south and exactly one office is furnished in Bauhaus among the offices facing north. If all of the other conditions remain the same, then which one of the following statements must be true?
    (A) Moderne furnishings are found in office 4.
    (B) Moderne furnishings are found in office 10.
    (C) Pop furnishings are found in office 1.
    (D) Bauhaus furnishings are found in office 6.
    (E) Bauhaus furnishings are found in office 9.

Cracking Game #3

Step 1: Draw your diagram

Each of our first two games was arranged in a grid, one with one level of information and the other with two. Each had a one-to-one correspondence between elements and slots. With this game, things get a little bit more complicated. No worries, though. All we have to do is follow the process and we'll be able to tackle it effectively. The setup tells us that this game has a particular spatial arrangement of the slots we'll assign elements to, but the process of assigning elements to spaces is still the same. So what will our diagram look like? Just take a cue from the setup and make it look the way it's described. We ended up with:

Don't forget to list the elements next to the diagram so that you'll have everything within easy reach. It's a pretty straightforward diagram. But it would be difficult to add rows in the way that we have with our previous games.

So instead, we'll use this as a template and then create another simple diagram—after all, it's only a few lines—to work each of the questions. We'll fill in the template with all of the concrete information that we have, effectively like a clue shelf. And then each of the new little diagrams that we create to work on the questions will just be a quick sketch that we can use as a framework to place our elements according to the restrictions of the question. And we still won't erase our previous work, for the same reason as before. If it's not clear, you'll see what we mean.

Notice that we only have three elements to be distributed among ten offices. That means that we'll have to repeat them. And based on how restrictive the clues are about the placement of elements of the same type in adjacent slots, we'll have to use all of the elements. Make a note of that.

Step 2: Symbolize the clues

Let's get right to it and make the restrictions visual.

> None of the offices is furnished in the same style as the office that is located directly across the hallway from it.

This tells us how elements *cannot* be arranged with respect to one another, so this is an antiblock clue, but it's broader than what we're used to. The antiblock clues we've seen so far have listed specific elements that can't be next to one another, but here it applies to all of the elements. No big deal. General clues—those that apply to all elements, all spaces, or even one entire type of element—are often the most powerful clues in a game. In this game, we only have three types of elements, so it would be easy enough to jot down the three possibilities as individual antiblocks. Because "facing" here is vertical, they would look like this:

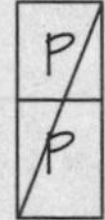

> None of the offices is furnished in the same style as any office adjacent to it.

We have another antiblock clue that applies to all of the elements. Adjacent means "right next to" so it's basically the same as our first clue, but horizontal. Like this:

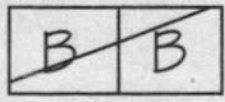

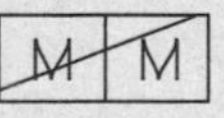

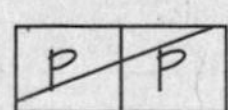

Bauhaus furnishings are found in exactly one office on each side of the hallway.

This is very specific about how many times we'll place B, but vague as to exactly where it will go within each row. So we'll jot down what we know. We'll use B exactly two times, so let's put two Bs down in our list of elements. And we'll make a note over to the side of our diagram to show that we must use B once in each row. We also know that we have eight slots to fill with M and P, so we'll have to use each more than once. Our symbol for "more than once" is a superscript 1+ next to each element in our list next to the diagram.

B B M^{1+} P^{1+}

B ⟶

1 2 3 4 5

6 7 8 9 10

B ⟶

Bauhaus furnishings are found in office number 3.

Notice how it's like falling dominoes...and how whether knowing that something is "out" is just as valuable as knowing that something is "in."

Aha! More about B. This time we are able to definitively place one of the Bs, so we'll go ahead and put it right into our diagram. We'll circle it the same way we did the permanently placed element in the first game, so that we never forget to place it in the same space for each question we work through. Keep in mind that we only have one more B to use and it'll have to go in the other row.

B ⟶ Ⓑ

1 2 3 4 5

6 7 8 9 10

B ⟶

Moderne furnishings are found in office number 7.

Another wonderfully restrictive clue. We can go ahead and drop that right into the diagram as well.

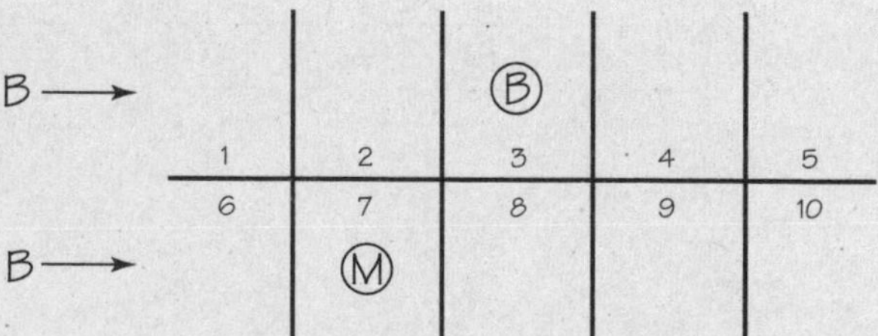

These are some pretty restrictive clues to work with. That should help to compensate for the fact that we don't have a one-to-one correspondence between elements and slots. Plus, we only have three possibilities (and in some cases fewer) for each space.

Step 3: Double-check your clues and make deductions

Did you remember to work backwards and check your clues against the grain? If so, things should have progressed pretty smoothly. Can we come up with any deductions? Those restrictive clues should yield something because we only have three elements in any one slot. There isn't really much overlap between the clues, but we should note that two of the clues put limitations on the placement of B. Let's start by looking for any further limitations that result from having B in office 3. We know that we can't have another B across from or next to 3, so we can show that we can't have B in 8, 2, or 4.

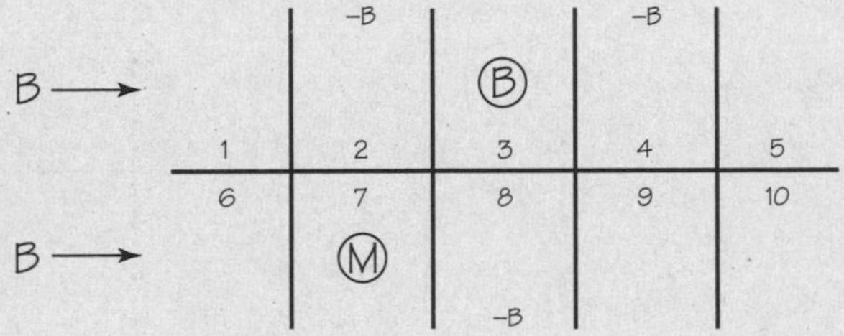

And we'll have similar results from the fact that M is placed in 7. That will eliminate the possibility of having another M in 2, 6, or 8.

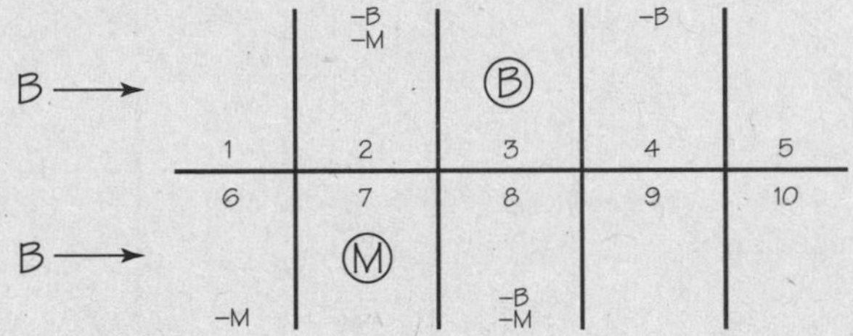

We now have two slots that can have neither B nor M, leaving only one element to place in 2 and 8. Let's put P in both of those offices.

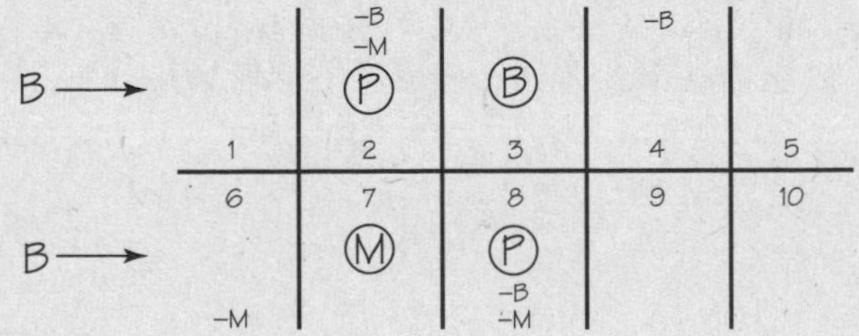

Placing P in 2 and 8 gives us further restrictions. After each new restriction, we can look for further impact. We can now eliminate the possibility of having P in either 1 or 9.

	1	2	3	4	5
B →	−P	−B −M (P)	(B)	−B	
	6	7	8	9	10
B →	−M	(M)	(P) −B −M	−P	

Which is the most restricted element in the top row? It's B, because we can only use it once in each row. That means that we can eliminate the possibility of having another B in the top row.

	1	2	3	4	5
B →	−P −B	−B −M (P)	(B)	−B	−B
	6	7	8	9	10
B →	−M	(M)	(P) −B −M	−P	

And now that we've eliminated both P and B from being placed in office 1, the only element left to go there is M.

	1	2	3	4	5
B →	−P −B (M)	−B −M (P)	(B)	−B	−B
	6	7	8	9	10
B →	−M	(M)	(P) −B −M	−P	

Is there anything else we know for sure? Notice that B is restricted from being in either 4 or 5, so that leaves only two elements (M or P) to go in each of those slots. And remember that we can't have the same elements in two adjacent slots. Because 4 and 5 can't be occupied by two Ms or by two Ps, we know that we'll have to have an M in one and a P in the other, right? We can't say for sure which element will be in which slot, but we can symbolize it in the same way we did before, using a slash between them.

	–P –B	–B –M		–B	–B
B ⟶	(M)	(P)	(B)	M/P	P/M
	1	2	3	4	5
	6	7	8	9	10
B ⟶		(M)	(P)		
	–M		–B –M	–P	

Anything else? Both slot 6 and slot 9 are limited to one of two elements, but we're not sure which one and they won't have any concrete impact on one another. We've reached a point at which we can come up with a few speculative deductions. For instance, *if* B was in 6, we would know that we can't use any more Bs in the bottom row and so we'd place M in office 9. But that's a big if. Once you've gotten to the point where you can't write down any more concrete information it's time to move on. You could spend all day running through the permutations, but that wouldn't be a good use of your limited time. The questions will give us more concrete information to work with, so let's get to them. We've got a ton of restrictions already, so we should be able to do some efficient POE in answering the questions.

Step 4: Attack the questions
You know what to do—head straight for the "if" questions.

Step 5: Use Process of Elimination
Now it's time to let our investment in Step 3 pay off. Let's get right to it. Question 2 is our first "if" question:

2. If Pop furnishings are found in exactly five of the offices along the hallway, then which one of the following statements must be true?
   (A) Moderne furnishings are found in office 6.
   (B) Moderne furnishings are found in office 4.
   (C) Pop furnishings are found in office 5.
   (D) Moderne furnishings are found in office 10.
   (E) Bauhaus furnishings are found in office 9.

What's the first thing we do? Put any new information the question gives us into the diagram. Until now, we've been working in our original template. Now that we'll be filling in information that won't be true for the whole game, it's time to draw a simple diagram for each question. Just draw a basic outline and carry along the elements we placed from our template.

M	P	B	M/P	P/M
	M	P		

We'll redraw one of these for each question. We can start by filling in the new information we were given in question 2: P occupies five slots. How can we make that happen? Well, we can already see 3 Ps from our template—one in office 2, one in office 8 and one in either office 4 or 5. Where can we put the last two? We know that we can't have one in office 9, so that only leaves 6 and 10. Once we put a P in 10, we know that we can't have one in 5 so that pushes P into 4 and M into 5. Now we only have one open slot. We know we can't use P so that leaves M or B. Can we tell which one it'll have to be? Remember that we have to use B twice so we can see that we'll have to put B in office 9. That's it. Our diagram's all filled in. We should be able to eliminate pretty easily.

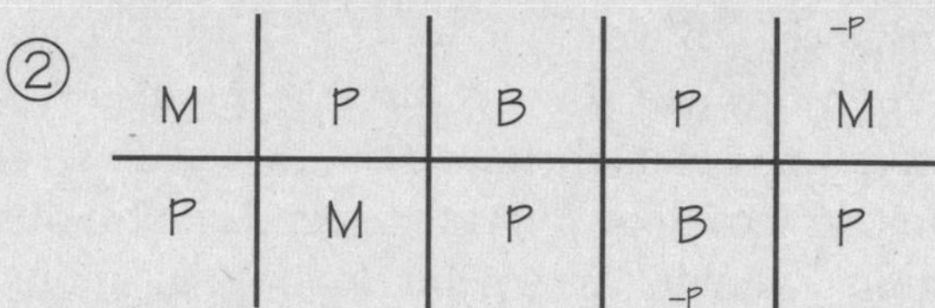

We're looking for the answer choice that *must be true* so we'll cross off any answers that could be false, even once. That eliminates all but (E). Circle it and move on. Our next "if" question is number 4.

4. If office 4 is furnished in Pop, then each of the following statements could be false, EXCEPT:

(A) Pop furnishings are found in office 10.
(B) Pop furnishings are found in office 6.
(C) Bauhaus furnishings are found in office 6.
(D) Moderne furnishings are found in office 5.
(E) Moderne furnishings are found in office 9.

We have an EXCEPT question here, so our answer will be the one that's not like the others. But first we have to draw another sketch and fill in the information we're given in the question.

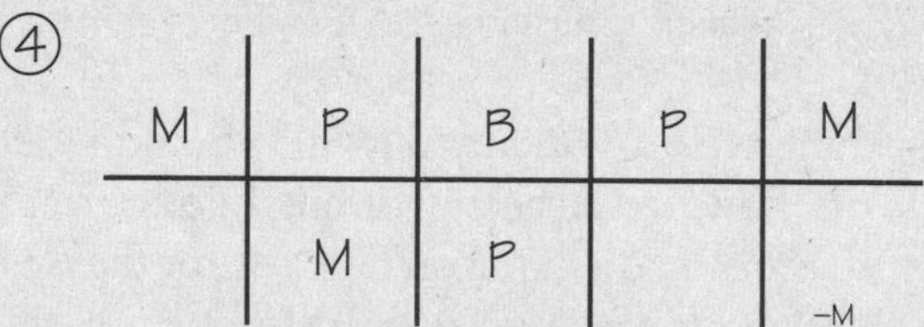

Once we put P in 4, we know that M will have to be in 5. That means no M in 10. Can we put down anything else that we know for sure? We know that we'll have to use our second B in the bottom row, but we don't know exactly where at this point. That looks like about all we can do. Let's see what we can eliminate.

Answer choice (A) could be false because we could put B in 10. Cross it off.
Answer choice (B) could be false because we could put B in 6. Eliminate.
Answer choice (C) could be false because we could put P in 6. Eliminate it.
Answer choice (D) has to be true from our diagram for this question.
Let's keep it.

Answer choice (E) could be false since, once again, we could also fill 9 with B. Eliminate it and we're done.

We're done with all of the "if" questions, so we'll move on to "which" questions. Question 1 is a partial grab-a-rule that applies only to the bottom row. Let's see what we can do with it.

1. Which one of the following could be an accurate list of the styles of furnishings found in offices 6, 7, 8, 9, and 10, respectively?
   (A) Pop, Moderne, Pop, Moderne, Pop
   (B) Pop, Moderne, Pop, Bauhaus, Moderne
   (C) Bauhaus, Pop, Moderne, Pop, Moderne
   (D) Bauhaus, Moderne, Pop, Moderne, Bauhaus
   (E) Pop, Moderne, Bauhaus, Pop, Moderne

Remember to start with the most restricted clues and slots first.

We know from our template that slots 7 and 8 have to be occupied by M and P, respectively. That eliminates answer choices (C) and (E).

What else do we know about the bottom row? You might have spent some time trying to get rid of the remaining choices if you forgot about the restriction on B. It's a big picture clue that's easy to lose sight of. If you find yourself struggling on a grab-a-rule question, look back to see if there are any of those big picture clues that you forgot to apply. Let's see if we can find violations of the rule that we have to use B once—and once only—in the bottom row. We sure can. That rule gets rid of (A) which has no B at all, and (D) which has two Bs. That only leaves (B), so we've got our answer. Let's move on to our next "which" question.

3. Which one of the following statements must be false?
   (A) Pop furnishings are found in office 10.
   (B) Pop furnishings are found in office 1.
   (C) Moderne furnishings are found in office 9.
   (D) Bauhaus furnishings are found in office 9.
   (E) Bauhaus furnishings are found in office 10.

Here we have to find the choice that *must be false*. You'll remember that we can eliminate any choice if it could be true, even one time. Let's see what we can do. Don't forget to use the good work you've done on the "if" questions to help with POE whenever possible.

We can use our work from question 2 to eliminate both (A) and (D). And we saw the possibility of both (C) and (E) in question 4, so we can get rid of those, too. If you were unsure about them, you could always draw another quick diagram and try them out. Answer choice (B) violates one of our deductions, so that's our answer. We only have one question left.

5. Suppose that exactly two offices are furnished in Bauhaus, rather than just one, among the offices facing south and exactly one office is furnished in Bauhaus among the offices facing north. If all of the other conditions remain the same, then which one of the following statements must be true?

(A) Moderne furnishings are found in office 4.
(B) Moderne furnishings are found in office 10.
(C) Pop furnishings are found in office 1.
(D) Bauhaus furnishings are found in office 6.
(E) Bauhaus furnishings are found in office 9.

This is one of those questions that changes one of our original conditions. It might impact our deductions, and we've had a number of them in this game, so we'll probably want to rebuild our template from scratch for this question. Yes, it's annoying, but rather than fretting, we'll just keep our pencils moving and get to it.

It turns out that because the new rule affects only the bottom row, our original deductions are still valid. The difference is that now we know that we have to place two Bs in the three remaining slots in the bottom row. Because we know that we can't have two adjacent Bs, they can't go in 9 *and* 10. So one of them will have to go in 6 and the other in either 9 or 10. We end up with something like this:

–P –B	–M –B		–B	–B
M	P	B	M/P	P/M
B	M	P	B/M	/B
–M		–M –B	–P	

Now that we've filled in everything we can, it's time to head to the answers. We're looking for the one that must be true, so if an answer choice *could be false*, even one time, we can cross it off. We found out when we were filling in the diagram that we have to have B in 6 and that's among the answers, so we've got a winner. If you'd feel more confident checking the rest of the choices, go ahead. If you're sure of your work, we're done. Just for the record, answer choices (A), (B), and (E) could be false and (C) must be false according to our diagram.

See, that wasn't so bad. We just followed the structure they gave us and got to work. You might think that redrawing the diagram for each question is too time consuming, but if you keep it simple you can create one quickly and then have a concrete space in which to work through the question. And you'll notice that making a new diagram for each question allowed us to use POE on the later questions quickly and painlessly. Our investment paid off.

Games Techniques: Drawing the Right Diagram

How can you tell when to use one of these template diagrams? The setup will let you know that you have a spatial arrangement that is not linear. Let's try it with another setup:

> Eight dishes—artichoke, beef, celery, danish, eggplant, fennel, grapes, and halibut—are being placed around a circular table.

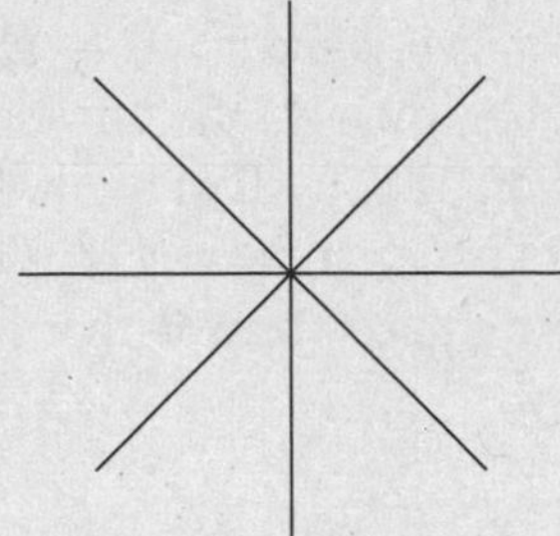

This is similar to what you just did, but here we are dealing with a circular diagram. The simplest way to deal with a circular diagram is to draw intersecting lines. Draw as many lines as you need so you have the appropriate number of spaces around the circle. Place each element at the end of a line. The basic idea is the same: Match what the setup tells you about the spatial arrangement. Remember to redraw the basic structure for each question you do. Don't erase!

Occasionally, the LSAT folks will surprise you with their generosity and will actually tell you how to draw the diagram. By all means, use their description. Copy it as many times as you need to. Draw it a bit more simply if necessary. Don't look a gift horse in the mouth.

Games Techniques: Question Strategy

Here are some guidelines for the most effective way to evaluate the answer choices when you encounter different tasks.

Make sure you've got this question strategy down COLD. Put it next to your Arguments chart on your refrigerator.

- When the task is to find the one that "must be true," you can eliminate any answer that *could be false*—even one time. First, look for the right answer that matches the deductions.
- When the task is to find the one that "must be false," you can eliminate any answer that *could be true*—even one time. Look for the right answer that contradicts a deduction.
- When the task is to find the one that "could be true," you can eliminate any answer that *must be false*—every time.
- When the task is to find the one that "could be false," you can eliminate any answer that *must be true*—every time.

- On grab-a-rule questions, use Process of Elimination. Start with the most restrictive clue and eliminate all answer choices that violate it. Do this with each clue.
- On questions that start with the word "suppose," either a new clue is added to the original clues or one of the original clues is removed. Do these questions last, because the change in the rules applies only to this question. Always remember to check to see whether any of your original deductions have changed.
- On except/cannot questions, circle the "EXCEPT/CANNOT" to help you remember, then do the question in reverse. For example, if the question asks, "All of the following could be true EXCEPT," eliminate every answer choice that could be true. Check every answer choice; the one that is not like the others is the correct answer.

GAME #4: HATS AND SCARVES

All of the games we've worked on so far have been *ordering* games. This one will be a bit different. Instead of having limitations on how the elements are arranged with respect to one another, we'll be told which elements have to be in a certain group. We'll call these *grouping* games. The order of the elements within each group won't matter. We'll just have to decide which elements make up a given group. Sometimes we'll know exactly how many elements are in each group, sometimes we won't. As you might imagine, the latter are trickier. But the process always remains the same. Let's try one.

A couple of tips before we start this game: One, re-read the section on "making deductions"; two, remember our old friend the contrapositive. Grab your pencil and get to work.

A store is creating a window display featuring four hats and three scarves. The only hats being considered are A, B, C, D, E, and F, and the only scarves being considered are J, K, L, M, and N.

If A is displayed, then neither B nor L can be displayed.
B is displayed only if D is displayed.
C cannot be displayed unless J is displayed.
D can only be displayed if K is displayed.
If L is displayed, then M must be displayed.
F cannot be displayed unless D is not displayed.

1. Which one of the following is a possible display of hats in the window?

   (A) A, B, C, F
   (B) A, C, D, E
   (C) A, D, E, F
   (D) B, C, D, F
   (E) B, C, E, F

2. If F is displayed, which one of the following must be true?

   (A) A is not displayed.
   (B) B is not displayed.
   (C) K is not displayed.
   (D) L is displayed.
   (E) M is displayed.

3. If both B and E are displayed, then which one of the following CANNOT be a partial list of items displayed?

   (A) C, D, E
   (B) C, J, M
   (C) C, D, F
   (D) C, J, K
   (E) D, K, M

4. Each of the following could be displayed together EXCEPT

   (A) B and K
   (B) B and F
   (C) B and M
   (D) E and F
   (E) E, J, and M

5. If B is displayed, which one of the following is a list of items that could also be displayed?

   (A) A, M, N
   (B) C, E, F
   (C) C, L, M
   (D) E, F, M
   (E) E, J, M

Cracking Game #4

Step 1: Draw your diagram

Well, we've got a lot going on here—first of all, we've got two sets of elements (hats ABCDEF and scarves jklmn). Next, we know that not all of the elements will be used, because only four out of the six hats are being displayed, and only three out of the five scarves are being displayed. However, we think it's important to keep track of all the elements. How would you do that? Create an "outbox" like the one on the following page.

IN (4+3) | OUT (2+2)   H: ABCDEF
s: jklmn

_ _ _ _ / _ _ _ | _ _ / _ _

When elements are either "in or out," or "selected or not selected," draw a two-column diagram.

As you can see, we created an "in" column and an "out" column. We've indicated the number of hats and the number of scarves in each column. This will allow us to keep track of all the elements, so if we are given information about whether something is in or whether something is out, we'll be able to use it. Now let's hit the clues.

Step 2: Symbolize the clues

We've got a whole mess of conditional clues here. Remember that every time you have a conditional clue, you also can deduce the contrapositive. Symbolize the contrapositive as soon as you've symbolized the clue. Here's what we have so far:

Go slowly with "if...then" clues and making contrapositives.

You can save a lot of time and effort by making antiblocks.

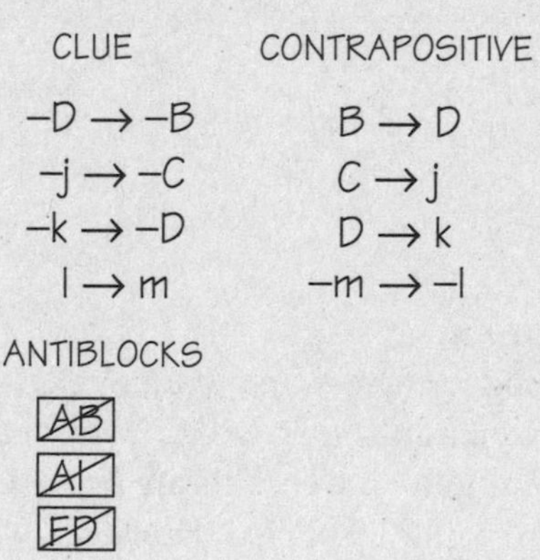

All right. Now let's look a little more closely at these clues. Consider the first clue:

A → –B   B → –A

So if A is displayed, B cannot be displayed, and if B is displayed, A cannot be displayed. The end effect is that there is no way both A and B can be displayed at the same time. That means that this is identical to [AB] because the [AB] also tells us that A and B cannot be displayed at the same time. So rather than writing out the clue and its contrapositive, we can save a lot of time and effort by just making antiblocks whenever we have a conditional clue like this one A → –B.

Step 3: Double-check your clues and make deductions

Did you go against the grain and work backward to make sure that you didn't make any errors in translating the clues into symbols? If not, repeat after me, "This is not a waste of time. This is NOT a waste of time." Good. Okay, now for the deductions. How can you make deductions with a string of "if…then" statements? By linking clues that share elements. If you see an element on one side of a conditional and the same element on the other side of another conditional, you can link them together. Do you see any two clues that can be linked? Take a look below:

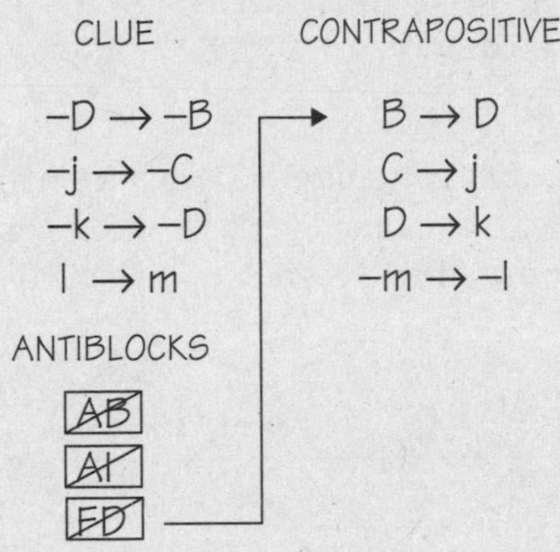

As you can see, there is one point of commonality—D is involved in both an F/D antiblock and a conditional clue. So what does that mean? Well, it means that you can make the following deduction:

F → –B

Why? Because if you have F, you cannot possibly have D, because they are involved in an antiblock. You further know that without D, you cannot possibly have B. Thus, if you have F, you cannot possibly have B. Now, what have we just learned about conditional clues that are formatted like this? That they are actually antiblocks in disguise. So this clue should read:

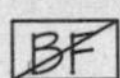

So now we have a fourth antiblock with which to work. Notice the fact that two of the elements (E and N) are not restricted at all. But if you get information about any of the other letters, you can begin to fill in pieces of your diagram. And by the way, a minus sign next to a letter in this game means that it's not displayed, so it goes in the "out" column.

Let's step back for a moment and see what we're going to be working with. Notice that the "out" column has fewer spaces than the "in" column. That means the "out" column is easier to fill, because it's a more restricted space. And notice how much information we have from our clues about elements that cannot appear together in the "in" column.

Any time you have an antiblock, you know for certain that one of those two elements must go in the "out" column. It's possible that both will be "out"—remember, the restrictions given by the clues apply to the elements that are in the "in" column, i.e., the ones that are displayed. The restrictions do not apply to the "out" column. But if you focus on antiblocks, you will quickly be able to determine when certain elements will be in the "out" column.

Step 4: Attack the questions
You guessed it—go for the "if" questions first.

Step 5: Use Process of Elimination
Here is our first "if" question. Let's see what we can do with this one.

2. If F is displayed, which one of the following must be true?
   (A) A is not displayed.
   (B) B is not displayed.
   (C) K is not displayed.
   (D) L is displayed.
   (E) M is displayed.

Here's how to crack it

We seem to have received only one paltry piece of information with this question. But remember that one of our deductions was about F, so now that we know where F is, we should know where several other elements can go:

IN (4+3)	OUT (2+2)	
____/___	__/__	
FACE/j__	BD/l_	②

That little piece of information ends up making a lot happen. Once F is "in" we know that both B and D are "out." Therefore, we know the exact composition of all of the "in" hats—A, C, E, and F. Once we know that, we can also see that l must be "out" because A is "in" and that j must be "in" because C is "in." We've filled in almost the entire diagram! So what's our answer? (A) can't be true, because A is "in." (B) must be true, because if F is "in," B is "out." Bingo! Let's go on to the next question.

Did we go too fast for you on that one? Take a look at the diagram on the next page to see exactly how we got from start to finish.

IN (4+3)	OUT (2+2)
_ _ _ _ / _ _ _	_ _ / _ _
F	
F	BD /
FACE / j_ _	BD /
FACE / j_ _	BD /l_

Notice how it's like falling dominoes...and how knowing that something is "out" is just as valuable as knowing that something is "in."

Now let's hit the next question.

3. If both B and E are displayed, then which one of the following CANNOT be a partial list of items displayed?

(A) C, D, E
(B) C, J, M
(C) C, D, F
(D) C, J, K
(E) D, K, M

Here's how to crack it

We've got two pieces of information in this question. Let's see what that gives us:

IN (4+3)	OUT (2+2)	
_ _ _ _ / _ _ _	_ _ / _ _	
FACE / j_ _	BD /l_	(2)
CDBE / jk_	FA /l_	(3)

Spending time making deductions will make doing the questions much easier.

Once again, we are able to fill in quite a lot here. Because the question tells us that four of the answer choices will work in our diagram (remember, we're looking for the one partial list that is invalid), take a look at the letters you placed in your "out" column (A, F, and l), and see if they appear in any of the choices. Choice (C) has F, doesn't it? It's our answer. Let's move on.

5. If B is displayed, which one of the following is a list of items that could also be displayed?

(A) A, M, N
(B) C, E, F
(C) C, L, M
(D) E, F, M
(E) E, J, M

Here's how to crack it

Only one piece of information again, but that doesn't seem to be stopping us, does it?

IN (4+3)	OUT (2+2)	
____/___	__/__	
FACE / j__	BD /l_	②
CDBE / jk_	FA /l_	③
CDBE / jk_	FA /l_	⑤

In composition, the arrangement of the letters looks suspiciously like the arrangement in number 3, doesn't it? Only now, we're looking for the only possibility that can work. Any answer choice that contains something in the "out" column should now be crossed off. (A), (B), (C), and (D) all contain an element that has been definitively placed in the "out" column. The answer is (E).

We're in the home stretch. Let's knock out the "which" questions.

The final two questions in this game are general questions. The first one is a partial possible-arrangement question. Here we're given only lists of hats that can go in the display. Remember that the hats displayed may have an impact on scarves that might prevent the display from being valid. First, attack it like a regular grab-a-rule question; if there are two or more answers remaining after you've done a round of elimination, start thinking about whether or not the scarves may be factoring in. A good second step on "which" questions like this one is very often to check prior work. Go to it!

1. Which one of the following is a possible display of hats in the window?

(A) A, B, C, F
(B) A, C, D, E
(C) A, D, E, F
(D) B, C, D, F
(E) B, C, E, F

Here's how to crack it

Take each of the clues from your list of symbols that have to do with the hats, and apply the clue to each answer choice, eliminating any choice that violates the clue. "If A then no B" knocks out (A). "If B then D" knocks out (E). "If F then no D" knocks out (C) and (D). The answer is (B). Sweet. Here's the final question:

4. Each of the following could be displayed together EXCEPT

(A) B and K
(B) B and F
(C) B and M
(D) E and F
(E) E, J, and M

Here's how to crack it

Well, there are several ways to attack this question. The first is to check your deductions and see if you know anything about any of these choices. In answer choice (B), we've got F and B together, which we know can't be true. If you didn't see that, you can look at your previous work to cross off answer choices you know can work. Your work from number 3 will eliminate (A); number 2 will eliminate (D). Both (C) and (E) seem possible given the work from number 3, but you can test them to be safe. If you try to make choice (B) work, you'll see that it violates a rule, so it's our answer.

GAMES TECHNIQUES: GETTING THE CONTRAPOSITIVE

You can't practice too much with "if...then" clues.

We just saw the importance of being able to work with conditional clues. And we found out that once you know how to symbolize them—and their contrapositives—even a game that has a bunch of conditionals can be approachable.

Let's take a look at how to symbolize a couple of other tricky conditional statements. We've already dealt with those that involve the word *unless*. You'll remember that when we see "unless" we substitute "if not" and start our symbol there. Now we're going to see what to do when we run across statements that include "only if." Here's an example:

> Novels will be on sale only if reference books are not on sale.

When you see the words *only if* substitute *if not*. You can rearrange the sentence to put the *if not* part first so that it reads like a regular "if...then" statement. So far, it's just like dealing with unless. But there's one more step. *You have to negate the other half of the statement*. So with our example, we would end up with:

> If not reference books are not on sale, novels will NOT be on sale.

The double negative can be a bit confusing, so we have to be careful. The first half is really: "If reference books are on sale." But once we have the statement clear we can simply symbolize the conditional and its contrapositive as we would any other conditional statement. Here's what we've got:

$$R \rightarrow -N$$
$$N \rightarrow -R$$

If you memorize the rule, these will become purely mechanical.

Let's look at one more interesting thing about conditionals. When you negate the part of a conditional that includes the word *and*, it becomes *or*. And when you negate the part of a conditional that includes the word *or*, it becomes *and*. Don't ask why, just learn the rule. Let's see how it works with an example:

> If A is chosen, either B or C must be chosen.

We would symbolize the statement in our usual manner, using the word *or* in our symbol:

$$A \rightarrow B \text{ or } C$$

The tricky part comes when we symbolize the contrapositive. Remember that "or" will become "and" once we negate it. Here's what it will look like:

–B and –C → –A

Notice that we had to negate each element as well as "or" when we symbolized. This is confusing at first, but once you practice, it will become second nature.

To recap:

When you see the words "only if" replace them with "if not," start your symbol there, and then negate the other half of the statement.

When you negate "and" it becomes "or."

When you negate "or" it becomes "and."

Below is a little chart that is going to drill you on just these skills. It's a five-column chart. Column 1 has clues. Put your symbols in column 2. Put the contrapositives of the clues in column 3. Columns 4 and 5 contain our symbols and contrapositives, so cover them up with a piece of paper before you start. Once you've finished all the symbols and contrapositives, uncover our answers and see how you fared. Got it? Go!

CLUE	YOUR SYMBOL	YOUR CONTRAPOSITIVE	OUR SYMBOL	OUR CONTRAPOSITIVE
If Jack attends, Mark must attend.			J → M	–M → –J
Ann will work only if Kate works.			–K → –A	A → K
Bob cannot work unless Gary is working.			–G → –B	B → G
If Will goes to the party, Cam won't go.*			W → –C	C → –W
Doug will not drive unless May also drives.			–M → –D	D → M
If Harry is invited, both Charles and Linda must be invited.			H → C and L	–C or –L → –H

*** This could be summed up as an antiblock** [WC (crossed out)] **.**

Games Techniques: Taking a Moment to Survey

Taking a moment to survey how the game is going to work is a worthwhile investment of time that many testers will skip in their rush to get to the questions. But it will help you get through the questions and answers much more efficiently. What exactly are you looking for? Well, we'll run through it again.

After you've marked your deductions in the diagram, look to see which elements and spaces have the most limitations. Look for the most restrictive clues and the most restricted spaces. Those are the ones that are likely to have the greatest impact on your placement of the elements for a given question.

Often, getting through a question efficiently will depend on knowing where to get started, so take a minute to acquaint yourself with the workings of the game before diving in. And once you get started, you'll find that a logical chain of events will follow.

Note that not all games will have deductions. If you've checked for overlap among the clues and between the clues and diagram and you still can't get anything concrete down, don't keep staring in the hope that something will appear. And don't get caught in the trap of listing deductions that *might* result *if* something were to happen. Once you've completed the process used to identify deductions and have taken a moment to survey how things are likely to work in the game, it's time to head to the questions.

GAME #5: THREE BUSES

Not all "grouping" type games will tell you exactly how many elements go in each of the columns, as was the case in the last game. Some games will involve the distribution of elements among various slots. You might have twelve animals to place in four cages, or ten people to place in seven houses, for instance. Your first goal is to attempt to figure out what the exact distribution is. If you can do that, the game becomes much easier. Look for information limiting the number of elements per group or distribution clues. On this game, give yourself 20 minutes or so—try figuring out the distribution for five minutes. If you get stuck, our solution is at the end!

Five girls—Fiorenza, Gladys, Helene, Jocelyn, and Kaitlin—and four boys—Abe, Bruce, Clive, and Doug—ride to school each day in three separate buses.

Abe and Fiorenza always ride together.
Gladys and Helene always ride together.
Jocelyn and Kaitlin never ride together.
Doug always rides in the bus with the fewest children.
Boys cannot outnumber girls in any bus.
The maximum number of children in any bus is four.

1. The bus in which Doug rides can hold how many children?

    (A) 1
    (B) 2
    (C) 3
    (D) 4
    (E) 5

2. Bruce can ride with each of the following EXCEPT

(A) Abe
(B) Clive
(C) Doug
(D) Fiorenza
(E) Helene

3. If Bruce and Clive ride in the same bus, which one of the following must also be in the bus?

(A) Abe
(B) Fiorenza
(C) Gladys
(D) Jocelyn
(E) Kaitlin

4. Which of the following could be a list of all the passengers in one bus?

(A) Doug, Gladys
(B) Fiorenza, Abe, Bruce
(C) Jocelyn, Kaitlin, Clive, Bruce
(D) Fiorenza, Gladys, Bruce, Clive
(E) Abe, Bruce, Fiorenza, Jocelyn

5. Abe can NEVER ride with which one of the following?

(A) Bruce
(B) Clive
(C) Gladys
(D) Jocelyn
(E) Kaitlin

6. If Bruce rides with Fiorenza, Gladys must ride with which one of the following?

(A) Clive
(B) Doug
(C) Fiorenza
(D) Jocelyn
(E) Kaitlin

Cracking Game #5

Step 1: Draw your diagram

First draw the diagram, then worry about distribution.

So we've got a total of nine children to place in three buses. Our diagram will consist of three columns—the only thing missing will be the exact number of children to be placed in each bus. We know that we'll need to use all of the elements and that we can't have any repeats, but uncertainty about the distribution of elements might make things complicated. Our diagram and elements are on the following page. Don't forget to distinguish between the two types (girls and boys).

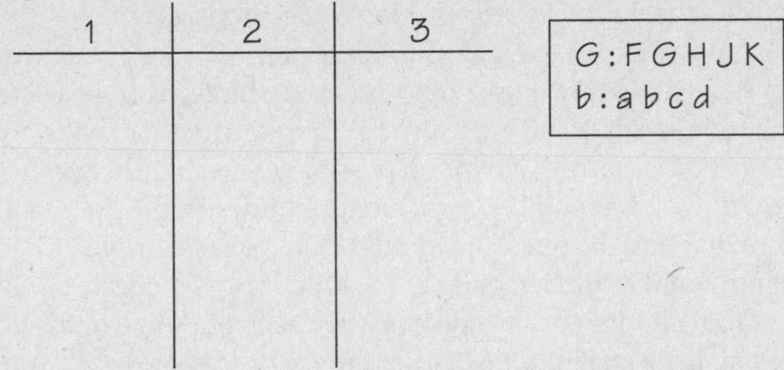

Step 2: Symbolize the clues

We've got several clues here; some should look familiar and some will be new. You should be comfortable by now with how the blocks and antiblocks work. We'll see how the others—known as distribution clues—work as we move through the rest of this game. Distribution clues give you information about how the elements will be distributed among the slots. In some cases, they may lead to only one possible distribution and in others they may merely limit the options, leaving a couple of different possible distributions. Let's get to work and see how it plays out.

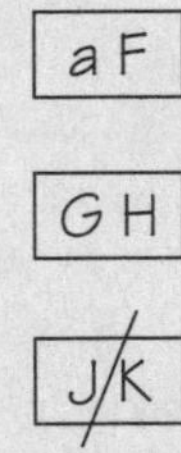

The first three clues are all pretty straightforward, right? We've already worked with similar clues and the symbols are becoming second nature. Now let's briefly symbolize our distribution clues to make sure we have a clear handle on how they work:

d = fewest

boys fewer than Girls

Maximum 4 per group

We are able to symbolize the information but it may not seem very useful at this point.

Step 3: Double-check your clues and make deductions

Spend a few minutes trying to narrow down the possible distributions—it's worth it!

As always, be sure to double-check against the grain. Now let's see if we can come up with any deductions. We'll use our standard methods because we're not sure of the distribution at this point. We'll also pay special attention to the distribution clues to see if we can narrow down the possible ways that the elements can be arranged in terms of the number of elements (children) in each group (bus). If we can figure that out, the questions should be a lot easier, right?

So which of the distribution clues is most limiting? The fact that there can't be more than four children in any one bus will knock out some of the possibilites right off the bat. Let's make a little distribution chart to see what the possibilities are. Remember that buses 1, 2, and 3 represent no particular buses, so it doesn't matter if the bus with four children is the first or second or third bus, or if there even will be a bus with four children. Check out our possibilities below:

1	2	3
③	③	③
④	③	②
④	④	①

As you can see above, limiting the maximum number of elements to four per group narrows the possibilities to three separate distributions: 3-3-3, 4-3-2, and 4-4-1. Let's take a look at our second distribution clue, the fact that boys cannot outnumber girls in any bus. Does this clue do anything to limit the number of distributions? It sure does. Take a look below:

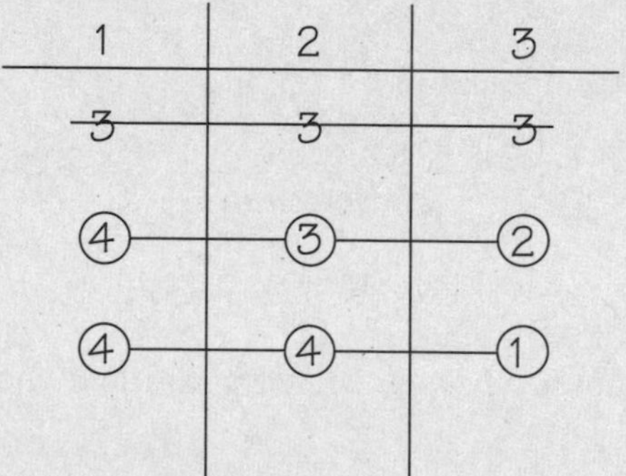

If boys cannot outnumber girls in any bus, and there are four boys, that means that the 3-3-3 distribution cannot be valid for this game. Why not? Because if the distribution is 3-3-3, then in one of the buses, there must be two boys and one girl, which we can't have. Another limitation. Now what about the final clue, that Doug must ride in the bus with the fewest children? Take a look:

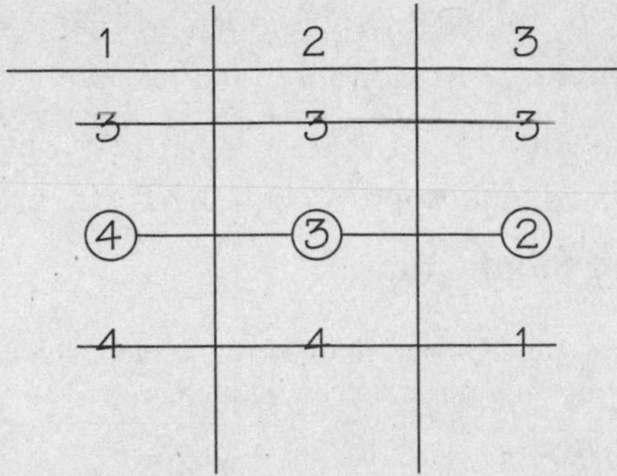

If Doug must ride in the bus with the fewest children, then the 4-4-1 distribution isn't possible in this game either. Doug would have to go alone. Doug is a boy, and we know that boys cannot outnumber girls in any bus, so he can't be the only rider. Therefore, after eliminating distributions that violate the rules, we're left with a diagram that will look like this:

1 (4)	2 (3)	3 (2)
_ _ _ _	_ _ _	_ d

Because there is no information to suggest that buses 1, 2, and 3 are distinguished from one another, as we just said above, we'll put four children in bus 1, three children in bus 2, and two children in bus 3. Any other deductions? Using the diagram above, go back to your relationship clues. Is there any more overlap that provides further limitations? Check this out:

1	2	3
		-G -H -F
b b G G	b G G	J/K over G, d over b

Yes; we've spent some precious minutes figuring out all this stuff. However, we now know the exact distribution of the children, how many of each gender are in every bus, the definitive placement of one child, and several other limiting factors—such as the fact that neither the G/H block nor the a/F block can go in bus 3, leaving d to go with either J or K only.

We've really narrowed things down. Remember that we'll keep an eye on the most restricted spots first as we deal with the questions.

Step 4: Attack the questions

We don't have a grab-a-rule question, so let's start with any "if" questions.

Step 5: Use Process of Elimination

3. If Bruce and Clive ride in the same bus, which one of the following must also be in the bus?
   (A) Abe
   (B) Fiorenza
   (C) Gladys
   (D) Jocelyn
   (E) Kaitlin

Here's how to crack it

Because boys cannot outnumber girls, we know where b and c have to go if they're together, right? Let's check it out:

1	2	3
b b G G	b G G	J/K d / G b
b c G H	a F _	_ d ③

As you can see, b and c in the first slot puts the a/F block in the second slot. This then forces the G/H block into slot 1 along with b and c. Looks like (C) is our answer. Now try this one:

6. If Bruce rides with Fiorenza, Gladys must ride with which one of the following?
   (A) Clive
   (B) Doug
   (C) Fiorenza
   (D) Jocelyn
   (E) Kaitlin

Here's how to crack it

Well, you know that a always comes with F, so you've once again got two boys (a and b) to place. Take a look at the following page.

1	2	3
b b G G	b G G	J/K over G, d over b
b a F _	c G H	_ d ⑥

Never forget that blocks are your best pieces of information—always remember to place them in the diagram.

So we've got b, a, and F all in bus 1, which means that the G/H block must go in bus 2. A boy must also go in bus 2, and the only one left is c. It's our answer—choice (A).

The final four questions in this game are general. However, you were able to deduce so much that they probably won't present too much of a problem. Let's do this one first:

4. Which of the following could be a list of all the passengers in one bus?
   (A) Doug, Gladys
   (B) Fiorenza, Abe, Bruce
   (C) Jocelyn, Kaitlin, Clive, Bruce
   (D) Fiorenza, Gladys, Bruce, Clive
   (E) Abe, Bruce, Fiorenza, Jocelyn

Here's how to crack it

This isn't quite a grab-a-rule question because it doesn't address all the elements in each answer choice. But we can probably eliminate at least a few answers by applying the clues to the answer choices and crossing off any violations. If more than one choice remains, we can see if there might be any violations in possible arrangements of the groups that are not shown in the answers, given what we know from this one group. The G/H block eliminates (A) and (D), the boys not being able to outnumber the girls eliminates (B), and the J/K antiblock eliminates (C). We're left with (E). Let's move on.

1. The bus in which Doug rides can hold how many children?
   (A) 1
   (B) 2
   (C) 3
   (D) 4
   (E) 5

Here's how to crack it

We've answered this one already because we made the proper deductions. It's (B), two children.

2. Bruce can ride with each of the following EXCEPT

    (A) Abe
    (B) Clive
    (C) Doug
    (D) Fiorenza
    (E) Helene

Here's how to crack it

Look at your diagram and your previous work. Is there anywhere b can't go? It can't go with d in bus 3, so (C) is our answer. Also note that you had b with a, c, F, and H in previous questions, so we can cross off (A), (B), and (D). Let's finish off the last question:

5. Abe can NEVER ride with which one of the following?

    (A) Bruce
    (B) Clive
    (C) Gladys
    (D) Jocelyn
    (E) Kaitlin

Here's how to crack it

We can attack this in several ways; using our previous work is one way. We've had a with both b and c in the past, so (A) and (B) are gone. And because J and K are interchangeable, neither (D) nor (E) can be the answer either. It's (C), Gladys, because you can't have a situation where both blocks are in the same bus. Try it if you need to, but it won't work because that leaves three boys left to place between buses 2 and 3, which we can't have. So you're done.

GAMES TECHNIQUES: INTERCHANGEABLE ELEMENTS

In the solution above, we mention that J and K are interchangeable, but what *are* interchangeable elements? Interchangeable elements are groups—usually pairs—of elements that have exactly the same restrictions (or no restrictions at all). In the game above, J and K are interchangeable because they are both girls and the only limitation on either is mutual: They cannot be in the same group. This means that unless a question gives us additional information about one or both of the elements, there is no reason why we couldn't switch J and K without affecting any other elements.

Interchangeable elements are important to identify because they often allow you to eliminate wrong answers and thus are useful for POE. As we just saw in question number 5, we were able to eliminate answers (D) and (E) because J and K are interchangeable, and therefore neither can be the answer to a question asking for something that *must be true*. In other words, if a could not ride with J, neither could he ride with K. Because it's not possible for both answers to be right, neither one can be. So make note of interchangeable elements and remember how they function.

GAMES TECHNIQUES: IDENTIFYING DIFFICULTY

In order to be successful on a Games section, it is important to be able to predict the relative difficulty of the games before you get started. How can you tell? There are several things to look for *after* you've read through the setup and the clues.

Start with the relationship between the elements and the places to which they'll be assigned. In an *ordering* game, you want a one-to-one correlation between elements and slots. In a *grouping* game, by definition, there will be more than one element in each group. In this case you want to know if there are a set number of elements per group. If there are multiple distributions, the game is more complicated than if everything is determined from the outset. Remember that having an "out" column will account for the elements that are not "in" the game, so if you know how many elements are not assigned, it becomes just like a *grouping* game with one more group.

Being able to predict the relative difficulty of games before you start working on them will have a significant impact on your games performance.

Then, you'll want to ask two important questions: Can we leave out any elements? Can there be any repeats? If the answer to either or both of those questions is yes, the game will be more complicated.

Next, you'll evaluate the clues. The more restrictive and concrete they are the better, because you'll have more limitations on the game to help in placing the elements. For instance a clue such as:

> Wednesday must be staffed by a member of the Quality committee.

will be much more useful than a clue such as:

> The juggler will perform at least once, but no more than three times during the week.

Finally, briefly scan the questions. The more "if" questions with straightforward tasks, the better. The more complicated or weird questions there are, the more complicated the game. And you'll definitely end up spending more time plugging away at the questions and answer choices to find the correct response.

We've presented these in order of importance; the characteristics near the top of the list are much more important predictors of a game's level of difficulty than the ones near the bottom. So a game that has great questions but allows you to use elements more than once and doesn't have a set distribution is still a bad choice to do early in the section.

The process of evaluating a game shouldn't take more than 15 or 20 seconds once you've had some practice. You'll want to spend enough time with the setup and clues so that you have a good grasp of the concepts mentioned above, but spending too much time sweating all the minor details will defeat the purpose of making you a more efficient "game player."

You should evaluate the level of difficulty even if you are planning to work through all four games. You always want to start with an easier game so that you can get into the groove. And if you get thrown by an early game, it can blow your confidence on the rest of the section and cost you points that you otherwise would have had in the bag; all the more reason to start with a more manageable game. Let's try another one.

GAME #6: BIRDS AND MAMMALS

Now we think you're ready to handle something a bit more complex. Remember that not all games will use each element only once. Sometimes you will not know how many times a given element might be used. However, your process remains exactly the same for these games as it is for all other games. Give yourself 20 minutes on this one and see how you do.

Elements used more than once? No big deal.

A zoomaster is deciding which birds and mammals will go in five consecutive cages, numbered 1 through 5, left to right. Each cage will contain one of three species of birds—egret, finch, or parrot—and one of three species of mammals—antelope, giraffe, or otter. The zoomaster must abide by the following conditions:

If finches are in a given cage, antelopes must also be placed in that cage.
If otters are in a given cage, egrets cannot be in that same cage.
In at least one cage, parrots and antelopes are together.
Parrots are never in consecutive cages.
If egrets and finches are both exhibited, the egrets must always be in lower-numbered cages than the finches.
The second cage contains otters.

1. Which one of the following must be true?
   (A) Egrets are exhibited in the first cage.
   (B) Parrots are exhibited in the second cage.
   (C) Parrots are exhibited in the third cage.
   (D) Antelopes are exhibited in the fourth cage.
   (E) Antelopes are exhibited in the fifth cage.

2. Each of the following is a possible line-up of mammals in the five cages EXCEPT
   (A) antelope, otter, antelope, giraffe, otter
   (B) antelope, otter, giraffe, antelope, antelope
   (C) antelope, otter, antelope, antelope, antelope
   (D) giraffe, otter, giraffe, giraffe, antelope
   (E) giraffe, otter, antelope, antelope, antelope

3. Which one of the following is not possible when both egrets and finches are exhibited?
   (A) Antelopes are exhibited in two consecutive cages.
   (B) Finches are exhibited in two consecutive cages.
   (C) Giraffes are not exhibited.
   (D) Otters are exhibited in the third cage.
   (E) Parrots are exhibited in two different cages.

4. If egrets are exhibited in the fifth cage, which one of the following must be true?
   (A) Antelopes are exhibited in the third cage.
   (B) Egrets are exhibited twice.
   (C) Finches are exhibited twice.
   (D) Giraffes are not exhibited in consecutively numbered cages.
   (E) If giraffes are exhibited, then they are exhibited in the fifth cage.

5. If egrets are exhibited exactly twice, each of the following must be true EXCEPT:

   (A) Antelopes are exhibited in the fourth cage.
   (B) Antelopes are exhibited in the fifth cage.
   (C) Egrets and finches are exhibited in consecutively numbered cages.
   (D) If antelopes are exhibited in as many cages as possible, then they are exhibited four times.
   (E) Giraffes cannot be exhibited in consecutively numbered cages.

6. If finches are exhibited exactly twice, it is possible to determine the types of mammals and birds for how many of the ten slots?

   (A) 7
   (B) 6
   (C) 5
   (D) 4
   (E) 3

Cracking Game #6

Step 1: Draw your diagram

Well, the diagram is pretty well laid out for you, isn't it? Five cages, with a bird and a mammal in each cage. Here's what we got:

Now let's hit the clues.

Step 2: Symbolize the clues

We've got lots of different types of clues, don't we? Clues 1, 2, and 5 are conditional; clue 3 is a block; clue 4 is an antiblock; and clue 6 definitively places something into our diagram. Remember when you have a conditional clue like o → –E, it's faster to write it as an antiblock so o → –E/E → –o is better written as

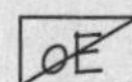

Here's what we got for the conditional clues:

F→ a   –a → –F

oE

E — F (if both)

You'll notice that our clue symbolizing egrets in lower-numbered cages is represented as a range clue with E to the left of F because lower-numbered cages are to the left of higher-numbered cages in our horizontal diagram.

Looks okay, right? Of course, we've added the contrapositives for each conditional clue. Here are the other two clues:

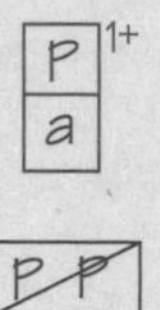

PP

There's a small wrinkle to the block, the fact that we know that there might be more than one of them. So we've added a little "+" after the block to indicate that there might be more than one. Finally, we've got a diagram that has an o placed in the mammal slot for cage 2.

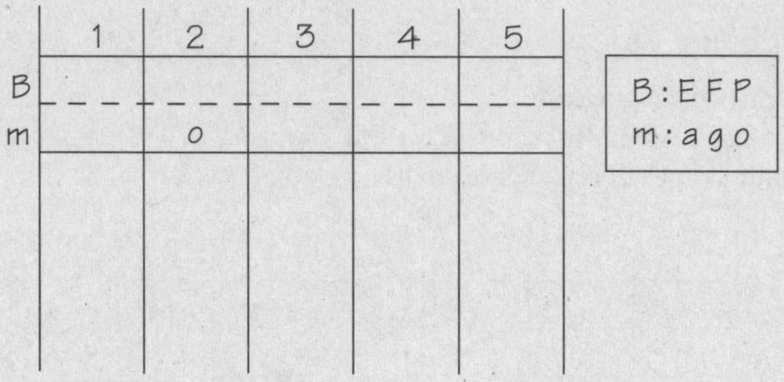

Step 3: Double-check your clues and make deductions

Have you re-read the clues to make sure you've symbolized correctly? The more complex the game, the greater the opportunity to make an error in symbolizing. If you'd gotten one thing even slightly wrong, everything could have fallen apart. If you're lucky, you'll notice the error while doing the first question, but you might find what appear to be valid answers for the first couple of questions and only realize the problem when the second or third question just doesn't work. At that point you'd have to fix the error and go back to re-work those first questions. What a nightmare. Not only does it waste valuable time, but you'd also become frustrated, and that can affect your performance on the next game or the next section. Avoid this by investing the time to double-check. As for deductions, there's a major one that you can find. Start by identifying elements that aren't able to go in certain cages, and also remember that there are only three possibilities for any given slot. Start by looking at the most restricted elements or places.

Here's what we got:

P 1+
a

	1	2	3	4	5
B	–P	–E –F P	–P		
m		o			

B:EFP
m:ago

Cool, right? We were able to definitively place P along with o in cage 2, because neither F nor E can go with o—because if you have o, you can't have E, and if you have F, you need to have a with it. In fact, if you have o in a column, you'll never be able to have F with it, so we can add another deduction to our list: an F/o antiblock. Take note of the other "minuses" in the diagram—i.e., cases in which certain elements are restricted from certain slots. These will all be very helpful because then you've only got at most two different elements that can go in those slots!

Also as a result of placing P definitively in slot 2, we know that P can be in neither slot 1 nor slot 3. That only leaves two slots for any other P to go in. And remember that we always have to place at least one P/a block. So that block will have to go in either slot 4 or slot 5, but not both. Let's make a note of that over the columns.

Now, let's consider our conditional clue about finches a little more carefully. If F is placed in a cage, a must also be placed in that cage. So suppose you have o in a cage. Could you have F? No. What about g? Again, no. So ultimately, you can also conceive of this clue as two separate antiblocks: F can be with neither g nor o, because the presence of an F requires an a as well. If you look at the contrapositive of the original you can see that –a → –F, and in this game –a is the same as either g or o. So that leads to another couple of antiblocks we'll need to keep in mind:

This is a way to show all of the ramifications of that clue. You might not realize this until you get into the game. No big deal; just jot it down when it becomes apparent. It makes clear just how restricted F is.

Let's step back and survey the big picture. In almost all games that contain two sets of elements, one set will be more restricted than the other. You will have more information on that set of elements, and when answering questions, that set of elements is *the* set you should focus on first. In this game, there are more restrictions and information about the birds than there are about the mammals.

Additionally, note the fact that you have a block you must place every time—the P/a block. Where can this block go? It can't go in cage 1, 2, or 3 anymore, right? Placing the P/a block is a major key to answering each question, then. Let's see what we can do with the questions.

Step 4: Attack the questions

We've got some "if" questions to attack, so let's get to 'em!

Step 5: Use Process of Elimination

4. If egrets are exhibited in the fifth cage, which one of the following must be true?
   - (A) Antelopes are exhibited in the third cage.
   - (B) Egrets are exhibited twice.
   - (C) Finches are exhibited twice.
   - (D) Giraffes are not exhibited in consecutively numbered cages.
   - (E) If giraffes are exhibited, then they are exhibited in the fifth cage.

Here's how to crack it

Well, we've got an E in the fifth cage, so that's going to determine the placement of our P/a block. Here's what we got:

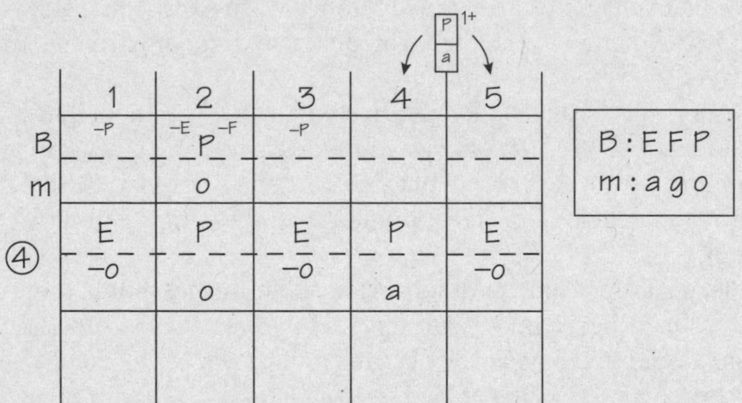

As you can see, putting E into the fifth slot forces our P/a block into cage 4. The other piece of information we want to focus on is the clue "If egrets and finches are both exhibited, the egrets must always be in lower-numbered cages than the finches." Because we've got an egret in cage 5, that means that no finches can be exhibited, because if you put a finch in a lower-numbered cage than an egret, it would violate this clue. Hey, wait a minute! Can we have an arrangement with no finches? Well, you'll notice that it was never mandated by the setup that we use all the elements, so it is a possibility. Hence, we've got egrets in cages 1, 3, and 5. We've wound up filling in seven out of our ten spaces. When we check the answer choices, the only thing that must be true is (D), the fact that giraffes can't be exhibited in consecutively numbered cages, because we've got an o in cage 2 and an a in cage 4. So it's our answer.

Here's the next "if" question:

5. If egrets are exhibited exactly twice, each of the following must be true EXCEPT:
   (A) Antelopes are exhibited in the fourth cage.
   (B) Antelopes are exhibited in the fifth cage.
   (C) Egrets and finches are exhibited in consecutively numbered cages.
   (D) If antelopes are exhibited in as many cages as possible, then they are exhibited four times.
   (E) Giraffes cannot be exhibited in consecutively numbered cages.

Here's how to crack it

You now know from the question the exact number of times each type of bird is exhibited—you've probably already figured out that P is always exhibited twice, because you need a P/a block and P/o is in cage 2. This question tells us that E is exhibited twice also, so you know that there is one F. And because we're using both E and F, we'll have to be sure that both Es come before the F. Here's our diagram:

P/a 1+

	1	2	3	4	5
B	−P	−E −F P	−P		
m		o			
④	E −o	P o	E −o	P a	E −o
⑤	E −o	P o	E −o	P/F a	F/P a

B: E F P
m: a g o

So we've got the Es definitively in cages 1 and 3. This means that P and F must be in cages 4 and 5—you don't know exactly where each one goes. Either way, however, an a must be in both cage 4 and cage 5, because a must always go with F and we already know the other spot is our P/a block. This means that the mammal slots for cages 1 and 3 must either be giraffes or antelopes. Thus, (A), (B), (D), and (E) must all be true. Only (C) can be false, so it's our answer. Let's hit the next question.

Question number 6 also starts with the word "if," but it's not one with a straight-ahead task like finding what *must be true* or what *could be false*. It sounds like it could be complicated, so we'll leave it for later.

Now we're on to the "which" questions. Let's take a look at number 1.

1. Which one of the following must be true?
   (A) Egrets are exhibited in the first cage.
   (B) Parrots are exhibited in the second cage.
   (C) Parrots are exhibited in the third cage.
   (D) Antelopes are exhibited in the fourth cage.
   (E) Antelopes are exhibited in the fifth cage.

Here's how to crack it

We've done a lot of work on this game, so chances are that our previous work will allow us to eliminate some answer choices by showing us that they could be false. In the questions we've worked through so far, E was in slot 1 but that doesn't necessarily mean it *must* be true every time, so let's leave answer choice (A) in for the moment. We know for sure that (B) must be true (it's our deduction) so it's our answer. If you're confident with that you can move on. If you'd feel better checking the last three answers it will only take a few seconds.

2. Each of the following is a possible line-up of mammals in the five cages EXCEPT

   (A) antelope, otter, antelope, giraffe, otter
   (B) antelope, otter, giraffe, antelope, antelope
   (C) antelope, otter, antelope, antelope, antelope
   (D) giraffe, otter, giraffe, giraffe, antelope
   (E) giraffe, otter, antelope, antelope, antelope

Here's how to crack it

On this question, you're looking for the one line-up that can't work. You can still use the Grab-a-Rule technique of applying the clues to the answer choices, but here a violation of the rule means you want to keep the answer rather than eliminate it. Your two best clues are of course: (1) an otter must be in cage 2 and (2) there is a P/a block in either cage 4 or cage 5. The P/a block in cage 4 or cage 5 means that line-up (A) can't work because it doesn't have a in either slot 4 or slot 5, so it's our answer. Here's the next question:

3. Which one of the following is not possible when both egrets and finches are exhibited?

   (A) Antelopes are exhibited in two consecutive cages.
   (B) Finches are exhibited in two consecutive cages.
   (C) Giraffes are not exhibited.
   (D) Otters are exhibited in the third cage.
   (E) Parrots are exhibited in two different cages.

Here's how to crack it

We're asked to find the one that's not possible, so really our task is to find the one that *must be false*. We've learned that we'll eliminate any answer that could be true. Take a look at previous scenarios in which you've had both egrets and finches exhibited. Then, run through the answer choices and see if you've already drawn any of them. You've had the possibility of (A), (C), and (E) in question 5. So now we have to try the last two. Let's see if we can make (B) work.

If we have F in two consecutive slots, they would have to be slots 3 and 4, forcing the P/a block into slot 5. Because we have to include E according to the question, we'll have to put it in slot 1. We can make it work once, so we can cross out (B). We know that P can't be in slot 3, so that leaves either E or F. If we have E in 3, we know that we can't use o. Likewise, if we have F in 3, we know that we must use a—which is the same as saying that we can't use o. So it looks like we can't use o in 3 no matter what. That's another deduction that we can put in our clue shelf. And we can circle (D). Nice work. Only one more question.

6. If finches are exhibited exactly twice, it is possible to determine the types of mammals and birds for how many of the ten slots?

(A) 7
(B) 6
(C) 5
(D) 4
(E) 3

Here's how to crack it

As with the last question, the information provided tells us the exact number of each type of bird. Because we always have two of P, and now we have two of F, we've got one E. That E must be in the first cage, because it has to go in a lower-numbered cage than any and all Fs. So here's our diagram:

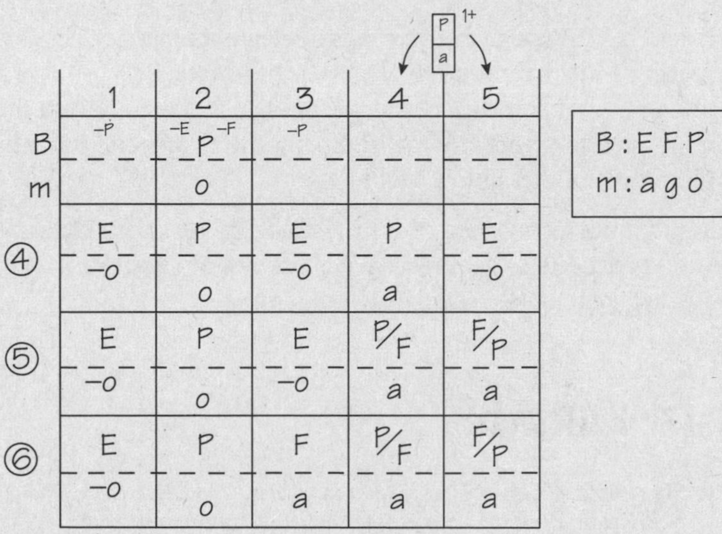

Fill in everything you can, then head to the answer choices.

We've wound up being able to definitively place only three birds, but because cages 4 and 5 contain either an F or a P, we know that the mammal exhibited must be an a. So we've got four mammals definitively placed as well, giving us seven total. Our answer here is (A).

GAMES TECHNIQUES: FLEXIBILITY

As you can see, the last game required a lot of flexibility. It had several types of clues, required that you keep track of ten slots, and didn't have a fixed number of each type of element. The key thing to remember, however, is that the process in attacking this game is exactly the same process as in every other game. Here's a brief run-down of some LSAT curve-balls, and how to hit them:

- If you have many more elements than spaces, focus on distribution. Chances are you'll be given distribution clues that may determine exactly how many elements will go in each space. This will make the game much easier because the number of possibilities will be greatly reduced.

- If you don't know the exact number of all types of elements, focus on making deductions and filling in slots. Typically, these types of games will provide you with spaces that can only have one of two or three types of elements anyway, so the number of possibilities for any one slot will be quite low. The more slots you're able to either definitively fill in or reduce to only one of two choices, the easier the game will be.
- If you have all conditional clues and no definitive information, focus on making sure you've diagrammed everything correctly and have gotten all the contrapositives possible. Then, look to link these conditional clues to see if you can make any deductions. Many times the questions will be mainly "if" questions, which will provide you with more concrete information.
- If you have more than two types of elements per slot, focus on finding and creating more blocks of information. These types of games will pair different types of elements together, so the more precisely you draw your blocks, the clearer the potential placement of these blocks will be.

One thing that the test writers can do to make games more challenging is to combine different aspects of games we have already discussed.

For instance, take a look at the following game:

GAME #7: KARAOKE

Six people—Kassia, Lani, Marco, Ox, Patty, and Shawn—participate in a karaoke contest. Each will sing exactly one song in one of two styles—pop or country. If more than one of the six people sings a song in one style, then the order in which they sing will be determined from first to last, with no two people singing at the same time. The following conditions must apply:

Ox sings a pop song.

Lani sings a country song.

No country singer sings before Lani.

If Marco sings a country song, then Patty and Shawn sing country songs, with Patty singing after Marco but before Shawn.

If Marco sings a pop song, then Shawn sings a pop song, with Shawn singing after Ox but before Marco.

If Patty sings a pop song, then so does Kassia, with Ox singing after Kassia but before Patty.

1. Which one of the following could be true?

(A) Marco sings a pop song and Shawn sings a country song.
(B) Patty sings a pop song and Kassia sings a country song.
(C) Kassia sings a pop song and Patty sings a country song.
(D) Patty and Ox sing pop songs, with Patty singing before Ox.
(E) Marco and Shawn sing pop songs, with Marco singing before Shawn.

2. Each of the following could be the last pop singer EXCEPT

(A) Shawn
(B) Kassia
(C) Ox
(D) Patty
(E) Marco

3. Which one of the following could be a complete and accurate list of the people who sing pop songs, listed in singing order from first to last?

(A) Shawn, Patty, Ox
(B) Ox, Patty, Kassia
(C) Shawn, Ox, Marco
(D) Ox, Shawn, Kassia, Marco
(E) Patty, Marco, Shawn, Kassia

4. If Shawn sings a country song, then each of the following are pairs of people who must sing in the same style as each other EXCEPT:

(A) Patty and Marco
(B) Patty and Shawn
(C) Kassia and Marco
(D) Patty and Lani
(E) Marco and Shawn

5. If Ox is the first pop singer, then which of the following must be true?

(A) Ox and Marco sing in the same style as each other.
(B) Patty and Lani sing in the same style as each other.
(C) Patty and Ox sing in the same style as each other.
(D) Kassia and Lani do not sing in the same style as each other.
(E) Kassia and Patty do not sing in the same style as each other.

6. Suppose that the condition is added that Shawn and Patty do not sing in the same style as each other. If all the other conditions remain in effect, then each of the following could be true EXCEPT:

(A) Marco and Kassia sing in the same style as each other.
(B) Patty and Kassia sing in the same style as each other.
(C) Patty and Marco sing in the same style as each other.
(D) Kassia and Patty do not sing in the same style as each other.
(E) Marco and Kassia do not sing in the same style as each other.

There are many ideas we're familiar with here, but they're jumbled all together in a way we haven't seen before. We call these *hybrid games*, and chances are good that you'll see some new combination of ideas on your actual LSAT.

This game, for example, is an In/Out type, because each person sings either rock or pop, but not both, and consequently you know that each element will be used exactly once. But there's a twist: each group is ordered from first to last, and we don't know how many people will be singing in each group. Furthermore, many of the clues are conditionals, but not all, and they're complicated because they involve ordering as well as grouping.

As we mentioned earlier, the key here is to stick to your basic steps, but remain flexible.

Cracking Game #7

Step 1: Draw your diagram

As we mentioned earlier, this is a grouping game in which each element is either a pop singer or a country singer. Here's what we got:

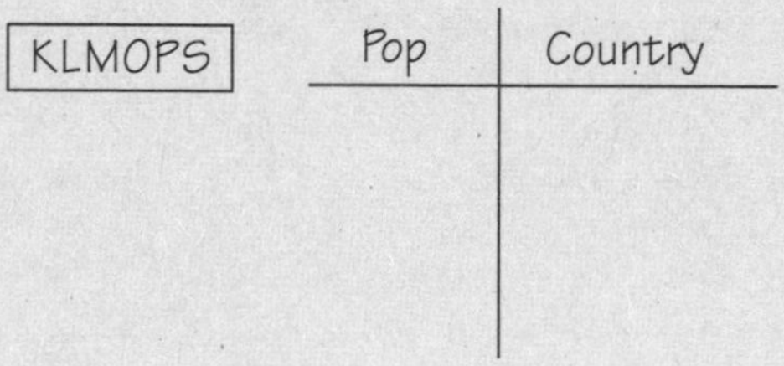

KLMOPS

Pop	Country

Step 2: Symbolize the clues

This is where some flexibility is required. The first two clues are very straightforward. The third one is harder, because we don't know how many other people, if any, will sing country songs. No matter what, though, Lani will come first.

So far, we have this:

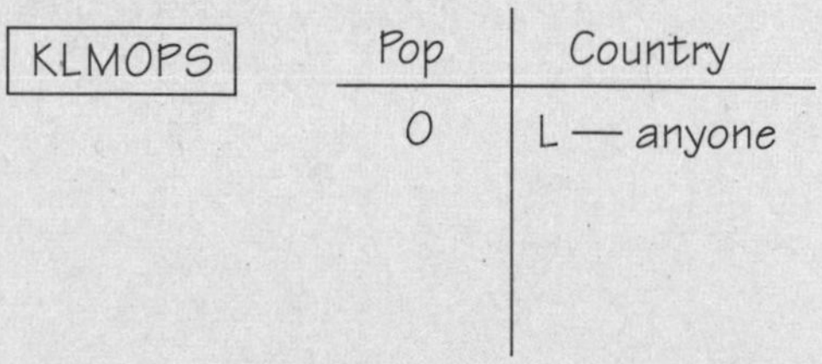

KLMOPS

Pop	Country
O	L — anyone

We've got two elements definitively placed, and notice we used a range clue to show that Lani sings first in the country group. But, the other clues are even stranger. If M sings country, then the order has to be M-P-S. Okay. But how would you diagram the contrapositive? If the country order isn't M-P-S, then M doesn't sing country (and must therefore sing pop). Is there an easy way to diagram that? Not really.

But wait—remember that although order is important, it's not the only thing going on here. This is ordering within an In/Out grouping. The other people (P and S) have to be on the country side before they can be placed in order, right? So a more useful way to think of the contrapositive in this case is to say that if P doesn't sing country, then M can't sing country and that if S doesn't sing country, then M can't sing country.

Because it's more useful to state these positively, we should say that if P sings pop then M sings pop and if S sings pop, then M sings pop. Because there are only two groups, if you're not in one, you're automatically in the other.

It's also more useful to write these on the sides of the diagram that they correspond to. So now we have:

KLMOPS

Pop	Country
O	L — anyone
S → M	M → M—P—S
P → M	

If we follow the same logic for the last two clues, we end up with the following:

KLMOPS

Pop	Country
O	L — anyone
	M → M—P—S
S → M	S → M
P → M	K → P
M → O—S—M	
P → K—O—P	

Notice that we don't end up with clues that start with "If O sings country," because that can never happen.

Step 3: Double-check your clues and make deductions

Carefully re-read the clues and make sure that you've written the contrapositives correctly. This is a complicated game, so there are many things to double-check.

There aren't a lot of useful individual deductions to be made here. There are many places you could connect conditional statements, but that's not terribly useful because you'll be able to do that easily if the need arises.

But don't forget to look at the big picture. It may have occurred to you that although there are six elements, two are already fixed, and it may also have occurred to you that we know a lot of information as soon as we find out where M belongs. In a situation like this, where there are a small number of free elements and a large number of restrictive clues centering around one element in particular, it's worth considering just how many different situations could arise.

In this case, we know that O and L are already placed. Then, because each element has to appear somewhere, we know that there are only two ways this can go: either M sings country, or M sings pop. Take these one at a time.

If M sings country, then he takes P and S along with him, in that order, and we already know that L belongs there (and must sing first). O is on the other side, and apparently K could sing either style, anytime, except for being the first country singer (that spot is already taken by L). We can collect all that information as follows:

Pop	Country
K	
—O—	L—M—P—S—

Now, let's look at the other possibility. What if M sings pop? That means O, S, and M all sing pop, in that order, and we already knew that L sings country. Hmm. That leaves two floaters in this case, P and K. We could leave it like this:

Pop	Country
K	
—O—	L—M—P—S—
P, K	
—O—S—M—	L—

But that's not really the whole story. We know a whole lot more if we know where P is, and, of course, P must be either a pop singer or a country singer. So let's try both of those:

If P sings pop, then it's K-O-P in that order, and O-S-M in order at the same time. So K and O must be the first two singers, and P can be wherever it likes with respect to S-M. L, of course, is by itself on the other side.

If P sings country, then it must come after L, and remember O-S-M are all still on the other side (because we already considered the case where M sings country). K, then, is unrestricted (except it couldn't be the first country singer, as usual).

We can encapsulate this as follows:

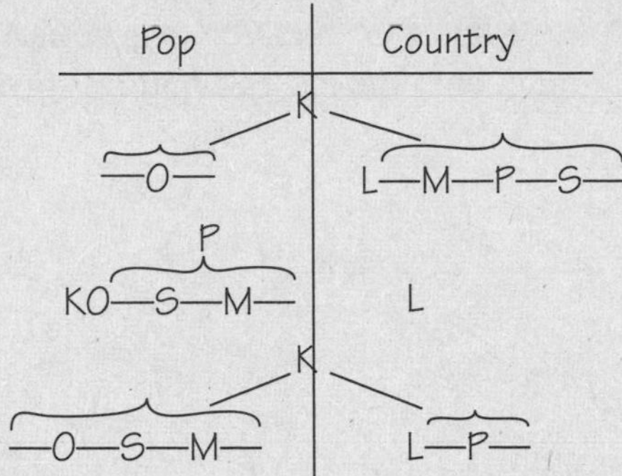

That's not bad. Except for K floating a little bit, there are really only three basic scenarios that can occur here. This is a valuable time-saver, as long as you're dealing with a game that has a small number of very restricted elements. You won't be able to approach most games with this technique (imagine trying to list out all the possibilities on some of the other games in this chapter!), but it makes your life easier when you can, because the questions go much faster.

Let's try it.

Step 4: Attack the questions
The first "if' question is number 4, so go to it.

Step 5: Use Process of Elimination

4. If Shawn sings a country song, then each of the following are pairs of people who must sing in the same style as each other EXCEPT

   (A) Patty and Marco
   (B) Patty and Shawn
   (C) Kassia and Marco
   (D) Patty and Lani
   (E) Marco and Shawn

Here's how to crack it

Compare the information given in the question to our diagram. Only the first row of our diagram has S on the country side, and everyone but O and K must sing country in that row. So the right answer must involve either O or K, and one of the other four. If you look at the answer choices, you'll see that only (C) fulfills that requirement.

Let's try number 5 (the next "if" question):

5. If Ox is the first pop singer, then which of the following must be true?

   (A) Ox and Marco sing in the same style as each other.
   (B) Patty and Lani sing in the same style as each other.
   (C) Patty and Ox sing in the same style as each other.
   (D) Kassia and Lani do not sing in the same style as each other.
   (E) Kassia and Patty do not sing in the same style as each other.

Here's how to crack it

There are two rows in our diagram where O could be the first pop singer: the top and the bottom. Because this is a "must be true" question, the right answer has to fit with the situation in both the top and bottom rows. Here's the diagram again:

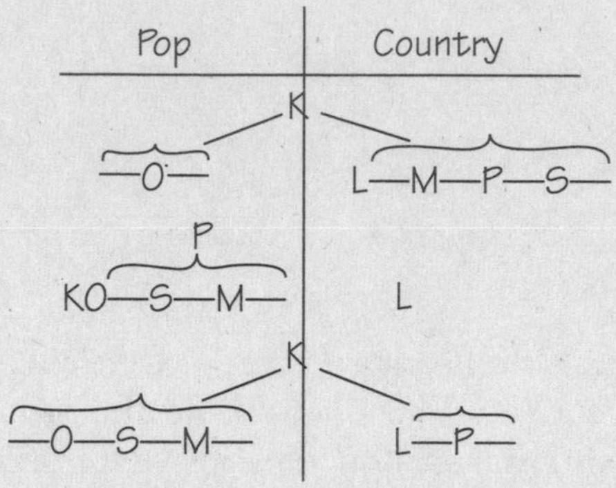

Pop | Country

K

—O— | L—M—P—S—

P

KO—S—M— | L

K

—O—S—M— | L—P—

Let's compare the answer choices to the diagram. In (A), O and M are together in the bottom row, but not the top row. Cross it off. Now compare (B) to the diagram. Yes, P and L are country singers in both rows. This is the right answer.

Moving right along to question 1:

1. Which one of the following could be true?
   (A) Marco sings a pop song and Shawn sings a country song.
   (B) Patty sings a pop song and Kassia sings a country song.
   (C) Kassia sings a pop song and Patty sings a country song.
   (D) Patty and Ox sing pop songs, with Patty singing before Ox.
   (E) Marco and Shawn sing pop songs, with Marco singing before Shawn.

Here's how to crack it

This is a "could be true" question, so we just need to find one example in any of the three rows.

What about (A)? No. M and S are always together. Choice (B)? Again no, because P sings pop only in the second row, and K is there, too. Aha! Look at (C)—yes, this could happen in either the first or third rows. That's the answer.

On to question 2:

2. Each of the following could be the last pop singer EXCEPT
   (A) Shawn
   (B) Kassia
   (C) Ox
   (D) Patty
   (E) Marco

Here's how to crack it

Try these one at a time. The one that can't be the last pop singer is the right answer.

Look at (A). S can't be the last pop singer, because in both situations where S sings pop (rows two and three), M (at least) must follow. This is the right answer.

Question 3 is next:

3. Which one of the following could be a complete and accurate list of the people who sing pop songs, listed in singing order from first to last?

    (A) Shawn, Patty, Ox
    (B) Ox, Patty, Kassia
    (C) Shawn, Ox, Marco
    (D) Ox, Shawn, Kassia, Marco
    (E) Patty, Marco, Shawn, Kassia

Here's how to crack it

This is another "could be" question, so we're just looking for one match.

On to choice (A). Nope. There is no row that has only S, P, and O on the pop side. There is also not a row that has only O, P and K on the pop side, so cross off (B). S is before O in the third row (the only one that has just O, S, and M), so (C) is also out. Choice (D)? Yup. In the bottom row, you could have exactly O, S, K, and M in that order. This is the right answer.

And finally, question 6:

6. Suppose that the condition is added that Shawn and Patty do not sing in the same style as each other. If all the other conditions remain in effect, then each of the following could be true EXCEPT

    (A) Marco and Kassia sing in the same style as each other.
    (B) Patty and Kassia sing in the same style as each other.
    (C) Patty and Marco sing in the same style as each other.
    (D) Kassia and Patty do not sing in the same style as each other.
    (E) Marco and Kassia do not sing in the same style as each other.

Here's how to crack it

This is actually very helpful, because all it says is that we don't need to pay attention to our first two rows any more. The only row we're concerned with is the last one, and we're looking for an answer choice that can't be true.

Let's look at (A): This could be true. K can be on either side. (B) could be true for the same reason. But (C)? No. They're on opposite sides. This is the right answer.

Ready for the last game? We hope so. Here it is:

GAME #8: COOKING CONTEST

Some games, like the game you're about to try, don't require one of our standard diagrams in which you fill in a different set of information for each possible arrangement of elements. What you'll see is a set of rules (usually two or three) for either mixing, combining, or switching elements from one position to another. Your goal here is to go slowly, making sure you understand the rules given. You can still use your pencil by drawing the "movements" the rules denote to make sure you can see what's going on. And you'll want to draw out what happens with the elements over the course of each question. Keep it visual even when it doesn't fit the most common models.

Billy, Carly, Debbie, and Ethan are competing in a cooking contest. In each round of the contest, different dishes are prepared. A contestant is eliminated the first time he or she fails to prepare a dish properly. The contestants will be reordered between rounds according to one of the following rules:

Rule X: Whoever was in third place moves in front of the contestant who was previously in second place.

Rule Y: Whoever was in third place moves in front of the contestant who was previously in first place.

Rule Z: Whoever was in last place moves into the first place position.

If reordering involves a place where a contestant has been eliminated, that reordering cannot occur.

If none of the reorderings can occur, the contestants will remain in the same order as they were in the preceding round.

1. If the order in one round is Ethan, Billy, Carly, Debbie, and if Carly alone is eliminated in that round, which one of the following must be the order of the contestants for the next round?

   (A) Billy, Debbie, Ethan
   (B) Billy, Ethan, Debbie
   (C) Debbie, Billy, Ethan
   (D) Debbie, Ethan, Billy
   (E) Ethan, Billy, Debbie

2. If the order in one round is Carly, Billy, Debbie, Ethan, and if no one is eliminated in that round, it must be true that in the next round

   (A) Billy is third
   (B) Carly is second
   (C) Debbie is first
   (D) Ethan is first
   (E) Ethan is fourth

3. If the order in a round is Billy, Debbie, Ethan, Carly, and no one is eliminated, which one of the following could be the order in the next round?

(A) Billy, Carly, Ethan, Debbie
(B) Carly, Billy, Ethan, Debbie
(C) Carly, Ethan, Billy, Debbie
(D) Debbie, Billy, Ethan, Carly
(E) Ethan, Billy, Debbie, Carly

4. If two rounds go by with no eliminations, and if the order of contestants in the third round is the same as it was in the first round, which one of the following represents the reorderings taking place so far?

(A) X, followed by Y
(B) X, followed by X
(C) Y, followed by X
(D) Z, followed by Y
(E) Z, followed by Z

Cracking Game #8

Step 1: Draw your diagram

We don't really have a diagram here, so all we should do is note the "contestants"—B, C, D, and E. Let's see what the rules are.

Step 2: Symbolize the clues

We can draw the three rules to see who goes where after a "round." Take a look at the diagram on the following page.

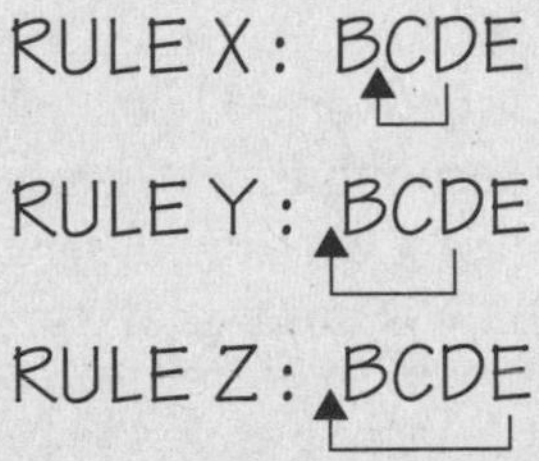

RULE X: BCDE

RULE Y: BCDE

RULE Z: BCDE

The final two clues talk about whether or not a reordering can occur based on the number of contestants left. Make sure you understand what this means before going to the questions!

Step 3: Double-check your clues and make deductions

Have you symbolized the rules correctly? Good. You want to look for questions that will tell you definitively whether someone has been eliminated and what the exact positions of the contestants are. That way, you'll be able to properly manipulate the rules and the contestants.

Step 4: Attack the questions

Fortunately there are only four questions and they are all "if" questions. Let's see how you do.

Step 5: Use Process of Elimination

1. If the order in one round is Ethan, Billy, Carly, Debbie, and if Carly alone is eliminated in that round, which one of the following must be the order of the contestants for the next round?

   (A) Billy, Debbie, Ethan
   (B) Billy, Ethan, Debbie
   (C) Debbie, Billy, Ethan
   (D) Debbie, Ethan, Billy
   (E) Ethan, Billy, Debbie

Here's how to crack it

If Carly is eliminated, and she was in the third position, no reordering that involves a contestant in the third position can take place, because all we have left is EBD. That means no Rule X and no Rule Y. So, we execute Rule Z, which puts our last contestant, Debbie, into the first position. Ethan and Billy don't move. The new order is Debbie, Ethan, Billy, or choice (D).

2. If the order in one round is Carly, Billy, Debbie, Ethan, and if no one is eliminated in that round, it must be true that in the next round

   (A) Billy is third
   (B) Carly is second
   (C) Debbie is first
   (D) Ethan is first
   (E) Ethan is fourth

Here's how to crack it

Try each move and see what happens. Executing Rule X produces the order Carly, Debbie, Billy, Ethan. Executing Rule Y produces the order Debbie, Carly, Billy, Ethan. Executing Rule Z produces the order Ethan, Carly, Billy, Debbie. In all three of those situations, Billy is third, so the answer is (A).

3. If the order in a round is Billy, Debbie, Ethan, Carly, and no one is eliminated, which one of the following could be the order in the next round?

   (A) Billy, Carly, Ethan, Debbie
   (B) Carly, Billy, Ethan, Debbie
   (C) Carly, Ethan, Billy, Debbie
   (D) Debbie, Billy, Ethan, Carly
   (E) Ethan, Billy, Debbie, Carly

Here's how to crack it

Try each move and see what happens. Executing Rule X produces the order Billy, Ethan, Debbie, Carly. There is no answer choice with that order. Executing Rule Y produces the order Ethan, Billy, Debbie, Carly, which appears in choice (E). That's our answer.

4. If two rounds go by with no eliminations, and if the order of contestants in the third round is the same as it was in the first round, which one of the following represents the reorderings taking place so far?

(A) X, followed by Y
(B) X, followed by X
(C) Y, followed by X
(D) Z, followed by Y
(E) Z, followed by Z

Here's how to crack it

Start with a random order: Billy, Carly, Debbie, Ethan. Now try the answers. We have to make sure that we end up with the same order in the third round that we have in the first round. Choice (A) suggests X, then Y. So if we started with B, C, D, E, Rule X produces B, D, C, E. Then execute Rule Y. That produces C, B, D, E. We do not have the same order in the third round as we did in the first round, do we? On to choice (B). If we started with B, C, D, E, Rule X produces B, D, C, E. Then execute Rule X again. That produces B, C, D, E. We have the same order in the third round as we did in the first round. (B) is our answer.

Why do we leave games like this until last in the section? They can often be complicated and time-consuming, because we can't really make any deductions before the game. In all the other games, there is a system: a diagram, clues, deductions. The worst thing about these games is that you usually have to test the answer choices, which is the biggest time-waster of all.

GAMES TECHNIQUES: ORDERING THE SECTION

We talked about how to predict the relative difficulty of the games in an earlier section of this chapter. Now let's make sure we're clear on how to put that knowledge to use.

Attacking the games in a "workable" order is the most powerful tool you can have for doing well on the section. Before you start working through any games, you should take a couple of minutes to look through all four games and evaluate them for difficulty. You should make a note on each game as to whether it's a game you'd like to work on now, later, or never. If you get to all four games, the Never game will be the one you do last. The LSAT rewards confidence and if you choose your first game well, you'll come away from it warmed up for the later games and fully confident that you'll be able to tackle them, too. And leaving the worst game for the end will ensure that you'll spend your time working through the questions that you'll best be able to answer; this will allow you to get as many points in those 35 minutes as you can.

GAMES TECHNIQUES: PRACTICING ON YOUR OWN

- Do everything in pencil, and don't erase your work.
- Work and write small—you will not be given a lot of space to draw your diagram.
- If a particular symbol isn't working, or is even causing mistakes, stop using it. Try something else.
- Do games over and over. If you had trouble with one, go back to it later and try it again until you get it.
- Practice games only when you are able to give them your full attention.
- *Very important:* Re-work all the games (including the games in this chapter) at least twice.
- Always keep in mind which games you're able to do most quickly. Look for those games and do those first on the real LSAT.

SUMMARY

Here's the step-by-step approach to ALL games:

Step 1: Draw your diagram

Step 2: Symbolize the clues

Step 3: Double-check your clues and make deductions

Step 4: Attack the questions

Step 5: Use Process of Elimination

On the following page is a summary chart of the games that you did in this section. When you re-work the games, note those that took you the least amount of time and analyze why. Also look at the games that took you the longest to do, and work on those skills that seem to be slowing you down. Find similar games in the two tests in the back of this book and on the real LSATs you've ordered, and work those games over and over. There's no substitute for practice. The chart is designed to give you a map of the games from this section, showing the basic characteristics of each game and how to attack it. Refer to the chart when working out games from previously released LSATs.

Game Name	Characteristics	How to Crack It
Days & Entrees	• One-to-one correspondence • Blocks • Grid format	Make sure you've drawn your blocks correctly, make deductions, and use the information provided to you in the "if" questions.
Tenant and Apartments	• Two tiers • Empty spaces • One-to-one correspondence	Remind yourself that the process is exactly the same for two tiers as for one. Keep your diagram very neat and very specific.
Office and Furnishings	• Template format • More spaces than elements • Many deductions	Be flexible with how you draw your diagram, and draw a new diagram for each question in the game.
Hats and Scarves	• Two columns only—in and out • All clues "if...then" format • Using the contrapositive	Make sure you' ve diagrammed all the contrapositives correctly, try to link clues together, and keep track of each "in" space and each "out" space.
Three Buses	• Distribution—many more elements than spaces • Blocks and anti-blocks • Distribution clues	Spend a minute or two trying to work out the distribution of elements to space—this will make the game go much smoother if you see it.
Birds and Mammals	• Two tiers • Multiple use of elements • Antiblocks • Some "if...then" clues	This tests your ability to pull several different types of clues together. Spend some time trying to link up these clues with each other—you'll get more deductions that way.
Karaoke	• Hybrid game—combination of more than one type of game • Flexible diagram • Unusual clues	Save this type of game for the end of the section. The key here is to understand what's going on in the game. Elements will be compared in more than one way, and one of those ways probably won't be fixed. Be very careful with your clues and deductions.
Cooking Contest	• No standard diagram • A set of rules to keep track of a fixed number of elements	Something you probably want to steer away from. Keep track of the rules and draw out the changes whenever you can.

4

Reading Comprehension

WHAT IS READING COMPREHENSION?

It's dull. Dull as dirt. There are of course other definitions, but the fact that Reading Comprehension is dull is probably the most accurate description we can think of. Why is it dull? For several reasons, but probably the most compelling is the fact that *no one actually writes like that.* It's true—you're not just being anti-intellectual when you're thinking these passages are boring.

So where do these passages come from? Well, most of the time they are culled from much longer passages. The LSAT writers then delete much of the introductory material. They also delete examples, illustrations, charts, pictures, transitions, and conclusions. What we're left with is information, and lots of it.

Thus, when you're reading a reading comprehension passage (like you've been doing since seventh grade on tests such as the SAT, the PSAT, the CAT, the Ohio tests, the ACT, the Regents, etc.), you probably do the following:

1. Read the first sentence of the passage.
2. Read the second sentence of the passage.
3. Read the third sentence of the passage.
4. Begin reading the fourth sentence of the passage, then realize that you've forgotten the information from the first sentence.
5. Go back and re-read the first three sentences of the passage.
6. Push on toward the middle of the passage, now both bored and frustrated out of your mind, anxious about how much time is left, and worried because you've once again forgotten the information in the first sentence of the passage.
7. Quickly finish reading the passage and start doing the questions in order, getting frustrated because you always have to go back to the passage to find the answers even though you just read the passage a few minutes ago.

There's no way that you can retain 60 or 70 lines' worth of information in such a short time.

Sound familiar? Well, because the passage is usually all information, that's about what *should* be happening. There's no way that you can retain sixty or seventy lines' worth of information in such a short period of time. You just can't do it. Especially when you've got no personal interest in the information being presented. You probably don't care about steel mills or water bugs or the painter Watteau, and you certainly wouldn't be reading a passage like the one on the LSAT if you were interested. You'd buy a book, or read an article in a magazine, or go to a museum, or whatever.

Naturally, we're going to provide you with a method to attack this section of the LSAT. We just wanted to let you know that you weren't the only one who felt this way.

WHAT DOES THIS SECTION TEST?

More than anything, Reading Comprehension tests your ability to answer questions about the author's big points and specific details scattered throughout the passage. Because the passages are presented in such a way as to hinder comprehension, this section also tests your ability to manage these tasks efficiently in a short period of time.

WHY IS THIS SECTION ON THE LSAT?

Reading Comprehension is on the LSAT to test your ability to read carefully and manage large amounts of information in a short period of time. This section also tests your ability to answer questions about a passage without bringing in any information from outside.

The section itself

The Reading Comprehension section contains four passages and each passage has five to eight questions attached to it, for a total of up to 27 questions. The passages are all typically between 55 and 65 lines.

Before we begin, take a moment to read the instructions to this section:

> Directions: Each passage in this section is followed by a group of questions to be answered on the basis of what is stated or implied in the passage. For some questions, more than one of the choices could conceivably answer the question. However, you are to choose the best answer, that is, the response that most accurately and completely answers the question, and blacken the corresponding space on your answer sheet.

These are the directions that will appear on your LSAT. As usual on the LSAT, the official directions provide very little help. Review them now. They will not change. Don't waste time reading them in the test room.

DON'T DESPAIR

We're about to give you a very simple four-step process for attacking the Reading Comprehension section of the LSAT. It may be a bit uncomfortable at first, but with practice, you'll be able to increase your reading comprehension score. Because this approach is likely to be different from what you're used to, you'll have to practice consistently to see the best results.

READING COMPREHENSION: GENERAL STRATEGIES

The following text is a list of general strategies that you should use when you are working on the Reading Comprehension section. Make sure you take these strategies seriously.

Take your time

If you rush through the Reading Comprehension section of the LSAT, you're going to make several mistakes. The questions and answer choices are just as difficult as in the Arguments section, and you've got more of them, too. So if you've been getting to all four reading comprehension passages but you're only getting 60 percent of the questions correct, slow down! Try attempting only three passages and see how your accuracy will increase. If you're getting more right than not, however, then you need to get to all four.

Your mantra: *I will slow down and focus on getting the questions I work on right, even if that means not getting to all the questions. I will increase my accuracy and thereby increase my score.*

Pick your passages

As in Games, you don't want to open up the Reading Comprehension section and just start doing the first passage. Look at all four passages—see which one or ones look easier to you, and start there. There are several criteria—organization of the passage, subject matter of the passage, number of questions, types of questions, length of the questions and answer choices, etc. We'll talk more about how to choose reading comprehension passages, but the point here is to find the passages that you think you'll be more effective on and do those first.

Your mantra: *I will evaluate the Reading Comprehension section and put the passages in my own order.*

Transfer your answers after each passage

Work *all* the questions on a particular passage and then transfer your answers to the bubble sheet. You need a few seconds to regroup after each passage, and transferring your answers allows your brain to do something mindless for a few seconds. When you're down to ten minutes, make sure you've got every single question bubbled in. Then, transfer your answers singly, changing whatever you might have bubbled in first. That way, if time is called early (remember, assume ineptitude on the part of all proctors), you've got an answer for every single question.

Your mantra: *I will transfer my answers in groups after each passage until ten minutes are left.*

Breathe

After you've completed each passage, use ten seconds to take three deep breaths. Transfer your answers from that passage, and then go and start another passage. You've cleared your mind and you're ready to push on.

Your mantra: *I will use ten seconds after each passage I complete to take some deep breaths.*

YOUR MANTRAS AND YOU

Here they are again:

> *I will slow down and focus on getting the questions I work on right, even if that means not getting to all the questions. I will increase my accuracy and thereby increase my score.*
>
> *I will evaluate the Reading Comprehension section and put the passages in my own order.*
>
> *I will transfer my answers in groups after each passage until ten minutes are left.*
>
> *I will use ten seconds after each passage I complete to take some deep breaths.*

Reading Comprehension: A Step-by-Step Process

We're about to give you a four-step process that will help you attack the Reading Comprehension section of the LSAT. Whenever you do a passage, follow these steps exactly. This process is designed to help you read the passage actively, searching for what you'll need to answer the questions. That's the key to working efficiently and effectively through this section of the LSAT.

Step 1: Preview the questions

When you read a book, do you just open it up to page one and begin reading? Hardly. You first read the back cover, the front cover, the blurbs, the paragraph about the author, etc. You also look to see how long the book is, and maybe see how it's organized—how long the chapters are, or how small the typeface is, etc. Yet, in Reading Comprehension, we're asked just to begin reading with absolutely no idea of what we're going to encounter in the next 60 lines.

So what can you do to solve this problem? Simple—*read the questions first*. By reading the questions, you'll know what the subject matter is in the passage, and you'll also know what specific issues are going to be important for you to know about. Look for repeated words or phrases; don't try to memorize the questions. For instance, if there is a passage about the poet James Merrill, and a question asks about his home in Stonington, Connecticut, you'll know in advance that the part of the passage that talks about this will be important. In addition, you'll know that anything about his apartment in New York City probably won't be important—unless another question asks about that.

Even knowing the general questions in a reading comprehension exercise can help—you'll know, for instance, that you will be asked about the author's tone or primary purpose, or the structure of the passage. Therefore, you can read with a specific goal in mind. This process of reading the questions and then noting what each one is asking (either by circling or underlining or re-writing) should really only take you 15 to 30 seconds with practice. Then, you can go to the passage.

A step-by-step process

The big money technique: Read the questions first.

Step 2: Work the passage

Great. You've read the questions, so now you can read the passage. However, most students try to memorize the passage. As we've already discussed, the passage contains too many facts to be able to memorize them, even for five minutes. So how should you read this passage? Should you just skim it? Or just read the first few sentences of each paragraph?

Here's your answer: Try to get through the passage fairly quickly—for fast readers, 90 seconds, and for slower readers, 3 minutes at most. You'll read every word of the passage, but you're only looking to do a few things in this time. Here they are:

1. Underline, circle, or star any word, phrase, or section of the passage that was mentioned in one of the questions.
2. Look for the underlying structure of the passage: Is the passage a description of three theories? Or is it merely mentioning one theory, and then refuting it?

3. Get the main idea of the passage—if four of the questions asked about the poet James Merrill, chances are he is part of the main idea of the passage—for instance, that James Merrill was a good poet although he could have been better, or that James Merrill was a great poet because he broke away from convention, etc.
4. Know the players in the passage. The author's opinion is always the most important, but often, it's conveyed by contrast with others' opinions, theories, or ideas. Knowing in which specific parts of the passage these other players' ideas are discussed can help you keep the author's point clear for yourself so you can zoom straight to the right part of the passage on more specific questions.

Don't try to find the actual answers to any of the specific questions—you're going to have to go back and re-read those parts when working each question. Just find out and note where the information is—so you can go back to the passage efficiently. While this process may take you more than three minutes the first few times around, you'll be able to pick up speed the more you practice it. So, you can now finally go to the questions, and you've only spent three to five minutes on the first two steps.

Step 3: Answer the questions in your own words
This step should really read as follows: Answer the questions in your own words *before you read the answer choices*. How are you able to do this? Simple. You read the question, go back to the passage, and then, for the first time, read the appropriate part of the passage *slowly* and *for specific content*.

Most of the time in reading comprehension questions, you should be able to know at least one word or idea that needs to be in the correct answer. You will see how this works in the following passage—how, by going back and reading the appropriate part of the passage carefully, you'll be able to come up with your own answer to each question.

Step 4: Use Process of Elimination
So now that you've got this wonderful answer, what do you do with it? You match it against the answer choices. The key here is to remain confident of what *you* said needs to be in the correct answer. Remember that four of the answer choices are wrong!

Something you'll notice about the wrong answer choices is that many of them will reference information contained in a different part of the passage. So the answer will look good because it's mentioning specific content from the passage, but in reality it's mentioning information that answers a totally different question. If you've come up with your own answer in Step 3, you won't be misled by these answer choices.

Let's Do a Reading Comprehension Passage

Okay, those are the steps. Now let's see how they work on a real reading comprehension passage. Try to complete all of this in about 15 minutes—don't worry if it takes you longer than that. With practice, you can get your speed down to 12 or even 9 minutes (i.e., three or four passages completed).

After the passage we'll give you some extra techniques for attacking this section of the LSAT, just as we did in the Arguments and Games discussions.

READING COMPREHENSION PASSAGE: *CELEBRITY LAW*

Recently, the right of public personalities to direct and profit from all commercial exploitations of their fame has gained widespread acceptance. Recognition of this "right of publicity," however, has raised difficult questions concerning the proper scope and duration of the right as well as its relationship to free speech and free trade interests. Often, the "type" of personality, be it an entertainer, politician, or athlete, also weighs on this decision-making process.

The right of publicity protects economic interests of celebrities in their own fame by allowing them to control and profit from the publicity values which they have created. Before courts recognized this right, celebrities' primary protection against the unauthorized commercial appropriation of their names or likenesses was a suit for invasion of privacy. Privacy law, however, proved to be an inadequate response to the legal questions presented by celebrities seeking to protect their economic interest in fame. Whereas privacy law protects a person's right to be left alone, publicity law proceeds from antithetical assumptions. Celebrities do not object to public attention—they thrive on it. However, they seek to benefit from any commercial use of their popularity.

A celebrity's public image has many aspects, each of which may be appropriated for a variety of purposes. Plaintiffs have sought to protect various attributes including: name, likeness, a particular routine or act, characters made famous by their celebrity, unique style, and biographical information. In deciding whether the right of publicity applies to a particular attribute, courts consider underlying legal and policy goals.

Two goals support recognition of the right of publicity: the promotion of creative endeavor and the prevention of unjust enrichment through the theft of goodwill. Courts determine the scope of publicity rights by balancing these policies against countervailing First Amendment and free trade interests. Recognizing the celebrity's ability to control the exercise of some personal attribute may limit the "speech" of would-be appropriators and give the celebrity a commercial monopoly. Thus, the value of promoting creativity and preventing unjust enrichment must outweigh negative constitutional and commercial repercussions before courts extend the right of publicity to any particular attribute.

The value of a publicity right in a particular attribute depends, in large part, on the length of time such a right is recognized and protected by the law. Courts disagree on whether publicity rights survive the death of their creators. Some courts advocate unconditional devisability. They emphasize that the ability to control exploitation of fame is a property right, carrying all the characteristics of the title. Other courts conclude that the right of publicity terminates at the celebrity's death. These courts fear that recognizing postmortem publicity rights would negatively affect free speech and free trade.

The right of publicity, especially in the cases of well-known politicians and statesmen, often conflicts with First Amendment interests and thus should be defined with care and precision.

1. Which of the following statements best summarizes the above passage?

    (A) An assessment of privacy law reveals that publicity law is a more appropriate legal remedy for public personalities.
    (B) The promotion of creative endeavor justifies the legal recognition of the right of publicity.
    (C) The courts, rather than the celebrities themselves, must determine the relative importance of commercial and constitutional concerns.
    (D) The legal issues regarding the right to publicity are complex and have yet to be fully resolved.
    (E) Widely accepted approaches to deciding publicity law cases conflict with First Amendment interests.

Focus first on the questions—they'll tell you what the passage is about.

2. According to the passage, the judicial response to "right of publicity" questions has been

   (A) theoretical
   (B) inconclusive
   (C) creative
   (D) disdainful
   (E) widely respected

3. It can be inferred from the passage that a characteristic of "devisability" (line 68) is the ability to be

   (A) commercially appropriated with the author's permission
   (B) divided into more than one legal entity
   (C) assigned by a will
   (D) recognized as a commercial monopoly
   (E) structured in several equal branches

4. Which one of the following can be inferred from the information in the passage?

   (A) First Amendment ramifications of extending the right of publicity to politicians should be analyzed.
   (B) There is rarely any provable nexus between exploitation during life and career incentive.
   (C) Celebrities invest substantial time and money to achieve uncertain success and are thus entitled to whatever value accrues from these efforts.
   (D) Concerns regarding unjust enrichment from biographical data outweigh the right to disseminate information under the First Amendment.
   (E) It is in the public interest to reward successful entertainers for their efforts and thereby encourage artists to devote their lives to creative endeavors.

5. According to the passage, privacy laws are inadequate as legal remedies for celebrities because

   (A) public personalities have no redress for unauthorized commercial appropriation of their images
   (B) private individuals waive privacy rights by becoming public figures
   (C) stars wish to be protected from the public only when they are not successful
   (D) the laws do not address the financial issues inherent in a public figure's fame
   (E) celebrities have a responsibility to the public to share their created personae and not avoid public attention

6. Which one of the following situations would most reasonably call upon the "right of publicity" as discussed in the passage?

   (A) A novelist objects to the unauthorized reprinting of a portion of his book in a student's paper.
   (B) An athlete plans to design and market, but not promote, a line of sportswear.
   (C) The well-known "catch-phrase" of a local talk-show host is used as part of an ad campaign for a supermarket.
   (D) The president of a small company bequeaths his business to an employee but his family contests the will.
   (E) The work of a celebrated screen actor is re-edited after the actor's death.

Step 1: Preview the questions
First we'll reprint each question and restate what it told us. Take a look at question 1:

1. Which of the following statements best summarizes the above passage?

This is a general question; it asks for the main idea of the passage. Most reading comprehension passages will include a main idea question, so you should always keep track of what the passage is saying as a whole while you read it.

2. According to the passage, the judicial response to "right of publicity" questions has been

All right. Now we know that the passage has something to do with right of publicity, and that we need to figure out how to characterize the judicial response to it.

3. It can be inferred from the passage that a characteristic of "devisability" (line 68) is the ability to be

This is a very specific question. We need to figure out what "devisability" is all about. Fortunately, the question gives us a line reference so we can quickly locate the word when we come back to work this question.

4. Which one of the following can be inferred from the information in the passage?

This is a general inference question. This type of question offers very little in the way of guidance; after all, from a given passage, we can infer any number of things. We'll discuss how to deal with this sort of question when we talk about POE.

5. According to the passage, privacy laws are inadequate as legal remedies for celebrities because

Another nice, specific question. Why are privacy laws inadequate as remedies for celebrities? We'll keep our eyes peeled for the answer to this question as we read the passage.

6. Which one of the following situations would most reasonably call upon the "right of publicity" as discussed in the passage?

This is kind of an odd question; though it refers to something specific in the passage (the "right of publicity"), it asks us to find which situation *outside* the passage is relevant to this right. We'll discuss how to approach this type of question later; all that's important now is that we know we need to understand what "right of publicity" is, and when it's applicable.

Great. So we know that the passage has something to do with publicity, privacy, celebrities, and the law. Sounds like we have all the makings of a bad made-for-TV-movie, but at least it might make for an almost interesting reading comp passage! And we also have a list of things to keep our eyes peeled for as we read: right of publicity, devisability, and the inadequacy of privacy laws for celebrities. We're ready for the next step.

Remember: This step should only take about 30 seconds.

Step 2: Work the passage
Below is a list of what each paragraph of the passage told us, and what we felt was important in it. Then we'll show you what we thought were the main idea and structure of the passage as a whole. Here we go:

Paragraph 1: Introduction of the concept of "right of publicity" and its problems.

Paragraph 2: Why right of publicity was needed: privacy laws didn't do the job.

Paragraph 3: What the right of publicity seeks to protect.

Paragraph 4: Pros and cons of the right of publicity.

Paragraph 5: How long does right of publicity apply: differing judicial perspectives.

Paragraph 6: Right of publicity and politicians: often a problem.

Break up the passage into smaller chunks of information—remember, it's easier to process a little at a time and then put it all together.

As you can see, we've retained very little information here; all we've done is created an outline of what each paragraph contributes to the passage as a whole. From this outline, however, we should be able to come up with the main idea of the passage, and describe its structure as a whole. You should always be able to state both the main idea and structure of a passage after you're finished reading it.

Main idea: *Something about the origins of "right to privacy," and how there are disagreements about how and when this right applies.*

Structure: *The concept of right to publicity is introduced, its origins are discussed, and several situations to which it applies are described.*

That's it. We'll save a more in-depth analysis of this for when we come up with our answers to the questions. And now that we know where the information is in the passage, we should be able to do that with efficiency. Let's go to Step 3.

Step 3: Answer the questions in your own words
Now let's look at the questions again and, whenever possible, come up with our own answers for them—before we look at the answer choices.

When you take the real test, you should think about each question and be ready with an answer before you look at any of the answer choices. That way you're much less likely to be sucked in by the seductive wrong answers they'll throw your way. To practice, let's come up with our own answers for all the questions we've seen, without looking at any of the answer choices.

1. Which of the following statements best summarizes the above passage?

We pretty much answered this question when we came up with our main idea. It has something to do with "right of publicity," and what a complicated issue it is.

2. According to the passage, the judicial response to "right of publicity" questions has been

Well, we know that the fifth paragraph has to do with differing judicial perspectives on right of publicity, and that the passage offers no resolution to the problems it addresses. So the judicial response did not lead to a resolution.

3. It can be inferred from the passage that a characteristic of "devisability" (line 68) is the ability to be

This is a specific question. Go back to the passage and study the context of the word; this will require you to read about five lines before and after the key word or phrase. We are told that "some courts advocate unconditional devisability" while "other courts conclude that the right of publicity terminates at the celebrity's death," so unconditional devisability implies that the right extends beyond death. This ought to be enough to help us find the right answer.

4. Which one of the following can be inferred from the information in the passage?

This is a general inference, and one of the few types of questions you can't really prepare an answer for ahead of time. We'll discuss how to deal with this when we get to Process of Elimination.

5. According to the passage, privacy laws are inadequate as legal remedies for celebrities because

Why are privacy laws inadequate? Well, we know that this is discussed in the second paragraph. Privacy laws (not surprisingly) protect a person's right to privacy, but the issue of publicity is not closely related to that of privacy.

6. Which one of the following situations would most reasonably call upon the "right of publicity" as discussed in the passage?

This is an unusual question. In order to answer it, we'll have to understand what "right of publicity" refers to, and find a situation where it would be applicable. It is clear from the passage that "right of publicity" refers to using someone's fame for commercial or financial gain, so we're looking for an answer that closely resembles this.

The key on reading comp is paraphrasing; answering in your own words involves boiling down a wordy passage into a simple phrase or concept. Looking for an answer that matches involves boiling down answer choices to a similar form, and seeing if the idea is the same.

Step 4: Use Process of Elimination

Now we're ready to see how well we did. For each question, we'll go through all the answer choices and check our answers against them, aggressively using Process of Elimination.

Keep it simple and trust your answers.

1. Which of the following statements best summarizes the above passage?

(A) An assessment of privacy law reveals that publicity law is a more appropriate legal remedy for public personalities.
(B) The promotion of creative endeavor justifies the legal recognition of the right of publicity.
(C) The courts, rather than the celebrities themselves, must determine the relative importance of commercial and constitutional concerns.
(D) The legal issues regarding the right to publicity are complex and have yet to be fully resolved.
(E) Widely accepted approaches to deciding publicity law cases conflict with First Amendment interests.

Our answer has something to do with right of publicity and all its problems. (A) is too specific. Privacy law is mentioned only briefly in the second paragraph. (B) is also too narrow; the promotion of creative endeavor is mentioned only in the fourth paragraph. While (C) is probably true, the passage is not about who must determine the relative importance of these concerns—it's about right of publicity. (D) looks pretty good; it mentions right of publicity, and the lack of complete resolution. (E) is just plain wrong, according to the passage; there are no widely accepted approaches to right of publicity.

2. According to the passage, the judicial response to "right of publicity" questions has been

(A) theoretical
(B) inconclusive
(C) creative
(D) disdainful
(E) widely respected

Our answer is that the judicial response has not led to any resolution, and (B), *inconclusive*, is the only answer that even comes close to this.

3. It can be inferred from the passage that a characteristic of "devisability" (line 68) is the ability to be

(A) commercially appropriated with the author's permission
(B) divided into more than one legal entity
(C) assigned by a will
(D) recognized as a commercial monopoly
(E) structured in several equal branches

Okay, so we inferred that the word had something to do with "rights of publicity" continuing after death. Now let's look at the answers. (A) mentions cases in which permission *has* been obtained from the author—this is not discussed anywhere in the passage. (B) is the sort of answer you might pick if you just looked at the word "devisability" and tried to guess its meaning; this pretty much guarantees that it isn't correct. Unless you're a *bona fide* expert in the field, chances are that the answer you would pick if you *didn't* read the passage is wrong. (C) talks about wills, so it might work, because wills have something to do with death. (D) brings up the concept of a commercial monopoly, which is used in a different context in the passage. (E) is out of scope—structuring something in branches is never mentioned. But this is another answer choice you might pick if you'd just looked at the word and tried to guess what it meant.

4. Which one of the following can be inferred from the information in the passage?

(A) First Amendment ramifications of extending the right of publicity to politicians should be analyzed.
(B) There is rarely any provable nexus between exploitation during life and career incentive.
(C) Celebrities invest substantial time and money to achieve uncertain success and are thus entitled to whatever value accrues from these efforts.
(D) Concerns regarding unjust enrichment from biographical data outweigh the right to disseminate information under the First Amendment.
(E) It is in the public interest to reward successful entertainers for their efforts and thereby encourage artists to devote their lives to creative endeavors.

All right. So how do we deal with general inference questions? Well, first of all, let's figure out what the question really asks. What it asks is, *What can you figure out based on the passage*, and the answer is *a lot*! We'll start by using some heavy-duty POE. First of all, eliminate any answers that are not relevant or go beyond what was stated in the passage. In other words, eliminate ones that bring up issues not mentioned in the passage. Well, guess what—that gets rid of every answer except (A). No mention is made of exploitation vs. career incentive (B), the time and money needed to achieve celebrity status (C), enrichment from biographical data (D), or what is in the public interest (E). So (A) must be the right answer, and this answer is, incidentally, clearly supported by the final paragraph of the passage. The lesson here is that, while these questions might *look* like a major pain, if you stick to your guns with POE, oftentimes they aren't so bad.

5. According to the passage, privacy laws are inadequate as legal remedies for celebrities because

(A) public personalities have no redress for unauthorized commercial appropriation of their images
(B) private individuals waive privacy rights by becoming public figures
(C) stars wish to be protected from the public only when they are not successful
(D) the laws do not address the financial issues inherent in a public figure's fame
(E) celebrities have a responsibility to the public to share their created personae and not avoid public attention

Why are privacy laws inadequate? They are inadequate because they deal only with people's privacy rights. Now let's go through the choices. (A) looks kind of good, so let's keep it for now. After all, privacy laws don't seem to help celebrities when their images are used without their authorization. (B) might also seem tempting, but the question is, *Why do we need "right of publicity" laws,* and the answer is: *Because privacy laws don't deal with financial issues, as publicity laws do.* (C) is not relevant, because right of publicity has to do with financial protection, not protection from the public. (D) looks like a solid answer, and it's superior to (A) because it is much broader; it covers the whole scope of financial issues relevant to right of publicity. (E) is not relevant; once again, the issue at hand is why we need "right to publicity" laws, not whether celebrities actually have a right to privacy.

6. Which one of the following situations would most reasonably call upon the "right of publicity" as discussed in the passage?

(A) A novelist objects to the unauthorized reprinting of a portion of his book in a student's paper.
(B) An athlete plans to design and market, but not promote, a line of sportswear.
(C) The well-known "catch-phrase" of a local talk-show host is used as part of an ad campaign for a supermarket.
(D) The president of a small company bequeaths his business to an employee but his family contests the will.
(E) The work of a celebrated screen actor is re-edited after the actor's death.

When can we call upon the right of publicity? When someone tries to make commercial use of a celebrity's fame. (A) is not appropriate, because the student is not writing the paper for financial gain. (B) is not appropriate, because the athlete has a right to his or her own fame. (C) looks good—the supermarket is making commercial use of the talk-show host's celebrity image. (D) has nothing to do with fame, and (E) is not a clear issue, since we do not know who is doing the re-editing and whether they have the right to do it.

So that's that. Now that you know the basic approach, you just need to practice, practice, practice. But first, a few more words of advice.

Reading Comprehension Techniques: Reading the Questions First

You might think that reading the questions *before* the passage is too time-consuming, but we strongly recommend that you do it. Keep in mind all the good things that can come from reading the questions first:

- You get a good idea of what the passage is about.
- You can generate a list of key words to look for as you read the passage.

- You can often recognize, while you read the passage, where you'll be likely to find the answer to a question later. Put a mark in the margin and you'll be able to find that information quickly and efficiently when you're working on the questions.
- You can also recognize which parts of the passage aren't as important. While you do want to read carefully enough to keep track of what's going on, there will be parts that you'll recognize as being less important if you read the questions first.

Despite all these advantages, you still might find reading the questions first too inconvenient. Practice it for a while, try it out, and compare it to reading the passage first, if you like. If you do decide to read the passage first, make sure you read closely enough to understand the main idea, the structure, and what each paragraph contributes to the passage. If you fail to get this kind of general understanding from reading the passage, you'll really be in trouble when you get to the questions.

Reading Comprehension Techniques: Process of Elimination

As you can see from the previous passage, coming up with your own answers helped you on many of the questions. You will still have to use Process of Elimination, however, in many instances. Just like in arguments, you can use several Process of Elimination techniques when working reading comprehension passages. The most important ones are described below.

Wrong part of the passage

As we mentioned earlier in the chapter, many of the wrong answer choices do contain content consistent with the passage. The problem is that this information is from a different part of the passage. For instance, if a passage is describing the properties of three different kinds of acids, and a question asks about the properties of the second acid, many of the wrong choices will be properties of the first and third acids. But as long as you focus on the information about the second acid only, you'll be able to eliminate any choices that talk about the first and third acids.

Extreme language

Here's a familiar technique from arguments. And as we mentioned in the arguments chapter, extreme language is usually very difficult to prove, so it's rarely contained in correct answers. The same rule applies to reading comprehension—if you're down to two choices, and one is wishy-washy and one is extreme, pick the wishy-washy choice.

In question 2 of the "right of publicity" passage, answer choices (D) and (E) are both excellent examples of strong wording. Also, in question 4, answer choices (D) and (E) contain language too definitive to match the author's viewpoint.

Relevance

Here's another familiar technique from arguments. Many answer choices in Reading Comprehension will either be too general or too specific. If the passage is about the poet James Merrill, and you're asked to come up with the main idea of the passage, the answer will not be that the passage is about "poetry," nor will it be that the passage is about "James Merrill's house in Connecticut."

Other answer choices will bring in information that was never mentioned in the passage. If the author didn't discuss it, it's not relevant. In question 6 of the "right of publicity" passage, answer choices (A), (B), and (D) all talk about issues not raised in the passage.

Too narrow

Main idea and primary purpose questions often have wrong answers that are too narrow or specific. Remember that the main idea should encompass the entire passage. Wrong answers to main idea questions are often true, but are subjects only discussed in one or two paragraphs. Similarly, the primary purpose describes the purpose of the entire passage, not of any one paragraph within the passage.

Not said

These answer choices are tempting because they may seem like reasonable projections from passage material, and often include key ideas or phrases mentioned in the passage. Often the problem is with one word, or is a problem of emphasis rather than gross content. These answers are often troublesome because people can write a two-page paper and persuade themselves it's "basically" in the passage.

READING COMPREHENSION TECHNIQUES: QUESTION TYPES

Reading comprehension questions fit into two main categories—general questions and specific questions. In the previous passage, questions 1 and 4 are general questions. All of the other questions are specific in nature, because they asked about a specific part of the passage or about a specific idea from the passage. On the following page is a chart showing the various types of reading comprehension questions and how you should attack each one.

General Questions	
Question Type	**Technique**
Main idea	Come up with your own main idea—what you think the passage is about. Be critical; any word or phrase or idea that you think is an essential part of the passage MUST be part of the answer you choose.
Structure of the passage	Write out what you think is the general flow of the passage. Did the author introduce three theories and then refute them all? If so, look for a similar choice. If any part of the choice is wrong, it's all wrong—cross it off.
Primary purpose	Decide what you feel the author was attempting to do in the passage. For example, was she debunking a myth, showing how a well-accepted theory is correct, or introducing a new theory? Then match your description to the answer choices.
Author's tone/attitude	Come up with your own description of what you felt was the author's attitude toward his subject. Typically, it's something pretty wishy-washy. LSAT Reading Comprehension authors don't get too worked up one way or the other. Words like "balanced" and "objective" are usually right; words like "enthusiastic" and "derogatory" are usually wrong. Words like "dispassionate" and "apathetic" are usually wrong, too. Why would an apathetic person write something to begin with?

Specific Questions	
Question Type	**Technique**
Specific word/phrase	Go back to the passage, find the paragraph that contains the information or the specific word or phrase in the question, and read it carefully. Then answer the question in your own words before going to the choices.
Line reference	Go back to the passage and read five lines above and five lines below the line reference given to you in the question. If it says "line 56," read lines 51–61. This should help you find out the purpose of the author's word or phrase—then match your answer to the choices.
Paragraph reference	Go back to the passage and read the paragraph referenced in the question. Also, note how that paragraph fits into the passage as a whole by checking what you said was the structure of the passage. Then, come up with your own answer and match it to the choices.

Some reading comprehension questions won't fall into either of these categories, and we call them "weird" questions. Most weird questions look like transplanted arguments questions: You'll be asked to strengthen or weaken one of the passage's ideas, or to resolve some paradox, or to find an assumption. Just apply the skills you learned in your arguments lesson to these questions. These questions will usually direct you to an idea presented in the passage. Go back, find the idea, find the premises that support that idea, find the assumptions, and you're good to go.

Weaken/strengthen

In some ways these types of questions are easier than the arguments versions of them. The key here is to identify the claim to be weakened or strengthened. Don't worry about assumptions; do look for choices that attack or support the statement directly, often by example or counter-example. Precise language of the claim can be extremely important.

Analogy

These questions will often ask which is most similar to a situation in the passage, or which can be substituted for a portion of the passage while retaining its meaning. It is extremely important to describe in your own words the purpose and key attributes of the original on the page—often there will be more than one aspect that is important. Eliminate anything that does not contain all of the key attributes you have identified.

Principle

These questions will ask you either to choose a specific case that illustrates a general statement made in the passage; or, alternatively, to choose a general principle consistent with a specific conclusion drawn in the passage. Find the collection of key ideas expressed or employed and make sure your answer choice matches them all.

Assumption

Sometimes you can predict the right answer, but not always. The key, as with weaken/strengthen questions, is to pay close attention to the claim. Often the contrary of the right answer (what you get when you negate it) will contradict the claim directly.

Reading Comprehension Techniques: Passage Selection

Reading comprehension passages fall within one of four broad categories:

1. **The law passage.** On each section, you'll see one passage that discusses some aspect of the law (the only place you can be sure to see law on the LSAT!). Law passages can deal with a wide variety of issues—most of which you've probably never heard of. And unfortunately, because they are often written in a stiff, academic style with a bevy of unfamiliar terms, law passages can be pretty challenging. It really pays to have solid technique on these!

2. **The science passage.** A lot of people are simply scared off by the science passage. But fear not! If you can cut through the unfamiliar terminology and read these carefully, you're set. Science passages pack a hidden benefit—most of the questions are specific retrieval questions or line references, which tend to be easier to do than other types of questions. So even if you don't completely understand all of the passage's nuances, you'll still be able to pick up a handful of points.

3. **The humanities passage.** On the whole, passages about art and literature are pretty readable. The only real downside to these is that you might end up having to answer a lot of author's attitude and inference questions. Translation: You'll probably end up spending longer on the questions than you would like. You won't be able to pick up points as quickly here, and make sure you're certain of the author's thesis before moving on to tackle the questions.

4. **The social science passage.** You should expect to see one passage that deals with anthropology, sociology, psychology, or some other social science. These passages are generally easier to read than the straight science passages, but they don't have the slew of specific questions to go with them. Attack them as you would any other passage.

So, how should this all figure into your reading comprehension strategy? Basically, it boils down to knowing your strengths and weaknesses. Most people don't read quickly enough to read all four passages and answer every single question within the time allotted, so it's important that you prioritize. If your strength is science, seek that passage out from the beginning and get it done first. Likewise, if you know you're not so hot at the law passage, avoid it until you've done the other three. This makes sense, right?

Also, knowing these passage types can help you out when you're in a pinch for time. For instance, let's say that you've completed two passages, you have time left to do one more, and you have to choose between the social science passage and the straight science passage. Which will it be? Chances are, the straight science passage will have more specific questions than the social science passage. Because specific questions take less time to do, you'll probably get more points by devoting your remaining minutes to the straight science passage. Guess on the remaining questions, and you'll pick up a couple of extra points there, too.

SUMMARY

Here's our step-by-step approach to the Reading Comprehension section:

Step 1: Preview the questions

Step 2: Work the passage

Step 3: Answer the questions in your own words

Step 4: Use Process of Elimination

5

The Writing Sample

The Writing Sample is a 30-minute ungraded essay whose topic is assigned. Your essay is supposed to be an argument supporting either of two given positions. You'll receive a booklet containing both the topic and the space in which to write your essay. You will also receive scratch paper.

Before we begin, take a moment to read the instructions to this section:

Don't devote too much study time to the writing sample.

> General Directions: You are to complete the brief writing exercise on the topic inside. You will have 30 minutes in which to plan and write the exercise. Read the topic carefully. You will probably find it best to spend a few minutes considering the topic and organizing your thoughts before you begin writing. **Do not write on a topic other than the one specified. Writing on a topic of your own choice is not acceptable.**
>
> There is no "right" or "wrong" position on the writing sample topic. Law schools are interested in how skillfully you support the position you take and how clearly you express that position. How well you write is much more important than what you write. No special knowledge is required or expected. Law schools are interested in organization, vocabulary, and writing mechanics. They understand the short time available to you and the pressure under which you are writing.
>
> Confine your writing to the lined area following the writing sample topic. You will find that you have enough space in this booklet if you plan your writing carefully, write on every line, avoid wide margins, and keep your handwriting a reasonable size. Be sure your writing is legible.
>
> Scratch paper is provided for use during the writing sample portion of the test only. Scratch paper cannot be used in other sections of the LSAT.
>
> The writing sample is photocopied and sent to law schools to which you direct your LSAT score. A pen will be provided at the test center, which must be used (for the writing sample only) to ensure a photocopy of high quality.

These are the instructions that will appear on the cover of your LSAT Writing Sample booklet. You'll be given a chance to read them before you write your essay.

THE WRITING TOPIC

Inside the booklet you'll find the assigned topic and about 30 blank lines on which to write your essay. You'll also get scratch paper on which to organize your essay. The assigned topics are innocuous. Expect a topic something like this:

> Karen Stratton is looking into buying a property with the plan to turn it into an animal-supply store. Write an essay in support of one of two proposed properties, the cost of which would be almost exactly the same, keeping in mind Karen's needs:
>
> - Karen needs to establish a market and begin making back her investment rather quickly, because she will put most of her money into buying the property.

- Karen wants her store to be different and memorable, so she can cultivate a loyal clientele.

Property One is a storefront in the middle of the main drag of the bustling downtown area. The outside of the storefront looks like the fronts of most of the other stores on the block. The central location would make shopping there convenient for people who work in the downtown area, and is accessible by all forms of public transportation.

Property Two is an old, renovated Victorian house on the outskirts of town. The design of the house is unique. It is six miles from the nearest public transport, making it accessible only by car and cab. It is closer to the farm country and has space for a garden, which Karen can use to grow organic products for her store.

Fill up the page when writing your LSAT essay.

How Much Will My Essay Affect My LSAT Score?

Not one bit.

Only four sections contribute to your LSAT score: one Games section, two Arguments sections, and one Reading Comprehension section. An unmarked photocopy of your essay will be sent to the law schools to which you apply.

Who Will Read My Essay?

Possibly no one.

How well or poorly you do on the Writing Sample will almost certainly not affect your admissions chances.

Then Why Do Law Schools Require It?

Law schools feel guilty about not being interested in anything about you other than your grades and LSAT scores. Knowing that you have spent 30 minutes writing an essay for them makes them feel better about having no interest in reading what you have written.

Future Changes?

Always be sure to check the LSAC website at www.lsac.org for any updates to the test.

If the Writing Sample Is So Unimportant, Why Discuss It?

Just for your own peace of mind. Once you have the rest of the test under control, look over the rest of this chapter. If you are short on time, you'd be better off practicing arguments.

There's also the possibility that a bored admissions officer will accidentally pass his or her eyes over what you have written. If your essay is ungrammatical, riddled with misspellings, off the topic, and wildly disorganized, the admissions officer may think less of you.

So we're going to assume that the Writing Sample counts a little bit. You should assume the same thing, but don't lose sleep over it. No one ever got into law school because of the LSAT Writing Sample; and it's doubtful that anyone ever got rejected because of it. Besides, good writing requires surprisingly few rules, and the rules we'll review will help your writing in general.

What Are They Looking For?

The general directions to the Writing Sample mention that law schools are interested in three things: essay organization, vocabulary, and writing mechanics. Presumably, writing mechanics covers grammar and style.

What they're *really* looking for

Researchers at the Educational Testing Service once did a study of essay-grading behavior. They wanted to find out what their graders really responded to when they marked papers, and which essay characteristics correlated most strongly with good scores.

The researchers discovered that the most important characteristic, other than "overall organization," is "essay length." Also highly correlated with good essay scores are the number of paragraphs, average sentence length, and average word length. The bottom line? *Students who filled in all the lines, indented frequently, and used big words earned higher scores than students who didn't.*

We will discuss these points in more detail later. Because organization is the most important characteristic, let's start with that.

ESSAY ORGANIZATION

Your essay should contain five paragraphs (remember high school?). In the first you state your opinion. In the last you restate your opinion, and the three middle paragraphs form the body of your argument.

Indent fully to set off each paragraph clearly.

State your actual argument in three paragraphs. Three paragraphs demonstrate that your argument is concise as well as organized. Of course, if you find that one of your major ideas has secondary ideas, you may have to subdivide one of the middle paragraphs.

So your essay should consist of an introductory paragraph, a conclusion paragraph, and three main paragraphs for your argument. The more you stick with a formula outline, the less thinking you'll have to do when you actually write.

What Am I Trying to Do?

You're trying to persuade your reader that one of two given alternatives is better. You cannot *prove* that one side is better; you can only make a case that it is. The test writers deliberately come up with boringly balanced alternatives so that you can argue for either one of them.

So choose a side and justify your choice.

Picking Sides

When choosing a side to write about, list pros and cons.

The directions stress that neither alternative is "correct." It doesn't matter which side you choose. Pick the alternative that gives you more to work with.

Another way to decide is to compile a little list of the pros and cons on your scratch paper. Then simply pick the alternative whose list of pros is longer. Let's see how you'd do this with the sample topic we've given you.

First, list each alternative (Property One, Property Two) as a heading. Underneath each heading draw two columns, one for the pros and one for the cons. Spend the first couple of minutes brainstorming the advantages and disadvantages of each choice. The key to brainstorming is *quantity,* not quality. You can select and discard points later.

Having brainstormed for pros and cons, select the ones you intend to keep and arrange them in order of importance, from *least* to *most* important.

For the purposes of this chapter, let's assume that we intend to give the nod to Property Two.

Don't forget the cons

Some students believe that if you're trying to make a case for something, you should bring up the advantages only. This is wrong.

To persuade readers that Property Two is the better choice, you must show that you have considered every argument that could be made for Property One, and found each one unconvincing.

Your argument, in other words, must show that you have weighed the pros and cons of *both* sides. The more forceful the objections you counter, the more compelling your position becomes.

Evaluating the pros and cons: the criteria

As you think of pros and cons for each position, keep in mind the given criteria. Here you have two considerations—getting money back and establishing a unique business. You must build your essay around these criteria, so don't ignore them. They give you the structure to follow.

The criteria may not be compatible. If so, weigh the pros and cons in light of this situation. In our example, an innovative-looking store might not attract other people. You may want to rank the two criteria in terms of importance. Perhaps getting money back is more important than establishing a unique business. Perhaps not. Decide which consideration is more important. If you cannot decide, state so explicitly.

Can I Raise Other Issues?

You *must* weigh the two stated considerations, but nothing prevents you from introducing additional considerations.

You need not raise additional considerations, but if one occurs to you, and you have the time, mention it in passing. If none occurs to you, mention in the conclusion that you have evaluated the two options in view of the two stated considerations only, acknowledging that other considerations may be important.

Property One Versus Property Two: Brainstorming the Pros and Cons

Remember: Brainstorm first. You will have blank space in your test booklet to jot down your ideas before you dive into writing the essay. Next, select the issues you intend to raise. Then rank the final issues, beginning with the least important.

To organize your brainstorming, use a rough chart like this one:

	Quick money	Unique business	Other factors
Property One	possible; central location good for exposure and quick purchases	looks like every other store front	size? use of space and light?
Property Two	possible, but it might take a while. Harder to get to, but could be a "specialty" shop	probably; unique-looking store, customers would have to be loyal because it's farther away	size? use of space and light?

Beginning Your Essay: Restating the Problem

Having brainstormed the pros and cons of each choice in light of the considerations, you are ready to start writing your essay.

Your first paragraph should do little more than state your argument. Try not to use a tedious grade school opening like, "The purpose of the essay I am about to write is to . . ."

There are several more interesting ways to introduce an argument. Which one you choose will influence how you organize the rest of your essay. Keep this in mind as you sketch your outline. We'll tell you more about this as we go along.

One possibility for an opening is simply to restate concisely the problem you are to address. Here's an example:

> Karen Stratton needs to buy a property for her animal-supply business. She must turn a profit quickly, but wants to establish a unique business. The two properties both have positive and negative aspects. We must weigh their respective strengths and weaknesses in light of Karen's needs.

This type of introduction sets up the conflict rather than immediately taking a side. The second, third, and fourth paragraphs are then devoted to weighing the specific advantages and disadvantages of each candidate. The author's preference isn't stated explicitly until the final paragraph, although a clear case for one should emerge as the essay progresses.

An essay like this is really just an organized written version of the mental processes you went through in deciding which candidate to choose. In the first paragraph you say, in effect, "Here are the problems, the choices, and my decision." In the second, third, and fourth paragraphs you say, "Here are the pros and cons I weighed." In the fifth and final paragraph you say, "So you can see why I decided as I did."

Your hope is that the reader, by following your reasoning step by step, will decide the same thing. The great advantage of this kind of organization is that it *does* follow your mental processes. That makes it a natural and relatively easy method.

Beginning Your Essay: Putting Your Cards on the Table

It's also possible to write an essay in which you begin by announcing your decision. You state your preference in the first paragraph, back it up in the middle paragraphs, and then restate your preference with a concluding flourish in the final paragraph.

Here's an example of such an opening paragraph:

> Property One is a centrally located storefront in a busy downtown area, which would probably bring in a lot of quick business. However, it looks like every other storefront, so it wouldn't stand out. Property Two, by contrast, would afford Karen Stratton an opportunity to create a unique-looking store that could be treated as a specialty shop that people would be willing to travel to. I believe that Karen should buy Property Two for her animal-supply store because it suits her needs.

By introducing your argument in this way, you leave yourself with a great deal of latitude for handling the succeeding paragraphs. For example, you might use the second paragraph to discuss both candidates in light of the first consideration, the third paragraph to discuss both candidates in light of the second consideration, the fourth paragraph to weigh the considerations themselves, and the fifth and final paragraph to summarize your argument and restate your preference.

The Body of Your Argument

We've discussed the introductory and concluding paragraphs. Depending on your preference, and depending on the essay topic you actually confront, we recommend three variations for the middle paragraphs.

Variation 1

Paragraph 2:	Both sides in light of the first consideration
Paragraph 3:	Both sides in light of the second consideration
Paragraph 4:	Weighing the two considerations (and other considerations?)

Variation 2

Paragraph 2:	Everything that can be said about Property One
Paragraph 3:	Everything that can be said about Property Two
Paragraph 4:	A sentence or two for Property One, followed by three or four sentences for Property Two

Variation 3

Paragraph 2:	A sentence or two for Property One, followed by three or four sentences for Property Two
Paragraph 3:	A sentence or two for Property One, followed by three or four sentences for Property Two
Paragraph 4:	A sentence or two for Property One, followed by three or four sentences for Property Two

Again, if necessary, you can divide any one of the three middle paragraphs into two paragraphs.

All three variations do the job. Choose a variation you feel comfortable with and memorize it. The less thinking you have to do on the actual exam, the better.

The Princeton Review Thesaurus of Pretty Impressive Words

The following list of words is not meant to be complete, nor is it in any particular order. Synonyms or related concepts are grouped where appropriate.

- example, instance, precedent, paradigm, archetype
- illustrate, demonstrate, highlight, acknowledge, exemplify, embody
- support, endorse, advocate, maintain, contend, espouse, champion
- supporter, proponent, advocate, adherent
- dispute, dismiss, outweigh, rebut, refute

Only use ten-dollar words if you can use and spell them correctly.

- propose, advance, submit, marshal, adduce
- premise, principle, presumption, assumption, proposition
- advantages, merits, benefits
- inherent, intrinsic, pertinent
- indisputable, incontrovertible, inarguable, unassailable, irrefutable, undeniable, unimpeachable
- unconvincing, inconclusive, dubious, specious
- compelling, cogent, persuasive
- empirical, hypothetical, theoretical

A note on diction

Make sure you don't spoil your display of verbal virtuosity by misusing or misspelling these or any other ten-dollar words. Also, get your idioms straight.

A final note on a common diction error. If, as in our writing sample, your choice involves only two options, *former* refers to the first and *latter* refers to the second. You cannot use these words to refer to more than two options.

Another common diction error occurs when comparing two or more things. The first option is *better* than the second, but it is not the *best*, which is used when discussing three or more options.

Rules to Write By

1. Write as if you were actually making the recommendation.
2. Write naturally, but don't use abbreviations or contractions.
3. Make sure your position is clear.
4. Write as neatly as possible.
5. Indent your paragraphs.
6. Don't use first person. The assignment is formal enough that it isn't appropriate here. The objective isn't to state what "I think," but to argue in favor of one option or the other. Personal experiance is not relevant.

One Final Reminder

Write legibly! If you can't, at least print.

A Sample Essay

Karen Stratton is looking for a property to buy for her animal-supply store, and has narrowed her search to two. Property One is centrally located and would allow Karen to make money quickly. Property Two is not centrally located, but would allow Karen to cultivate a special business. In view of those considerations, she should buy Property Two

Property One would certainly be convenient for shoppers. It is also accessible by all forms of public transportation, making it even easier to get to. Karen could certainly make back some money quickly by the location alone. But her store would not be unique; it would look like every other store in the area. People wouldn't be going there for any reason but its location, which means they might not be loyal customers. Also, being in the downtown area, the store might not be big enough for Karen to feature all of the items that would make her store unique, and the outside would not suggest uniqueness either.

Property Two, on the other hand, is certainly unique-looking. It's true that people would have to travel to get there, but Karen could make it into a specialty shop, by growing her own products in the garden, for example, and would make her store worth the trip. These types of stores inspire loyalty for customers looking for hard-to-find items, and thought Karen might not make back her investment right away, she would over time. Her store could also serve the farm community, whose residents might not want to travel downtown.

Another thing Property Two has in its favor is that it is probably bigger than Property One, or if not, it at least would afford Karen creative ways to use space and natural light that a downtown storefront would not. If Karen can afford to be a little patient money-wise, she could end up with a memorable, unique, lucrative business for herself.

Both properties have strengths and deficiencies as far as meeting Karen's needs. Karen should buy Property Two for her animal-supply store because its strengths outweigh its deficiencies.

6

Putting It All Together

Well, you've worked through five pretty arduous chapters of *Cracking the LSAT*. How should you feel? Answer: CONFIDENT. Why? Because you've been given a specific process for each section of the LSAT. You've got a good game plan—and the team with the good game plan usually wins the game. So here's a quick review of your game plan for each section of the exam.

ARGUMENTS

Step 1: Read the question and identify your task

Step 2: Work the argument

Step 3: Answer the question in your own words as best you can

Step 4: Use Process of Elimination

Pretty simple, right? Well, many people begin to get anxious and they tend to skip Step 3. They want to get right to the answer choices so they can start getting confused and frustrated. However, Step 3 is the most important step in this process. If you come up with your own ideas about what should be the right answer before looking at any of the choices, you'll be misled less often by those appealing but wrong answer choices.

GAMES

You should have these steps down cold by now.

Step 1: Draw your diagram

Step 2: Symbolize the clues

Step 3: Double-check your clues and make deductions

Step 4: Attack the questions

Step 5: Use Process of Elimination

As in arguments, many students tend to skip an essential step in the games process. That step is Step 3 (again). Students usually see how necessary it is to draw a diagram and symbolize the clues, but then get nervous that they've spent so much time drawing and symbolizing that they go straight to the questions. However, looking at the diagram and the symbols you've drawn for 30 seconds before going to the questions will invariably make the game easier—any deduction you make will actually save you time by making you more efficient in answering the questions.

READING COMPREHENSION

Step 1: Preview the questions

Step 2: Work the passage

Step 3: Answer the questions in your own words

Step 4: Use Process of Elimination

Well, here we've once again highlighted Step 3, because it's the most important step and it's the one students tend to skip. Again, nervousness about time is the culprit. But as you learned in the reading comprehension chapter, pinpointing the correct answer choice becomes much easier when you've already got an idea of what you should be looking for. Don't wait for the answer choices to confuse you—attack the test questions by being ready before you go wallow in the mire of the answer choices.

PACING

Believe it or not, even after you've aced the techniques and you're raking in the points like never before, there's still more you can do to improve your score.

The speed at which you work through the test makes a huge difference in how many points you get. How does this happen? It all boils down to this: The faster you work, the more likely it is that you're going to make careless errors. You've probably seen it more times than you'd like to admit. Maybe you bubbled in the wrong answer choice, or you crossed out the right answer instead of the one you wanted to eliminate, or you simply overlooked some key fact that was right there all along. But all of these mistakes are preventable!

Your mantra: *If you want to get more points, stay focused and directed but don't rush.*

Remember that the test is *designed* so that the vast majority of testers won't be able to answer all the questions. Fight the urge to rush. Use all the knowledge you've gained during your preparation for the test to make good choices about which questions to work and which questions to skip. But also, don't second-guess yourself; some questions on the test are really easy. Slow down for the tougher situations when you're only able to narrow down the answer choices to two or three, but move quickly and confidently when you predict the answer and find it in the answer choices. Depending on your most effective pace, you may find that your best results come from skipping an entire game. Or, you may find that you only need to leave off a couple of the trickiest arguments in order to maximize your effectiveness on the rest. Wherever you fall on the continuum, you'll still get some extra points by using your "letter of the day" to guess on any questions you don't work.

Take full advantage of the opportunity to work through each section in the order that's most suited to your own strengths. Each question is worth one raw point, so spend your time on the ones that will net you the most gain.

And one final note on pacing: Many test takers develop an effective method only to fall prey to the anxiety invoked by the intimidating environment on test day. Once you've learned and practiced the methods, don't abandon them on the real LSAT. Sure, you'll be stressed and worried about your score. But don't rush. Be flexible. You are armed with a strategy that you've proven to be successful through all your practice. You know what to do; don't change horses in midstream. If you find yourself feeling overwhelmed, take a deep breath and remember your mantras. Focus on the process for solving whatever type of question you're working on and don't stray from the techniques you've mastered. The process is always there to fall back on. Concentrate and take it one step at a time.

This is a general chart. Don't worry about being so exact here.

Here's a chart to help you assess your performance on the practice tests.

Pacing Yourself			
If you received . . .	**Your first goal is . . .**	**Your intermediate goal is . . .**	**Your final goal is . . .**
25–45% correct on Arguments	Work 12–15 arguments and try to get 10–12 right in 35 minutes	Work 15–18 arguments and try to get 12–15 right in 35 minutes	Work 18–21 arguments and try to get 15–18 right in 35 minutes
45–65% correct on Arguments	Work 15–18 arguments and try to get 12–15 right in 35 minutes	Work 18–21 arguments and try to get 15–18 right in 35 minutes	Work 21–24 arguments and try to get 18–21 right in 35 minutes
65–85% correct on Arguments	Work 18–21 arguments and try to get 15–18 right in 35 minutes	Work 21–24 arguments and try to get 18–21 right in 35 minutes	Work all the arguments and try to get 20–23 right in 35 minutes
25–45% correct on Games	Do two games correctly in 35 minutes	Get through two full games and halfway through a third one in 35 minutes	Do three games correctly in 35 minutes
45–65% correct on Games	Do two games correctly in 35 minutes	Get through three complete games in 35 minutes, missing only one or two questions	Get through three full games and half of a fourth game in 35 minutes
65–85% correct on Games	Get through two full games and half of a third game in 35 minutes	Do three complete games in 35 minutes and get halfway through the fourth game	Get through the entire section only missing a few questions in 35 minutes
20–40% correct on Reading Comprehension	Do two reading comprehension passages in 35 minutes, trying only to miss one question per passage	Do two full reading comprehension passages and get halfway through a third passage in 35 minutes	Do three full reading comprehension passages in 35 minutes
40–60% correct on Reading Comprehension	Do two full reading comprehension passages and get halfway through a third passage in 35 minutes	Do three full reading comprehension passages in 35 minutes	Do three full reading comprehension passages and get halfway through the fourth passage in 35 minutes
60–80% correct on Reading Comprehension	Do three reading comprehension passages in 35 minutes, trying only to miss one question per passage	Do three full reading comprehension passages and get halfway through the fourth passage in 35 minutes	Do four full reading comprehension passages in 35 minutes

THE DAY OF THE TEST

There is probably just as much bad advice as good advice dispensed about what to do on test day. A lot of the good advice is just common sense, but we're going to give it to you here just in case you're a bit distracted.

Visit your test center before test day

Why worry on test day about the best way to get to the test center? Visit the test center a few weeks or days before the test so you know exactly where to go on test day. Better yet, go there with a practice LSAT and try to get into the room where you're going to take the LSAT. Work the test in that room, if possible, so you're on familiar ground the day of the test. This will do wonders for your comfort and confidence. You'll know if the room is hot or cold, what the lighting is like, whether you'll be working at an individual desk or a long table, etc. Use the boy scout motto here: Be prepared.

Eat and drink what you normally eat and drink

People have many different ideas about what to eat and drink on the morning of the test. The most important thing is not to vary dramatically from what you normally ingest. Don't eat a big, heavy breakfast that will leave you sluggish. Don't skip breakfast completely. Eat a reasonable meal that will prepare you for a grueling three-and-a-half hour test. And don't experiment with caffeine. If you don't normally have coffee in the morning, don't start on test day. If you do normally have coffee in the morning, don't stop on test day. The same advice applies if you get your caffeine from soda or any other caffeinated beverage.

Bring a snack

Maybe your proctor won't let you munch on anything during the break, but maybe he or she will. If so, be prepared by bringing a bottle of water and some granola bars or a banana. If you're subtle about it, chances are no one will care one way or the other. Even if you're not allowed to eat in the testing room, you can always go outside and fuel up for the second half of the test.

Bring a nonbeeping digital timer

Spend the 10 or 15 dollars and get yourself a digital timer. Use it as you practice so that you'll be familiar with it on test day. You can't use a timer that beeps, so either find one that doesn't or have someone disable the speaker. It's amazing what you can do with a small screwdriver, a pair of scissors, and some tape. If you absolutely *insist* on using an analog watch, do yourself a favor and reset it to twelve o'clock at the beginning of each section. That will take the guesswork out of determining when the section will be over. And don't forget the ten minute drill: Bubble in your "letter of the day" for any questions you haven't worked and then change them one at a time as you pick up those last few questions.

Bring everything you'll need

Yes, you will be fingerprinted and asked for proper identification. You'll also need your registration ticket. Refer to the registration booklet and follow the procedures outlined there. You'll also want to have plenty of sharp pencils and a separate eraser. Don't leave any room for the unexpected.

Get there nice and early and warm up your brain

You're going to be stressed out enough on test day without worrying that you'll be late for the test. Get there nice and early and warm up your brain by working out a game that you've already done and perhaps by running through a few arguments. And don't bother to check the answers; the purpose is warming up, not diagnosis. That way, you'll already be in gear by the time you open up section 1. You want to hit the ground running so you won't be warming up on questions that count toward your score.

Some stress good, much stress bad

We know you're going to be stressed the day of the exam, and a little stress is not a bad thing—it will keep you on your toes. But if you tend to get *really* stressed by standardized tests, try a yoga or meditation class, or some other type of relaxation therapy, preferably a month before the test. This way, you'll have some techniques to calm you down, taught to you by people who know what they're doing. One Princeton Review student had a dream about test day—she went into the test, and the bubbles were about five feet in diameter. She hadn't even finished bubbling in one bubble before the proctor called time. If you're having dreams like this, relaxation therapy might help.

Wear layered clothing

Who knows how cold or how warm the test center will be on test day? Wear your most comfortable layered clothing, so you can put more layers on if you're cold or take layers off if you're hot.

Be confident, be aggressive, never say die

Sometimes we'll talk to students after they've taken the LSAT and they'll say: "By the time I got to section 5, I just didn't care anymore. I just filled in whatever." Don't say that, don't think that—section 5 will probably count, because the experimental section is usually in the first three sections of the exam. So when you open up your test to section 5, keep in mind that it's most likely a real section that will count toward your score. Your goal is to take three deep breaths and to fight your way through that last section, and attack it just as aggressively as you attacked the other sections of the exam. It's going to count—don't lose your confidence and your energy here, because it's almost over!

Here is another problem students have reported: "I was doing fine until I hit section 3. I didn't know how to do any of the games and I couldn't concentrate on the last two sections of the test." Well, guess what? That was probably the experimental section! Don't let a weird or tough section get you down, especially if it's early in the test. Remember, they are using the experimental sections to test new questions—some of them invariably will be a bit strange. And even if it is a section that ultimately counts toward your score, getting stressed out over it will only hurt your performance on that section and potentially on subsequent scored sections as well. Just roll with the punches.

Always keep your pencil moving

Actively using your pencil will help you to stay engaged. Cross off all the wrong answer choices; circle and underline key words in reading comprehension and arguments passages; always diagram and symbolize in games. By constantly keeping your pencil moving, you'll be keeping your brain moving as well.

If you find that you're losing focus, stop working for a second and regroup. Never waste time working on a question if your mind has gone astray or if you find that you can't focus on the task at hand. The few seconds you invest in a short break will pay off in the long run.

And remember that you can always come back to a question that is giving you grief. Just mark it so that you can find it later if you have time to come back to it. Don't spend too much time on any one question. It will only lead to frustration and lost points.

YOUR TEST DAY "TOP TEN"

Here are the tips mentioned above in a handy numbered list. Find some room on the fridge.

1. Visit your test center before test day.
2. Eat and drink what you normally eat and drink.
3. Bring a snack.
4. Bring a nonbeeping digital timer.
5. Bring everything you'll need.
6. Get there nice and early and warm up your brain.
7. Some stress good, much stress bad.
8. Wear layered clothing.
9. Be confident, be aggressive, never say die.
10. Always keep your pencil moving.

Good luck on test day!

7

Law School Admissions

INTRODUCTION

The process of applying to law school, while simple enough in theory, is viewed by many to be about as painful as a root canal. The best way to avoid the pain is to start early. If you're reading this in December, hope to get into a law school for the following year and haven't done anything about it, you're in big trouble. If you've got an LSAT score that you're happy with, you're in less trouble. However, your applications will get to the law schools after the optimum time and the applications themselves, even with the most cursory glance by an admissions officer, may appear rushed. The best way to think about applying is to start early in the year, take care of one thing at a time, and be totally finished by December.

This chapter will be mainly a nuts-and-bolts manual on how to apply to law school and when to do it. There will be a checklist, information about Law School Forums, fee waivers, the Law School Data Assembly Service (LSDAS), and several admissions calendars, which will show you when you need to take which step.

LSAC, LSAT, LSDAS

The Law School Admission Council (LSAC), headquartered in Newtown, Pennsylvania, is the governing body that oversees the creation, testing, and administration of the LSAT (Law School Admission Test). The LSAC also runs the Law School Data Assembly Service (LSDAS), which provides information (in a standard format) on law school applicants to the schools themselves. All American Bar Association (ABA)-approved law schools are members of LSAC. Fascinating.

LSAT SCORE DISTRIBUTION

Most test takers are interested in knowing where their LSAT scores fall within the distribution of all scores. This chart should help you determine how well you did in comparison to fellow test takers over the last few years. Please be aware, however, that percentiles are not fixed values that remain constant over time. Unlike an LSAT score, a percentile rank associated with a given test score may vary slightly depending on the year in which it is reported. This is just to give you a roughly accurate idea where you rank compared to those competing for the same spot in law school.

LSAT Score	Percent Below	LSAT Score	Percent Below
180	99.9	160	83.1
179	99.9	159	80.6
178	99.9	158	77.4
177	99.9	157	74.2
176	99.8	156	70.7
175	99.7	155	67.1
174	99.5	154	63.3
173	99.3	153	59.3
172	99.1	152	55.2
171	98.7	151	51.5
170	98.2	150	47.3
169	97.5	149	43.2
168	97.0	148	39.3
167	95.9	147	35.6
166	94.8	146	32.2
165	93.5	145	28.4
164	91.9	144	25.5
163	90.0	143	22.2
162	88.2	142	19.6
161	85.7	141	16.9

Source: *The Complete Book of Law Schools*, 2003 Ed.

When to Apply

Consider these application deadlines for fall admission: Yale Law School, on or about January 10; New York University (NYU) Law School, on or about February 1; Loyola University Chicago School of Law, on or about April 1. While some of this information may make starting the application process in December seem like a viable option, remember that law schools don't wait until they've received every application to start selecting students. In fact, the longer you wait to apply to a school, the worse your chances are of getting into that school. Maybe your chances will go only from 90 percent to 85 percent, but you shouldn't risk it if you don't have to.

Additionally, some schools have "early admissions decisions" options, so that you may know by December if you've been accepted (for instance, NYU's early admission deadline is on or about October 15). This option is good for a few reasons: It can give you an indication of what your chances are at other schools; it can relieve the stress of waiting until April to see where you're going to school; and, if you're waitlisted the first time around, you might be accepted a bit later on in the process—i.e., when everyone else is hearing from law schools for the first time. However, not every school has an early admission option, and not every school's option is the same, so check with your prospective institutions' policies before you write any deadlines on your calendar.

Law School Forums

Law School Forums are an excellent way to talk with representatives and gather information on almost every law school in the country simultaneously. More than 150 schools send admissions officers to these forums, which take place in major cities around the country between July and November. If possible, GO. For information about forum dates and locations check the LSAC website at www.lsac.org

Let's take a look at the major steps in the application process:

- **Take the LSAT**. All ABA-approved and most non-ABA-approved law schools in the United States and Canada require an LSAT score from each applicant. The LSAT is given in February, June, October (occasionally very late September), and December of each year.
- **Register for LSDAS**. You can register for the Law School Data Assembly Service at the same time you register to take the LSAT—both forms are contained in the *LSAT & LSDAS Registration Information Book* (hence the name).
- **Select approximately seven schools**. After you've selected your schools, you'll be able to see which schools want what types of things on their applications—though almost all of them will want three basic things: a personal statement, recommendations, and a résumé. Each applicant should be thinking about putting law schools into three categories: (1) "reach" schools, (2) schools where you've got a good chance of being accepted, and (3) "safety" schools. As a minimum, each applicant should apply to two to three schools in each category. (Most admissions experts will say either 2-2-3 or 2-3-2. It is not uncommon for those with extremely low grades or low LSAT scores (or both) to apply to 15 or 20 schools.
- **Write your personal statement(s)**. It may be that you'll only need to write one personal statement (many schools will ask that your personal statement be about why you want to obtain a law degree), but you may need to write several—which is why you need to select your schools fairly early.
- **Obtain two or three recommendations**. Some schools will ask for two recommendations, both of which must be academic. Others want more than two recommendations and want at least one of your recommenders to be someone who knows you outside traditional academic circles.

- **Update/create a résumé**. Most law school applications ask that you submit a résumé. Make sure yours is up to date and suitable for submission to an academic institution.
- **Get your academic transcripts sent to LSDAS**. A minor administrative detail, seemingly, but then again, if you forget to do this, LSDAS will not send your information to the law schools. LSDAS helps the law schools by acting as a clearinghouse for information—LSDAS, not you, sends the law schools your undergraduate and graduate school transcripts, your LSAT score(s), and an undergraduate academic summary.

Those are the major steps in applying to law school. From reading this chapter, or from reading the *LSAT & LSDAS Registration Information Book*, you might discover that there are other steps you need to take—such as preparing an addendum to your application, asking for application fee waivers, applying for a special administration of the LSAT, etc. If you sense that you might need to do anything special, start your application process even earlier than what is recommended in the *LSAT & LSDAS Registration Information Book*, which is unquestionably the most useful tool in applying to law school. This information book not only contains the forms to apply for the LSAT and LSDAS, but also has a sample LSAT, admissions information, the Law School Forum schedule, and two sample application schedules. These schedules are very useful. For instance, one sample schedule recommends taking the June LSAT for fall admission. This schedule allows you to focus on the LSAT in the spring and early summer and then start the rest of your application process rolling. That's good advice—as mentioned in the LSAT chapter in this book, the LSAT is the most important factor in getting into the best law school possible.

The sample schedule also indicates that you should research schools in late July/early August. While you are doing this, go ahead and subscribe to LSDAS and send your transcript request forms to your undergraduate and any other educational institutions—there's no reason to wait until September to do this (you should pay LSDAS for seven law school applications, unless you're positive you want to apply to only a few schools). Why do this? Because undergraduate institutions can and will screw up and delay the transcript process—even when you go there personally and pay them to provide your records. This is essential if you're applying for early decision at some law schools—the transcript process can be a nightmare. Your undergraduate institution already has all your money; why should they care about administrative matters like transcripts?

Average LSAT Scores

Law School	Scores
Widener University, School of Law	146–151
The John Marshall Law School	145–152
University of North Dakota, School of Law	148–155
Gonzaga University, School of Law	149–155
Rutgers University-Newark, Rutgers School of Law	154–160
Northeastern University, School of Law	152–160
University of Florida, Levin College of Law	154–160
University of Missouri-Columbia, School of Law	154–160
University of Pittsburgh, School of Law	154–161
Temple University, James E. Beasley School of Law	154–160
University of Tennessee, College of Law	155–160
Case Western Reserve University, School of Law	155–160
Loyola University Chicago, School of Law	157–161
Southern Methodist University, School of Law	156–161
University of Alabama, School of Law	157–162
Brigham Young University, J. Reuben Clark School	158–164
Emory University, School of Law	160–165
University of Southern California, The Law School	163–166
George Washington University, Law School	160–164
Boston University, School of Law	163–166
Duke University, School of Law	164–169
University of Michigan, Law School	163–168
Stanford University, School of Law	165–170
University of Chicago, Law School	165–172
New York University, School of Law	167–171
Yale University, Yale Law School	168–174

Source: *The Complete Book of Law Schools*, 2003 Ed.

Finally, you should send your applications to law schools between late September and early November. Naturally, if you bombed the LSAT the first time around, you're still in good shape to take the test again in October. Another good piece of news on that front is that more and more law schools are now just simply taking the highest LSAT score that each applicant has, rather than averaging multiple scores. If you've got to take the LSAT again, this is good news—but with proper preparation you can avoid having to spend too much quality time with the LSAT.

A simple checklist

The following is a simple checklist for the major steps of the application process. Each shaded box indicates the recommended month during which you should complete that action.

	Jan.	Feb.	Mar.	Apr.	May	June	July	Aug.	Sept.	Oct.	Nov.	Dec.
Take practice LSAT												
Research LSAT prep companies												
Obtain *Registration Information Book**												
Register for June LSAT												
Take LSAT prep course												
Take LSAT												
Register for LSDAS												
Research law schools												
Obtain law school applications												
Get transcripts sent to LSDAS												
Write personal statement(s)												
Update/create résumé												
Get recommendations												
Send early decision applications												
Finish sending all applications												
Relax												

*The *LSAT & LSDAS Registration Information Book* is traditionally published in March of each year. Call 215-968-1001 to order your materials.

Helpful Hints on Personal Statements, Recommendations, Résumés, and Addenda

While your LSAT score is the most important factor in the admissions process, you should still present a professional résumé, get excellent recommendations, and hone your personal statement when preparing your law school applications.

Many law schools still employ the "three-pile" system in the application process:

Pile 1 contains applicants with high enough LSAT scores and GPAs to admit them pretty much automatically.

Pile 2 contains applicants who are "borderline"—decent enough LSAT scores and GPAs for that school, but not high enough for automatic admission. Admissions officers look at these applications thoroughly to sort out the best candidates.

Pile 3 contains applicants with "substandard" LSAT scores and GPAs for that school. These applicants are usually rejected without much further ado. There are circumstances in which admissions officers will look through pile 3 for any extraordinary applications, but it doesn't happen very often.

What does this mean? Well, if you're lucky, you are in pile 2 (and not pile 3!) for at least one of your "reach" schools. And if you are, there's a good possibility that your application will be thoroughly scrutinized by the admissions committee. Consequently, make sure the following four elements of your application are as strong as you can possibly make them.

Personal statement

Ideally, your personal statement should be two pages long. Often, law schools will ask you to identify exactly why you want to go to law school and obtain a law degree. "I love 'The Practice'" is not the answer to this question. There should be some moment in your life, some experience that you had, or some intellectual slant that you are interested in that is directing you to law school. Identify that, write about it, and make it compelling. Then you should have three or four people read your personal statement and critique it. You should select people whom you respect intellectually, not people who will merely say, "Yeah, that looks cool." Also, your personal statement is not the place to make excuses, get on your soapbox, or try your hand at alliterative verse. Make it intelligent, persuasive, short, and powerful—those are the writing and analytical qualities law schools are looking for.

Make your personal statement intelligent, persuasive, short, and powerful—those are the writing and analytical qualities law schools are looking for.

Recommendations

Most law schools ask for two or three recommendations. Typically, the longer it has been since you've graduated, the tougher it is to obtain academic recommendations. However, if you've kept your papers and if your professors were tenured, chances are you'll still be able to find them and obtain good recommendations—just present your selected prof with your personal statement and a decent paper you did in his or her course. That way, the recommender has something tangible to work from. And that's the simple secret to great recommendations—if the people you're asking for recommendations don't know anything specific about you, how can the recommendation possibly be compelling? Getting the mayor of your town or a state senator to write a recommendation only helps if you have a personal and professional connection to them in some way. That way, the recommender will be able to present to the admissions committee actual qualities and accomplishments you have demonstrated. If you've been out of school for some time and are having trouble finding academic recommendations, choose people from your workplace, from the community, or from any other area of your life that is important to you. You should respect the people you choose—you should view them as quality individuals who have in some way shaped your life. If they're half as good as you think they are, they will know, at least intuitively, that they in some way were responsible for part of your development or education, and they will then be able to talk intelligently about it. Simply put, these people should know who you are, where you live, what your background is, and what your desires and motivations are—otherwise, your recommendations will not distinguish you from the ten-foot-high pile that's on the admissions committee desk.

Fee waivers

Even though the cost of taking the LSAT, subscribing to LSDAS, paying for LSAT prep materials, and paying application fees will probably be one-hundredth of your total law school outlay, it's still not just a drop in the bucket. The LSAT is $108 (late registrants must pay an additional $54), LSDAS is $99 (includes one report sent to an LSDAS-requiring law school and three letters of recommendation), plus $10 for each additional school you are applying to when ordered at the time that you register for LSDAS, and $12 for each additional report ordered after you register for LSDAS. And law school applications themselves are typically around $50 each. As a result, LSAC, as well as most law schools, offers a fee waiver program. If you're accepted into the LSAC program, you get one free LSAT per year, one LSDAS subscription, three LSDAS law school reports, and one TriplePrep Plus (which contains three previously administered LSATs). With proper documentation, you can also waive a good portion of your law school application fees. You can request a fee waiver packet from Law Services at 215-968-1001, or write to them at: Law Services, Attn: Fee Waiver Packet, Box 2000, 661 Penn Street, Newtown, PA, 18940-0998. You can also download a packet at www.lsac.org.

Résumés

Résumés are a fairly simple part of your application, but make sure yours is updated and proofed correctly. Errors on your résumé (and, indeed, anywhere on your application) will make you look as if you don't really care too much about going to law school. Just remember that this should be a more academically oriented résumé, because you are applying to an academic institution. Put your academic credentials and experiences first—no matter what they are.

Addenda

If your personal and academic life has run fairly smoothly, you shouldn't need to include any addenda with your application. Addenda are brief explanatory letters written to explain or support a "deficient" portion of your application. Some legitimate addenda topics are: academic probation, low/discrepant GPA, low/discrepant LSAT score, arrests/convictions, DUI/DWI suspensions, a leave of absence or other "time gap," etc. The addenda is not the place to go off on polemics about standardized testing—if you've taken the LSAT two or three times and simply did not do very well, after spending time preparing with a test prep company or private tutor, merely tell the admissions committee that that's what you've done—you worked as hard as you could to achieve a high score and explored all possibilities to help you achieve that goal. Then let them draw their own conclusions. Additionally, addenda should be brief and balanced—do not go into detailed descriptions of things. Explain the problem and state what you did about it. Simply put, do not whine.

GATHERING INFORMATION AND MAKING DECISIONS

There are some key questions that you should ask before randomly selecting law schools around the country or submitting your application to someone or other's list of the "top ten" law schools and saying, "If I don't get in to one of these schools, I'll go to B-School instead." Here are some questions to think about:

Where would you like to practice law?

For instance, if you were born and bred in the state of Nebraska, care deeply about it, wish to practice law there, and want to someday be governor, then it might be a better move to go to the University of Nebraska School of Law than, say, University of Virginia, even though UVA is considered a "top ten" law school. A law school's reputation is usually greater on its home turf than anywhere else (except for Harvard and Yale). Apply to the schools in the geographic area where you wish to practice law. You'll be integrated into the community, you may gain some experience in the region doing clinics during law school, and it should be easier for you to get more interviews and position yourself as someone who already knows, for instance, Nebraska.

Applying by computer

Almost all law schools want their applications typed. While typing is not exactly rocket science, it can be annoying.
The Princeton Review's very own www.Princetonreview.com will allow you to fill out law school applications for free on its site. The LSACD, a CD-ROM online service (215-968-1001 or www.lsac.org; $59), has a searchable database and applications to ABA-approved schools.

What type of law would you like to practice?

Law schools *do* have specialties. For instance, if you are very interested in environmental law, it might be better to go to the University of Vermont School of Law than to go to NYU. The University of Vermont is one of the most highly regarded schools in the country when it comes to environmental law. So look at what you want to do in addition to where you want to do it.

Can you get in?

Many people apply to Harvard. Very few get in. Go right ahead and apply, if you wish, but unless you've got killer scores and/or have done some very outstanding things in your life (it's okay if you haven't; really it is) your chances are, well, *slim*. Apply to a few reach schools, but make sure they are schools you really want to go to.

Did you like the school when you went there?

What if you decided to go to Stanford, got in, went to Palo Alto, California, and decided that you hated it? The weather was horrible! The architecture was mundane! There's nothing to do nearby! Well, maybe Stanford wasn't the best example—but you get the point. Go to the school and check it out. Talk to students and faculty. Walk around. Kick the tires. *Then* make a decision.

CONCLUSION

The application process, though detailed, is a lot easier than taking the extremely stressful LSAT, which in turn will be a lot easier than your first year of law school—no matter where you go. However, you've still got to want to go to law school. Otherwise, your applications will be sloppy and late, and you won't be accepted by the schools that you really want to go to. If all this administrative stuff seems overwhelming (i.e., you're the type of person who dreads filling out a deposit slip), the major test-prep companies have designed law school application courses that force you to think about where you want to go and make sure you've got all your recommendations, résumés, personal statements, addenda, and everything else together.

Whatever your level of administrative facility, the choice of where you want to go to school is yours. You'll probably be paying a lot of money to go, so you should really make sure you go to the place that's best for you. Take the time to do research on the schools, because you'll be paying for law school for a long, long time.

8

The Princeton Review LSAT Practice Test 1

ABOUT OUR PRINCETON REVIEW LSAT PRACTICE TEST

If you can't get your hands on some actual LSATs, our practice test is the next best thing. As we said in Chapter 1, you should practice on real LSATs only. Don't be fooled by the sample questions in the other books, which are only superficially similar to actual LSAT questions.

We have constructed our practice test using the same sophisticated procedures and statistical methods used in creating actual LSATs. Thousands of Princeton Review students have taken this test, so we know it is an excellent predictor of LSAT scores. It includes the four sections that contribute to your LSAT score; we have spared you the trouble of taking the unscored experimental section and Writing Sample.

HOW TO TAKE THIS TEST

Be sure to review the chapters in this book before sitting down to take this test. Clear some table space, take your phone off the hook, and try to complete these sections in one sitting. You may want to take a break after completing the first three sections. If possible, have a friend time you. Trust us: Timing yourself is not nearly the same experience.

SECTION I

Time—35 Minutes

24 Questions

Directions: Each group of questions in this section is based on a set of conditions. In answering some of the questions, it may be useful to draw a rough diagram. Choose the response that most accurately and completely answers each question and blacken the corresponding space on your answer sheet.

Questions 1–5

A veterinarian will be using four large animal cages for transport: Cage 1, Cage 2, Cage 3, and Cage 4. Each cage has an upper berth and a lower berth, and each berth will be occupied by exactly one animal, either male or female. The following rules govern assignment of animals to cage berths:

Exactly three berths will contain males.
The upper berths of Cages 1 and 2 will contain females.
If a cage has a male in one of its berths, it will carry a female in the other.
If a male is assigned to the lower berth of Cage 3, then the upper berth of Cage 4 will contain a male.

1. If a female is assigned to both berths of Cage 3, then which one of the following could be two other berths that also contain females?

(A) The upper berth of Cage 1 and the lower berth of Cage 2
(B) The lower berth of Cage 1 and the upper berth of Cage 4
(C) The lower berth of Cage 1 and the upper berth of Cage 2
(D) The upper berth of Cage 2 and the lower berth of Cage 4
(E) The lower berth of Cage 2 and the lower berth of Cage 4

2. It CANNOT be true that females are assigned to both

(A) the lower berth of Cage 1 and the lower berth of Cage 4
(B) the lower berth of Cage 1 and the lower berth of Cage 2
(C) the lower berth of Cage 1 and the upper berth of Cage 3
(D) the lower berth of Cage 2 and the lower berth of Cage 4
(E) the upper berth of Cage 3 and the lower berth of Cage 4

3. If the upper berth of Cage 4 contains a female, then a female must also be assigned to which one of the following berths?

(A) The lower berth of Cage 1
(B) The lower berth of Cage 4
(C) The lower berth of Cage 2
(D) The lower berth of Cage 3
(E) The upper berth of Cage 3

4. If a male is assigned to the lower berth of Cage 3, which one of the following is a complete and accurate list of the berths that CANNOT be assigned males?

(A) The upper berth of Cage 1, the upper berth of Cage 2
(B) The upper berth of Cage 1, the upper berth of Cage 2, the upper berth of Cage 3
(C) The upper berth of Cage 1, the upper berth of Cage 2, the lower berth of Cage 4
(D) The upper berth of Cage 1, the upper berth of Cage 2, the upper berth of Cage 3, the lower berth of Cage 4
(E) The upper berth of Cage 1, the lower berth of Cage 1, the upper berth of Cage 2, the upper berth of Cage 3, the lower berth of Cage 4

5. If the lower berth of Cage 2 contains a female, then it could be true that females are assigned to both

(A) the lower berth of Cage 1 and the upper berth of Cage 4
(B) the lower berth of Cage 1 and the lower berth of Cage 4
(C) the upper berth of Cage 3 and the upper berth of Cage 4
(D) the lower berth of Cage 3 and the lower berth of Cage 4
(E) the lower berth of Cage 3 and the upper berth of Cage 3

GO ON TO THE NEXT PAGE.

Questions 6–11

In a single day, exactly seven airplanes—J, K, L, M, N, P, and Q—are the only arrivals at an airport. No airplane arrives at the same time as any other plane, and no plane arrives more than once that day. Each airplane is either a prop or a jet (but not both). The following conditions apply:

No two consecutive arrivals are jets.
P arrives some time before both K and M.
Exactly two of the planes that arrive before P are jets.
J is the sixth arrival.
Q arrives sometime before L.

6. Which one of the following could be the order, from first to last, in which the airplanes arrive?

(A) N, Q, L, P, M, J, K
(B) N, P, Q, L, M, J, K
(C) Q, M, L, K, P, J, N
(D) Q, L, K, P, M, J, N
(E) L, Q, P, K, J, M, N

7. For which one of the following pairs of airplanes is it the case that they CANNOT both be jets?

(A) J and N
(B) K and J
(C) L and M
(D) M and K
(E) N and Q

8. If N is the third arrival, then which of the following airplanes must be a prop?

(A) J
(B) K
(C) L
(D) M
(E) Q

9. If exactly three of the airplanes are props, then which one of the following airplanes must be a prop?

(A) J
(B) K
(C) L
(D) M
(E) Q

10. For how many of the seven airplanes can one determine exactly how many airplanes arrived before it?

(A) one
(B) two
(C) three
(D) four
(E) five

11. Which one of the following pairs of airplanes CANNOT arrive consecutively at the airport?

(A) L and P
(B) N and P
(C) P and K
(D) P and M
(E) P and Q

GO ON TO THE NEXT PAGE.

Questions 12–18

A total of six pieces of fruit are found in three small baskets: one in the first basket, two in the second basket, and three in the third basket. Two of the fruits are pears—one Bosc, the other Forelle. Two others are apples—one Cortland, one Dudley. The remaining two fruits are oranges—one navel, one Valencia. The fruits' placement is consistent with the following:

There is at least one orange in the same basket as the Bosc pear.
The apples are not in the same basket.
The navel orange is not in the same basket as either apple.

12. Which of the following could be an accurate matching of the baskets to the pieces of fruit in each of them?

(A) basket one: Forelle pear
basket two: Dudley apple, navel orange
basket three: Bosc pear, Cortland apple, Valencia orange
(B) basket one: Dudley apple
basket two: Bosc pear, navel orange
basket three: Forelle pear, Cortland apple, Valencia orange
(C) basket one: navel orange
basket two: Cortland apple, Bosc pear
basket three: Forelle pear, Dudley apple, Valencia orange
(D) basket one: Valencia orange
basket two: Cortland and Dudley apples
basket three: navel orange, Bosc and Forelle pears
(E) basket one: Valencia orange
basket two: Bosc pear, navel orange
basket three: Forelle pear, Cortland and Dudley apples

13. Which one of the following CANNOT be true?

(A) A pear is in the first basket.
(B) An apple is in the same basket as the Forelle pear.
(C) An orange is in the first basket.
(D) The oranges are in the same basket as each other.
(E) Neither apple is in the first basket.

14. Which one of the following must be true?

(A) An apple and a pear are in the second basket.
(B) An orange and a pear are in the second basket.
(C) At least one apple and at least one pear are in the third basket.
(D) At least one orange and at least one pear are in the third basket.
(E) At least one orange and at least one apple are in the third basket.

15. If both pears are in the same basket, which one of the following could be true?

(A) The Cortland apple is in the third basket.
(B) An orange is in the first basket.
(C) Both oranges are in the second basket.
(D) The Bosc pear is in the second basket.
(E) The Cortland apple is in the first basket.

16. Which one of the following must be true?

(A) An apple is in the first basket.
(B) No more than one orange is in each basket.
(C) The pears are not in the same basket.
(D) The Dudley apple is not in the same basket as the Valencia orange.
(E) The Valencia orange is not in the first basket.

17. If the Bosc pear is not in the third basket, which of the following could be true?

(A) The Cortland apple is in the second basket.
(B) The Forelle pear is in the second basket.
(C) The Dudley apple is in the third basket.
(D) The navel orange is in the third basket.
(E) The Valencia orange is in the second basket.

18. If the Forelle pear and the Cortland apple are in the same basket, which one of the following must be true?

(A) The Cortland apple is in the second basket.
(B) The Valencia orange is in the second basket.
(C) The Dudley apple is in the second basket.
(D) The Dudley apple is in the first basket.
(E) The Valencia orange is in the third basket.

GO ON TO THE NEXT PAGE.

Questions 19–25

A live radio show features five bands—the Foghorns, the Geriatrics, the Hollowmen, the Inkstains, and the Jarheads—that will sing ten songs. Each band performs exactly two of the songs: one band performs songs 1 and 6, one band performs songs 2 and 7, one band performs songs 3 and 8, one band performs songs 4 and 9, and one band performs songs 5 and 10. The following conditions apply:

Neither of the Geriatrics' songs is performed immediately before either of the Hollowmen's.

The Foghorns do not sing the ninth song.

The Jarheads' first song is after (but not necessarily immediately after) the Inkstains' first song.

At least one of the Foghorns' songs is immediately after one of the Jarheads' songs.

19. Which one of the following could be an accurate list of the bands performing the first five songs, in order from song 1 to song 5?

(A) Foghorns, Geriatrics, Inkstains, Hollowmen, Jarheads
(B) Geriatrics, Inkstains, Jarheads, Foghorns, Hollowmen
(C) Hollowmen, Inkstains, Foghorns, Geriatrics, Jarheads
(D) Jarheads, Geriatrics, Inkstains, Hollowmen, Foghorns
(E) Inkstains, Jarheads, Foghorns, Geriatrics, Hollowmen

20. If the Foghorns sing the eighth song, then for exactly how many of the ten songs can one determine which band sings the song?

(A) ten
(B) eight
(C) six
(D) four
(E) two

21. If the Jarheads sing the fourth song, then which one of the following could be true?

(A) The Foghorns sing song 1.
(B) The Foghorns sing song 3.
(C) The Geriatrics sing song 5.
(D) The Hollowmen sing song 3.
(E) The Inkstains sing song 5.

22. Which one of the following could be true?

(A) The Foghorns sing song 4.
(B) The Geriatrics sing song 5.
(C) The Hollowmen sing song 5.
(D) The Inkstains sing song 10.
(E) The Jarheads sing song 6.

23. The Foghorns CANNOT perform which one of the following songs?

(A) song 1
(B) song 2
(C) song 3
(D) song 6
(E) song 10

24. Which one of the following could be an accurate list of the bands performing the last five songs, in order from song 6 to song 10?

(A) Foghorns, Inkstains, Geriatrics, Jarheads, Hollowmen
(B) Geriatrics, Hollowmen, Inkstains, Jarheads, Foghorns
(C) Hollowmen, Geriatrics, Inkstains, Jarheads, Foghorns
(D) Inkstains, Geriatrics, Jarheads, Foghorns, Hollowmen
(E) Jarheads, Foghorns, Geriatrics, Inkstains, Hollowmen

STOP

IF YOU FINISH BEFORE TIME IS CALLED, YOU MAY CHECK YOUR WORK ON THIS SECTION ONLY. DO NOT WORK ON ANY OTHER SECTION IN THE TEST.

SECTION II

Time—35 Minutes

27 Questions

Directions: Each passage in this section is followed by a group of questions to be answered on the basis of what is stated or implied in the passage. For some questions, more than one of the choices could conceivably answer the question. However, you are to choose the best answer, that is, the response that most accurately and completely answers the question, and blacken the corresponding space on your answer sheet.

Questions 1–6 are based on the following passage:

It is commonly asserted that an ideology is powerless against political interest groups and against the unflagging tendency of established social institutions to expand. To dispute this claim, however, we need only look to the present day political situation. There is, at the present time, an unfortunate political revolution under way among Western countries that is occurring in spite of potent political opposition.

For most of the postwar period, there was a proliferation of government social welfare programs designed to raise the income share of the poor. Such programs serve, in various forms, to redistribute wealth among the population at large, generally taking from those who are better situated and giving to those who are economically disadvantaged. As a result of their implementation, the plight of the poor was ameliorated to an even greater degree than was expected.

Despite these positive advances, one school of ideology, known as *redistributional retrenchment,* has long argued that the gains from redistribution programs are far outweighed by adverse economic side effects. In the wake of the worldwide slowdown in economic growth following the first oil embargo of 1973, these arguments have been treated with increasing respect, resulting in deliberate government curtailing of social welfare spending. As a consequence, in the United States, England, Germany, and even in the Netherlands and Scandinavia, public income transfer programs have been or are being cut back. On the face of it, only France and Italy seem to be resisting the trend; Switzerland, though it partook in the rapid expansion of the earlier period, has temporarily reached a plateau in spending. The political mentality that supports redistributional retrenchment now holds considerable sway. As a consequence of the deliberate government curtailment of social welfare spending, the Western poor are measurably worse off today than they were just a decade ago.

In addition, every dollar cut from the budget of such programs reduces the government payroll by twenty cents. Thus, the curtailment of social welfare programs has caused a decrease in the number of government jobs. The resulting unemployment has not been fully absorbed by the private sector. There is, then, in addition to the many poor whose benefits have been cut, a large number of middle-income citizens who oppose redistributional retrenchment.

Given those facts, one would expect everyday political forces to reverse this trend of social welfare cutbacks. Yet no reversal has occurred. Counting on fundamental principles of democracy and the ultimate power of the vote, political hopefuls have sought to attain office by appealing to such people and addressing the genuine economic distress they are experiencing. Their efforts have, for the most part, failed. Indeed, those government legislators, administrators, and executives who felt confident that they would succeed in abating the trend, simply because the number of voting citizens who stood to suffer was so large, underestimated the power of the redistributional-retrenchment ideology. It continues to advance notwithstanding the adverse effect it has had on huge sectors of the population.

1. Which one of the following best states the main idea of the passage?

(A) We must determine whether redistribution offers more benefit than cost.
(B) For a number of reasons, political pressures have failed to slow government redistribution programs.
(C) The ideology behind redistributional retrenchment is currently more powerful than the political forces opposing it.
(D) Governments have curtailed social welfare spending deliberately in order to worsen the plight of the poor.
(E) Redistributional retrenchment is contrary to democratic ideals.

GO ON TO THE NEXT PAGE.

2. According to the passage, which one of the following was most important in creating the modern trend toward redistributional retrenchment?

(A) arguments that suggest that redistribution programs have negative economic consequences
(B) the fact that most social welfare programs did not actually serve society's welfare
(C) the unexpected discovery that redistribution programs raised the income share of the poor
(D) the tendency of institutions and procedures to maintain themselves
(E) the fact that most industrialized nations have reached a permanent plateau in their ability to spend

3. In the fourth paragraph of the passage, the author attempts to

(A) prove that democracy is more potent than any individual ideology
(B) indicate that not only poor citizens are harmed by redistributional retrenchment
(C) argue that in a democracy the vote is not as powerful as it is thought to be
(D) illustrate that government officials do not always understand the political process
(E) highlight the failure of ordinary political forces to overcome redistributional retrenchment

4. It can be inferred from the passage that the author

(A) favors redistributional retrenchment but is concerned about its effect on the poor
(B) opposes redistributional retrenchment because of its effect on the poor and working class
(C) does not believe democracy can effectively represent the interests of the poor
(D) thinks redistributional retrenchment is appropriate to some nations but not to others
(E) believes that redistributional retrenchment was a hasty reaction to a temporary economic slowdown

5. The phrase "potent political opposition" (line 8) refers to

(A) the ideology that favors taking wealth from the more fortunate and distributing it to the less fortunate
(B) the political view that opposes redistribution on a large scale
(C) the adverse effects of redistribution programs on international economic transactions
(D) the large number of eligible voters who benefit from the existence of social welfare programs
(E) the large number of political officials who support redistributional retrenchment

6. It can be inferred from the information in the passage that the author believes that redistributional retrenchment

(A) has reduced profits for private industry
(B) exerts its most serious effects on public employees
(C) has produced only 20 percent of the savings its supporters expected
(D) has left private industry unable to find qualified workers to fill its needs
(E) has caused unemployment among some citizens who would otherwise have jobs

GO ON TO THE NEXT PAGE.

Questions 7–13 are based on the following passage:

A fundamental element of the American criminal justice system is trial by an impartial jury. This constitutionally protected guarantee is made meaningful by allowing the defendant to challenge and have removed from the panel those prospective jurors who are demonstrably prejudiced in the case. Such prejudice may be based on a juror's having some tangible interest in the case or on his relationship to the participants. Beyond this, a juror may be challenged if the defendant can show that the juror has preconceptions about the issues or parties that would prevent him from rendering a verdict based solely on the law and the evidence put forth at trial. In order to enable the defendant to discover these disqualifying factors, prospective jurors are subjected to questioning by the court or counsel or both. This interrogation is known as the *voir dire* examination.

Generally, the courts have recognized that any prejudice affecting the ability of a juror to decide a case fairly is a sufficient ground for a challenge. Such prejudices can be categorized in two basic ways: as a bias implied as a matter of law and as actual bias. The former may include such objective factors as a juror's relationship to a participant in the trial, whereas the latter may involve such subjective characteristics as racial, religious, economic, social, or political prejudices that would prevent the juror from trying the case fairly.

There is, however, a fundamental disagreement as to the extent to which the *voir dire* examination does, in fact, uncover juror prejudice. It has been suggested that once the prospective jurors are in the courtroom, they feel that disqualification for bias would impugn their integrity and may, therefore, be willing to lie to avoid removal from the panel.

While it may be true that people will not invariably answer truthfully on *voir dire*, the same may be said of other stages of the trial. That witnesses do not always testify truthfully at trial compels neither the conclusion that it is useless to examine or cross-examine them nor the conclusion that the trial process itself is invalid. Similarly, the recognition that prospective jurors may at times suppress what they know to be their own weaknesses need not lead to the determination that the *voir dire* process itself is worthless.

There is, for the most part, an absence of both explicit statutory guidelines and clear Supreme Court rulings indicating what specific inquiries must be made if *voir dire* is to fulfill its constitutional function. What the Constitution requires, and will be held to require, of juror interrogation as to, for example, racial prejudice is unclear. Recent case law suggests, however, that policy considerations and perhaps the Constitution itself call for some degree of direct and specific questioning as to not only racial bias, but also as to other common sources of prejudice as well.

7. The primary purpose of this passage is to

(A) criticize a constitutionally guaranteed right
(B) show how the Constitution fails to protect racial minorities
(C) examine the problems inherent in a legal process
(D) illustrate the weakness that qualifies an otherwise flawless process
(E) compare two criteria that define a legal process

8. The passage suggests that *voir dire* fails in regard to which one of the following issues?

(A) whether counsel or the court should conduct interrogations
(B) determining whether a juror is actually prejudiced with regard to a certain case
(C) the lack of specific statutory guidelines that designate when inquiries should be made
(D) the need to keep issues of law free of social, religious, racial, or economic issues
(E) the objectivity of counsel when interrogating potential jurors

9. The author states that "witnesses do not always testify truthfully" (lines 38–39) in order to highlight the fact that

(A) lying on the part of trial participants is inevitable
(B) distinguishing what is true from what is false is one of a juror's duties
(C) *voir dire* is yet another opportunity for citizens to suppress their prejudices
(D) witness testimony should not represent the exclusive premise upon which a defendant rests his or her case
(E) many levels of the judicial process can be marred by suppression of the truth

GO ON TO THE NEXT PAGE.

10. It can be inferred from the passage that *voir dire*, while possessing specific flaws, is designed to

(A) aid the defendant by providing him with a trial by an impartial jury
(B) weed out jurors who do not support the defendant's point of view
(C) reveal a potential juror's racist inclinations
(D) persuade a prospective juror that his or her duty is to reach a verdict based on the law
(E) interrogate potential jurors and make them testify to their own prejudices

11. With which one of the following statements would the author be most likely to agree?

(A) Prospective jurors should be subjected to rigorous questioning regarding their feelings toward specific social, ethnic, and economic groups.
(B) The virtues of *voir dire* need to be carefully weighed against the limitations before the process is constitutionally mandated.
(C) Because people can be depended upon to lie during a *voir dire* interrogation, the process itself should be deemed unconstitutional by the Supreme Court.
(D) Courts should clarify which prejudices constitute sufficient grounds for a challenge.
(E) While a trial by an impartial jury is a fundamental element of the criminal justice system, the *voir dire* process is the most limited way of approaching the idea.

12. Based on the information in the passage, in which one of the following circumstances might a defendant effectively challenge a prospective juror?

(A) the prosecutor and the juror share the same racial background
(B) the juror is ignorant of the laws applicable to the case
(C) the juror is shown to be a habitual liar
(D) the juror is casually acquainted with the prosecuting party
(E) the juror has been disqualified from previous *voir dire* examinations

13. As stated by the author, which one of the following might be a prospective juror's reason for suppressing information that might prejudice him or her from participating in a trial?

(A) the prospective juror's actual bias with regard to issues such as race, economics, and religion
(B) the desire to avoid maligning one's own reputation as an objective, bias-free citizen
(C) the need to feel accepted by an institution of the U.S. government
(D) the truth is considered less dangerous outside of an actual trial situation
(E) the prospective juror's desire to mask his or her relationship to trial participants

GO ON TO THE NEXT PAGE.

Questions 14–20 are based on the following passage:

Late in the nineteenth century, land reform emerged as a dominant concern of the Liberal Party in England. During this time, many prominent thinkers dissented from mainstream liberal ideology by questioning the justification of individual ownership. To John Stuart Mill, Henry George, and Herbert Spencer, for example, land represented something unique among ownable goods as "a thing not made by man, a thing necessary to life, and of which there is not enough for all." With these attributes—naturalness of origin, absolute scarcity, and centrality to all productive life-sustaining activity—land and land ownership, it was asserted, could be considered indefensible rights based upon personal labor or achievement.

Prior to the emergence of these political analysts, the *laissez-faire* views of Adam Smith were the dominant liberal position. Smith asserted that "the interests of the state require that land should be as much in commerce as any other good." The "new liberal" thinking, however, rejected this traditional notion and attacked the institutions of primogeniture and strict family settlement that enabled the landed class to maintain their estates from one generation to the next. The new liberal ideology encompassed both economic and social goals. They envisioned a break with the static conditions of primogeniture and its replacement with a more egalitarian and morally vigorous society of peasant proprietors.

In addressing the dilemma of land ownership, proponents of the new liberal thinking offered several different strategies. Herbert Spencer's proposal sought to make land the joint property of society in which all land would be confiscated by the (democratic) state. Individuals might then lease parts of it through competitive bidding. By paying rent, tenants would thus compensate all non-owners for having relinquished their claim.

John Stuart Mill employed the law of rent to show that increased land values cannot be attributed to the exertions undertaken by owners; most often, rather, such increases are the function of the "mere progress of wealth and population." In his *Political Economy*, Mill held that private property is justified only insofar as the proprietor of land is its improver. Some policies advocated by Mill included a special tax on rent, the protection of tenants' rights, state land purchases, and the prohibition of any further enclosures of common lands. While supporting some land reform measures, however, Mill insisted that present owners were owed compensation. His proposal of a special tax on land pertained to future unearned income without disturbing past acquisitions.

According to Henry George, another prominent new liberal, virtually all social and moral ills of modern society could be traced to private ownership of land. In *Progress and Poverty*, George rejects the inevitability of poverty and deprivation as remedial defects of society. In his view, rent represented not only unearned income, but a deleterious drain on much of society's earned income that absorbed the disposable surplus created by society's cooperative efforts. George's solution lay in the socialization of rent. He proposed that the community recapture its entitlement through a special tax on the rental value of land; a levy—known as the "single tax"—would eliminate the need for taxing productive enterprises and would eventually replace all other taxes.

14. The primary purpose of the passage is to

(A) discuss contrasting views on land reform among nineteenth-century English liberals
(B) trace the development of land ownership laws in England
(C) describe a current debate on land ownership
(D) prove that Adam Smith was not truly a *laissez-faire* liberal
(E) suggest a new political approach to the problem of land scarcity

15. According to the passage, all of the following characteristics were ascribed to land as justification for its special treatment EXCEPT

(A) the limited availability of land as a resource
(B) its nonartificial essence
(C) the integral nature of the commodity to human existence
(D) the effort required to increase its value
(E) the historical precedent for private property

GO ON TO THE NEXT PAGE.

16. According to thc passage, Henry George considered economic deprivation to be

(A) an unfortunate but necessary global condition
(B) a temporary state that would inevitably be reversed
(C) a condition that varied according to the policies of the ruling elites
(D) a situation that could be rectified by employing certain policies
(E) a condition that was unlikely to be alleviated

17. In addressing the issue of land reform, Mill prescribed that the unearned benefits accrued to landowners from prior transactions should be

(A) unlike future transactions in that they should not be taxed
(B) considered invalid and used for the benefits of all citizens
(C) left undisturbed by the society at large
(D) confiscated and distributed to the neediest members of society
(E) dealt with on a case-by-case basis in determining their disposal

18. The author introduces the term "new liberal" (line 19) in order to

(A) delineate the dominant political parties of the time
(B) compare the views of Adam Smith to conservative land theories
(C) present a view that differed from traditional liberal thinking
(D) differentiate between U.S. liberals and English liberals
(E) explain the traditional opposition to the institution of primogeniture

19. According to the passage, Mill believed that a landowner would be entitled to profit from his holdings as long as he

(A) did so without taking unfair advantage of the less fortunate
(B) offered some of the profits to be used for the public betterment
(C) was prepared to pay substantial taxes on his past and present holdings
(D) was directly responsible for improving the condition of the land
(E) supplied parts of the land for communal use

20. Based on the content of the passage, one can infer that, according to the traditional liberal outlook prior to the late nineteenth century, land was viewed as

(A) an entity that should be used for the benefit of the entire society
(B) a means by which wealth could be redistributed
(C) a valid, but potentially deleterious, means of producing wealth
(D) a private commodity to be bought and sold without outside interference
(E) an area that developed mysteriously even without human interference

GO ON TO THE NEXT PAGE.

Questions 21–27 are based on the following passage:

In both developed and developing nations, governments finance, produce, and distribute various goods and services. In recent years, the range of goods provided by the government has extended broadly, encompassing many goods that do not meet the economic purist's definition of "public goods." As the size of the public sector has increased steadily, there has been a growing concern about the effectiveness of the public sector's performance as producer.

Critics argue that the public provision of certain goods is inefficient and have proposed that the private sector should replace many current public sector activities, that is, these services should be privatized. Since the Reagan administration, greater privatization efforts have been pursued in the United States. Concurrent with this trend has been a strong endorsement by international bilateral donor agencies for heavier reliance on the private sector in developing countries. The underlying claim is that the private sector can improve the quality of outputs and deliver goods more quickly and less expensively than the public sector in these countries.

This claim, however, has mixed theoretical support and little empirical verification in the Third World. The political, institutional, and economic environments of developing nations are markedly different from those of developed countries. It is not clear that the theories and empirical evidence that purport to justify privatization in developed countries are applicable to developing countries. Often policy makers in developing nations do not have sufficient information to design effective policy shifts to increase efficiency of providing goods through private initiatives. Additionally, there is a lack of basic understanding about what policy variables need to be altered to attain desired outcomes of privatization in developing countries.

One study of privatization in Honduras examined the policy shift from "direct administration" to "contracting out" for three construction activities: urban upgrading for housing projects, rural primary schools, and rural roads. It tested key hypotheses pertaining to the effectiveness of privatization, focusing on three aspects: cost, time, and quality.

The main finding was that contracting out in Honduras did not lead to the common expectations of its proponents because institutional barriers and limited competitiveness in the marketplace have prevented private contractors from improving quality and reducing the time and cost required for construction.

Privatization in developing countries cannot produce goods and services efficiently without substantial reform in the market and regulatory procedures. Policy makers interested in privatization as a policy measure should consider carefully the multiple objectives at the national level.

21. The author's primary purpose in the passage is to

(A) outline some of the shortcomings of privatization in developing nations
(B) contrast the public sector's performance as producer in the United States and Honduras
(C) explain the conditions that are necessary for privatization in Third World nations
(D) justify heavier reliance on the private sector in developing countries
(E) offer a solution for the future course of Honduran economic policy

22. It can be inferred by the author's assessment of the Honduras study that a problem with introducing privatization in developing nations is that

(A) most leaders of developing nations did not concur with the policies begun during the Reagan administration
(B) the direct administration of services requires more capital than contracting out does
(C) many developing nations lack the necessary competition between contractors in the marketplace
(D) privatization of services is not politically acceptable in the struggling economies of Third World nations
(E) contracting out is limited to upgrading facilities and most developing nations need to concentrate on constructing new facilities

GO ON TO THE NEXT PAGE.

23. Which one of the following would weaken the author's statements about privatization in developing nations?

(A) The leading industrial nations have all benefited from the improved efficiency of privatization.
(B) International bilateral donor agencies have endorsed privatization efforts in developing nations.
(C) Many international economists favor the policies begun during the Reagan administration.
(D) A recent study of ten Third World nations found evidence contrary to the Honduran example.
(E) The citizens of developing nations use the term "public goods" differently than Americans do.

24. It could be inferred from the passage that which one of the following groups would most likely have an increased role in the privatized Honduran economy?

(A) U.S. banks
(B) Honduran entrepreneurs
(C) U.S. corporations
(D) international bilateral donor agencies
(E) Honduran economists

25. Based on the passage, it can be inferred that economic purists

(A) have a strict interpretation of what constitutes public goods
(B) endorse privatization only in developed nations
(C) are proponents of Honduran efforts to privatize
(D) feel that contracting out in Honduras has not led to diminished expectations
(E) disapprove of the shifting of responsibility for providing public services from the public to the private sector

26. "Desired outcomes" (line 35) partially refers to which one of the following?

(A) effective policy shifts
(B) urban upgrading
(C) political stability
(D) improved quality of outputs
(E) greater reliance on the public sectors

27. According to the passage, since the Reagan administration, there has been

(A) broad international support for privatization
(B) demand from U.S. banks for diversification of Third World debt
(C) encouragement for privatization of international donor agencies
(D) a greater privatization effort pursued in Honduras
(E) much evidence justifying privatization in developing nations

STOP

IF YOU FINISH BEFORE TIME IS CALLED, YOU MAY CHECK YOUR WORK ON THIS SECTION ONLY. DO NOT WORK ON ANY OTHER SECTION IN THE TEST.

SECTION III

Time—35 Minutes

25 Questions

Directions: The questions in this section are based on the reasoning contained in brief statements or passages. For some questions, more than one of the choices could conceivably answer the question. However, you are to choose the best answer; that is, the response that most accurately and completely answers the question. You should not make assumptions that are by commonsense standards implausible, superfluous, or incompatible with the passage. After you have chosen the best answer, blacken the corresponding space on your answer sheet.

1. The best professors never tell their students what to write. They strive instead to establish an intellectually critical environment conducive to thorough and creative scholarship, because training a student through indoctrination is never as effective as encouraging a student to develop his faculties independently. Truly impressive scholarly work can be produced only by the student who feels that he is breaking new ground, or at least treating familiar ground in a fresh and original manner.

   Which one of the following statements is assumed by the argument above?

   (A) Most students who are not told what to write produce great scholarly work.
   (B) Professors who do not enjoy the security of tenure have no incentive to teach in the fashion described above.
   (C) A student cannot create impressive scholarly work if he has been instructed on what he should write.
   (D) Many great professors do not use an authoritative and dogmatic style of teaching.
   (E) Many good students prefer being told what to write to the pressure of being encouraged to formulate their own, however original, ideas.

2. Although all prisons have some system of social hierarchy among prisoners, there are some social hierarchies in prisons that are based neither on physical strength nor on length of incarceration. However, there is no such thing as a system of social hierarchy in which no distinction is made between those who have influence over the actions of others and those who do not.

   Which one of the following can be inferred from the passage above?

   (A) The ability to measure personal influence is derived from the need for social hierarchy.
   (B) All prison hierarchies have a system with which to identify whether a given individual has influence over the actions of another.
   (C) Each individual prison community has its own unique set of criteria by which to measure social status.
   (D) There are certain aspects of social status that are common among all social hierarchies.
   (E) There are certain aspects of social status that are common among all hierarchies.

GO ON TO THE NEXT PAGE.

3. Early in this century Heisenberg stated that it is impossible to know with certainty both the position and the velocity of an electron at any specific instant. Initially, this theory was rejected by the scientific community because there was no accurate way to measure the movement of electrons. Now, however, the theory is accepted as true, not because we can measure the movement of electrons, but because no other theory of merit has been able to explain the myriad observable inconsistencies of electron behavior.

The author appeals to which one of the following principles in establishing his conclusion?

(A) The goal of science is to conscribe the vast variation apparent in nature in one comprehensive theory.
(B) Through the acceptance of mathematical models that describe observable phenomena, scientists have come to a greater understanding of the uncertainties of nature.
(C) Standard scientific method is to accept the best known explanation for an observable phenomenon regardless of its inconsistencies.
(D) Science, through the study of probabilistic phenomena, transforms the complexities of nature into easily quantifiable terms.
(E) A theory need not be supported by observational data to be accepted by the scientific community.

4. Concerned citizen: The county government's new ordinance limiting the types of materials that can be disposed of in trash fires violates our rights as citizens. The fact that local environmental damage results from the burning of certain inorganic materials is not the primary issue. The real concern is the government's flagrant disregard for the right of the individual to establish what is acceptable on his or her own property.

Which one of the following principles, if accepted, would enable the concerned citizen's conclusion to be properly drawn?

(A) Legislative violation of an individual's right to privacy is not justifiable unless the actions of that individual put others at risk.
(B) The right of an individual to live in a safe environment takes precedence over the right of an individual to be exempt from legislative intrusion.
(C) An individual's personal rights supersede any right or responsibility the government may have to protect a community from harm.
(D) An individual has a moral obligation to act in the best interest of the community as a whole.
(E) A compromise must be found when the right of an individual to act independently conflicts with the responsibility of the government to provide protection for the local environment.

GO ON TO THE NEXT PAGE.

5. As part of a new commitment to customer satisfaction, an electronics company sent a survey to all customers who had purchased its electronic personal organizer in the previous month. The survey, which was sent through the mail, asked customers to give personal information and to rate their satisfaction with the product. Of customers who returned the survey, more indicated that they had a negative opinion of the product's performance than indicated a neutral or positive opinion. On the basis of these results, the company, hoping to increase customer satisfaction, decided to allocate a large amount of capital to redesigning the product.

Which one of the following, if true, indicates the most serious flaw in the method of research used by the company?

(A) The company relied on a numerical system of rating responses rather than on open-ended questions that allow for more detailed feedback.
(B) Customers who were dissatisfied with the information display of the organizer outnumbered customers who were dissatisfied with the variety of functions offered by the organizer.
(C) Studies show that customer dissatisfaction with a new product is highest during the first year of the product's release and gradually decreases over the following years.
(D) The marketing division has found that responses to their mail-in surveys are generally accurate.
(E) People who are satisfied with a product or have no strong opinion about it are less likely to be motivated to return a mail-in questionnaire.

6. In an attempt to restructure the city's transit system, the head of the Mass Transit Authority has announced plans to cut services substantially and to increase fares on the subway and bus systems. He stated that the proposed changes represent the only means available to increase revenue and allow the Transit Authority to serve citizens better.

Opponents of the head of the Mass Transit Authority's plan would be best served if which one of the following were shown to be true?

(A) The installation of a new, more efficient turnstile system would eliminate fare evasion, saving more money than the proposed changes would raise.
(B) The revenue from the proposed changes would not be sufficient to prevent further fare increases in the future.
(C) The financial problems faced by the Mass Transit Authority were caused by a variety of factors, many of them legal as well as financial.
(D) A planned conversion from old, heavy steel cars to newer, lighter alloy cars has been factored into the Mass Transit Authority's budget, but has yet to be approved by the city council.
(E) The citizens of the city would be better served if people relied more on other means of transportation such as walking and biking.

GO ON TO THE NEXT PAGE.

7. If the water level of the reservoir falls below the "safe line," then either the amount of water being consumed has increased or the amount of rainfall in the area has been below normal. If the amount of rainfall has been below normal, then the native plant life cannot be perfectly healthy.

Assume that the reservoir level falls below the safe line. According to the passage, which one of the following statements cannot be true?

(A) The amount of water being consumed has decreased.
(B) The amount of rainfall has been below normal, and the native plant life is not perfectly healthy.
(C) The amount of water being consumed has increased, the amount of rainfall has been below normal, and some of the native plant life is perfectly healthy.
(D) The amount of water being consumed has decreased, the amount of rainfall has been below normal, and the native plant life is perfectly healthy.
(E) The amount of water being consumed has increased, the amount of rainfall has been higher than normal, and the native plant life is not perfectly healthy.

8. If we are to improve the status of our college in the public's perception, our next promotional campaign should appear in the form of full-page advertisements placed in nationally circulated magazines, rather than in radio advertisements broadcast to a variety of stations. Although advertising fees for both campaigns are roughly equivalent, the production costs of the print advertisement campaign are nearly half those of the radio campaign. Therefore, our next promotional campaign should be a print advertisement campaign.

Which one of the following, if true, would most help to explain the difference in production costs of the two campaigns?

(A) More man-hours would be required in the preparation of the magazine advertisement than in the preparation of the radio advertisement.
(B) The number of people involved in the creation of a national ad campaign is greater than the number of people involved in the creation of a local ad campaign.
(C) The layout of the print ad campaign could potentially be reused in another campaign at a later date.
(D) The perceived impact of a magazine advertisement is greater than that of a radio advertisement.
(E) The creation of the layout for the magazine advertisement can be done in house at no extra cost to the college, whereas the creation of a radio advertisement requires scheduling many hours of expensive time at a recording studio.

GO ON TO THE NEXT PAGE.

9. Schools that train students in technical skills for a specific field of work are more successful, as measured by the percentage of students that gain employment in full-time jobs in the six-month period following graduation, than are institutions that teach a liberal arts curriculum. Technical schools have a student employment rate of approximately 65 percent, whereas liberal arts schools have a rate of only 56 percent. This difference reveals that technical schools are more effectively meeting the challenge of providing education than are liberal arts schools.

Which one of the following is an assumption on which the above argument rests?

(A) Schools will not accurately report information if they believe that information will reflect poorly on them.
(B) The curriculum of a school can be evaluated by examining the number and types of job placements achieved by its students.
(C) The percent of students that gain employment following graduation is a measurement of that school's ability to provide education.
(D) The sole function of education is to help students gain employment.
(E) Technical schools and liberal arts schools serve different educational purposes.

10. Scientists have long dreamed of the technological possibilities of nuclear fusion, a process in which the nuclei of two atoms are fused together. The energy that would be generated by this process would far surpass that of nuclear fission. However, years of research have failed to produce any tangible results and, as a result, funding for fusion projects has been drastically reduced. Nonetheless, some scientists continue to believe that fusion is possible. Unfortunately, the one team that claimed to have achieved "cold" fusion failed to replicate its experimental results, and scientists believe that other explanations can be found for the results the team initially observed. Therefore, it is unwise to conclude that nuclear fusion will be achieved in the immediate future.

In the passage above, the author reaches his conclusion by

(A) criticizing the premises on which the opposing side bases its view
(B) basing his conclusion upon experimental results
(C) drawing a conclusion based on a lack of evidence for the opposing view
(D) questioning the opposing view's use of the indefinite term "cold"
(E) reaching a conclusion that is incompatible with his premises

11. At one time, nutritionists fervently advocated the consumption of large quantities of vitamins to correct certain minor health problems. They justified these claims by citing the negative effects of vitamin deficiency and by pointing out that the Recommended Daily Allowance specifies only the minimum amount of a vitamin required for normal health rather than the amount that would lead to optimal health. Recent studies, however, have discredited those recommendations by showing that high dosages can have detrimental effects.

The argument above best supports which one of the following claims?

(A) A person suffering from a minor ailment will always benefit from medical attention.
(B) Ingesting large doses of vitamins is the best way to treat minor ailments.
(C) A person suffering from a minor health problem would probably do best to avoid excessive doses of vitamins.
(D) Nutritionists were more motivated by their opposition to the Recommended Daily Allowance than by evidence of medical benefit.
(E) All minor health problems should be treated promptly, regardless of the method by which they are treated.

12. Recent studies of preventive dental care have clearly established the positive effects of regular dental care. While the frequency of visits to the dentist varies throughout the population, a general trend has emerged: Those who visit the dentist at least twice a year have significantly fewer dental problems than those who do not.

Which one of the following is most clearly implied in the argument above?

(A) An individual with few dental problems is likely to have recently visited the dentist.
(B) If one has a significant number of dental problems, it is likely that one has visited the dentist fewer than two times a year.
(C) Most people visit their dentists semiannually, and thus have little reason to worry about cavities.
(D) In order to have fewer dental problems, one need only visit the dentist twice a year.
(E) Frequency of dental care can affect the number of dental problems experienced by an individual.

GO ON TO THE NEXT PAGE.

13. In recent years, the number of reported cases of ethical misconduct in the telemarketing of stocks, securities, and other investments has risen dramatically. In answer to the growing demand for regulation of this industry, federal agencies are formulating an approach to the problem that would entail close supervision of the activities of the investment houses that use telemarketing. Such government involvement in private industry is, however, antithetical to private industry and would surely dampen the spirit of free enterprise. Clearly, in order to prevent government interference, investment houses should cease the practice of paying telemarketers on commission.

Which one of the following is an assumption upon which the argument above is based?

(A) Successful capitalism is dependent upon a governmental policy of noninterference and furthered by pro-business regulations.
(B) The government's ability to detect misconduct, even with close supervision, is minimal, and therefore useless.
(C) If judged by contemporary standards, many of these so-called violations are considered ethical.
(D) Earning a high commission as a telemarketer is not proof of one's abilities as an investment broker.
(E) The incidence of ethical misconduct is directly related to the telemarketers' desire for larger commissions.

14. A study of former college athletes revealed that, as a group, they are five times less likely to die before the age of fifty than are members of the population at large. The advice to derive from this is clear: Colleges should vastly expand their athletic departments so as to allow a greater proportion of all students to participate in athletics, thereby increasing the overall life expectancy of their student population.

Which one of the following, if true, most seriously weakens the argument above?

(A) Because participation in college athletics requires tremendous academic discipline, college athletes are better suited to succeed in society than are students who do not participate in college athletics.
(B) The students who voluntarily compete in college athletics are more predisposed to good health than are those who do not.
(C) Few colleges have the resources to increase spending on athletics, a nonessential university program.
(D) People who become active after leading sedentary lives can remarkably decrease their chances of contracting heart disease.
(E) Women, whose average life expectancies exceed men's by seven years, have traditionally had fewer opportunities to participate in college athletics than have men.

GO ON TO THE NEXT PAGE.

Questions 15–16

Dear Sirs,

In your letter, which detailed the many reasons you were not able to offer me the position at this time, you mentioned that my color blindness was the central factor in your decision. In the hope that you may reconsider, I am writing to explain that my overall vision is actually quite good. Enclosed you will find letters from three different optometrists confirming that I have never required any kind of corrective eyewear whatsoever.

Mark Furnace

15. Which one of the following would best highlight the flaw in Mr. Furnace's logic?

(A) Mr. Furnace had not been administered a complete eye examination before he wrote the letter.
(B) The evidence that Mr. Furnace mentions is not relevant to the decision made.
(C) In addressing only one of the many reasons why he was rejected, Mr. Furnace undermines his own intentions.
(D) The extent to which his color blindness was responsible for his being rejected is not made clear.
(E) Doctors' records are not considered official documentation of a person's well-being.

16. Which one of the following is an assumption upon which Mr. Furnace's letter is based?

(A) A deal can be struck with his potential employers.
(B) A person wearing corrective eyewear should not be hired for certain positions.
(C) Color blindness is not a fair criterion upon which to base hiring decisions.
(D) A note from a doctor can be sufficient to change a potential employer's opinion.
(E) His color blindness is not affected by corrective eyewear.

17. An airline representative announced the introduction of a new pricing system that uses sophisticated computer technology. Based on up-to-the-minute information on sales, the system identifies and continually updates peak times of high demand and off-peak times of low demand, keeping prices high when demand is high and lowering prices to attract customers when demand is low. As a result, the airline anticipates that large numbers of customers will choose to travel off-peak in order to experience savings, while those who wish to travel at peak times will enjoy greater availability due to higher prices. The airline therefore anticipates that the majority of customers will experience significant benefits as a result of the new system.

Which one of the following indicates an error in the reasoning on the part of the airline?

(A) The airline's conclusion is based on an unproven premise.
(B) The airline displays a naive trust in the possibilities of technology.
(C) The airline fails to factor in the cost of implementing the new system.
(D) The airline's conclusion rests on a result that would necessarily cancel out the anticipated benefit.
(E) The airline fails to establish the percentage of customers who would benefit from the change.

GO ON TO THE NEXT PAGE.

Question 18

Kristen:

Compared to a direct business tax cut, a personal income tax cut is a better way to stimulate our state's economy. A personal income tax cut would give residents greater in-pocket income. With this increase in income, individuals will be encouraged to start their own businesses. In addition, individuals will be more likely to spend more money at existing businesses.

Mark:

A personal income tax cut is not the most effective way to help business. There is no guarantee that individuals will in fact start new businesses, and the additional income may be used to purchase products from a different state or even a different country.

18. Mark objects to Kristen's argument by

(A) suggesting that a personal income tax cut is no more important than a direct business tax cut
(B) claiming that Kristen has reached a premature conclusion based on an inadequate understanding of the consequences of a business tax cut
(C) demonstrating that the negative impact of a personal income tax outweighs the positive effects
(D) questioning Kristen's use of the ambiguous phrase "in-pocket income"
(E) indicating that the positive consequences that Kristen predicts may not occur

19. Observation reveals that as children become physically exhausted, they become more prone to crying and temper tantrums. Thus, an occurrence of screaming or yelling in a small child is best remedied by providing physical rest.

Which one of the following uses the same pattern of reasoning as the argument above?

(A) People who feel insecure often compensate by acting in an aggressive manner. A person who is not acting in an aggressive manner is therefore unlikely to be insecure.
(B) Scientists establish the validity of their theories by conducting meticulously controlled experiments. Thus, a scientist who is conducting a meticulously controlled experiment is well on his way to establishing the validity of his theory.
(C) Completion of a four-year college program leads to an improvement in standard of living. A person who has not attended a four-year college program will not experience a comparable improvement in standard of living.
(D) The best way to avoid the common cold is to observe simple rules of hygiene, like washing one's hands. After all, people who don't wash their hands are far more likely to contract a cold.
(E) Habitual lack of sleep leads to a condition known as "chronic exhaustion." A person who is not chronically exhausted is likely to get regular and sufficient sleep.

GO ON TO THE NEXT PAGE.

20. Statistics show that there is a direct correlation between the ammonia content and the cleaning power of industrial-strength floor and tile cleaners; simply stated, the more ammonia, the better the cleaner. However, in a nationwide survey of commercial food services, cleaning supervisors uniformly replied that in order for any floor and tile cleaner to be effective, it must be used on a given surface twice a day with the right proportion of cleaner to water, and must be applied with well-maintained mops. The survey thus proves that ammonia content is not relevant to the efficacy of floor and tile cleaners after all.

Which one of the following best identifies the flawed reasoning in the passage above?

(A) There is no reason to assume that effective floor and tile cleaning is the only use for floor and tile cleaner.
(B) It cannot be assumed that industrial-strength floor and tile cleaners contain comparable levels of ammonia.
(C) It is unreasonable to conclude that the ammonia content is not relevant to a cleaner's efficacy just because there are requirements for the proper use of industrial-strength floor and tile cleaners.
(D) It cannot be assumed that the efficacy of all industrial-strength floor and tile cleaners depends on the same procedures for use.
(E) It is unreasonable to assume that the makers of industrial-strength floor and tile cleaners are unaware that food services don't always use them properly.

21. Products containing naproxen sodium produce relief from pain and fever by blocking prostaglandins. As a consequence of recent technological advances, production costs for pain and fever medications containing naproxen sodium, allowing for both packaging and marketing costs, are one-fifth of what they were ten years ago, while the corresponding cost for medications using the ingredient ibuprofen, which is produced by different means, has increased. Therefore, naproxen sodium is a less costly ingredient to use in medication for the prevention of pain and fever relief than ibuprofen.

The conclusion of the argument is properly drawn if which one of the following is assumed?

(A) The cost of producing pain and fever medication containing ibuprofen has increased over the past ten years.
(B) Ten years ago, ibuprofen was used more than five times as often as naproxen sodium.
(C) None of the recent technological advances in producing pain and fever medication with naproxen sodium can be applied to the production of medication using ibuprofen.
(D) Ten years ago, the cost of producing pain and fever medication with the ingredient naproxen sodium was less than five times the cost of producing medications with ibuprofen.
(E) The cost of producing pain and fever medication with naproxen sodium is expected to decrease further, while the cost of producing similar medications using ibuprofen is not expected to decrease.

22. Below is an excerpt from a letter that a medical school sent to an applicant:

We regret that we will not be offering you a position at our school. The committee has been forced to reject many highly qualified applicants because we must restrict our class size to fewer than two hundred students.

Which one of the following can be logically inferred from the information in the letter above?

(A) Only highly qualified applicants were accepted by the medical school.
(B) The applicant was considered to be highly qualified.
(C) The school had already taken its maximum number of students.
(D) Most of the applicants were highly qualified.
(E) The qualifications of applicants were not the only factor affecting admissions.

GO ON TO THE NEXT PAGE.

23. Many Americans are required to spend at least two years studying a foreign language as part of their high school or college educations. As a result of this classroom study, students are usually able to conjugate verbs, define words, and write simple sentences. Yet because even those students who received good grades during their foreign language training find themselves unable to hold a brief, unrehearsed conversation in that language, classroom training is clearly insufficient in transmitting the essential principles of another language.

Which one of the following principles, if accepted, would provide the most justification for the conclusion?

(A) If a student cannot adequately conjugate verbs or write simple sentences in a foreign language, he has not grasped the essential principles of that language.
(B) Anyone who can converse fluently in another language is likely to have the ability to conjugate verbs and define words in that language.
(C) Students grasp the essential principles of a foreign language by living in the country where that language is spoken, not by studying it in the classroom.
(D) Someone can be said to understand the basic principles of a foreign language only when she is able to converse spontaneously in that language.
(E) Any person who has not grown up speaking a given language will never truly grasp the essential principles of that language.

24. Jane Anne: Feeling frightened and delighted are mutually exclusive. Therefore, a person's behavior cannot both strike fear and evoke delight simultaneously.

Clive: That's not true. Many people love to go to horror movies. The movies frighten them and amuse them. They simultaneously cringe and laugh.

Clive has weakened Jane Anne's argument by

(A) showing that Jane Anne's argument is based on circular reasoning
(B) demonstrating that two feelings are not mutually exclusive
(C) qualifying Jane Anne's usage of the term "simultaneously"
(D) pointing out the inherent ambiguity in the relationship between "fear" and "delight"
(E) changing an argument by analogy into one based on a more reliable sample

25. Journalistic criticism of literature is falling victim to its own efforts to justify its existence. Critics believe that they garner respect from their readers by ignoring objective description in favor of opinionated commentary. Any new work is given the briefest of summaries and then mercilessly carved up in an effort to divine its deeper meaning. But the best journalist simply presents facts and allows her audience to decide their meanings independently. Critics should convey the truest possible form of the works in question; let the art, and not the art critic, speak to us.

Which one of the following statements best lends support to the argument presented above?

(A) Libraries make all new work available to the interested public without regard to critical opinions.
(B) Because space is limited, it is not practical to reproduce completely every work that is criticized in print.
(C) Writers would likely alter their style if they knew that their works would simply be read rather than criticized.
(D) Because most people have the capacity to appreciate art to some degree, it is superfluous to criticize art and a mistake not to allow people to decide for themselves.
(E) In the context described, only parts of a work could be presented, and this would lead to an increased role for the critic, who would have to decide which parts would be shown.

STOP

IF YOU FINISH BEFORE TIME IS CALLED, YOU MAY CHECK YOUR WORK ON THIS SECTION ONLY. DO NOT WORK ON ANY OTHER SECTION IN THE TEST.

SECTION IV

Time—35 Minutes

25 Questions

Directions: The questions in this section are based on the reasoning contained in brief statements or passages. For some questions, more than one of the choices could conceivably answer the question. However, you are to choose the best answer; that is, the response that most accurately and completely answers the question. You should not make assumptions that are by commonsense standards implausible, superfluous, or incompatible with the passage. After you have chosen the best answer, blacken the corresponding space on your answer sheet.

1. In France, children in preschool programs spend a portion of each day engaged in a program of stretching and exercise. Preschool programs in the United States, however, seldom devote time to a daily stretching and exercise program. In tests designed to measure cardiovascular fitness, children in the United States were outperformed by their French counterparts. It can therefore be determined that children attending preschool programs in the United States can achieve cardiovascular fitness only by engaging in a daily school program of stretching and exercise.

   Which one of the following is an assumption on which the argument depends?

   (A) A daily program of stretching and exercise will allow all children to achieve cardiovascular fitness.
   (B) Cardiovascular fitness is integral to one's overall health.
   (C) It has been proven that children who participate in stretching and exercise programs in preschool have better cardiovascular fitness as adults.
   (D) Stretching and exercise are necessary components of French children's superior cardiovascular fitness programs.
   (E) United States preschool children could make healthful dietary changes as well as changes to their daily fitness regimens.

2. In an effort to lessen the risk of liability, fertility clinics are seeking new methods of record keeping and storage that would help avoid donor sperm that might contain dangerous genes. Toward this end, a database is being developed to aid the clients in their screening of donor sperm. The database is exhaustively thorough, containing the medical histories of more than twenty thousand people, approximately half of them men.

   Which one of the following, if true, best explains why the database contains the records of almost ten thousand women?

   (A) Small fertility clinics, located in remote areas, wish to have access to a large selection of donor sperm.
   (B) Keeping genetic information on women is a standard procedure for many scientific clinics.
   (C) Some genetic disorders are not expressed until the onset of puberty.
   (D) Some genetic disorders may be carried by, but not manifested in, men who inherited the dangerous gene from their mothers.
   (E) Some genetic disorders are due to the effects of drugs and alcohol during puberty.

GO ON TO THE NEXT PAGE.

3. If the Food and Drug Administration (FDA) does not relax some of its regulations governing the testing of experimental drugs, tens of thousands of U.S. citizens are sure to die as a result of certain diseases before an effective treatment is found and made generally available.

   It follows logically from the statement above that if the FDA does relax some of its regulations governing the testing of experimental drugs, then tens of thousands of U.S. citizens

   (A) will definitely die of certain diseases
   (B) will probably die of certain diseases
   (C) will probably not die of certain diseases
   (D) will not die of certain diseases
   (E) may still die of certain diseases

4. The level of blood sugar for many patients suffering from disease *Q* is slightly higher than the level of blood sugar in the general population. Nonetheless, most medical professionals believe that slightly increasing blood sugar levels is a successful means by which to treat disease *Q*.

   This apparently contradictory argument can best be resolved by which one of the following statements?

   (A) Blood sugar levels for patients who have been cured of disease *Q* are virtually identical to the levels of blood sugar found in the general population.
   (B) Many of the symptoms associated with severe cases of disease *Q* have been recognized in laboratory animals with experimentally induced high blood pressure, but none of the animals developed disease *Q*.
   (C) The movement from inactive to advanced states of disease *Q* often occurs because the virus that causes *Q* flourishes during periods when blood sugar levels are slightly low.
   (D) The blood sugar level in patients with disease *Q* fluctuates abnormally in response to changes in blood chemistry.
   (E) Low levels of blood sugar are symptomatic of many other diseases that are even more serious than disease *Q*.

<u>Questions 5–6</u>

Many people, in the wake of an exceedingly large number of deaths in the United States caused by handguns, have argued for a federal law making handguns illegal for ordinary citizens anywhere in the United States. However, it is clear that any such proposal would be completely counterproductive. For instance, when handguns were outlawed in the city of Clarksville in 1998, the number of handgun deaths actually increased by 10 percent by 1999. Furthermore, such a proposal clearly violates the Second Amendment, which ensures every citizen's right to bear arms.

5. The above argument is vulnerable to criticism on the grounds that it

   (A) fails to consider the fact that other cities may have had different results with handgun bans
   (B) fails to define precisely the ambiguous term "handgun"
   (C) assumes that the aim of the Clarksville handgun ban was to reduce the number of handgun deaths
   (D) assumes that the Clarksville police were not responsible for a larger number of handgun deaths in 1999 than in previous years
   (E) fails to cite a legitimate authority in support of its interpretation of the Second Amendment

6. Which one of the following, if true, would most strongly support the conclusion above?

   (A) The number of handgun deaths in Clarksville increased by 20 percent from 1997 to 1998.
   (B) The number of handgun deaths in the United States increased by 2 percent from 1998 to 1999.
   (C) The number of handgun deaths in Clarksville in 1999 was not as great as the number of handgun deaths in the entire country.
   (D) The attempt to ban handguns in Brazil in 1985 also led to a drastically increased number of handgun deaths.
   (E) Canada, which has a handgun ban, has a faster growing rate of deaths from firearms than does the United States.

GO ON TO THE NEXT PAGE.

7. For our protein needs, sea plankton has none of the drawbacks that meat has. Plankton contains neither the high levels of saturated animal fat nor the dangerous hormones that commercially available meats do, and its harvest does not require the massive waste of natural and agricultural resources that meat production does. In light of these facts, it is clear that people must stop getting their protein from meat and start getting it from plankton.

Which one of the following statements, if true, most seriously weakens the argument above?

(A) Relatively few scientific studies have been done on people's willingness to make radical changes in their dietary habits.
(B) The only reports containing information on the drawbacks of plankton as a meat substitute have been funded by the United States Department of Agriculture.
(C) Greater governmental regulation of the meat industry could significantly reduce the use of dangerous chemicals and hormones in meat production.
(D) The costs incurred in the harvest of sea plankton in amounts large enough to meet the average person's annual protein needs exceed the costs incurred in the production of a similar amount of meat.
(E) As of yet, no effective means of making sea plankton commercially available for consumption have been developed.

8. Tenant Representative: Residents of units in the West Building of the Fife Arms apartment complex were recently subjected to rent increases averaging 12.5 percent, while residents of identical apartments in the East Building were given increases of, on the average, only 7 percent. Do our landlords really think that the residents of Fife Arms will believe that the maintenance costs on units in the West Building have risen more than one and a half times as quickly as the maintenance costs on units in the East Building? It seems to us that these identical units, which were built at the same time, have deteriorated equally, and we certainly haven't seen any better service here in the West Building than they have in the East Building.

Which one of the following statements would most seriously weaken the tenant representative's argument that the recent rent increases are inequitable?

(A) Before the recent increases were announced, residents of units in the West Building, who were the first to occupy Fife Arms, were not sharing the burden of the cost of maintenance of the entire complex equally with the residents of units in the East Building.
(B) Before the recent increases were announced, residents of units in the West Building, who were the first to occupy Fife Arms, were paying substantially less for the cost of the maintenance of the entire complex than were the residents of the units of the East Building.
(C) Although the units are identical in age, the rate of occupancy for units in the West Building has been higher than that for units in the East Building, resulting in more wear and tear on units in the West Building.
(D) The increases in rent were not determined by the landlords, but imposed by changes in the city regulations regarding landlord-owned residences.
(E) An independent appraiser judged units in the West Building in the Fife Arms to be one and a half times more valuable than units in the East Building.

GO ON TO THE NEXT PAGE.

9. It has long been thought that the ancestors of the human race who lived prior to the Ice Age did not have the aid of the many useful inventions characteristic of post–Ice Age humans. In particular, it has long been believed that they did not have the advantages of sharp cutting tools. Such people supposedly had to manage by tearing things, such as the animal skins that they needed for warmth, with their teeth and fingernails. However, the recent discovery of the well-preserved remains of a pre–Ice Age woman has shown this to be false. The woman was wearing a number of animal skins and carried in her hand a number of sharp-edged stones, which scientists discovered could cut through animal skins remarkably well.

A flaw in the above argument is that it

(A) makes an appeal to the authority of scientists, without giving sufficient justification for that appeal
(B) assumes that the stones were sharpened by the woman herself
(C) assumes that if a thing can be used for a certain purpose, then that purpose must be what the thing in fact was used for
(D) ignores the fact that many pre–Ice Age people used skins for other reasons besides warmth
(E) assumes that any object that could be used for cutting animal skins would be good for cutting all kinds of things

10. The accountant for a large retail store warned that more than half of the accounts receivable for the previous quarter were delinquent. He suggested that the store hire a collection agency to collect the debt immediately. His suggestion was not followed, however, when it was noted that the store had already received more than two-thirds of the total dollar amount of the outstanding accounts.

If the statements above are true, they most strongly support which one of the following?

(A) The store had already collected on twice as many accounts as remained unpaid.
(B) At least one-third of the accounts had been paid before the beginning of the last quarter.
(C) Two-thirds of the total number of delinquent accounts must have been collected by the store.
(D) The total dollar amount and the total number of delinquent accounts are not necessarily proportional.
(E) If each account paid in installments, then all the accounts paid at least two-thirds of the individual bill.

GO ON TO THE NEXT PAGE.

11. Statistics recently compiled from Fortune 500 companies seem to suggest that, in the top levels of management, those with a Masters in Business Administration (MBA) face fewer obstacles than do non-MBAs in becoming vice presidents and thus positioning themselves for further advancement. Fully 7 percent of all MBAs within the companies surveyed are vice presidents, while only 2 percent of all non-MBAs have achieved that status. Anyone planning a career in top-level management would be wise to go to graduate school for an MBA.

Information about which one of the following would be most helpful in evaluating the validity of the argument above?

(A) the percentages of eligible MBAs and eligible non-MBAs who have recently become corporate vice presidents
(B) the percentage of vice-president positions in non–Fortune 500 companies that are held by non-MBAs
(C) whether other opportunities for advancement below the rank of vice president exist in Fortune 500 companies
(D) the actual number of non-MBAs who have recently become vice presidents in Fortune 500 companies versus the actual number of MBAs who have recently become vice presidents in those companies
(E) the percentage of people with MBAs versus the percentage of people without MBAs who seek employment in Fortune 500 companies

12. Concerns about the quality of domestic motorcycles drove many consumers to purchase foreign bikes in the 1990s. But here is a motorcycle that will change all that. According to the J.P.R. Glowers customer satisfaction survey, a survey that asks motorcycle owners how they feel about their bikes after the first year of ownership, the Acme Chopper scored highest of all motorcycles in quality for the second year in a row. It also scored very high in safety features, look, and feel. It is clear that this is a bike that represents the new domestic standard: high quality for many years of enjoyable riding.

Which one of the following arguments contains a flaw that is most similar to the one in the argument above?

(A) There is no doubt that these are the finest roses in the country. Eight out of nine growers surveyed rated these the most colorful in their class.
(B) This house paint will last for decades. When it was tested on several houses it showed barely a crack after ten years.
(C) This new skyscraper will be one of the sturdiest buildings ever built. It has three separate stabilization systems, which will allow it to withstand even significant earthquakes.
(D) Even though the domestic tea market has been depressed for years, it should be coming out with some better teas soon, which will increase its market share dramatically.
(E) The best boats in the world are built by domestic boat manufacturers. We know they are the best because they last the longest of any boats in the world.

GO ON TO THE NEXT PAGE.

Questions 13–14

For many years, skeptics scoffed at the idea that plants respond to environmental stimuli other than those that directly affect the process of photosynthesis. Recent studies, however, offer contradictory evidence that seems to suggest that music, for instance, can have a direct and positive effect on plant development. Plants that were kept in the presence of music during the first six weeks of development grew considerably faster and showed fewer signs of disease than those plants developed in silence. The "music-advantaged" plants were also 35 percent more likely to survive the process of transplantation initially than were the "music-disadvantaged" plants.

13. Which one of the following is an assumption upon which the above argument is based?

(A) Many skeptics still do not believe that music is beneficial to plant development.
(B) Plants that do not thrive have been deprived of music during the first six weeks of their development.
(C) Plants that were exposed to music for longer periods of time were healthier and grew faster than those with less exposure.
(D) Some kinds of music are more beneficial to plants than others.
(E) Music does not significantly damage a plant's ability to photosynthesize.

14. A logical critique of the study cited above would most likely raise which one of the following questions?

(A) Was the type of music used during the experiment consistent over time?
(B) Were both plant groups raised in the same quality soil?
(C) Did the "music-advantaged" plants that survived transplantation live longer than the "music-disadvantaged" plants that survived transplantation?
(D) Is the idea that plants respond to environmental stimuli other than those traditionally accepted as aiding growth now accepted by the scientific community?
(E) What types of plants were used in the experiment?

15. Max: It's a travesty that our government gives away billions of dollars every year to foreign countries while people in this country are poor, starving, and living in inadequate housing. Many foreigners now live far better than the majority of our own people, courtesy of our leaders. This is clearly wrong. A government is obligated to serve its own citizens' interests first, before trying to further the interests of other people in other countries.

Alex: But that is precisely what our government is doing in giving large amounts of foreign aid. Giving such money to foreign countries ensures their loyalty to us, so that we will have their help in furthering our international goals. Thus, even though the poor people in this country may not believe that the government is serving them, it most certainly is.

Which one of the following is the point at issue between Max and Alex?

(A) whether or not foreign governments ought to give money away to other countries
(B) what should be considered in the citizens' interests, when judging the actions of a government
(C) whether or not the government should consider the interests of foreign people before the interests of its own citizens
(D) whether or not providing food and adequate housing are important functions of a government
(E) how much of the government's money should be allowed to go to foreign aid

GO ON TO THE NEXT PAGE.

16. Excessive logging has led to a sharp drop in the available supply and an increase in the price of hardwood lumber such as oak and maple. This same pattern has occurred with far too many of our scarce and vital natural resources, resulting in high prices for many products. It is likely, then, that the prices of new hardwood furniture will rise in the near future.

In making the argument above, the author relies on all of the following assumptions EXCEPT:

(A) The price of raw materials is a determining factor in the cost of new furniture.
(B) An increase in the price of lumber usually leads to an increase in the price of newly produced furniture.
(C) There will not be any substantial decrease in other costs to furniture producers that could keep the price of newly produced furniture from increasing.
(D) The cost of new hardwood furniture is affected by an increase in the price of hardwood lumber.
(E) Logging practices can substantially influence the demand for wooden manufactured goods.

Questions 17–18

Dr. Ronson: These animal tracks exhibit some interesting and strange characteristics. This first footprint appears to have two toes, whereas this second footprint appears to have three. And while this first footprint is facing north, this second footprint is facing east. Due to the weight of this evidence, we can safely conclude that these prints were made by two different animals.

Dr. Martinson: These tracks may indeed have been made by two different animals, but your evidence does not conclusively demonstrate that fact. A slight twist of the foot can make a print that seems to have extra toes. And some animals have feet that are oriented at right angles to one another, such that when they walk, their footprints face different directions. Now, if one footprint had claws while the other one did not, I would find your case more persuasive.

17. Drs. Ronson and Martinson disagree about which of the following?

(A) Any group of tracks can be determined as having been made by a single animal or more than one animal, based on the shapes of the footprints and the directions that they are facing.
(B) Any group of tracks made by a single individual would have similarly shaped footprints and would be facing in the same direction.
(C) Each kind of animal leaves a distinct kind of footprint by which it can be uniquely identified.
(D) The shapes and directions of the footprints in groups of tracks can be used to determine the number of animals who made them.
(E) It is not possible for a single animal to leave both a two-toed and a three-toed footprint.

18. Dr. Martinson does which one of the following?

(A) argues that one can never conclusively determine how many animals made a given group of tracks
(B) criticizes Ronson's conclusion based on other known facts about footprints and the properties of some animals' feet
(C) attacks Ronson's authority as a scientist
(D) disputes Ronson's reasoning by giving an explanation of the facts
(E) states an alternative criterion that would conclusively determine whether one or more animals made a given group of tracks

GO ON TO THE NEXT PAGE.

19. At current rates of emission, a tax of one cent per pound of pollutant released into the air or water would raise $15 billion. This seems to be an ideal way to pay for the new environmental cleanup program that was recently instituted by the government. Not only that, but this tax would also help prevent further need for such cleanup efforts by encouraging companies to install more modern, less environmentally damaging equipment, and in the future, the money collected from the tax could support programs such as the National Park Service.

Which one of the following most clearly identifies a flaw in the author's reasoning?

(A) The author makes a generalization based on insufficient data.
(B) The author fails to consider other possible ways to accomplish the same end.
(C) The author mistakes an effect for a cause.
(D) The author makes incompatible assumptions.
(E) The author fails to consider a possible result of the plan.

20. Vaccines have allowed us to eradicate diseases such as smallpox, polio, and diptheria. Vaccines work by the injection of a weak or harmless version of a certain virus or bacteria in order to allow the body to learn to recognize it and build a defense against it, so that if a full-strength version of the virus ever enters the body, it will be recognized and attacked before it can do serious damage. Recently, vaccine therapy itself has undergone a major change. The old polio vaccine, for instance, actually required the injection of live (although severely weakened) polio virus into the subject, thereby causing polio in about 3 percent of the subjects. However, today's more modern polio vaccine works by administering a completely crippled polio vaccine: one that has had its genetic information removed so that it can never reproduce itself or cause polio. This new vaccine is at least as effective as the old one, and it has not caused polio in a single patient since it began to be used nearly a decade ago.

If all of the above statements are true, which one of the following must also be true?

(A) Aside from the few cases of polio caused by the administration of the old vaccine, the old vaccine was completely effective in preventing polio.
(B) The body must learn to recognize viruses by some other factor than their genetic information.
(C) Once we are able to manufacture a vaccine for a certain virus, the disease caused by that virus will be eradicated within a period of years.
(D) Vaccines will only work if your body's own immune system is in perfect shape.
(E) Except for cases of polio caused by the administration of the old vaccine, the old polio vaccine was no less effective than the new one.

GO ON TO THE NEXT PAGE.

21. In order to lose body fat, you have to raise your metabolism. If you run six hours per week, you'll be able to lose body fat. Therefore, if you lose body fat, you must be running six hours per week.

Which one of the following best describes the flaw in the argument?

(A) Some people might not want to run six hours per week.
(B) Although running six hours per week may be sufficient to raise your metabolism, it may not be necessary.
(C) If you don't run at least six hours per week, you will not raise your metabolism.
(D) Some people may want to run more than six hours per week in order to get in shape more quickly.
(E) Some people are not marathon runners and may take years to lose a significant amount of body fat.

22. The current notion of corporate liability holds that no corporate head can be sued unless criminal misconduct is established. Thus the corporate head cannot be held individually responsible but is viewed simply as a part of the corporate body, rather than as a distinct entity. This makes it difficult to recover compensation for corporate negligence from a corporate head who may ultimately have been responsible for his company's negligence, and may very well be directly responsible for implementation of the negligent act.

Which one of the following best supports the argument that corporate liability should be extended to corporate heads?

(A) The assets of negligent small corporations are often sufficient to compensate for damages awarded in negligence suits.
(B) The assets of heads of small corporations are often insufficient to compensate for damages awarded in negligence suits.
(C) The threat of personal liability will dissuade corporate heads from discharging their duties improperly.
(D) Threats of corporate liability are necessary in order to recover compensation for corporate negligence.
(E) Statistics indicate that where threats of personal liability are present, corporations are more likely to violate regulations that could lead to liability disputes.

23. Sarah, a surgeon at a large hospital, asked a hospital administrator for permission to take the vital organs from a man who had just died in an accident, in order to use his organs to save the lives of several other people who needed immediate organ transplants to survive. The man carried neither identification with which to attempt to contact his family, nor anything that specifically authorized the use of his organs, such as an organ donor card. But the man did have a Goose Lodge lapel pin, and the Goose Lodge had long been in favor of encouraging its members to be organ donors.

Which one of the following principles, if accepted, would determine either that the man's organs should be used or that they should not be used?

(A) If using parts of a dead body can save people's lives, and if members of the dead person's family are notified and do not object, then those parts can be used.
(B) The fact that someone belongs to a group that encourages organ donations does not constitute consent on the part of that person to have his organs used.
(C) Authorization from a person's family, an organ donor card, or other authorizing document signed by that person is always sufficient to give permission to take that person's vital organs.
(D) If no relatives can be found after a period of 30 days, then a dead body can be used for whatever purposes its possessors see fit.
(E) Only if members of a dead person's family consent can that person's organs be used to save other lives.

GO ON TO THE NEXT PAGE.

24. A survey of urban middle-class citizens revealed some inconsistencies in their attitudes toward the homeless. More than 75 percent of those who responded said that they believed the general public to be sympathetic toward the plight of the homeless. Ironically, an overwhelming majority of the respondents confessed to going to great lengths to avoid homeless people on the street.

Which one of the following, if true, would explain the apparent paradox in the results reported in the passage above?

(A) Having sympathy for homeless people and wanting to avoid them on the street are not necessarily incompatible positions.
(B) Sympathizing with one person who has no home is easier than dealing with homelessness as an abstract concept.
(C) There was a wide variety of sentiment regarding homelessness among the respondents themselves.
(D) Many of the respondents had once been homeless people themselves.
(E) The general public is not aware of government programs designed to implement low-income housing.

25. As a result of studies that successfully established that drinking a glass of red wine with dinner can reduce the risk of heart disease, doctors have been recommending that their patients consume red wine with their evening meals. Surprisingly, according to research intended to track the effectiveness of such recommendations, many patients who followed these recommendations continued to be vulnerable to heart disease.

Which one of the following, if true, would explain the unexpected result described above?

(A) Many patients ignore their doctors' recommendations to drink wine with meals.
(B) A greater number of people are likely to drink red wine than did before the results of the study were known.
(C) The high cost of red wine has discouraged many people from consuming it regularly.
(D) Red wine is not believed to prevent all types of diseases, so it is to be expected that people will continue to have some types of diseases.
(E) The beneficial effects of drinking red wine are incurred only when the wine is drunk in moderation, which many patients fail to do.

S T O P

IF YOU FINISH BEFORE TIME IS CALLED, YOU MAY CHECK YOUR WORK ON THIS SECTION ONLY. DO NOT WORK ON ANY OTHER SECTION IN THE TEST.

The Princeton Review

Completely darken bubbles with a No. 2 pencil. If you make a mistake, be sure to erase mark completely.

1. YOUR NAME: ______________________________
(Print) Last First M.I.

SIGNATURE: ______________________________ DATE: ___/___/___

HOME ADDRESS: ______________________________
(Print) Number

____
City State Zip Code

PHONE NO.: ______________________________
(Print)

IMPORTANT: Please fill in these boxes exactly as shown on the back cover of your test book.

2. TEST FORM

3. TEST CODE

0	A	0	0	0
1	B	1	1	1
2	C	2	2	2
3	D	3	3	3
4	E	4	4	4
5	F	5	5	5
6	G	6	6	6
7		7	7	7
8		8	8	8
9		9	9	9

4. REGISTRATION NUMBER

0	0	0	0	0	0
1	1	1	1	1	1
2	2	2	2	2	2
3	3	3	3	3	3
4	4	4	4	4	4
5	5	5	5	5	5
6	6	6	6	6	6
7	7	7	7	7	7
8	8	8	8	8	8
9	9	9	9	9	9

5. YOUR NAME

First 4 letters of last name					FIRST INIT	MID INIT
A	A	A	A		A	A
B	B	B	B		B	B
C	C	C	C		C	C
D	D	D	D		D	D
E	E	E	E		E	E
F	F	F	F		F	F
G	G	G	G		G	G
H	H	H	H		H	H
I	I	I	I		I	I
J	J	J	J		J	J
K	K	K	K		K	K
L	L	L	L		L	L
M	M	M	M		M	M
N	N	N	N		N	N
O	O	O	O		O	O
P	P	P	P		P	P
Q	Q	Q	Q		Q	Q
R	R	R	R		R	R
S	S	S	S		S	S
T	T	T	T		T	T
U	U	U	U		U	U
V	V	V	V		V	V
W	W	W	W		W	W
X	X	X	X		X	X
Y	Y	Y	Y		Y	Y
Z	Z	Z	Z		Z	Z

6. DATE OF BIRTH

Month	Day		Year	
JAN				
FEB				
MAR	0	0	0	0
APR	1	1	1	1
MAY	2	2	2	2
JUN	3	3	3	3
JUL		4	4	4
AUG		5	5	5
SEP		6	6	6
OCT		7	7	7
NOV		8	8	8
DEC		9	9	9

7. SEX
MALE
FEMALE

The Princeton Review

FORM NO. 00001-PR

Test 1 Start with number 1 for each new section.
If a section has fewer questions than answer spaces, leave the extra answer spaces blank.

1. A B C D E
2. A B C D E
3. A B C D E
4. A B C D E
5. A B C D E
6. A B C D E
7. A B C D E
8. A B C D E
9. A B C D E
10. A B C D E
11. A B C D E
12. A B C D E
13. A B C D E
14. A B C D E
15. A B C D E
16. A B C D E
17. A B C D E
18. A B C D E
19. A B C D E
20. A B C D E
21. A B C D E
22. A B C D E
23. A B C D E
24. A B C D E

1. A B C D E
2. A B C D E
3. A B C D E
4. A B C D E
5. A B C D E
6. A B C D E
7. A B C D E
8. A B C D E
9. A B C D E
10. A B C D E
11. A B C D E
12. A B C D E
13. A B C D E
14. A B C D E
15. A B C D E
16. A B C D E
17. A B C D E
18. A B C D E
19. A B C D E
20. A B C D E
21. A B C D E
22. A B C D E
23. A B C D E
24. A B C D E
25. A B C D E
26. A B C D E
27. A B C D E

1. A B C D E
2. A B C D E
3. A B C D E
4. A B C D E
5. A B C D E
6. A B C D E
7. A B C D E
8. A B C D E
9. A B C D E
10. A B C D E
11. A B C D E
12. A B C D E
13. A B C D E
14. A B C D E
15. A B C D E
16. A B C D E
17. A B C D E
18. A B C D E
19. A B C D E
20. A B C D E
21. A B C D E
22. A B C D E
23. A B C D E
24. A B C D E
25. A B C D E

1. A B C D E
2. A B C D E
3. A B C D E
4. A B C D E
5. A B C D E
6. A B C D E
7. A B C D E
8. A B C D E
9. A B C D E
10. A B C D E
11. A B C D E
12. A B C D E
13. A B C D E
14. A B C D E
15. A B C D E
16. A B C D E
17. A B C D E
18. A B C D E
19. A B C D E
20. A B C D E
21. A B C D E
22. A B C D E
23. A B C D E
24. A B C D E
25. A B C D E

COMPUTING YOUR SCORE

Directions

1. Use the Answer Key on the next page to check your answers.
2. Use the Scoring Worksheet below to compute your raw score.
3. Use the Score Conversion Chart to convert your raw score into the 120–180 LSAT scale.

Your scaled score on this virtual test is for general guidance only.

Scores obtained by using the Score Conversion Chart can only approximate the score you would receive if this virtual test were an actual LSAT. Your score on an actual LSAT may differ from the score obtained on this virtual test.

In an actual test, final scores are computed using an equating method that makes scores earned on different editions of the LSAT comparable to one another. This virtual test has been constructed to reflect an actual LSAT as closely as possible, and the conversion of raw scores to the LSAT scale has been approximated.

What this means is that the Conversion Chart reflects only an estimate of how raw scores would translate into final LSAT scores.

Scoring Worksheet

1. Enter the number of questions you answered correctly in each section.

	Number Correct
Section I	______
Section II.	______
Section III	______
Section IV	______

2. Enter the sum here: ______

This is your raw score.

SCORE CONVERSION CHART

For Converting Raw Scores to the 120–180 LSAT Scaled Score

Reported Score	Raw Score Lowest	Raw Score Highest
180	99	101
179	—*	—*
178	98	98
177	97	97
176	96	96
175	95	95
174	94	94
173	93	93
172	92	92
171	91	91
170	90	90
169	89	89
168	88	88
167	86	87
166	85	85
165	84	84
164	82	83
163	81	81
162	79	80
161	77	78
160	76	76
159	74	75
158	72	73
157	71	71
156	69	70
155	67	68
154	65	66
153	63	64
152	61	62
151	59	60
150	58	58
149	56	57
148	54	55
147	52	53
146	50	51
145	48	49
144	46	47
143	44	45
142	43	43
141	41	42
140	39	40
139	37	38
138	36	36
137	34	35
136	32	33
135	30	31
134	29	29
133	27	28
132	26	26
131	24	25
130	23	23
129	22	22
128	20	21
127	19	19
126	18	18
125	17	17
124	16	16
123	15	15
122	14	14
121	13	13
120	0	12

*There is no raw score that will produce this scaled score for this form.

SECTION I

1. D	8. C	15. E	22. B
2. B	9. A	16. E	23. B
3. D	10. B	17. C	24. C
4. D	11. E	18. E	
5. D	12. B	19. A	
6. A	13. A	20. A	
7. B	14. D	21. D	

SECTION II

1. C	8. B	15. E	22. C
2. A	9. E	16. D	23. D
3. B	10. A	17. A	24. B
4. B	11. A	18. C	25. A
5. D	12. D	19. D	26. D
6. E	13. B	20. D	27. A
7. C	14. A	21. A	

SECTION III

1. C	8. E	15. B	22. E
2. D	9. C	16. D	23. D
3. E	10. C	17. D	24. B
4. C	11. C	18. E	25. D
5. E	12. E	19. D	
6. A	13. E	20. C	
7. D	14. B	21. D	

SECTION IV

1. D	8. A	15. B	22. C
2. D	9. C	16. E	23. E
3. E	10. D	17. A	24. A
4. C	11. A	18. B	25. E
5. D	12. B	19. E	
6. B	13. E	20. B	
7. E	14. B	21. B	

9

Answers and Explanations to Practice Test 1

SECTION I

QUESTIONS	EXPLANATIONS

Questions 1–5

A veterinarian will be using four large animal cages for transport: Cage 1, Cage 2, Cage 3, and Cage 4. Each cage has an upper berth and a lower berth, and each berth will be occupied by exactly one animal, either male or female. The following rules govern assignment of animals to cage berths:

Exactly three berths will contain males.
The upper berths of Cages 1 and 2 will contain females.
If a cage has a male in one of its berths, it will carry a female in the other.
If a male is assigned to the lower berth of Cage 3, then the upper berth of Cage 4 will contain a male.

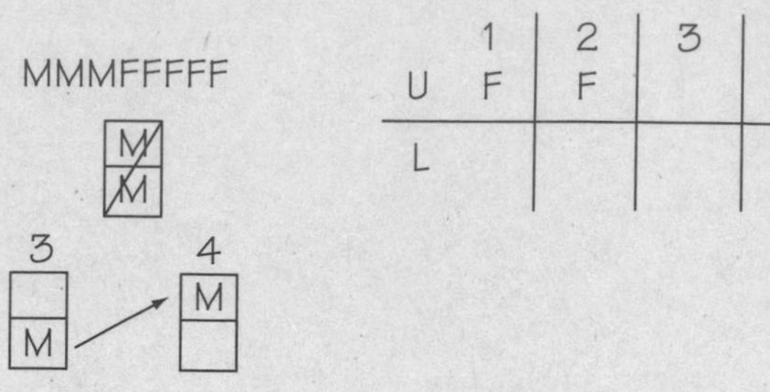

1. If a female is assigned to both berths of Cage 3, then which one of the following could be two other berths that also contain females?
   (A) The upper berth of Cage 1 and the lower berth of Cage 2
   (B) The lower berth of Cage 1 and the upper berth of Cage 4
   (C) The lower berth of Cage 1 and the upper berth of Cage 2
   (D) The upper berth of Cage 2 and the lower berth of Cage 4
   (E) The lower berth of Cage 2 and the lower berth of Cage 4

1. (A) No. This would leave two males in Cage 4.
   (B) No. This would make a total of six females.
   (C) No. This would leave two males in Cage 4.
   (D) Right. This is possible.
   (E) No. This would make a total of six females.

2. It CANNOT be true that females are assigned to both
   (A) the lower berth of Cage 1 and the lower berth of Cage 4
   (B) the lower berth of Cage 1 and the lower berth of Cage 2
   (C) the lower berth of Cage 1 and the upper berth of Cage 3
   (D) the lower berth of Cage 2 and the lower berth of Cage 4
   (E) the upper berth of Cage 3 and the lower berth of Cage 4

2. (A) No. This is possible.
   (B) Right. That would force males to double up in 3 or 4.
   (C) No. This is possible.
   (D) No. This is possible.
   (E) No. This is possible.

SECTION I

QUESTIONS

3. If the upper berth of Cage 4 contains a female, then a female must also be assigned to which one of the following berths?

   (A) The lower berth of Cage 1
   (B) The lower berth of Cage 4
   (C) The lower berth of Cage 2
   (D) The lower berth of Cage 3
   (E) The upper berth of Cage 3

4. If a male is assigned to the lower berth of Cage 3, which one of the following is a complete and accurate list of the berths that CANNOT be assigned males?

   (A) The upper berth of Cage 1, the upper berth of Cage 2
   (B) The upper berth of Cage 1, the upper berth of Cage 2, the upper berth of Cage 3
   (C) The upper berth of Cage 1, the upper berth of Cage 2, the lower berth of Cage 4
   (D) The upper berth of Cage 1, the upper berth of Cage 2, the upper berth of Cage 3, the lower berth of Cage 4
   (E) The upper berth of Cage 1, the lower berth of Cage 1, the upper berth of Cage 2, the upper berth of Cage 3, the lower berth of Cage 4

5. If the lower berth of Cage 2 contains a female, then it could be true that females are assigned to both

   (A) the lower berth of Cage 1 and the upper berth of Cage 4
   (B) the lower berth of Cage 1 and the lower berth of Cage 4
   (C) the upper berth of Cage 3 and the upper berth of Cage 4
   (D) the lower berth of Cage 3 and the lower berth of Cage 4
   (E) the lower berth of Cage 3 and the upper berth of Cage 3

EXPLANATIONS

3. (A) No. A male could go there.
   (B) No. A male could go there.
   (C) No. A male could go there.
   (D) Right. A male can't go there because of the conditional clue.
   (E) No. A male could go there.

4. (A) This list is incomplete.
   (B) A male cannot go in the upper berth of Cage 3.
   (C) A male cannot go in the lower berth of Cage 4.
   (D) Right.
   (E) A male can go in the lower berth of Cage 1.

5. (A) No. A female in the lower berth of Cage 1 would force males to double up somewhere else.
   (B) No. A female in the lower berth of Cage 1 would force males to double up somewhere else.
   (C) No. That would leave a male in the lower berth of 3, which would force a male into the upper berth of 4.
   (D) Right.
   (E) No. That would force males to double up in Cage 4.

SECTION I

QUESTIONS

EXPLANATIONS

Questions 6–11

In a single day, exactly seven airplanes—J, K, L, M, N, P, and Q—are the only arrivals at an airport. No airplane arrives at the same time as any other plane, and no plane arrives more than once that day. Each airplane is either a prop or a jet (but not both). The following conditions apply:

> No two consecutive arrivals are jets.
> P arrives some time before both K and M.
> Exactly two of the planes that arrive before P are jets.
> J is the sixth arrival.
> Q arrives sometime before L.

JKLMNPQ
j/p
~~jj~~
P—K
P—M
jjP
Q—L

	–L		–Q		–P		–Q –P
	1	2	3	4	5	6	7
				P	K/M	J	M/K
j/p:	j	p	j	p			

Many deductions can be made at the very beginning. Take a look at the chart above:

6. Which one of the following could be the order, from first to last, in which the airplanes arrive?

   (A) N, Q, L, P, M, J, K
   (B) N, P, Q, L, M, J, K
   (C) Q, M, L, K, P, J, N
   (D) Q, L, K, P, M, J, N
   (E) L, Q, P, K, J, M, N

6. (A) Right. This is possible.
   (B) No. P must be fourth.
   (C) No. P must be fourth.
   (D) No. M and K must be 5th and 7th in some order.
   (E) No. P must be fourth.

7. For which one of the following pairs of airplanes is it the case that they CANNOT both be jets?

   (A) J and N
   (B) K and J
   (C) L and M
   (D) M and K
   (E) N and Q

7. (A) No. They could both be jets.
   (B) Right. Either way, they must be next to each other.
   (C) No. They could both be jets.
   (D) No. They could both be jets.
   (E) No. They could both be jets.

8. If N is the third arrival, then which of the following airplanes must be a prop?

   (A) J
   (B) K
   (C) L
   (D) M
   (E) Q

8. (A) No. J could be either.
   (B) No. K could be either.
   (C) Yes. L must be second, and is therefore a prop.
   (D) No. M could be either.
   (E) No. Q could be either.

9. If exactly three of the airplanes are props, then which one of the following airplanes must be a prop?

   (A) J
   (B) K
   (C) L
   (D) M
   (E) Q

9. (A) Yes. J would have to be between two jets.
   (B) No. It would have to be a jet.
   (C) No. It could be either.
   (D) No. It would have to be a jet.
   (E) No. It could be either.

SECTION I

QUESTIONS	EXPLANATIONS

10. For how many of the seven airplanes can one determine exactly how many airplanes arrived before it?

    (A) one
    (B) two
    (C) three
    (D) four
    (E) five

10. (A) No. You can deduce both P and J's locations.
    (B) Right. You can deduce both P and J's locations.
    (C) No. You can deduce only P and J's locations.
    (D) No. You can deduce only P and J's locations.
    (E) No. You can deduce only P and J's locations.

11. Which one of the following pairs of airplanes CANNOT arrive consecutively at the airport?

    (A) L and P
    (B) N and P
    (C) P and K
    (D) P and M
    (E) P and Q

11. (A) No. They could arrive consecutively.
    (B) No. They could arrive consecutively.
    (C) No. They could arrive consecutively.
    (D) No. They could arrive consecutively.
    (E) Right. Q can't be third.

QUESTIONS	EXPLANATIONS

Questions 12–18

A total of six pieces of fruit are found in three small baskets: one in the first basket, two in the second basket, and three in the third basket. Two of the fruits are pears—one Bosc, the other Forelle. Two others are apples—one Cortland, one Dudley. The remaining two fruits are oranges—one navel, one Valencia. The fruits' placement is consistent with the following:

> There is at least one orange in the same basket as the Bosc pear.
> The apples are not in the same basket.
> The navel orange is not in the same basket as either apple.

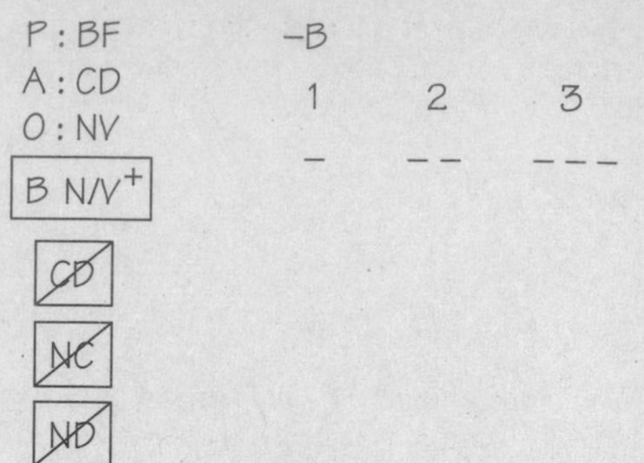

The most important deduction is that the navel orange, Cortland apple, and Dudley apple must all be in separate baskets.

12. Which of the following could be an accurate matching of the baskets to the pieces of fruit in each of them?
    (A) basket one: Forelle pear
    basket two: Dudley apple, navel orange
    basket three: Bosc pear, Cortland apple, Valencia orange
    (B) basket one: Dudley apple
    basket two: Bosc pear, navel orange
    basket three: Forelle pear, Cortland apple, Valencia orange
    (C) basket one: navel orange
    basket two: Cortland apple, Bosc pear
    basket three: Forelle pear, Dudley apple, Valencia orange
    (D) basket one: Valencia orange
    basket two: Cortland and Dudley apples
    basket three: navel orange, Bosc and Forelle pears
    (E) basket one: Valencia orange
    basket two: Bosc pear, navel orange
    basket three: Forelle pear, Cortland and Dudley apples

12. (A) No. D and N can't be together.
    (B) Right. This is possible.
    (C) No. B must be with at least one of the oranges.
    (D) No. C and D can't be together.
    (E) No. C and D can't be together.

13. Which one of the following CANNOT be true?
    (A) A pear is in the first basket.
    (B) An apple is in the same basket as the Forelle pear.
    (C) An orange is in the first basket.
    (D) The oranges are in the same basket as each other.
    (E) Neither apple is in the first basket.

13. (A) Right. Because N, C, and D must be separated, one of them must be in the first basket.
    (B) No. This is possible.
    (C) No. This is possible.
    (D) No. This is possible.
    (E) No. This is possible.

SECTION I

QUESTIONS

14. Which one of thc following must be true?

(A) An apple and a pear are in the second basket.
(B) An orange and a pear are in the second basket.
(C) At least one apple and at least one pear are in the third basket.
(D) At least one orange and at least one pear are in the third basket.
(E) At least one orange and at least one apple are in the third basket.

15. If both pears are in the same basket, which one of the following could be true?

(A) The Cortland apple is in the third basket.
(B) An orange is in the first basket.
(C) Both oranges are in the second basket.
(D) The Bosc pear is in the second basket.
(E) The Cortland apple is in the first basket.

16. Which one of the following must be true?

(A) An apple is in the first basket.
(B) No more than one orange is in each basket.
(C) The pears are not in the same basket.
(D) The Dudley apple is not in the same basket as the Valencia orange.
(E) The Valencia orange is not in the first basket.

17. If the Bosc pear is not in the third basket, which of the following could be true?

(A) The Cortland apple is in the second basket.
(B) The Forelle pear is in the second basket.
(C) The Dudley apple is in the third basket.
(D) The navel orange is in the third basket.
(E) The Valencia orange is in the second basket.

18. If the Forelle pear and the Cortland apple are in the same basket, which one of the following must be true?

(A) The Cortland apple is in the second basket.
(B) The Valencia orange is in the second basket.
(C) The Dudley apple is in the second basket.
(D) The Dudley apple is in the first basket.
(E) The Valencia orange is in the third basket.

EXPLANATIONS

14. (A) Not necessarily.
(B) Not necessarily.
(C) Not necessarily.
(D) Right.
(E) Not necessarily.

15. (A) No. This can't be true.
(B) No. An apple must be in the first basket.
(C) No. The navel orange must be in the third basket.
(D) No. The Bosc pear must be in the third basket.
(E) Right. This is possible.

16. Which one of the following must be true?

(A) No. The navel orange could be, too.
(B) No. This is possible.
(C) No. This is possible.
(D) No. This is possible.
(E) Right. N, C, and D must be separated, so one of them must be in the first basket.

17. (A) No. The second basket must hold B and N.
(B) No. The second basket must hold B and N.
(C) Right. This could bc truc.
(D) No. N must be in the second basket.
(E) No. The second basket must hold B and N.

18. (A) No. It could be in the third basket, too.
(B) No. This can't be true.
(C) No. This can't be true.
(D) No. It could be in the third basket, too.
(E) Right. This must be true.

SECTION I

QUESTIONS

EXPLANATIONS

Questions 19–25

A live radio show features five bands—the Foghorns, the Geriatrics, the Hollowmen, the Inkstains, and the Jarheads—that will sing ten songs. Each band performs exactly two of the songs: one band performs songs 1 and 6, one band performs songs 2 and 7, one band performs songs 3 and 8, one band performs songs 4 and 9, and one band performs songs 5 and 10. The following conditions apply:

Neither of the Geriatrics' songs is performed immediately before either of the Hollowmen's.
The Foghorns do not sing the ninth song.
The Jarheads' first song is after (but not necessarily immediately after) the Inkstains' first song.
At least one of the Foghorns' songs is immediately after one of the Jarheads' songs.

FGHIJ

~~GH~~

I—J

[JF]+

	–J 1/6	–F 2/7	–J 3/8	–F 4/9	–I 5/10
(20)	I	J	F	H	G
(21)				J	F

You can deduce that J can only be 2/7, 4/9, or 5/10.

19. Which one of the following could be an accurate list of the bands performing the first five songs, in order from song 1 to song 5?

(A) Foghorns, Geriatrics, Inkstains, Hollowmen, Jarheads
(B) Geriatrics, Inkstains, Jarheads, Foghorns, Hollowmen
(C) Hollowmen, Inkstains, Foghorns, Geriatrics, Jarheads
(D) Jarheads, Geriatrics, Inkstains, Hollowmen, Foghorns
(E) Inkstains, Jarheads, Foghorns, Geriatrics, Hollowmen

19. (A) Right. This is possible. Remember that this would still put one of the Foghorns' songs (the sixth) immediately after one of the Jarheads' (the fifth).
(B) No. Jarheads can't be 3/8.
(C) No. Jarheads must immediately precede Foghorns at least once.
(D) No. Jarheads can't be 1/6.
(E) No. Geriatrics can't immediately precede Hollowmen.

20. If the Foghorns sing the eighth song, then for exactly how many of the ten songs can one determine which band sings the song?

(A) ten
(B) eight
(C) six
(D) four
(E) two

20. (A) Right. You can determine them all. See diagram.
(B) No. You can determine them all.
(C) No. You can determine them all.
(D) No. You can determine them all.
(E) No. You can determine them all.

21. If the Jarheads sing the fourth song, then which one of the following could be true?

(A) The Foghorns sing song 1.
(B) The Foghorns sing song 3.
(C) The Geriatrics sing song 5.
(D) The Hollowmen sing song 3.
(E) The Inkstains sing song 5.

21. (A) No. They must sing songs 5/10.
(B) No. They must sing songs 5/10.
(C) No. The Foghorns sing song 5.
(D) Right. This is possible.
(E) No. The Foghorns sing song 5.

SECTION I

QUESTIONS	EXPLANATIONS

22. Which one of the following could be true?

(A) The Foghorns sing song 4.
(B) The Geriatrics sing song 5.
(C) The Hollowmen sing song 5.
(D) The Inkstains sing song 10.
(E) The Jarheads sing song 6.

22. (A) No. This can't happen.
(B) Right. We've already shown in our diagram that this could happen.
(C) No. This can't happen.
(D) No. This can't happen.
(E) No. This can't happen.

23. The Foghorns CANNOT perform which one of the following songs?

(A) song 1
(B) song 2
(C) song 3
(D) song 6
(E) song 10

23. (A) No. This could happen.
(B) Right. This can't happen.
(C) No. This could happen.
(D) No. This could happen.
(E) No. This could happen.

24. Which one of the following could be an accurate list of the bands performing the last five songs, in order from song 6 to song 10?

(A) Foghorns, Inkstains, Geriatrics, Jarheads, Hollowmen
(B) Geriatrics, Hollowmen, Inkstains, Jarheads, Foghorns
(C) Hollowmen, Geriatrics, Inkstains, Jarheads, Foghorns
(D) Inkstains, Geriatrics, Jarheads, Foghorns, Hollowmen
(E) Jarheads, Foghorns, Geriatrics, Inkstains, Hollowmen

24. (A) No. Forghorns must immediately follow Jarheads at least once.
(B) No. Geriatrics cannot immediately precede Hollowmen.
(C) Right. This is possible.
(D) No. Foghorns can't sing ninth.
(E) No. Inkstains must always precede Jarheads.

SECTION II

Directions: Each passage in this section is followed by a group of questions to be answered on the basis of what is stated or implied in the passage. For some questions, more than one of the choices could conceivably answer the question. However, you are to choose the best answer, that is, the response that most accurately and completely answers the question, and blacken the corresponding space on your answer sheet.

Questions 1–6 are based on the following passage:

It is commonly asserted that an ideology is powerless against political interest groups and against the unflagging tendency of established social institutions to expand. To dispute this claim, however, we need only look to the present day political situation. There is, at the present time, an unfortunate political revolution under way among Western countries that is occurring in spite of potent political opposition.

For most of the postwar period, there was a proliferation of government social welfare programs designed to raise the income share of the poor. Such programs serve, in various forms, to redistribute wealth among the population at large, generally taking from those who are better situated and giving to those who are economically disadvantaged. As a result of their implementation, the plight of the poor was ameliorated to an even greater degree than was expected.

Despite these positive advances, one school of ideology, known as *redistributional retrenchment,* has long argued that the gains from redistribution programs are far outweighed by adverse economic side effects. In the wake of the worldwide slowdown in economic growth following the first oil embargo of 1973, these arguments have been treated with increasing respect, resulting in deliberate government curtailing of social welfare spending. As a consequence, in the United States, England, Germany, and even in the Netherlands and Scandinavia, public income transfer programs have been or are being cut back. On the face of it, only France and Italy seem to be resisting the trend; Switzerland, though it partook in the rapid expansion of the earlier period, has temporarily reached a plateau in spending. The political mentality that supports redistributional retrenchment now holds considerable sway. As a consequence of the deliberate government curtailment of social welfare spending, the Western poor are measurably worse off today than they were just a decade ago.

In addition, every dollar cut from the budget of such programs reduces the government payroll by twenty cents. Thus, the curtailment of social welfare programs has caused a decrease in the number of government jobs. The resulting unemployment has not been fully absorbed by the private sector. There is, then, in addition to the many poor whose benefits have been cut, a large number of middle-income citizens who oppose redistributional retrenchment.

Given those facts, one would expect everyday political forces to reverse this trend of social welfare cutbacks. Yet no reversal has occurred. Counting on fundamental principles of democracy and the ultimate power of the vote, political hopefuls have sought to attain office by appealing to such people and addressing the genuine economic distress they are experiencing. Their efforts have, for the most part, failed. Indeed, those government legislators, administrators, and executives who felt confident that they would succeed in abating the trend, simply because the number of voting citizens who stood to suffer was so large, underestimated the power of the redistributional-retrenchment ideology. It continues to advance notwithstanding the adverse effect it has had on huge sectors of the population.

SECTION II

QUESTIONS

1. Which one of the following best states the main idea of the passage?

   (A) We must determine whether redistribution offers more benefit than cost.
   (B) For a number of reasons, political pressures have failed to slow government redistribution programs.
   (C) The ideology behind redistributional retrenchment is currently more powerful than the political forces opposing it.
   (D) Governments have curtailed social welfare spending deliberately in order to worsen the plight of the poor.
   (E) Redistributional retrenchment is contrary to democratic ideals.

2. According to the passage, which one of the following was most important in creating the modern trend toward redistributional retrenchment?

   (A) arguments that suggest that redistribution programs have negative economic consequences
   (B) the fact that most social welfare programs did not actually serve society's welfare
   (C) the unexpected discovery that redistribution programs raised the income share of the poor
   (D) the tendency of institutions and procedures to maintain themselves
   (E) the fact that most industrialized nations have reached a permanent plateau in their ability to spend

EXPLANATIONS

1. This is a MAIN IDEA question. Come up with your own main idea before you go to the answer choices.

   (A) No, it's pretty clear that the author thinks redistribution is a good thing and that redistributional retrenchment is a bad thing. If you're not convinced, re-read the last paragraph.
   (B) No, they have failed to slow redistributional retrenchment.
   (C) Yes. Redistributional retrenchment is still plowing away even though it's bad.
   (D) The author doesn't say that governments deliberately hurt the poor.
   (E) Maybe, but the author doesn't mention democratic ideals—he just thinks that redistributional retrenchment is a bad idea.

2. This is a SPECIFIC question. Find the part of the passage that first mentions redistributional retrenchment.

   (A) Yes, this is mentioned in lines 18–21.
   (B) They do serve society's welfare—see lines 15–17.
   (C) It was hardly unexpected—it was the goal of the redistribution programs.
   (D) This has nothing to do with anything. Classic LSAT gibberish.
   (E) This is referencing the wrong part of the passage. It's referring to the part about Switzerland. Eliminate it.

SECTION II

QUESTIONS

3. In the fourth paragraph of the passage, the author attempts to

(A) prove that democracy is more potent than any individual ideology
(B) indicate that not only poor citizens are harmed by redistributional retrenchment
(C) argue that in a democracy the vote is not as powerful as it is thought to be
(D) illustrate that government officials do not always understand the political process
(E) highlight the failure of ordinary political forces to overcome redistributional retrenchment

4. It can be inferred from the passage that the author

(A) favors redistributional retrenchment but is concerned about its effect on the poor
(B) opposes redistributional retrenchment because of its effect on the poor and working class
(C) does not believe democracy can effectively represent the interests of the poor
(D) thinks redistributional retrenchment is appropriate to some nations but not to others
(E) believes that redistributional retrenchment was a hasty reaction to a temporary economic slowdown

EXPLANATIONS

3. This is a PARAGRAPH REFERENCE question. Reread paragraph four and see what its purpose was.

(A) The words "prove" and "any" are too extreme here.
(B) Yes. The author shows how the middle class was affected as well.
(C) This is discussed in paragraph five.
(D) Understanding the political process is not mentioned in the paragraph.
(E) This is discussed in paragraph five.

4. This is a GENERAL question. You have to read the choices and see which is closest to what the author thinks.

(A) The author opposes redistributional retrenchment. Eliminate it.
(B) Yes. See paragraph 4 and the last line of the passage.
(C) The author's not talking about democracy, but about redistributional retrenchment.
(D) The author never gives any examples of how it is a good thing anywhere.
(E) No, the author says that the redistributional retrenchment school has "long argued" for it. See line 20.

SECTION II

QUESTIONS

5. The phrase "potent political opposition" (line 8) refers to

    (A) the ideology that favors taking wealth from the more fortunate and distributing it to the less fortunate
    (B) the political view that opposes redistribution on a large scale
    (C) the adverse effects of redistribution programs on international economic transactions
    (D) the large number of eligible voters who benefit from the existence of social welfare programs
    (E) the large number of political officials who support redistributional retrenchment

6. It can be inferred from the information in the passage that the author believes that redistributional retrenchment

    (A) has reduced profits for private industry
    (B) exerts its most serious effects on public employees
    (C) has produced only 20 percent of the savings its supporters expected
    (D) has left private industry unable to find qualified workers to fill its needs
    (E) has caused unemployment among some citizens who would otherwise have jobs

EXPLANATIONS

5. This is a LINE REFERENCE question. Read five lines above and five lines below the line reference.

    (A) An ideology isn't political opposition, people are.
    (B) This is the opposite of what you are looking for. "Potent political opposition" refers to those who oppose redistributional retrenchment.
    (C) An effect isn't political opposition, people are.
    (D) Right. Here are the people who support redistribution and make up the "political opposition" to retrenchment.
    (E) No, we learn that many officials don't support it. But it's continuing anyway.

6. This is a SPECIFIC question. Answer in your own words what the author thinks redistributional retrenchment has caused.

    (A) No, it has just not increased the number of jobs in private industry substantially.
    (B) No, "most serious effects" is too extreme.
    (C) This is not mentioned anywhere in the passage.
    (D) No, an inability to find qualified workers isn't mentioned.
    (E) Right. There are more middle-class people out of work because of it.

SECTION II

Questions 7–13 are based on the following passage:

A fundamental element of the American criminal justice system is trial by an impartial jury. This constitutionally protected guarantee is made meaningful by allowing the defendant to challenge and have removed from the panel those prospective jurors who are demonstrably prejudiced in the case. Such prejudice may be based on a juror's having some tangible interest in the case or on his relationship to the participants. Beyond this, a juror may be challenged if the defendant can show that the juror has preconceptions about the issues or parties that would prevent him from rendering a verdict based solely on the law and the evidence put forth at trial. In order to enable the defendant to discover these disqualifying factors, prospective jurors are subjected to questioning by the court or counsel or both. This interrogation is known as the *voir dire* examination.

Generally, the courts have recognized that any prejudice affecting the ability of a juror to decide a case fairly is a sufficient ground for a challenge. Such prejudices can be categorized in two basic ways: as a bias implied as a matter of law and as actual bias. The former may include such objective factors as a juror's relationship to a participant in the trial, whereas the latter may involve such subjective characteristics as racial, religious, economic, social, or political prejudices that would prevent the juror from trying the case fairly.

There is, however, a fundamental disagreement as to the extent to which the *voir dire* examination does, in fact, uncover juror prejudice. It has been suggested that once the prospective jurors are in the courtroom, they feel that disqualification for bias would impugn their integrity and may, therefore, be willing to lie to avoid removal from the panel.

While it may be true that people will not invariably answer truthfully on *voir dire*, the same may be said of other stages of the trial. That witnesses do not always testify truthfully at trial compels neither the conclusion that it is useless to examine or cross-examine them nor the conclusion that the trial process itself is invalid. Similarly, the recognition that prospective jurors may at times suppress what they know to be their own weaknesses need not lead to the determination that the *voir dire* process itself is worthless.

There is, for the most part, an absence of both explicit statutory guidelines and clear Supreme Court rulings indicating what specific inquiries must be made if *voir dire* is to fulfill its constitutional function. What the Constitution requires, and will be held to require, of juror interrogation as to, for example, racial prejudice is unclear. Recent case law suggests, however, that policy considerations and perhaps the Constitution itself call for some degree of direct and specific questioning as to not only racial bias, but also as to other common sources of prejudice as well.

SECTION II

QUESTIONS	EXPLANATIONS

7. The primary purpose of this passage is to

(A) criticize a constitutionally guaranteed right
(B) show how the Constitution fails to protect racial minorities
(C) examine the problems inherent in a legal process
(D) illustrate the weakness that qualifies an otherwise flawless process
(E) compare two criteria that define a legal process

7. This is a PRIMARY PURPOSE question. Answer in your own words first and then look at the choices.

(A) No, overall the author thinks the *voir dire* process is a good one.
(B) No, the correct answer should reference the *voir dire* process.
(C) Yes. "A legal process" is referring to the *voir dire* process.
(D) "Flawless process" is a bit too enthusiastic for this passage.
(E) What two criteria? The *voir dire* process is more complex than that.

8. The passage suggests that *voir dire* fails in regard to which one of the following issues?

(A) whether counsel or the court should conduct interrogations
(B) determining whether a juror is actually prejudiced with regard to a certain case
(C) the lack of specific statutory guidelines that designate when inquiries should be made
(D) the need to keep issues of law free of social, religious, racial, or economic issues
(E) the objectivity of counsel when interrogating potential jurors

8. This is a SPECIFIC question. Find a part of the passage that talks about when *voir dire* doesn't work.

(A) No, it doesn't matter who conducts the investigations.
(B) Yes, see lines 29–31. It doesn't always work.
(C) Not *when* inquiries should be made, but *what* inquiries should be made. See line 48.
(D) This is way too general; we're only talking about *voir dire* here.
(E) Counsel objectivity is not an issue that was raised in the passage. Eliminate it.

9. The author states that "witnesses do not always testify truthfully" (lines 38–39) in order to highlight the fact that

(A) lying on the part of trial participants is inevitable
(B) distinguishing what is true from what is false is one of a juror's duties
(C) *voir dire* is yet another opportunity for citizens to suppress their prejudices
(D) witness testimony should not represent the exclusive premise upon which a defendant rests his or her case
(E) many levels of the judicial process can be marred by suppression of the truth

9. This is a LINE REFERENCE question. Read five lines above and five lines below the line reference.

(A) This is a bit too extreme. Is it really inevitable? In all cases?
(B) The author's not talking about jurors' duties in this passage. Eliminate it.
(C) This answer choice was written by a conspiracy theorist. Eliminate it.
(D) This is true but that's not why it was mentioned. It is an example used to illustrate something about the *voir dire* process.
(E) Yes—suppression of the truth affects both the testimony of witnesses on the stand AND the claims of prospective jurors during the *voir dire* process.

QUESTIONS	EXPLANATIONS

10. It can be inferred from the passage that *voir dire*, while possessing specific flaws, is designed to

(A) aid the defendant by providing him with a trial by an impartial jury
(B) weed out jurors who do not support the defendant's point of view
(C) reveal a potential juror's racist inclinations
(D) persuade a prospective juror that his or her duty is to reach a verdict based on the law
(E) interrogate potential jurors and make them testify to their own prejudices

10. This is a SPECIFIC question asking about the purpose of the *voir dire* process. Find the part about the *voir dire* process in the passage.

(A) This is right. We're using the *voir dire* process to weed out prejudiced people. Re-read the first paragraph.
(B) No, the process is to find impartial people. Eliminate it.
(C) The purpose of the *voir dire* process is a bit broader than this. Eliminate it.
(D) The *voir dire* process is not related to convincing anybody. Eliminate it.
(E) This is a bit harsh. We don't want to torture these people. Eliminate it.

11. With which one of the following statements would the author be most likely to agree?

(A) Prospective jurors should be subjected to rigorous questioning regarding their feelings toward specific social, ethnic, and economic groups.
(B) The virtues of *voir dire* need to be carefully weighed against the limitations before the process is constitutionally mandated.
(C) Because people can be depended upon to lie during a *voir dire* interrogation, the process itself should be deemed unconstitutional by the Supreme Court.
(D) Courts should clarify which prejudices constitute sufficient grounds for a challenge.
(E) While a trial by an impartial jury is a fundamental element of the criminal justice system, the *voir dire* process is the most limited way of approaching the idea.

11. This is a GENERAL question. Find the choice that is most in line with the main idea of the author and the primary purpose of the passage.

(A) Yes, this should be done to make sure that the jurors aren't prejudiced.
(B) There's nothing in the passage about whether or not the author thinks the *voir dire* process should be constitutionally mandated. Eliminate it.
(C) Remember, the author likes the process overall. This is too extreme.
(D) Which courts? You can't prove this choice with information from the passage. Eliminate it.
(E) Remember, the author likes the process and doesn't think it's all that limiting.

SECTION II

QUESTIONS	EXPLANATIONS

12. Based on the information in the passage, in which one of the following circumstances might a defendant effectively challenge a prospective juror?

(A) the prosecutor and the juror share the same racial background
(B) the juror is ignorant of the laws applicable to the case
(C) the juror is shown to be a habitual liar
(D) the juror is casually acquainted with the prosecuting party
(E) the juror has been disqualified from previous *voir dire* examinations

13. As stated by the author, which one of the following might be a prospective juror's reason for suppressing information that might prejudice him or her from participating in a trial?

(A) the prospective juror's actual bias with regard to issues such as race, economics, and religion
(B) the desire to avoid maligning one's own reputation as an objective, bias-free citizen
(C) the need to feel accepted by an institution of the U.S. government
(D) the truth is considered less dangerous outside of an actual trial situation
(E) the prospective juror's desire to mask his or her relationship to trial participants

12. This is a SPECIFIC question. Find the part of the passage that talks about challenges.

(A) Nope. The issue is racial bias, not racial similarity.
(B) No, that's what the trial is for. The *voir dire* process is not an educational one.
(C) This looks good, but it's a bit extreme and you can't find it in the passage.
(D) Bingo. See lines 7–8. A juror shouldn't have a relationship with anyone involved in the trial.
(E) This is not mentioned in the passage as grounds for a challenge. Eliminate it.

13. This is a SPECIFIC question. Find the part of the passage that talks about the ulterior motives of a juror.

(A) This was not mentioned as the reason. See lines 31–34.
(B) Bingo. See lines 31–34. This is a paraphrase of "impugn their integrity." It's the answer.
(C) This was not mentioned as the reason. See lines 31–34.
(D) This was not mentioned as the reason. See lines 31–34.
(E) This was not mentioned as the reason. See lines 31–34.

SECTION II

Questions 14–20 are based on the following passage:

Late in the nineteenth century, land reform emerged as a dominant concern of the Liberal Party in England. During this time, many prominent thinkers dissented from mainstream liberal ideology by questioning the justification of individual ownership. To John Stuart Mill, Henry George, and Herbert Spencer, for example, land represented something unique among ownable goods as "a thing not made by man, a thing necessary to life, and of which there is not enough for all." With these attributes—naturalness of origin, absolute scarcity, and centrality to all productive life-sustaining activity—land and land ownership, it was asserted, could be considered indefensible rights based upon personal labor or achievement.

Prior to the emergence of these political analysts, the *laissez-faire* views of Adam Smith were the dominant liberal position. Smith asserted that "the interests of the state require that land should be as much in commerce as any other good." The "new liberal" thinking, however, rejected this traditional notion and attacked the institutions of primogeniture and strict family settlement that enabled the landed class to maintain their estates from one generation to the next. The new liberal ideology encompassed both economic and social goals. They envisioned a break with the static conditions of primogeniture and its replacement with a more egalitarian and morally vigorous society of peasant proprietors.

In addressing the dilemma of land ownership, proponents of the new liberal thinking offered several different strategies. Herbert Spencer's proposal sought to make land the joint property of society in which all land would be confiscated by the (democratic) state. Individuals might then lease parts of it through competitive bidding. By paying rent, tenants would thus compensate all non-owners for having relinquished their claim.

John Stuart Mill employed the law of rent to show that increased land values cannot be attributed to the exertions undertaken by owners; most often, rather, such increases are the function of the "mere progress of wealth and population." In his *Political Economy*, Mill held that private property is justified only insofar as the proprietor of land is its improver. Some policies advocated by Mill included a special tax on rent, the protection of tenants' rights, state land purchases, and the prohibition of any further enclosures of common lands. While supporting some land reform measures, however, Mill insisted that present owners were owed compensation. His proposal of a special tax on land pertained to future unearned income without disturbing past acquisitions.

According to Henry George, another prominent new liberal, virtually all social and moral ills of modern society could be traced to private ownership of land. In *Progress and Poverty*, George rejects the inevitability of poverty and deprivation as remedial defects of society. In his view, rent represented not only unearned income, but a deleterious drain on much of society's earned income that absorbed the disposable surplus created by society's cooperative efforts. George's solution lay in the socialization of rent. He proposed that the community recapture its entitlement through a special tax on the rental value of land; a levy—known as the "single tax"—would eliminate the need for taxing productive enterprises and would eventually replace all other taxes.

SECTION II

QUESTIONS	EXPLANATIONS

14. The primary purpose of the passage is to

(A) discuss contrasting views on land reform among nineteenth-century English liberals
(B) trace the development of land ownership laws in England
(C) describe a current debate on land ownership
(D) prove that Adam Smith was not truly a *laissez-faire* liberal
(E) suggest a new political approach to the problem of land scarcity

14. This is a PRIMARY PURPOSE question. Answer in your own words first and then look at the choices.

(A) Right. There are a bunch of liberals, and they are talking about land reform.
(B) This would take several pages, if not several books, to accomplish. Too broad; eliminate it.
(C) No, the passage is talking about the debate during the nineteenth century.
(D) The question is about the entire passage. This is way too specific, not to mention wrong.
(E) The author's talking about the nineteenth century, which is hardly new. Eliminate it.

15. According to the passage, all of the following characteristics were ascribed to land as justification for its special treatment EXCEPT

(A) the limited availability of land as a resource
(B) its nonartificial essence
(C) the integral nature of the commodity to human existence
(D) the effort required to increase its value
(E) the historical precedent for private property

15. This is a SPECIFIC question. Go and find the four things that were mentioned and eliminate the one that was not.

(A) Mentioned in line 9. Eliminate it.
(B) Mentioned in line 10. Eliminate it.
(C) Mentioned in line 11. Eliminate it.
(D) Mentioned in lines 13–14. Eliminate it.
(E) This is referring to a different part of the passage, so it's our answer.

16. According to the passage, Henry George considered economic deprivation to be

(A) an unfortunate but necessary global condition
(B) a temporary state that would inevitably be reversed
(C) a condition that varied according to the policies of the ruling elites
(D) a situation that could be rectified by employing certain policies
(E) a condition that was unlikely to be alleviated

16. This is a SPECIFIC question. Read the paragraph on Henry George and then answer the question.

(A) He thinks we can beat it. See lines 56–57.
(B) He thinks we *can* beat it, not that we *will* beat it. See lines 56–57.
(C) Never mentioned anywhere. Eliminate it.
(D) Yes. See lines 56–68.
(E) We don't really know how likely he thought it was, just that he thought it was possible. Not as good as (D).

SECTION II

QUESTIONS	EXPLANATIONS

17. In addressing the issue of land reform, Mill prescribed that the unearned benefits accrued to landowners from prior transactions should be

(A) unlike future transactions in that they should not be taxed
(B) considered invalid and used for the benefits of all citizens
(C) left undisturbed by the society at large
(D) confiscated and distributed to the neediest members of society
(E) dealt with on a case-by-case basis in determining their disposal

17. This is a SPECIFIC question. Read the paragraph on John Stuart Mill and then answer the question.

(A) Yes. See lines 51–52.
(B) He never said this. Eliminate it.
(C) He never said this. Eliminate it.
(D) He never said this. Eliminate it.
(E) He never said this. Eliminate it.

18. The author introduces the term "new liberal" (line 19) in order to

(A) delineate the dominant political parties of the time
(B) compare the views of Adam Smith to conservative land theories
(C) present a view that differed from traditional liberal thinking
(D) differentiate between U.S. liberals and English liberals
(E) explain the traditional opposition to the institution of primogeniture

18. This is a LINE REFERENCE question. Read five lines above and five lines below the line reference.

(A) We're not talking about parties but ideologies. Eliminate it.
(B) No, Adam Smith is not a new liberal—he's an old one.
(C) Yes, guys like Mill and George and Spencer were coming up with new theories. This is the answer.
(D) "U.S. liberals" is totally out of the scope of this passage, orbiting Pluto somewhere.
(E) This is not why he mentions new liberals. Eliminate it.

SECTION II

QUESTIONS	EXPLANATIONS

19. According to the passage, Mill believed that a landowner would be entitled to profit from his holdings as long as he

    (A) did so without taking unfair advantage of the less fortunate
    (B) offered some of the profits to be used for the public betterment
    (C) was prepared to pay substantial taxes on his past and present holdings
    (D) was directly responsible for improving the condition of the land
    (E) supplied parts of the land for communal use

19. This is a SPECIFIC question. Read the paragraph on John Stuart Mill and then answer the question.

    (A) He never said this. Eliminate it.
    (B) He never said this. Eliminate it.
    (C) He never said past holdings, only present ones. Eliminate it.
    (D) Yes. See lines 43–44. It's the answer.
    (E) He never said this. Eliminate it.

20. Based on the content of the passage, one can infer that, according to the traditional liberal outlook prior to the late nineteenth century, land was viewed as

    (A) an entity that should be used for the benefit of the entire society
    (B) a means by which wealth could be redistributed
    (C) a valid, but potentially deleterious, means of producing wealth
    (D) a private commodity to be bought and sold without outside interference
    (E) an area that developed mysteriously even without human interference

20. This is a SPECIFIC question. Go back to where the passage talked about what was happening before these guys.

    (A) Nope. That's the radical view of the new guys.
    (B) Nope. Same problem as (A).
    (C) Hardly. No one before these guys thought that owning a lot of land was deleterious.
    (D) Bingo. Pure Adam Smith—it's pretty much exactly what he said. See lines 16–19.
    (E) Ah, yes, the mysterious nature of land ownership. Consult your local Psychic Friends Network representative. Eliminate it.

SECTION II

Questions 21–27 are based on the following passage:

In both developed and developing nations, governments finance, produce, and distribute various goods and services. In recent years, the range of goods provided by the government has extended broadly, encompassing many goods that do not meet the economic purist's definition of "public goods." As the size of the public sector has increased steadily, there has been a growing concern about the effectiveness of the public sector's performance as producer.

Critics argue that the public provision of certain goods is inefficient and have proposed that the private sector should replace many current public sector activities, that is, these services should be privatized. Since the Reagan administration, greater privatization efforts have been pursued in the United States. Concurrent with this trend has been a strong endorsement by international bilateral donor agencies for heavier reliance on the private sector in developing countries. The underlying claim is that the private sector can improve the quality of outputs and deliver goods more quickly and less expensively than the public sector in these countries.

This claim, however, has mixed theoretical support and little empirical verification in the Third World. The political, institutional, and economic environments of developing nations are markedly different from those of developed countries. It is not clear that the theories and empirical evidence that purport to justify privatization in developed countries are applicable to developing countries. Often policy makers in developing nations do not have sufficient information to design effective policy shifts to increase efficiency of providing goods through private initiatives. Additionally, there is a lack of basic understanding about what policy variables need to be altered to attain desired outcomes of privatization in developing countries.

One study of privatization in Honduras examined the policy shift from "direct administration" to "contracting out" for three construction activities: urban upgrading for housing projects, rural primary schools, and rural roads. It tested key hypotheses pertaining to the effectiveness of privatization, focusing on three aspects: cost, time, and quality.

The main finding was that contracting out in Honduras did not lead to the common expectations of its proponents because institutional barriers and limited competitiveness in the marketplace have prevented private contractors from improving quality and reducing the time and cost required for construction.

Privatization in developing countries cannot produce goods and services efficiently without substantial reform in the market and regulatory procedures. Policy makers interested in privatization as a policy measure should consider carefully the multiple objectives at the national level.

SECTION II

QUESTIONS	EXPLANATIONS

21. The author's primary purpose in the passage is to

(A) outline some of the shortcomings of privatization in developing nations
(B) contrast the public sector's performance as producer in the United States and Honduras
(C) explain the conditions that are necessary for privatization in Third World nations
(D) justify heavier reliance on the private sector in developing countries
(E) offer a solution for the future course of Honduran economic policy

21. This is a PRIMARY PURPOSE question. Answer in your own words first and then look at the choices.

(A) Right. Privatization might be okay, but so far we've had no evidence that it's good for developing countries. That's why the author uses the Honduras example.
(B) Too specific. And it should say something about privatization. Eliminate it.
(C) This looks good, but it's a bit too broad. The author talks more about why it fails than about what is necessary for it to succeed. It would take more space than this paragraph if this were to be done. Eliminate it.
(D) Hardly. The author doesn't think it works in developing countries.
(E) Too specific. The author's only using Honduras as an example here. Eliminate it.

22. It can be inferred by the author's assessment of the Honduras study that a problem with introducing privatization in developing nations is that

(A) most leaders of developing nations did not concur with the policies begun during Reagan administration
(B) the direct administration of services requires more capital than contracting out does
(C) many developing nations lack the necessary competition between contractors in the marketplace
(D) privatization of services is not politically acceptable in the struggling economies of Third World nations
(E) contracting out is limited to upgrading facilities and most developing nations need to concentrate on constructing new facilities

22. This is a SPECIFIC question. Read the stuff about Honduras. Now.

(A) We have no idea from the passage what these people thought. Eliminate it.
(B) The passage never says anything about more capital. Eliminate it.
(C) Yes. See lines 46–47. This is our answer.
(D) The author never says this. Eliminate it.
(E) The author never says anything about new facilities. Eliminate it.

SECTION II

QUESTIONS

23. Which one of the following would weaken the author's statements about privatization in developing nations?

(A) The leading industrial nations have all benefited from the improved efficiency of privatization.
(B) International bilateral donor agencies have endorsed privatization efforts in developing nations.
(C) Many international economists favor the policies begun during the Reagan administration.
(D) A recent study of ten Third World nations found evidence contrary to the Honduran example.
(E) The citizens of developing nations use the term "public goods" differently than Americans do.

24. It could be inferred from the passage that which one of the following groups would most likely have an increased role in the privatized Honduran economy?

(A) U.S. banks
(B) Honduran entrepreneurs
(C) U.S. corporations
(D) international bilateral donor agencies
(E) Honduran economists

25. Based on the passage, it can be inferred that economic purists

(A) have a strict interpretation of what constitutes public goods
(B) endorse privatization only in developed nations
(C) are proponents of Honduran efforts to privatize
(D) feel that contracting out in Honduras has not led to diminished expectations
(E) disapprove of the shifting of responsibility for providing public services from the public to the private sector

EXPLANATIONS

23. This is a WEAKEN question. We know the author thinks privatization in developing countries isn't a good thing. What would weaken that?

(A) This has no impact because it's talking about industrialized nations.
(B) We know they like it, but the author already disagreed with them. Opinions don't matter—facts do.
(C) See (B). Same problem. We need an actual fact.
(D) Oops. Some evidence that it's working somewhere, which would weaken the author's argument. It's the correct answer.
(E) Huh? This doesn't give us any evidence that privatization is working somewhere. Eliminate it.

24. This is a SPECIFIC question. Read the stuff about Honduras. Now.

(A) Not mentioned.
(B) These people would be examples of private sector people in Honduras. It's the answer.
(C) Not mentioned.
(D) Mentioned, but we're looking for Honduran people here.
(E) We're looking for contractors, not economists. Eliminate it.

25. This is a SPECIFIC question. Find the part of the passage that mentions what the economic purists would think.

(A) Right. See lines 3–6. They have a definition, and it's more strict than the government's definition.
(B) No, that's what the author does. Eliminate it.
(C) No, the author says that the claim has "mixed theoretical support." Eliminate it.
(D) We don't know what they think about Honduras. Eliminate it.
(E) We have no idea what they think about this. Eliminate it.

SECTION II

QUESTIONS	EXPLANATIONS

26. "Desired outcomes" (line 35) partially refers to which one of the following?

    (A) effective policy shifts
    (B) urban upgrading
    (C) political stability
    (D) improved quality of outputs
    (E) greater reliance on the public sectors

26. This is a LINE REFERENCE question. Read five lines above and five lines below the line reference.

    (A) No, we're looking for a positive outcome of privatization. Eliminate it.
    (B) This refers to Honduras, which is later in the passage. Eliminate it.
    (C) Not an outcome of privatization. Eliminate it.
    (D) Yes, see lines 19–20. This is a pretty tricky line reference because the answer is so far above the reference. But this is a desired outcome of privatization.
    (E) Not a desired outcome of privatization—in fact, it's the opposite.

27. According to the passage, since the Reagan administration, there has been

    (A) broad international support for privatization
    (B) demand from U.S. banks for diversification of Third World debt
    (C) encouragement for privatization of international donor agencies
    (D) a greater privatization effort pursued in Honduras
    (E) much evidence justifying privatization in developing nations

27. This is a SPECIFIC question. Find the part of the passage that mentions the Reagan administration.

    (A) Sure. Look at all those bilateral donor agencies in line 17.
    (B) Banks are never mentioned in the passage. Eliminate it.
    (C) No, the agencies are encouraging governments to privatize, not the other way around.
    (D) We don't know when exactly the Honduras effort took place.
    (E) There isn't any, which is why the author is against it.

SECTION III

QUESTIONS

1. The best professors never tell their students what to write. They strive instead to establish an intellectually critical environment conducive to thorough and creative scholarship, because training a student through indoctrination is never as effective as encouraging a student to develop his faculties independently. Truly impressive scholarly work can be produced only by the student who feels that he is breaking new ground, or at least treating familiar ground in a fresh and original manner.

   Which one of the following statements is assumed by the argument above?

   (A) Most students who are not told what to write produce great scholarly work.
   (B) Professors who do not enjoy the security of tenure have no incentive to teach in the fashion described above.
   (C) A student cannot create impressive scholarly work if he has been instructed on what he should write.
   (D) Many great professors do not use an authoritative and dogmatic style of teaching.
   (E) Many good students prefer being told what to write to the pressure of being encouraged to formulate their own, however original, ideas.

EXPLANATIONS

1. This is an ASSUMPTION question. The correct answer will be something necessary for the conclusion to be true, and, if made false, will make the argument fall apart.

   (A) The amount or percentage of students who produce great scholarly work is not necessary for the author's conclusion to be true.
   (B) Tenure is totally out of the scope of this argument.
   (C) Yes. The argument says that independent thinking is what's important. If you make this choice false, the argument will totally fall apart.
   (D) Authoritative and dogmatic styles are outside the scope of the argument.
   (E) What the students would actually prefer is outside the scope of the argument.

SECTION III

QUESTIONS	EXPLANATIONS

2. Although all prisons have some system of social hierarchy among prisoners, there are some social hierarchies in prisons that are based neither on physical strength nor on length of incarceration. However, there is no such thing as a system of social hierarchy in which no distinction is made between those who have influence over the actions of others and those who do not.

   Which one of the following can be inferred from the passage above?

   (A) The ability to measure personal influence is derived from the need for social hierarchy.
   (B) All prison hierarchies have a system with which to identify whether a given individual has influence over the actions of another.
   (C) Each individual prison community has its own unique set of criteria by which to measure social status.
   (D) There are certain aspects of social status that are common among all social hierarchies.
   (E) There are certain aspects of social status that are common among all hierarchies.

2. This is an INFERENCE question. Your goal is to find the one choice that must be true based on the information in the passage.

   (A) We have no idea whether the connection between these two ideas must be true.
   (B) The language of this answer choice is extreme, plus it seems to be confusing what exactly is a "system" and what is a "distinction." Let's eliminate it.
   (C) The argument doesn't say whether or not each prison system is "unique."
   (D) What could this be referring to? The fact that in every social hierarchy, a distinction of some sort is made in social status. Therefore, that's an aspect common among all social hierarchies, and it's the answer.
   (E) We are only concerned with social hierarchies, not all hierarchies.

3. Early in this century Heisenberg stated that it is impossible to know with certainty both the position and the velocity of an electron at any specific instant. Initially, this theory was rejected by the scientific community because there was no accurate way to measure the movement of electrons. Now, however, the theory is accepted as true, not because we can measure the movement of electrons, but because no other theory of merit has been able to explain the myriad observable inconsistencies of electron behavior.

   The author appeals to which one of the following principles in establishing his conclusion?

   (A) The goal of science is to conscribe the vast variation apparent in nature in one comprehensive theory.
   (B) Through the acceptance of mathematical models that describe observable phenomena, scientists have come to a greater understanding of the uncertainties of nature.
   (C) Standard scientific method is to accept the best known explanation for an observable phenomenon regardless of its inconsistencies.
   (D) Science, through the study of probabilistic phenomena, transforms the complexities of nature into easily quantifiable terms.
   (E) A theory need not be supported by observational data to be accepted by the scientific community.

3. This is a PRINCIPLE question. We are given five principles in the answer choices for this specific question, so we should come up with our own principle for the actions in the argument and match it to the answer choices.

   (A) The goal of science is much too vast for this argument.
   (B) This is also too general a principle—remember, we're looking for something that says that sometimes the best theory is the only theory that just simply can't be refuted, even though there's no evidence for it.
   (C) While it's true that no one's come up with anything better than Heisenberg, we don't know one way or the other whether his theory contains inconsistencies or not.
   (D) If this were true, then Heisenberg would have already figured everything out to the last detail.
   (E) This is nice and basic, because it merely states that we can accept something even though we can't measure it, just like the current state of Heisenberg's theory. It's the answer.

SECTION III

QUESTIONS

4. Concerned citizen: The county government's new ordinance limiting the types of materials that can be disposed of in trash fires violates our rights as citizens. The fact that local environmental damage results from the burning of certain inorganic materials is not the primary issue. The real concern is the government's flagrant disregard for the right of the individual to establish what is acceptable on his or her own property.

Which one of the following principles, if accepted, would enable the concerned citizen's conclusion to be properly drawn?

(A) Legislative violation of an individual's right to privacy is not justifiable unless the actions of that individual put others at risk.
(B) The right of an individual to live in a safe environment takes precedence over the right of an individual to be exempt from legislative intrusion.
(C) An individual's personal rights supersede any right or responsibility the government may have to protect a community from harm.
(D) An individual has a moral obligation to act in the best interest of the community as a whole.
(E) A compromise must be found when the right of an individual to act independently conflicts with the responsibility of the government to provide protection for the local environment.

EXPLANATIONS

4. This is a PRINCIPLE question. We are given five principles in the answer choices for this specific question, so we should come up with our own principle for the actions in the argument and match it to the answer choices.

(A) If this were true, it would not match with the actions in the argument, because the argument says the local environmentenal risk isn't as important as individual rights.
(B) This has the same problem as answer choice (A). It's the opposite of what the argument is saying.
(C) Bingo. An individual's rights (such as privacy) are more important than environmental rights.
(D) This would also go in the opposite direction from the argument.
(E) This is nice, but it's not something that would strengthen the citizen's viewpoint. This is the politically correct response. Watch out—it's a trap.

SECTION III

QUESTIONS

5. As part of a new commitment to customer satisfaction, an electronics company sent a survey to all customers who had purchased its electronic personal organizer in the previous month. The survey, which was sent through the mail, asked customers to give personal information and to rate their satisfaction with the product. Of customers who returned the survey, more indicated that they had a negative opinion of the product's performance than indicated a neutral or positive opinion. On the basis of these results, the company, hoping to increase customer satisfaction, decided to allocate a large amount of capital to redesigning the product.

   Which one of the following, if true, indicates the most serious flaw in the method of research used by the company?

   (A) The company relied on a numerical system of rating responses rather than on open-ended questions that allow for more detailed feedback.

   (B) Customers who were dissatisfied with the information display of the organizer outnumbered customers who were dissatisfied with the variety of functions offered by the organizer.

   (C) Studies show that customer dissatisfaction with a new product is highest during the first year of the product's release and gradually decreases over the following years.

   (D) The marketing division has found that responses to their mail-in surveys are generally accurate.

   (E) People who are satisfied with a product or have no strong opinion about it are less likely to be motivated to return a mail-in questionnaire.

EXPLANATIONS

5. **Conclusion:** The company is going to redesign the product.

   Premise: The surveys indicate that more people have a negative opinion of the product than have a neutral or positive one.

   Assumption: The survey is representative of the opinions of all people who have used the product.

   This is a WEAKEN question. Try and see which answer choice has the most negative impact on the conclusion of the argument. Remember to assume the hypothetical truth of each choice and apply it to the argument.

   (A) We have no idea whether a numerical system or an open-ended system would be more appropriate for this survey.

   (B) We're not concerned with what exactly about the product these customers didn't like. We're looking for something that would show why the conclusion might be wrong.

   (C) This looks okay, but it doesn't really show that we should ignore the dissatisfaction of the customers. Let's eliminate it.

   (D) This would strengthen the argument by showing how the survey was representative. It's the opposite of what we want in this case.

   (E) This shows how the survey was not representative because there's a lot of happy, or at least not unhappy, people who aren't sending back the questionnaires, thereby skewing the data. It's the answer.

SECTION III

QUESTIONS

6. In an attempt to restructure the city's transit system, the head of the Mass Transit Authority has announced plans to cut services substantially and to increase fares on the subway and bus systems. He stated that the proposed changes represent the only means available to increase revenue and allow the Transit Authority to serve citizens better.

Opponents of the head of the Mass Transit Authority's plan would be best served if which one of the following were shown to be true?

(A) The installation of a new, more efficient turnstile system would eliminate fare evasion, saving more money than the proposed changes would raise.
(B) The revenue from the proposed changes would not be sufficient to prevent further fare increases in the future.
(C) The financial problems faced by the Mass Transit Authority were caused by a variety of factors, many of them legal as well as financial.
(D) A planned conversion from old, heavy steel cars to newer, lighter alloy cars has been factored into the Mass Transit Authority's budget, but has yet to be approved by the city council.
(E) The citizens of the city would be better served if people relied more on other means of transportation such as walking and biking.

EXPLANATIONS

6. **Conclusion:** The changes are the only means available to increase revenue and allow the Transit Authority to serve citizens better.

Premise: No reason is given.

Assumption: Really, there is no assumption beyond what is already stated in the conclusion; this weaken question directly attacks the conclusion.

This is a WEAKEN question. Try and see which answer choice has the most negative impact on the conclusion of the argument. Remember to assume the hypothetical truth of each choice and apply it to the argument.

(A) Here's an alternate solution to the problem of insubstantial revenue. Let's leave it.
(B) What happens in the future has no impact one way or another on the argument. Eliminate it.
(C) The causes of the lack of revenue have no impact on whether the head of the Mass Transit Authority's plan is good or bad. Eliminate it.
(D) The issue of the weight of the subway cars has no impact on the plan. Eliminate it.
(E) Here's another politically correct response for you tree-huggers out there. It tells us nothing about whether or not the plan is a good one though. Therefore, our answer is (A).

SECTION III

QUESTIONS

7. If the water level of the reservoir falls below the "safe line," then either the amount of water being consumed has increased or the amount of rainfall in the area has been below normal. If the amount of rainfall has been below normal, then the native plant life cannot be perfectly healthy.

Assume that the reservoir level falls below the safe line. According to the passage, which one of the following statements cannot be true?

(A) The amount of water being consumed has decreased.
(B) The amount of rainfall has been below normal, and the native plant life is not perfectly healthy.
(C) The amount of water being consumed has increased, the amount of rainfall has been below normal, and some of the native plant life is perfectly healthy.
(D) The amount of water being consumed has decreased, the amount of rainfall has been below normal, and the native plant life is perfectly healthy.
(E) The amount of water being consumed has increased, the amount of rainfall has been higher than normal, and the native plant life is not perfectly healthy.

EXPLANATIONS

7. This is an INFERENCE question. Your goal is to find the one choice that can't be true based on the information in the passage.

(A) This can be true, because the amount of rainfall could still be very far below normal, thereby making the reservoir level fall below a safe level even though the amount of water being consumed has decreased. So we eliminate this choice, because we're looking for what can't be true.
(B) This can be true, because the amount of rainfall decreasing leads to native plant life not being perfectly healthy.
(C) The first two parts of this three-part answer choice are fine, but we can't have perfectly healthy plant life if the amount of rainfall has been below normal, according to the argument. Therefore this answer choice might not be able to be true, although the last part of the answer choice is pretty wishy-washy because of the use of "some." Let's see if there's something better.
(D) There's no way that this answer choice can be true, because we are told in the argument that "if the amount of rainfall has been below normal, then the native plant life cannot be perfectly healthy," and this choice says the opposite. It's much worse than (C), so it's the answer.
(E) This can be true, because it's possible that the plant life is not healthy for some other reason.

SECTION III

QUESTIONS

8. If we are to improve the status of our college in the public's perception, our next promotional campaign should appear in the form of full-page advertisements placed in nationally circulated magazines, rather than in radio advertisements broadcast to a variety of stations. Although advertising fees for both campaigns are roughly equivalent, the production costs of the print advertisement campaign are nearly half those of the radio campaign. Therefore, our next promotional campaign should be a print advertisement campaign.

   Which one of the following, if true, would most help to explain the difference in production costs of the two campaigns?

   (A) More man-hours would be required in the preparation of the magazine advertisement than in the preparation of the radio advertisement.
   (B) The number of people involved in the creation of a national ad campaign is greater than the number of people involved in the creation of a local ad campaign.
   (C) The layout of the print ad campaign could potentially be reused in another campaign at a later date.
   (D) The perceived impact of a magazine advertisement is greater than that of a radio advertisement.
   (E) The creation of the layout for the magazine advertisement can be done in house at no extra cost to the college, whereas the creation of a radio advertisement requires scheduling many hours of expensive time at a recording studio.

EXPLANATIONS

8. This is a PARADOX question. Look for an answer choice that allows both parts of the argument to be true, and remember to assume the hypothetical truth of each of the answer choices.

   (A) This choice would exacerbate the paradox. It's the opposite of what we want. Eliminate it.
   (B) This has no impact on the argument because we're not talking about local campaigns.
   (C) While this is nice, it doesn't explain why it's cheaper to create a print campaign than a radio campaign.
   (D) This also doesn't explain why it's cheaper to produce a print campaign than a radio campaign.
   (E) This explains the difference in cost pretty clearly. It's the answer.

SECTION III

QUESTIONS

9. Schools that train students in technical skills for a specific field of work are more successful, as measured by the percentage of students that gain employment in full-time jobs in the six-month period following graduation, than are institutions that teach a liberal arts curriculum. Technical schools have a student employment rate of approximately 65 percent, whereas liberal arts schools have a rate of only 56 percent. This difference reveals that technical schools are more effectively meeting the challenge of providing education than are liberal arts schools.

   Which one of the following is an assumption on which the above argument rests?

   (A) Schools will not accurately report information if they believe that information will reflect poorly on them.
   (B) The curriculum of a school can be evaluated by examining the number and types of job placements achieved by its students.
   (C) The percent of students that gain employment following graduation is a measurement of that school's ability to provide education.
   (D) The sole function of education is to help students gain employment.
   (E) Technical schools and liberal arts schools serve different educational purposes.

10. Scientists have long dreamed of the technological possibilities of nuclear fusion, a process in which the nuclei of two atoms are fused together. The energy that would be generated by this process would far surpass that of nuclear fission. However, years of research have failed to produce any tangible results and, as a result, funding for fusion projects has been drastically reduced. Nonetheless, some scientists continue to believe that fusion is possible. Unfortunately, the one team that claimed to have achieved "cold" fusion failed to replicate its experimental results, and scientists believe that other explanations can be found for the results the team initially observed. Therefore, it is unwise to conclude that nuclear fusion will be achieved in the immediate future.

    In the passage above, the author reaches his conclusion by

    (A) criticizing the premises on which the opposing side bases its view
    (B) basing his conclusion upon experimental results
    (C) drawing a conclusion based on a lack of evidence for the opposing view
    (D) questioning the opposing view's use of the indefinite term "cold"
    (E) reaching a conclusion that is incompatible with his premises

EXPLANATIONS

9. **Conclusion:** Technical schools are providing better education than liberal arts schools.

   Premise: A greater proportion of technical school graduates find jobs.

   Assumption: Education is indicated by success at finding jobs.

   This is an ASSUMPTION question. The correct answer will be something necessary for the conclusion to be true, and, if made false, will make the argument fall apart.

   (A) This means that perhaps someone is lying, but we don't know who. It's certainly not an assumption of the argument. Eliminate it.
   (B) We're not concerned with evaluating the curriculum of a school—we're looking to see how getting a full-time job is linked with education. Eliminate it.
   (C) Bingo. This provides the link between having a full-time job and being educated. If this were false, then there would be no evidence that the technical schools are providing a better education than liberal arts schools.
   (D) This is too extreme. Education can still have other functions—it's just that the most relevant one is to get a job.
   (E) If this were true, it would weaken the argument. Eliminate it.

10. This is a REASONING question. Come up with your own description of how the author reaches his conclusion before you go to the answer choices, and then match your description to the choices.

    (A) The author is not saying that fusion isn't possible ever, just not soon. Eliminate it.
    (B) No, it was those wacky cold fusion scientists who based their conclusions on experimental results, not the author.
    (C) The opposing view states that we can achieve fusion soon, so by showing how everything up to this point has failed, the author feels he's supported his conclusion. This is pretty much what happened in the argument. It's the answer.
    (D) The author doesn't really care about the "cold" issue. It's certainly not a basis for his conclusion.
    (E) No, he's pretty solid here. Plus, if it were flawed reasoning, the question would've tipped us off to that in advance. Eliminate it.

SECTION III

QUESTIONS

11. At one time, nutritionists fervently advocated the consumption of large quantities of vitamins to correct certain minor health problems. They justified these claims by citing the negative effects of vitamin deficiency and by pointing out that the Recommended Daily Allowance specifies only the minimum amount of a vitamin required for normal health rather than the amount that would lead to optimal health. Recent studies, however, have discredited those recommendations by showing that high dosages can have detrimental effects.

The argument above best supports which one of the following claims?

(A) A person suffering from a minor ailment will always benefit from medical attention.
(B) Ingesting large doses of vitamins is the best way to treat minor ailments.
(C) A person suffering from a minor health problem would probably do best to avoid excessive doses of vitamins.
(D) Nutritionists were more motivated by their opposition to the Recommended Daily Allowance than by evidence of medical benefit.
(E) All minor health problems should be treated promptly, regardless of the method by which they are treated.

12. Recent studies of preventive dental care have clearly established the positive effects of regular dental care. While the frequency of visits to the dentist varies throughout the population, a general trend has emerged: Those who visit the dentist at least twice a year have significantly fewer dental problems than those who do not.

Which one of the following is most clearly implied in the argument above?

(A) An individual with few dental problems is likely to have recently visited the dentist.
(B) If one has a significant number of dental problems, it is likely that one has visited the dentist fewer than two times a year.
(C) Most people visit their dentists semiannually, and thus have little reason to worry about cavities.
(D) In order to have fewer dental problems, one need only visit the dentist twice a year.
(E) Frequency of dental care can affect the number of dental problems experienced by an individual.

EXPLANATIONS

11. This is an INFERENCE question. Your goal is to find the one choice that must be true based on the information in the passage.

(A) Too extreme and out of the scope of the argument. Eliminate it.
(B) No, that's the opposite of what the author is saying.
(C) Nice and wishy-washy, and it's pretty much a restatement of the last sentence. It's the answer.
(D) We have no idea about the true motivations of the nutritionists, or anyone else for that matter.
(E) Too extreme. Eliminate it.

12. This is an INFERENCE question. Your goal is to find the one choice that must be true based on the information in the passage.

(A) Not necessarily. Eliminate it.
(B) Not necessarily. Eliminate it.
(C) Cavities and patient worry are outside the scope of the argument. Eliminate it.
(D) The word "only" is too extreme. For a given individual other steps might be needed to reduce dental problems.
(E) Nice and wishy-washy again, right? ("…can affect the number…") It's the answer.

SECTION III

QUESTIONS	EXPLANATIONS

13. In recent years, the number of reported cases of ethical misconduct in the telemarketing of stocks, securities, and other investments has risen dramatically. In answer to the growing demand for regulation of this industry, federal agencies are formulating an approach to the problem that would entail close supervision of the activities of the investment houses that use telemarketing. Such government involvement in private industry is, however, antithetical to private industry and would surely dampen the spirit of free enterprise. Clearly, in order to prevent government interference, investment houses should cease the practice of paying telemarketers on commission.

    Which one of the following is an assumption upon which the argument above is based?

    (A) Successful capitalism is dependent upon a governmental policy of noninterference and furthered by pro-business regulations.
    (B) The government's ability to detect misconduct, even with close supervision, is minimal, and therefore useless.
    (C) If judged by contemporary standards, many of these so-called violations are considered ethical.
    (D) Earning a high commission as a telemarketer is not proof of one's abilities as an investment broker.
    (E) The incidence of ethical misconduct is directly related to the telemarketers' desire for larger commissions.

13. **Conclusion:** Investment houses should stop paying telemarketers on commission.

    Premises: They want to avoid government interference, and the government will interfere if there continues to be ethical misconduct.

    Assumption: The ethical misconduct is somehow related to the fact that telemarketers get paid on commission.

    This is an ASSUMPTION question. The correct answer will be something necessary for the conclusion to be true, and, if made false, will make the argument fall apart.

    (A) This doesn't address the gap in the argument between ethical misconduct and paying telemarketers on commission. Also, successful capitalism is out of the scope here. Eliminate it.
    (B) This is not necessary for the conclusion to be true—the author's saying that the government shouldn't interfere whether or not they'd be successful.
    (C) This is also not necessary for the conclusion to be true—the author's admitting that there is some ethical misconduct, and is just saying that government control isn't the answer on how to stop it.
    (D) Whether or not you can prove you're a good broker is totally out of the scope of this argument.
    (E) If there were no link between the ethical misconduct and the desire for large commissions, the argument would totally fall apart. This is our answer.

QUESTIONS

14. A study of former college athletes revealed that, as a group, they are five times less likely to die before the age of fifty than are members of the population at large. The advice to derive from this is clear: Colleges should vastly expand their athletic departments so as to allow a greater proportion of all students to participate in athletics, thereby increasing the overall life expectancy of their student population.

Which one of the following, if true, most seriously weakens the argument above?

(A) Because participation in college athletics requires tremendous academic discipline, college athletes are better suited to succeed in society than are students who do not participate in college athletics.
(B) The students who voluntarily compete in college athletics are more predisposed to good health than are those who do not.
(C) Few colleges have the resources to increase spending on athletics, a nonessential university program.
(D) People who become active after leading sedentary lives can remarkably decrease their chances of contracting heart disease.
(E) Women, whose average life expectancies exceed men's by seven years, have traditionally had fewer opportunities to participate in college athletics than have men.

EXPLANATIONS

14. **Conclusion:** Colleges should expand their athletic departments.

Premises: College athletes are less likely to die young; expanded departments would allow more people to participate in college athletics.

Assumption: That it is participation in athletics that makes people live longer, rather than something inherent in the people who currently compete in college athletics.

This is a WEAKEN question. Figure out which answer choice has the most negative impact on the conclusion of the argument. Remember to assume the hypothetical truth of each choice and apply it to the argument.

(A) Succeeding in society has no impact on this argument. Eliminate this choice.
(B) Let's leave this choice, because it seems to be saying that the existing athlete population is different health-wise than the college population at large, which would weaken the argument that if we included more people in the program, more people would be healthy.
(C) This doesn't impact the argument that if colleges were able to expand athletic departments, people would be healthier.
(D) This would strengthen the argument, if anything, if we made nonathletes into athletes when they entered college.
(E) Comparing women to men is not revelant. There could be biological (or other) reasons why women live longer than men that are completely unrelated to athletics. For this answer to be relevant, it would need to compare women athletes to women nonathletetes.

SECTION III

QUESTIONS	EXPLANATIONS

Questions 15–16

Dear Sirs,

In your letter, which detailed the many reasons you were not able to offer me the position at this time, you mentioned that my colorblindness was the central factor in your decision. In the hope that you may reconsider, I am writing to explain that my overall vision is actually quite good. Enclosed you will find letters from three different optometrists confirming that I have never required any kind of corrective eyewear whatsoever.

Mark Furnace

15. Which one of the following would best highlight the flaw in Mr. Furnace's logic?

(A) Mr. Furnace had not been administered a complete eye examination before he wrote the letter.
(B) The evidence that Mr. Furnace mentions is not relevant to the decision made.
(C) In addressing only one of the many reasons why he was rejected, Mr. Furnace undermines his own intentions.
(D) The extent to which his colorblindness was responsible for his being rejected is not made clear.
(E) Doctors' records are not considered official documentation of a person's well-being.

15. **Conclusion:** You should reconsider your decision not to hire me.

Premise: My overall vision is quite good.

Assumption: There is no reason why colorblindness in particular would be a problem for working this job.

This is a FLAW question. Come up with your own description of why the author's conclusion is flawed before you go to the answer choices, and then match your description to the choices.

(A) We have no idea whether he was administered one or not. Eliminate it.
(B) It sure looks that way. The company only cares about whether he can distinguish colors. It's the answer.
(C) While he should have addressed all the points, that's not why this one point is wrong. Eliminate it.
(D) That might be a reason why the company's decision is bad, but not a reason for why Furnace's logic is bad. Eliminate it.
(E) A person's "well-being" is outside the scope of this argument. Eliminate it.

16. Which one of the following is an assumption upon which Mr. Furnace's letter is based?

(A) A deal can be struck with his potential employers.
(B) A person wearing corrective eyewear should not be hired for certain positions.
(C) Colorblindness is not a fair criterion upon which to base hiring decisions.
(D) A note from a doctor can be sufficient to change a potential employer's opinion.
(E) His colorblindness is not affected by corrective eyewear.

16. This is an ASSUMPTION question. The correct answer will be something necessary for the conclusion to be true, and, if made false, will make the argument fall apart.

(A) What is this? Vegas? A "deal" is outside the scope of the argument.
(B) This would weaken his argument, if anything. Eliminate it.
(C) He's not saying that it's not a valid criticism, just that the good points of his vision outweigh this one detriment. Eliminate it.
(D) This looks pretty good. That's the whole point of his writing this letter—if this weren't true, the letter would have no purpose. It's the answer.
(E) We have no information about this. Eliminate it.

QUESTIONS

17. An airline representative announced the introduction of a new pricing system that uses sophisticated computer technology. Based on up-to-the-minute information on sales, the system identifies and continually updates peak times of high demand and off-peak times of low demand, keeping prices high when demand is high and lowering prices to attract customers when demand is low. As a result, the airline anticipates that large numbers of customers will choose to travel off-peak in order to experience savings, while those who wish to travel at peak times will enjoy greater availability due to higher prices. The airline therefore anticipates that the majority of customers will experience significant benefits as a result of the new system.

Which one of the following indicates an error in the reasoning on the part of the airline?

(A) The airline's conclusion is based on an unproven premise.
(B) The airline displays a naive trust in the possibilities of technology.
(C) The airline fails to factor in the cost of implementing the new system.
(D) The airline's conclusion rests on a result that would necessarily cancel out the anticipated benefit.
(E) The airline fails to establish the percentage of customers who would benefit from the change.

EXPLANATIONS

17. **Conclusion:** People will be tempted to buy tickets at off-peak times since prices will be lower and will not buy at peak times since prices will be higher.

Premise: The computer will set the prices so that they are high when demand is high and low when demand is low.

Assumptions: That prices will stay low at off-peak times even though lots of people will want tickets, and will stay high at peak times even though fewer people will want tickets.

This is a FLAW question. Come up with your own description of why the author's conclusion is flawed before you go to the answer choices, and then match your description to the choices.

(A) No, the reason that this argument is flawed is actually much worse than this—the fact that the argument makes no sense, perhaps. Eliminate it.
(B) Assuming that the technology will work is not what's wrong with this line of reasoning. Eliminate it.
(C) This has no impact on the goal of the airline—to pass savings on to its customers. Eliminate it.
(D) Yes. The result, that a large number of people would choose to travel at off-peak times, would cancel the benefit that off-peak times would be cheaper because the system would increase the number of flights as a larger number of people sought to buy tickets.
(E) We're not concerned with the overall percentages here. Eliminate it.

SECTION III

QUESTIONS

Question 18

Kristen: Compared to a direct business tax cut, a personal income tax cut is a better way to stimulate our state's economy. A personal income tax cut would give residents greater in-pocket income. With this increase in income, individuals will be encouraged to start their own businesses. In addition, individuals will be more likely to spend more money at existing businesses.

Mark: A personal income tax cut is not the most effective way to help business. There is no guarantee that individuals will in fact start new businesses, and the additional income may be used to purchase products from a different state or even a different country.

18. Mark objects to Kristen's argument by

(A) suggesting that a personal income tax cut is no more important than a direct business tax cut
(B) claiming that Kristen has reached a premature conclusion based on an inadequate understanding of the consequences of a business tax cut
(C) demonstrating that the negative impact of a personal income tax outweighs the positive effects
(D) questioning Kristen's use of the ambiguous phrase "in-pocket income"
(E) indicating that the positive consequences that Kristen predicts may not occur

EXPLANATIONS

18. This is a REASONING question. Come up with your own description of how Mark objects to Kristen before you go to the answer choices, and then match your description to the choices.

(A) Importance is not the issue here—effectiveness is. Eliminate it.
(B) No, she's making a mistake with regard to the personal income tax cut—not the business one. Eliminate it.
(C) He doesn't point out any negative impacts of the personal income tax. He just shows that Kristen's positive points may not be so positive.
(D) He doesn't ever question that.
(E) Exactly. He shows how it's possible that neither of Kristen's good outcomes could occur. It's the answer.

SECTION III

QUESTIONS

19. Observation reveals that as children become physically exhausted, they become more prone to crying and temper tantrums. Thus, an occurrence of screaming or yelling in a small child is best remedied by providing physical rest.

Which one of the following uses the same pattern of reasoning as the argument above?

(A) People who feel insecure often compensate by acting in an aggressive manner. A person who is not acting in an aggressive manner is therefore unlikely to be insecure.

(B) Scientists establish the validity of their theories by conducting meticulously controlled experiments. Thus, a scientist who is conducting a meticulously controlled experiment is well on his way to establishing the validity of his theory.

(C) Completion of a four-year college program leads to an improvement in standard of living. A person who has not attended a four-year college program will not experience a comparable improvement in standard of living.

(D) The best way to avoid the common cold is to observe simple rules of hygiene, like washing one's hands. After all, people who don't wash their hands are far more likely to contract a cold.

(E) Habitual lack of sleep leads to a condition known as "chronic exhaustion." A person who is not chronically exhausted is likely to get regular and sufficient sleep.

EXPLANATIONS

19. This is a PARALLEL-THE-REASONING question. Try to get the theme or diagram of the logic and then match it to each answer choice.

(A) We need something that says you can stop a behavior by preventing its cause, because that's what the original argument says.

(B) We need something that says you can stop a behavior by preventing its cause, because that's what the original argument says.

(C) We need something that says you can stop a behavior by preventing its cause, because that's what the original argument says.

(D) This is closest to the logic in the argument. It's the answer.

(E) We need something that says you can stop a behavior by preventing its cause, because that's what the original argument says.

SECTION III

QUESTIONS

20. Statistics show that there is a direct correlation between the ammonia content and the cleaning power of industrial-strength floor and tile cleaners; simply stated, the more ammonia, the better the cleaner. However, in a nationwide survey of commercial food services, cleaning supervisors uniformly replied that in order for any floor and tile cleaner to be effective, it must be used on a given surface twice a day with the right proportion of cleaner to water, and must be applied with well-maintained mops. The survey thus proves that ammonia content is not relevant to the efficacy of floor and tile cleaners after all.

Which one of the following best identifies the flawed reasoning in the passage above?

(A) There is no reason to assume that effective floor and tile cleaning is the only use for floor and tile cleaner.

(B) It cannot be assumed that industrial-strength floor and tile cleaners contain comparable levels of ammonia.

(C) It is unreasonable to conclude that the ammonia content is not relevant to a cleaner's efficacy just because there are requirements for the proper use of industrial-strength floor and tile cleaners.

(D) It cannot be assumed that the efficacy of all industrial-strength floor and tile cleaners depends on the same procedures for use.

(E) It is unreasonable to assume that the makers of industrial-strength floor and tile cleaners are unaware that food services don't always use them properly.

EXPLANATIONS

20. **Conclusion:** Ammonia content is not relevant to cleaner efficacy.

Premise: For a cleaner to be effective, it must be used with the right proportion of water and applied with a mop twice a day.

Assumption: That because you must do other things to make a cleaner effective, ammonia has nothing to do with cleaner effectiveness.

This is a FLAW question. Come up with your own description of why the author's conclusion is flawed before you go to the answer choices, and then match your description to the choices.

(A) This answer choice is an excellent example of LSAT gibberish. Eliminate it.

(B) Why not? Because you know that's true in life? We're talking about the argument. Eliminate it.

(C) That's right. The other requirements don't just make the ammonia issue evaporate. No pun intended.

(D) The author is flawed in assuming that ammonia content isn't relevant, not in discussing procedure.

(E) The awareness of the cleaner makers is out of the scope of this argument.

SECTION III

QUESTIONS

21. Products containing naproxen sodium produce relief from pain and fever by blocking prostaglandins. As a consequence of recent technological advances, production costs for pain and fever medications containing naproxen sodium, allowing for both packaging and marketing costs, are one-fifth of what they were ten years ago, while the corresponding cost for medications using the ingredient ibuprofen, which is produced by different means, has increased. Therefore, naproxen sodium is a less costly ingredient to use in medication for the prevention of pain and fever relief than ibuprofen.

    The conclusion of the argument is properly drawn if which one of the following is assumed?

    (A) The cost of producing pain and fever medication containing ibuprofen has increased over the past ten years.
    (B) Ten years ago, ibuprofen was used more than five times as often as naproxen sodium.
    (C) None of the recent technological advances in producing pain and fever medication with naproxen sodium can be applied to the production of medication using ibuprofen.
    (D) Ten years ago, the cost of producing pain and fever medication with the ingredient naproxen sodium was less than five times the cost of producing medications with ibuprofen.
    (E) The cost of producing pain and fever medication with naproxen sodium is expected to decrease further, while the cost of producing similar medications using ibuprofen is not expected to decrease.

EXPLANATIONS

21. **Conclusion:** Naproxen sodium is less costly than is ibuprofen.

    Premises: Naproxen sodium costs one fifth what it did ten years ago, while ibuprofen costs somewhat more.

    Assumption: Naproxen sodium was not five times as expensive or more than was ibuprofen ten years ago.

    This is a STRENGTHEN question. Figure out which answer choice has the most positive impact on the conclusion of the argument. Remember to assume the hypothetical truth of each choice and apply it to the argument.

    (A) Nope. We need something that links the price of naproxen and ibuprofen. Eliminate it.
    (B) The frequency of use of either product is outside the scope of the argument.
    (C) Bummer, but we're not trying to help the ibuprofen makers here anyway. Eliminate it.
    (D) Bingo. If you work out the math, you'll see that it's now a certainty that naproxen is less costly than ibuprofen.
    (E) But if naproxen were *really* expensive as compared to the possibly super-cheap ibuprofen originally, this wouldn't necessarily make the conclusion work.

SECTION III

QUESTIONS

22. Below is an excerpt from a letter that a medical school sent to an applicant:

We regret that we will not be offering you a position at our school. The committee has been forced to reject many highly qualified applicants because we must restrict our class size to fewer than two hundred students.

Which one of the following can be logically inferred from the information in the letter above?

(A) Only highly qualified applicants were accepted by the medical school.
(B) The applicant was considered to be highly qualified.
(C) The school had already taken its maximum number of students.
(D) Most of the applicants were highly qualified.
(E) The qualifications of applicants were not the only factor affecting admissions.

23. Many Americans are required to spend at least two years studying a foreign language as part of their high school or college educations. As a result of this classroom study, students are usually able to conjugate verbs, define words, and write simple sentences. Yet because even those students who received good grades during their foreign language training find themselves unable to hold a brief, unrehearsed conversation in that language, classroom training is clearly insufficient in transmitting the essential principles of another language.

Which one of the following principles, if accepted, would provide the most justification for the conclusion?

(A) If a student cannot adequately conjugate verbs or write simple sentences in a foreign language, he has not grasped the essential principles of that language.
(B) Anyone who can converse fluently in another language is likely to have the ability to conjugate verbs and define words in that language.
(C) Students grasp the essential principles of a foreign language by living in the country where that language is spoken, not by studying it in the classroom.
(D) Someone can be said to understand the basic principles of a foreign language only when she is able to converse spontaneously in that language.
(E) Any person who has not grown up speaking a given language will never truly grasp the essential principles of that language.

EXPLANATIONS

22. This is an INFERENCE question. Your goal is to find the one choice that must be true based on the information in the passage.

(A) This does not necessarily have to be true. They could have admitted two hundred boneheads. The others that weren't admitted were just bigger boneheads.
(B) This does not necessarily have to be true. The letter doesn't specifically say that this particular applicant was highly qualified.
(C) We don't know this for sure. It could be that this guy was a major moron and was rejected for that.
(D) We have no idea how many were qualified out of the total pool of applicants.
(E) Obviously not, because it said right in the letter that class size was also an issue. Thus, it's the answer.

23. This is a PRINCIPLE question. We are given five principles in the answer choices for this specific question, so we should come up with our own principle for the actions in the argument and match it to the answer choices.

(A) No, all the argument is saying is that conversation is an essential part of knowing another language.
(B) Probably, but this doesn't help the conclusion out any. Eliminate it.
(C) This looks pretty good, but it actually doesn't talk at all about conversation, which is a key element to the author's argument. Eliminate it.
(D) If this is true, then it helps strengthen the author's claim that classroom training is insufficient. It's the answer.
(E) Bummer, but then there's no solution, which is not the author's point. Eliminate it.

SECTION III

QUESTIONS

24. Jane Anne: Feeling frightened and delighted are mutually exclusive. Therefore, a person's behavior cannot both strike fear and evoke delight simultaneously.

    Clive: That's not true. Many people love to go to horror movies. The movies frighten them and amuse them. They simultaneously cringe and laugh.

    Clive has weakened Jane Anne's argument by

    (A) showing that Jane Anne's argument is based on circular reasoning
    (B) demonstrating that two feelings are not mutually exclusive
    (C) qualifying Jane Anne's usage of the term "simultaneously"
    (D) pointing out the inherent ambiguity in the relationship between "fear" and "delight"
    (E) changing an argument by analogy into one based on a more reliable sample

EXPLANATIONS

24. This is a REASONING question. Come up with your own description of how Clive weakened Jane Anne's argument before you go to the answer choices, and then match your description to the choices.

    (A) Jane Anne's argument, while inane, is not circular. Eliminate it.
    (B) Yep. Clive actually provides an example of this—people who go to horror movies.
    (C) He doesn't qualify or expand or do anything else to Jane Anne's use of that term. Eliminate it.
    (D) He does not see these things as ambiguous. Eliminate it.
    (E) No, he's the one who made the analogy, not Jane Anne. Eliminate it.

SECTION III

QUESTIONS

25. Journalistic criticism of literature is falling victim to its own efforts to justify its existence. Critics believe that they garner respect from their readers by ignoring objective description in favor of opinionated commentary. Any new work is given the briefest of summaries and then mercilessly carved up in an effort to divine its deeper meaning. But the best journalist simply presents facts and allows her audience to decide their meanings independently. Critics should convey the truest possible form of the works in question; let the art, and not the art critic, speak to us.

    Which one of the following statements best lends support to the argument presented above?

    (A) Libraries make all new work available to the interested public without regard to critical opinions.
    (B) Because space is limited, it is not practical to reproduce completely every work that is criticized in print.
    (C) Writers would likely alter their style if they knew that their works would simply be read rather than criticized.
    (D) Because most people have the capacity to appreciate art to some degree, it is superfluous to criticize art and a mistake not to allow people to decide for themselves.
    (E) In the context described, only parts of a work could be presented, and this would lead to an increased role for the critic, who would have to decide which parts would be shown.

EXPLANATIONS

25. **Conclusion:** Critics should convey the form of artworks and let the art speak for itself.

    Premise: Offering opinionated critiques of artwork is less valuable.

    Assumption: Opinionated critiques of artwork also do not serve an important purpose.

    This is a STRENGTHEN question. Figure out which answer choice has the most positive impact on the conclusion of the argument. Remember to assume the hypothetical truth of each choice and apply it to the argument.

    (A) Libraries have no impact on this argument either way. Eliminate it.
    (B) This, if anything, would weaken the argument, although it really has no impact either. Eliminate it.
    (C) This choice makes no sense and has no impact. Eliminate it.
    (D) This statement lends support to the argument that criticism isn't the point, merely presenting the work is. It's the answer.
    (E) Giving the critic an increased role wouldn't help strengthen the conclusion. Eliminate it.

SECTION IV

QUESTIONS

1. In France, children in preschool programs spend a portion of each day engaged in a program of stretching and exercise. Preschool programs in the United States, however, seldom devote time to a daily stretching and exercise program. In tests designed to measure cardiovascular fitness, children in the United States were outperformed by their French counterparts. It can therefore be determined that children attending preschool programs in the United States can achieve cardiovascular fitness only by engaging in a daily school program of stretching and exercise.

   Which one of the following is an assumption on which the argument depends?

   (A) A daily program of stretching and exercise will allow all children to achieve cardiovascular fitness.
   (B) Cardiovascular fitness is integral to one's overall health.
   (C) It has been proven that children who participate in stretching and exercise programs in preschool have better cardiovascular fitness as adults.
   (D) Stretching and exercise are necessary components of French children's superior cardiovascular fitness programs.
   (E) United States preschool children could make healthful dietary changes as well as changes to their daily fitness regimens.

EXPLANATIONS

1. **Conclusion:** U.S. children can achieve cardiovascular fitness only by engaging in daily stretching and exercise.

   Premises: French children are more fit than are U.S. children, and French children engage in daily stretching and exercise.

   Assumptions: There is no other reason that French children have greater cardiovascular fitness; if U.S. children start such a program, they will achieve greater fitness; the reason French children are more fit has something to do with daily stretching and exercise.

   This is an ASSUMPTION question. The correct answer will be something necessary for the conclusion to be true, and, if made false, will make the argument fall apart.

   (A) This certainly strengthens the conclusion that stretching and fitness, applied to children anywhere, will help them achieve cardiovascular nirvana. Is it necessary though? We're only concerned with kids in the United States, so "all" is too extreme.
   (B) We're not concerned with the overall health of the children in this argument. Eliminate it.
   (C) We're not concerned with how fit the children will become when they are adults. Eliminate it.
   (D) If stretching *weren't* a necessary part of the French children's fitness, then the argument that doing the same thing in the United States would have the same result would fall apart. So it's the answer.
   (E) Dietary changes are outside the scope of the argument. Eliminate it.

SECTION IV

QUESTIONS

2. In an effort to lessen the risk of liability, fertility clinics are seeking new methods of record keeping and storage that would help avoid donor sperm that might contain dangerous genes. Toward this end, a database is being developed to aid the clients in their screening of donor sperm. The database is exhaustively thorough, containing the medical histories of more than twenty thousand people, approximately half of them men.

   Which one of the following, if true, best explains why the database contains the records of almost ten thousand women?

   (A) Small fertility clinics, located in remote areas, wish to have access to a large selection of donor sperm.
   (B) Keeping genetic information on women is a standard procedure for many scientific clinics.
   (C) Some genetic disorders are not expressed until the onset of puberty.
   (D) Some genetic disorders may be carried by, but not manifested in, men who inherited the dangerous gene from their mothers.
   (E) Some genetic disorders are due to the effects of drugs and alcohol during puberty.

EXPLANATIONS

2. This is a PARADOX question. Look for an answer choice that allows both parts of the argument to be true, and remember to assume the hypothetical truth of each of the answer choices.

   (A) This doesn't explain why half the records are of women. Eliminate it.
   (B) This looks pretty good, but it doesn't actually explain why this is "standard procedure." Also, it's a bit too general, because it says "scientific clinics," and we're talking specifically about fertility clinics. Eliminate it.
   (C) Puberty is outside the scope of the argument. Eliminate it.
   (D) Ah, so we have an example of why the records of the same number of women are kept as of men. It's the answer.
   (E) Puberty is outside the scope of the argument. Eliminate it.

QUESTIONS

3. If the Food and Drug Administration (FDA) does not relax some of its regulations governing the testing of experimental drugs, tens of thousands of U.S. citizens are sure to die as a result of certain diseases before an effective treatment is found and made generally available.

   It follows logically from the statement above that if the FDA does relax some of its regulations governing the testing of experimental drugs, then tens of thousands of U.S. citizens

   (A) will definitely die of certain diseases
   (B) will probably die of certain diseases
   (C) will probably not die of certain diseases
   (D) will not die of certain diseases
   (E) may still die of certain diseases

EXPLANATIONS

3. This is an INFERENCE question. Your goal is to find the one choice that must be true based on the information in the passage.

   (A) We don't know for sure what will happen if they do relax regulations, only what will happen if they don't. Therefore, look for a wishy-washy answer. This is too extreme.
   (B) This is less extreme than (A), so let's leave it in for right now.
   (C) This has a similar structure to (B), so we now have to eliminate both (B) and (C).
   (D) Too extreme. Eliminate.
   (E) This is the most wishy-washy choice, and therefore, it's the answer.

QUESTIONS

4. The level of blood sugar for many patients suffering from disease *Q* is slightly higher than the level of blood sugar in the general population. Nonetheless, most medical professionals believe that slightly increasing blood sugar levels is a successful means by which to treat disease *Q*.

This apparently contradictory argument can best be resolved by which one of the following statements?

(A) Blood sugar levels for patients who have been cured of disease *Q* are virtually identical to the levels of blood sugar found in the general population.
(B) Many of the symptoms associated with severe cases of disease *Q* have been recognized in laboratory animals with experimentally induced high blood pressure, but none of the animals developed disease *Q*.
(C) The movement from inactive to advanced states of disease *Q* often occurs because the virus that causes *Q* flourishes during periods when blood sugar levels are slightly low.
(D) The blood sugar level in patients with disease *Q* fluctuates abnormally in response to changes in blood chemistry.
(E) Low levels of blood sugar are symptomatic of many other diseases that are even more serious than disease *Q*.

EXPLANATIONS

4. This is a PARADOX question. Look for an answer choice that allows both parts of the argument to be true, and remember to assume the hypothetical truth of each of the answer choices.

(A) This would exacerbate the paradox, if anything. Eliminate it.
(B) This doesn't do anything to explain the paradox, and blood pressure is out of the scope here. Eliminate it.
(C) So if we are always making sure to keep blood sugar levels high, then we won't ever have these slightly low periods where the virus will flourish. It's the answer.
(D) We don't care why the blood sugar fluctuates. We just want to know why we should keep it high.
(E) Other diseases are outside the scope of the argument.

SECTION IV

QUESTIONS

Questions 5–6

Many people, in the wake of an exceedingly large number of deaths in the United States caused by handguns, have argued for a federal law making handguns illegal for ordinary citizens anywhere in the United States. However, it is clear that any such proposal would be completely counterproductive. For instance, when handguns were outlawed in the city of Clarksville in 1998, the number of handgun deaths actually increased by 10 percent by 1999. Furthermore, such a proposal clearly violates the Second Amendment, which ensures every citizen's right to bear arms.

5. The above argument is vulnerable to criticism on the grounds that it

(A) fails to consider the fact that other cities may have had different results with handgun bans
(B) fails to define precisely the ambiguous term "handgun"
(C) assumes that the aim of the Clarksville handgun ban was to reduce the number of handgun deaths
(D) assumes that the Clarksville police were not responsible for a larger number of handgun deaths in 1999 than in previous years
(E) fails to cite a legitimate authority in support of its interpretation of the Second Amendment

EXPLANATIONS

5. **Conclusion:** A ban on handguns for private citizens would be counterproductive.

Premise: They had such a ban in Clarksville, and handgun deaths increased by 10 percent.

Assumptions: Handgun deaths would not have increased by even more had there not been a ban; private citizens with handguns were the reason for the increase in handgun deaths; if handguns are banned elsewhere, handgun deaths would similarly increase.

This is a FLAW question. Come up with your own description of why the author's conclusion is flawed before you go to the answer choices, and then match your description to the choices.

(A) What's happened in other cities doesn't necessarily have an impact on why the Clarksville example is a bad one. Eliminate it.
(B) "Handgun" is *not* an ambiguous term.
(C) The argument does make this assumption but that's not why the argument is bad. Eliminate it.
(D) Bingo—this points out that the author has failed to consider a possible alternate cause.
(E) We don't need experts to prove anything about the Second Amendment. These types of answer choices are almost always wrong on the LSAT—choices that say an argument is bad because the author doesn't bring in an expert to validate assumptions. Eliminate it.

QUESTIONS	EXPLANATIONS

6. Which one of the following, if true, would most strongly support the conclusion above?

(A) The number of handgun deaths in Clarksville increased by 20 percent from 1997 to 1998.
(B) The number of handgun deaths in the United States increased by 2 percent from 1998 to 1999.
(C) The number of handgun deaths in Clarksville in 1999 was not as great as the number of handgun deaths in the entire country.
(D) The attempt to ban handguns in Brazil in 1985 also led to a drastically increased number of handgun deaths.
(E) Canada, which has a handgun ban, has a faster growing rate of deaths from firearms than does the United States.

6. This is a STRENGTHEN question. Figure out which answer choice has the most positive impact on the conclusion of the argument. Remember to assume the hypothetical truth of each choice and apply it to the argument.

(A) This would weaken the conclusion by showing that after the law was passed in Clarksville, the rate of handgun deaths was actually increasing at a greater rate than before the law was passed.
(B) So there's something seriously wrong in Clarksville, which is why the Monkees waited to take the last train there. Thus, the law had the opposite effect than what was intended. This is the answer.
(C) The number of deaths in Clarksville as compared to everywhere else isn't the point—we want to look for something that shows us the law isn't effective.
(D) What happened in Brazil, while interesting, is outside the scope of the argument.
(E) "Firearms" is too general here. Our argument is only talking about handguns. Eliminate it.

SECTION IV

QUESTIONS

7. For our protein needs, sea plankton has none of the drawbacks that meat has. Plankton contains neither the high levels of saturated animal fat nor the dangerous hormones that commercially available meats do, and its harvest does not require the massive waste of natural and agricultural resources that meat production does. In light of these facts, it is clear that people must stop getting their protein from meat and start getting it from plankton.

Which one of the following statements, if true, most seriously weakens the argument above?

(A) Relatively few scientific studies have been done on people's willingness to make radical changes in their dietary habits.
(B) The only reports containing information on the drawbacks of plankton as a meat substitute have been funded by the United States Department of Agriculture.
(C) Greater governmental regulation of the meat industry could significantly reduce the use of dangerous chemicals and hormones in meat production.
(D) The costs incurred in the harvest of sea plankton in amounts large enough to meet the average person's annual protein needs exceed the costs incurred in the production of a similar amount of meat.
(E) As of yet, no effective means of making sea plankton commercially available for consumption have been developed.

EXPLANATIONS

7. **Conclusion:** People need to start getting their protein from plankton.

Premise: Plankton doesn't have high levels of saturated fat or dangerous hormones.

Assumptions: There's not some other drawback to plankton; there's enough plankton available to meet our protein needs.

This is a WEAKEN question. Figure out which answer choice has the most negative impact on the conclusion of the argument. Remember to assume the hypothetical truth of each choice and apply it to the argument.

(A) People's willingness to start eating plankton burgers has no impact on the argument, which merely says it would be a good thing to do, and makes no claims as to whether people would actually like it.
(B) So what's in these reports? We don't know, so how can we see if they would weaken the argument? Eliminate it.
(C) Better government regulation of the meat industry wouldn't weaken the argument that we should be eating plankton. Eliminate it.
(D) This is one piece of negative information about switching to plankton. You still don't know how wasteful it is. Also, how much more expensive? One penny? One million dollars? Let's see if (E) is better.
(E) Well, if it's not available to the people, the whole argument is moot. This is the answer.

SECTION IV

QUESTIONS

8. Tenant Representative: Residents of units in the West Building of the Fife Arms apartment complex were recently subjected to rent increases averaging 12.5 percent, while residents of identical apartments in the East Building were given increases of, on the average, only 7 percent. Do our landlords really think that the residents of Fife Arms will believe that the maintenance costs on units in the West Building have risen more than one and a half times as quickly as the maintenance costs on units in the East Building? It seems to us that these identical units, which were built at the same time, have deteriorated equally, and we certainly haven't seen any better service here in the West Building than they have in the East Building.

Which one of the following statements would most seriously weaken the tenant representative's argument that the recent rent increases are inequitable?

(A) Before the recent increases were announced, residents of units in the West Building, who were the first to occupy Fife Arms, were not sharing the burden of the cost of maintenance of the entire complex equally with the residents of units in the East Building.
(B) Before the recent increases were announced, residents of units in the West Building, who were the first to occupy Fife Arms, were paying substantially less for the cost of the maintenance of the entire complex than were the residents of the units of the East Building.
(C) Although the units are identical in age, the rate of occupancy for units in the West Building has been higher than that for units in the East Building, resulting in more wear and tear on units in the West Building.
(D) The increases in rent were not determined by the landlords, but imposed by changes in the city regulations regarding landlord-owned residences.
(E) An independent appraiser judged units in the West Building in the Fife Arms to be one and a half times more valuable than units in the East Building.

EXPLANATIONS

8. **Conclusion:** The recent rent increases are inequitable.

Premises: The West Building's rent went up by 12.5 percent, but the East Building only went up by 7 percent, even though the units are of equal age, the units are identical, and the service is not better.

Assumption: There is not some factor besides size of unit, age of building, and quality of service that would justify one building's rent going up more than the other's.

This is a WEAKEN question. Figure out which answer choice has the most negative impact on the conclusion of the argument. Remember to assume the hypothetical truth of each choice and apply it to the argument.

(A) This looks pretty good, because it gives us a reason why the West Building people are now asked to pay a higher rate of maintenance than the East Building people do. Let's leave it.
(B) This would only weaken it if you knew that both sets of tenants were paying the same amount before the East Building got an increase.
(C) This looks pretty good too, but just because we've got more wear and tear in the West Building doesn't mean that those people should necessarily have to pay more. Besides, the argument says the units have deteriorated equally. Therefore, (A) is better.
(D) We don't care who actually determined the increases. Eliminate it.
(E) The value of the apartments is outside the scope of the argument.

SECTION IV

QUESTIONS

9. It has long been thought that the ancestors of the human race who lived prior to the Ice Age did not have the aid of the many useful inventions characteristic of post–Ice Age humans. In particular, it has long been believed that they did not have the advantages of sharp cutting tools. Such people supposedly had to manage by tearing things, such as the animal skins that they needed for warmth, with their teeth and fingernails. However, the recent discovery of the well-preserved remains of a pre–Ice Age woman has shown this to be false. The woman was wearing a number of animal skins and carried in her hand a number of sharp-edged stones, which scientists discovered could cut through animal skins remarkably well.

   A flaw in the above argument is that it

   (A) makes an appeal to the authority of scientists, without giving sufficient justification for that appeal
   (B) assumes that the stones were sharpened by the woman herself
   (C) assumes that if a thing can be used for a certain purpose, then that purpose must be what the thing in fact was used for
   (D) ignores the fact that many pre–Ice Age people used skins for other reasons besides warmth
   (E) assumes that any object that could be used for cutting animal skins would be good for cutting all kinds of things

EXPLANATIONS

9. **Conclusion:** The belief that pre–Ice Age humans did not have sharp cutting tools is mistaken.

   Premise: The well-preserved remains of a pre–Ice Age woman was wearing animal skins and carrying stones sharp enough to cut the skins.

   Assumption: Just because the stones could be used to cut, they were used to cut.

   This is a FLAW question. Try to come up with your own description why the author's conclusion is flawed before you go to the answer choices, and then try to match your description to the choices.

   (A) If the scientists have something valuable to contribute, then it's a good thing. That's not why the argument is flawed. Eliminate it.
   (B) No, the question is whether or not she actually used the stones for cutting things. Eliminate it.
   (C) This is the answer, because the arguer and the scientists have no proof that the woman was actually using the stones to cut things—she might have been using them for a game of pre–Ice Age ping pong, for instance.
   (D) The skins aren't the issue here; the sharp stones are. Eliminate it.
   (E) He didn't claim that the stones were used to cut everything. Be wary of the extreme language of the choice here. Eliminate it.

QUESTIONS

10. The accountant for a large retail store warned that more than half of the accounts receivable for the previous quarter were delinquent. He suggested that the store hire a collection agency to collect the debt immediately. His suggestion was not followed, however, when it was noted that the store had already received more than two-thirds of the total dollar amount of the outstanding accounts.

    If the statements above are true, they most strongly support which one of the following?

    (A) The store had already collected on twice as many accounts as remained unpaid.
    (B) At least one-third of the accounts had been paid before the beginning of the last quarter.
    (C) Two-thirds of the total number of delinquent accounts must have been collected by the store.
    (D) The total dollar amount and the total number of delinquent accounts are not necessarily proportional.
    (E) If each account paid in installments, then all the accounts paid at least two-thirds of the individual bill.

EXPLANATIONS

10. This is an INFERENCE question. Your goal is to find the one choice that must be true based on the information in the passage.

    (A) We have no idea as to the actual number of accounts collected. Eliminate it.
    (B) We have no idea as to the actual number of accounts at the beginning of the last quarter. Eliminate it.
    (C) We have no idea as to the actual number of accounts collected. Eliminate it.
    (D) Nice and wishy-washy. They could be proportional, they could not be proportional. This statement must be true even independently of the information provided in the argument, it's so wishy-washy. It's the answer.
    (E) We have no idea about the percentage of installment payments as related to each person's account balance as a whole. Eliminate it.

QUESTIONS

11. Statistics recently compiled from Fortune 500 companies seem to suggest that, in the top levels of management, those with a Masters in Business Administration (MBA) face fewer obstacles than do non-MBAs in becoming vice presidents and thus positioning themselves for further advancement. Fully 7 percent of all MBAs within the companies surveyed are vice presidents, while only 2 percent of all non-MBAs have achieved that status. Anyone planning a career in top-level management would be wise to go to graduate school for an MBA.

    Information about which one of the following would be most helpful in evaluating the validity of the argument above?

    (A) the percentages of eligible MBAs and eligible non-MBAs who have recently become corporate vice presidents
    (B) the percentage of vice-president positions in non–Fortune 500 companies that are held by non-MBAs
    (C) whether other opportunities for advancement below the rank of vice president exist in Fortune 500 companies
    (D) the actual number of non-MBAs who have recently become vice presidents in Fortune 500 companies versus the actual number of MBAs who have recently become vice presidents in those companies
    (E) the percentage of people with MBAs versus the percentage of people without MBAs who seek employment in Fortune 500 companies

EXPLANATIONS

11. **Conclusion:** Anyone who wants a career in top-level management should get an MBA.

    Premise: 7 percent of all MBAs in companies were vice presidents, while only 2 percent of non-MBAs were vice presidents.

    Assumption: All employees are equally eligible to become vice presidents (in other words, if the non-MBAs surveyed included people on the maintenance crew, that would skew the results of the survey in favor of MBAs).

    This is most like an ASSUMPTION question, because you are looking for a fact that will help you to evaluate the validity of the assumption.

    (A) This looks good—if all MBAs were vice presidents before going to business school it weakens the argument; if not, it strengthens it.
    (B) Remember, we're concerned with Fortune 500 companies. Let's eliminate this.
    (C) We're concerned with top-level management only. Eliminate it.
    (D) The numbers don't matter if the percentages are already established, which they are. Eliminate it.
    (E) The number of prospective candidates in each group won't help us to find out whether they get top-level managerial positions. Eliminate it.

SECTION IV

QUESTIONS

12. Concerns about the quality of domestic motorcycles drove many consumers to purchase foreign bikes in the 1990s. But here is a motorcycle that will change all that. According to the J.P.R. Glowers customer satisfaction survey, a survey that asks motorcycle owners how they feel about their bikes after the first year of ownership, the Acme Chopper scored highest of all motorcycles in quality for the second year in a row. It also scored very high in features, look, and feel. It is clear that this is a bike that represents the new domestic standard: high quality for many years of enjoyable riding.

    Which one of the following arguments contains a flaw that is most similar to the one in the argument above?

    (A) There is no doubt that these are the finest roses in the country. Eight out of nine growers surveyed rated these the most colorful in their class.
    (B) This house paint will last for decades. When it was tested on several houses it showed barely a crack after ten years.
    (C) This new skyscraper will be one of the sturdiest buildings ever built. It has three separate stabilization systems, which will allow it to withstand even significant earthquakes.
    (D) Even though the domestic tea market has been depressed for years, it should be coming out with some better teas soon, which will increase its market share dramatically.
    (E) The best boats in the world are built by domestic boat manufacturers. We know they are the best because they last the longest of any boats in the world.

EXPLANATIONS

12. This is a PARALLEL-THE-REASONING question. Figure out the theme or diagram of the logic and then match it to each answer choice.

    (A) We need to find something that shows that good performance in the short run proves good performance in the long run. This choice doesn't do that.
    (B) This says ten years is equal to "decades," which does the same thing as the argument. It's the answer.
    (C) The skyscraper as yet hasn't been proven to be sturdy at all because it's new. Therefore, it's not parallel to the argument.
    (D) This has no relevance to the theme in the argument. Eliminate it.
    (E) We have proof of long-standing performance here, so eliminate it.

SECTION IV

QUESTIONS

Questions 13–14

For many years, skeptics scoffed at the idea that plants respond to environmental stimuli other than those that directly affect the process of photosynthesis. Recent studies, however, offer contradictory evidence that seems to suggest that music, for instance, can have a direct and positive effect on plant development. Plants that were kept in the presence of music during the first six weeks of development grew considerably faster and showed fewer signs of disease than those plants developed in silence. The "music-advantaged" plants were also 35 percent more likely to survive the process of transplantation initially than were the "music-disadvantaged" plants.

13. Which one of the following is an assumption upon which the above argument is based?

(A) Many skeptics still do not believe that music is beneficial to plant development.
(B) Plants that do not thrive have been deprived of music during the first six weeks of their development.
(C) Plants that were exposed to music for longer periods of time were healthier and grew faster than those with less exposure.
(D) Some kinds of music are more beneficial to plants than others.
(E) Music does not significantly damage a plant's ability to photosynthesize.

EXPLANATIONS

13. **Conclusion:** Music can have a direct effect on plant development.

Premise: Plants kept in the presence of music during the first six weeks of development grow faster, show fewer signs of disease, and survive transplants more often than those that grow up in silence.

Assumptions: There are no negative effects to exposing plants to music; there was no other factor that favored the music-exposed plants over the other plants.

This is an ASSUMPTION question. The correct answer will be something necessary for the conclusion to be true, and, if made false, will make the argument fall apart.

(A) What skeptics believe or don't believe is outside the scope of the argument.
(B) This is not essential to the argument—we're just looking to see something that strengthens the fact that music helps.
(C) This is nice, but it's not an underlying assumption of the argument. We don't know anything about longer periods of time.
(D) A specific type of music isn't the issue.
(E) This is definitely an assumption. Make this choice false—what would happen to the argument if music damaged the photosynthetic ability of plants? The argument would crumble. So it's the answer.

SECTION IV

QUESTIONS

14. A logical critique of the study cited above would most likely raise which one of the following questions?

(A) Was the type of music used during the experiment consistent over time?
(B) Were both plant groups raised in the same quality soil?
(C) Did the "music-advantaged" plants that survived transplantation live longer than the "music-disadvantaged" plants that survived transplantation?
(D) Is the idea that plants respond to environmental stimuli other than those traditionally accepted as aiding growth now accepted by the scientific community?
(E) What types of plants were used in the experiment?

15. Max: It's a travesty that our government gives away billions of dollars every year to foreign countries while people in this country are poor, starving, and living in inadequate housing. Many foreigners now live far better than the majority of our own people, courtesy of our leaders. This is clearly wrong. A government is obligated to serve its own citizens' interests first, before trying to further the interests of other people in other countries.

Alex: But that is precisely what our government is doing in giving large amounts of foreign aid. Giving such money to foreign countries ensures their loyalty to us, so that we will have their help in furthering our international goals. Thus, even though the poor people in this country may not believe that the government is serving them, it most certainly is.

Which one of the following is the point at issue between Max and Alex?

(A) whether or not foreign governments ought to give money away to other countries
(B) what should be considered in the citizens' interests, when judging the actions of a government
(C) whether or not the government should consider the interests of foreign people before the interests of its own citizens
(D) whether or not providing food and adequate housing are important functions of a government
(E) how much of the government's money should be allowed to go to foreign aid

EXPLANATIONS

14. This is a FLAW question. Come up with your own description of why the author's conclusion is flawed before you go to the answer choices, and then match your description to the choices.

(A) A specific type of music isn't the issue.
(B) Exactly. Do we know for sure that all the conditions of the experiment other than music were identical? If not, the results are garbage. This is a classic LSAT issue—learn it well!
(C) The life expectancy of the plants isn't the issue here; their healthfulness and ability to survive transplantation is.
(D) What the scientific community thinks is irrelevant if we actually have proof of something. A classic LSAT trap. Eliminate it.
(E) The types of plants used aren't important as long as the same types were used for both the control and experimental groups. Eliminate it.

15. This is a REASONING question. Come up with your own description of what they're arguing about before you go to the answer choices, and then match your description to the choices.

(A) Foreign government isn't what they're talking about. Eliminate it.
(B) Right. Max is claiming foreign aid isn't in the interest of citizens, and Alex is claiming that it is.
(C) No, because both are claiming that the government should care more about its own citizens.
(D) No, because we have no idea whether Alex thinks this is important or not.
(E) Not how much, but whether they should be giving any money at all. Eliminate it.

SECTION IV

QUESTIONS

16. Excessive logging has led to a sharp drop in the available supply and an increase in the price of hardwood lumber such as oak and maple. This same pattern has occurred with far too many of our scarce and vital natural resources, resulting in high prices for many products. It is likely, then, that the prices of new hardwood furniture will rise in the near future.

In making the argument above, the author relies on all of the following assumptions EXCEPT:

(A) The price of raw materials is a determining factor in the cost of new furniture.
(B) An increase in the price of lumber usually leads to an increase in the price of newly produced furniture.
(C) There will not be any substantial decrease in other costs to furniture producers that could keep the price of newly produced furniture from increasing.
(D) The cost of new hardwood furniture is affected by an increase in the price of hardwood lumber.
(E) Logging practices can substantially influence the demand for wooden manufactured goods.

EXPLANATIONS

16. **Conclusion:** It is likely that the price of hardwood furniture will increase.

Premise: Excessive logging has led to a sharp decrease in supply and increase in price of hardwood. This same pattern has resulted in increased prices for other products.

Assumptions: The price of raw materials affects the price of products made from those materials; the pattern that affected other products will affect products made from hardwood; other costs related to furniture manufacturing have not decreased substantially.

This is an ASSUMPTION question. Four answers will be something necessary for the conclusion to be true, and, if made false, will make the argument fall apart.

(A) This is an assumption, because if the price of the raw materials weren't a factor, then the price of the furniture wouldn't necessarily rise. Eliminate it.
(B) This is an assumption, because if this weren't true, the price wouldn't necessarily rise. Eliminate it.
(C) This is an assumption, because if prices of things like glue and screws and saws all decreased a lot, then the price of newly produced furniture wouldn't necessarily rise. Eliminate it.
(D) This is an assumption; it says the same thing as (B). Eliminate it.
(E) The demand for furniture isn't an issue here; the price is. This isn't a necessary assumption and therefore it's the answer.

SECTION IV

QUESTIONS

Questions 17–18

Dr. Ronson: These animal tracks exhibit some interesting and strange characteristics. This first footprint appears to have two toes, whereas this second footprint appears to have three. And while this first footprint is facing north, this second footprint is facing east. Due to the weight of this evidence, we can safely conclude that these prints were made by two different animals.

Dr. Martinson: These tracks may indeed have been made by two different animals, but your evidence does not conclusively demonstrate that fact. A slight twist of the foot can make a print that seems to have extra toes. And some animals have feet that are oriented at right angles to one another, such that when they walk, their footprints face different directions. Now, if one footprint had claws while the other one did not, I would find your case more persuasive.

17. Drs. Ronson and Martinson disagree about which of the following?

(A) Any group of tracks can be determined as having been made by a single animal or more than one animal, based on the shapes of the footprints and the directions that they are facing.
(B) Any group of tracks made by a single individual would have similarly shaped footprints and would be facing in the same direction.
(C) Each kind of animal leaves a distinct kind of footprint by which it can be uniquely identified.
(D) The shapes and directions of the footprints in groups of tracks can be used to determine the number of animals who made them.
(E) It is not possible for a single animal to leave both a two-toed and a three-toed footprint.

18. Dr. Martinson does which one of the following?

(A) argues that one can never conclusively determine how many animals made a given group of tracks
(B) criticizes Ronson's conclusion based on other known facts about footprints and the properties of some animals' feet
(C) attacks Ronson's authority as a scientist
(D) disputes Ronson's reasoning by giving an explanation of the facts
(E) states an alternative criterion that would conclusively determine whether one or more animals made a given group of tracks

EXPLANATIONS

17. This is a REASONING question. Come up with your own idea of what they're arguing about before you go to the answer choices, and then match your description to the choices.

(A) Ronson says it's possible in this case; Martinson says it isn't. Therefore, they would disagree about this statement. It's the answer.
(B) They're not disagreeing about this.
(C) That's not what they are arguing about. Eliminate it.
(D) In all cases? They're only talking about this one specific instance.
(E) They're not arguing about whether the animal is a freak. Eliminate it.

18. This is a REASONING question. Come up with your own description of what Dr. Martinson does before you go to the answer choices, and then match your description to the choices.

(A) "Never" is too extreme here. We're only talking about one specific set of tracks. Eliminate it.
(B) Bingo. He calls into question the two pieces of evidence Ronson brings up. It's the answer.
(C) He doesn't do this. Eliminate it.
(D) He gives an *alternative* explanation. Eliminate it.
(E) "Conclusively" is too extreme here. (B) is the better answer; it's more wishy-washy and therefore more easily provable.

SECTION IV

QUESTIONS

19. At current rates of emission, a tax of one cent per pound of pollutant released into the air or water would raise $15 billion. This seems to be an ideal way to pay for the new environmental cleanup program that was recently instituted by the government. Not only that, but this tax would also help prevent further need for such cleanup efforts by encouraging companies to install more modern, less environmentally damaging equipment, and in the future, the money collected from the tax could support programs such as the National Park Service.

    Which one of the following most clearly identifies a flaw in the author's reasoning?

    (A) The author makes a generalization based on insufficient data.
    (B) The author fails to consider other possible ways to accomplish the same end.
    (C) The author mistakes an effect for a cause.
    (D) The author makes incompatible assumptions.
    (E) The author fails to consider a possible result of the plan.

EXPLANATIONS

19. **Conclusion:** We should institute a tax on pollutants.

    Premises: A tax charging a penny per pound of pollutant released would raise $15 billion to help aid environmental cleanup then fund the National Park Service once the pollution is cleaned up, and would provide incentive for companies to be less environmentally damaging, thus reducing the rate of pollution.

    Assumption: That the level of pollutants would somehow both remain constant (allowing $15 billion dollars to be raised for national parks) and be reduced.

    This is a FLAW question. Come up with your own description of what's wrong with the argument before you go to the answer choices, and then match your description to the choices.

    (A) There's no generalization here. The author's actually talking about a specific plan. Eliminate it.
    (B) This isn't necessarily bad as long as the plan is a good one. Eliminate it.
    (C) The author's not confused to this degree. Eliminate it.
    (D) The argument isn't contradictory, just weak. Eliminate it.
    (E) Yep—the result that if companies don't pollute much anymore by installing less damaging equipment, there won't *be* any tax money with which to fund the National Park Service. Oops. It's the answer.

SECTION IV

QUESTIONS

20. Vaccines have allowed us to eradicate diseases such as smallpox, polio, and diptheria. Vaccines work by the injection of a weak or harmless version of a certain virus or bacteria in order to allow the body to learn to recognize it and build a defense against it, so that if a full-strength version of the virus ever enters the body, it will be recognized and attacked before it can do serious damage. Recently, vaccine therapy itself has undergone a major change. The old polio vaccine, for instance, actually required the injection of live (although severely weakened) polio virus into the subject, thereby causing polio in about 3 percent of the subjects. However, today's more modern polio vaccine works by administering a completely crippled polio vaccine: one that has had its genetic information removed so that it can never reproduce itself or cause polio. This new vaccine is at least as effective as the old one, and it has not caused polio in a single patient since it began to be used nearly a decade ago.

If all of the above statements are true, which one of the following must also be true?

(A) Aside from the few cases of polio caused by the administration of the old vaccine, the old vaccine was completely effective in preventing polio.
(B) The body must learn to recognize viruses by some other factor than their genetic information.
(C) Once we are able to manufacture a vaccine for a certain virus, the disease caused by that virus will be eradicated within a period of years.
(D) Vaccines will only work if your body's own immune system is in perfect shape.
(E) Except for cases of polio caused by the administration of the old vaccine, the old polio vaccine was no less effective than the new one.

EXPLANATIONS

20. This is an INFERENCE question. Your goal is to find the one choice that must be true based on the information in the passage.

(A) We don't know if this must be true or not. Eliminate it.
(B) This must be true, because if the body recognized viruses by their genetic information, then there's no way that the new genetic-information–free virus would be recognized by the body. It's the answer.
(C) This is too extreme. Eliminate it.
(D) This is too extreme. Eliminate it.
(E) This is the opposite of what the argument said, which was that the new one is at least as effective as the old one, not the other way around.

SECTION IV

QUESTIONS

21. In order to lose body fat, you have to raise your metabolism. If you run six hours per week, you'll be able to lose body fat. Therefore, if you lose body fat, you must be running six hours per week.

Which one of the following best describes the flaw in the argument?

(A) Some people might not want to run six hours per week.
(B) Although running six hours per week may be sufficient to raise your metabolism, it may not be necessary.
(C) If you don't run at least six hours per week, you will not raise your metabolism.
(D) Some people may want to run more than six hours per week in order to get in shape more quickly.
(E) Some people are not marathon runners and may take years to lose a significant amount of body fat.

22. The current notion of corporate liability holds that no corporate head can be sued unless criminal misconduct is established. Thus the corporate head cannot be held individually responsible but is viewed simply as a part of the corporate body, rather than as a distinct entity. This makes it difficult to recover compensation for corporate negligence from a corporate head who may ultimately have been responsible for his company's negligence, and may very well be directly responsible for implementation of the negligent act.

Which one of the following best supports the argument that corporate liability should be extended to corporate heads?

(A) The assets of negligent small corporations are often sufficient to compensate for damages awarded in negligence suits.
(B) The assets of heads of small corporations are often insufficient to compensate for damages awarded in negligence suits.
(C) The threat of personal liability will dissuade corporate heads from discharging their duties improperly.
(D) Threats of corporate liability are necessary in order to recover compensation for corporate negligence.
(E) Statistics indicate that where threats of personal liability are present, corporations are more likely to violate regulations that could lead to liability disputes.

EXPLANATIONS

21. **Conclusion:** If you lose fat, you must be running six hours a week.

Premise: If you run six hours a week, you'll be able to lose fat.

Assumption: Running six hours a week is the only way you can lose fat.

This is a FLAW question. Come up with your own description of what's wrong with the argument before you go to the answer choices, and then match your description to the choices.

(A) The desire of people to run is not what's wrong with the argument. Eliminate it.
(B) Exactly. The argument flip-flops the logic on itself, saying that the only way to lose body fat is to run six hours a week, eliminating all other possibilities.
(C) This is merely repeating the mistake the argument makes. Eliminate it.
(D) Once again, desire isn't the issue, and we don't know what happens if you run more than six hours.
(E) Marathon runners aren't the issue here. Eliminate it.

22. **Conclusion:** Corporate liability should be extended to corporate heads.

Premise: It is difficult to receive compensation from the corporate heads under the current system. You must instead sue the corporate body.

Assumption: There is some advantage to holding the corporate head personally liable rather than suing the corporation as a whole.

This is a STRENGTHEN question. Figure out which answer choice has the most positive impact on the conclusion of the argument. Remember to assume the hypothetical truth of each choice and apply it to the argument.

(A) This, if anything, would weaken the argument. Eliminate it.
(B) This would also weaken the argument because it says you wouldn't get any money even if you were able to sue corporate heads directly. Eliminate it.
(C) This would definitely help the conclusion that making corporate heads personally responsible would be a good thing. Let's keep it.
(D) If this choice said *personal* liability, then it might make sense. As of now, it doesn't. Eliminate it.
(E) This would also weaken the argument because it would have the opposite effect desired. Eliminate it.

SECTION IV

QUESTIONS

23. Sarah, a surgeon at a large hospital, asked a hospital administrator for permission to take the vital organs from a man who had just died in an accident, in order to use his organs to save the lives of several other people who needed immediate organ transplants to survive. The man carried neither identification with which to attempt to contact his family, nor anything that specifically authorized the use of his organs, such as an organ donor card. But the man did have a Goose Lodge lapel pin, and the Goose Lodge had long been in favor of encouraging its members to be organ donors.

Which one of the following principles, if accepted, would determine either that the man's organs should be used or that they should not be used?

(A) If using parts of a dead body can save people's lives, and if members of the dead person's family are notified and do not object, then those parts can be used.

(B) The fact that someone belongs to a group that encourages organ donations does not constitute consent on the part of that person to have his organs used.

(C) Authorization from a person's family, an organ donor card, or other authorizing document signed by that person is always sufficient to give permission to take that person's vital organs.

(D) If no relatives can be found after a period of 30 days, then a dead body can be used for whatever purposes its possessors see fit.

(E) Only if members of a dead person's family consent can that person's organs be used to save other lives.

EXPLANATIONS

23. This is a PRINCIPLE question. We are given five principles in the answer choices for this specific question, so we should come up with our own principle for the actions in the argument and match it to the answer choices.

(A) This wouldn't work because we can't contact the family of the guy.

(B) All this tells us is that we can't make a decision based on the pin. This is no help in deciding whether we should or should not use the organs.

(C) Because we don't have any of this, it doesn't help make our decision for us.

(D) This answer just says that in 30 days, we can use the organs if we want to. But the question is *should* we use the organs or not, not *can* we use the organs.

(E) This is much more powerful than (B) because it says the *only* way for us to take the organs is through family consent. Therefore, it's the answer.

SECTION IV

QUESTIONS

24. A survey of urban middle-class citizens revealed some inconsistencies in their attitudes toward the homeless. More than 75 percent of those who responded said that they believed the general public to be sympathetic toward the plight of the homeless. Ironically, an overwhelming majority of the respondents confessed to going to great lengths to avoid homeless people on the street.

Which one of the following, if true, would explain the apparent paradox in the results reported in the passage above?

(A) Having sympathy for homeless people and wanting to avoid them on the street are not necessarily incompatible positions.
(B) Sympathizing with one person who has no home is easier than dealing with homelessness as an abstract concept.
(C) There was a wide variety of sentiment regarding homelessness among the respondents themselves.
(D) Many of the respondents had once been homeless people themselves.
(E) The general public is not aware of government programs designed to implement low-income housing.

25. As a result of studies that successfully established that drinking a glass of red wine with dinner can reduce the risk of heart disease, doctors have been recommending that their patients consume red wine with their evening meals. Surprisingly, according to research intended to track the effectiveness of such recommendations, many patients who followed these recommendations continued to be vulnerable to heart disease.

Which one of the following, if true, would explain the unexpected result described above?

(A) Many patients ignore their doctors' recommendations to drink wine with meals.
(B) A greater number of people are likely to drink red wine than did before the results of the study were known.
(C) The high cost of red wine has discouraged many people from consuming it regularly.
(D) Red wine is not believed to prevent all types of diseases, so it is to be expected that people will continue to have some types of diseases.
(E) The beneficial effects of drinking red wine are incurred only when the wine is drunk in moderation, which many patients fail to do.

EXPLANATIONS

24. This is a PARADOX question. Look for an answer choice that allows both parts of the argument to be true, and remember to assume the hypothetical truth of each of the answer choices.

(A) Bingo. This allows both facts from the argument to be true.
(B) We're not talking about an abstract concept here. This has no impact. Eliminate it.
(C) That's nice, but it doesn't help to explain the seeming discrepancy. Eliminate it.
(D) Wow. Interesting, but it doesn't help to explain the discrepancy. In fact, it would exacerbate it, if anything.
(E) Government programs are really, really far outside the scope of this argument. Like, in Andromeda.

25. This is a PARADOX question. Look for an answer choice that allows both parts of the argument to be true, and remember to assume the hypothetical truth of each of the answer choices.

(A) But we're told in the argument that these patients have actually followed the recommendations.
(B) But we still have lots of people with heart disease.
(C) This is the same problem as (A).
(D) This is too general and therefore has no impact, because the argument is specifically talking about heart disease.
(E) Oops. Everyone's boozing it up! Therefore, this can explain why the treatment isn't working. It's the answer.

10

The Princeton Review LSAT Practice Test 2

SECTION I

Time—35 Minutes

27 Questions

Directions: Each passage in this section is followed by a group of questions to be answered on the basis of what is stated or implied in the passage. For some questions, more than one of the choices could conceivably answer the question. However, you are to choose the best answer, that is, the response that most accurately and completely answers the question, and blacken the corresponding space on your answer sheet.

Questions 1–6 are based on the following passage:

Conventionally, the landowner wishing to build on his land has the structure designed by one entity and then built by another; the design and build functions are viewed as separate. With the innovative "design-build" construction arrangement, however, a single entity performs both the design and construction functions. That single entity may be a joint venture between an architect or engineer and general contractor, a design-build firm that employs both professionals and contractors, or a general contracting firm subcontracting with an architectural or engineering firm. Design-build contracts appeal to owners because they require only one entity for performance; if a problem arises, the owner does not have to decide whether the architect or the contractor is the culprit. From the standpoint of the contractor, design-build contracts are advantageous because they secure both design fees and construction profits. In addition, many design-build contracts are calculated on a cost-plus basis and are therefore less risky than fixed-price work.

A design-build job may be carried out like a traditional project, in which the contractor prepares design documents and obtains owner approval before construction commences, or as a series of tasks entailing the preparation of design documents in phases, with construction beginning as each phase of the design is completed. The process of starting construction before the overall design is complete is known as the "fast-track" construction plan. Often, the design-build and fast-track concepts are employed together.

Fast-track construction appeals to owners because it reduces the time between a project's conception and its completion, thus minimizing finance costs and the often disastrous effects of inflation and increasing the likelihood that the budget will be adequate to complete the project. On the other hand, the fast-track approach presents problems to owners seeking construction changes. Normally, a builder is obliged to conform to designs and, with compensation for extra expense, to owner-requested changes when such changes are within the "scope of the project"; while in the traditional format, determining whether or not a change is within the scope of the project is relatively simple.

On a fast-track job, however, the finishing details of the job are defined after construction begins. Thus, there is more room for misunderstanding between the owner and the contractor as to whether design changes are within the scope of the project.

In this regard, a contractor should define the parameters of his obligations as early as possible. For example, the parties should be able to agree on the type and function of the structure, the number of stories, and the approximate area before any construction commences. Once building has begun, the keys to minimizing disputes are constant communication with the owner regarding what the contractor deems the scope of his work, and prompt notice if the contractor perceives that these bounds are being overstepped.

1. According to the passage, the design-build method of construction is attractive to a landowner who wishes to build on her land because

(A) she no longer needs to work with two separate entities
(B) it allows earlier marketing, thereby reducing finance costs
(C) its speed of construction protects her against inflation
(D) when problems develop, she has financial recourse
(E) it enables her to make changes even after the building has begun

GO ON TO THE NEXT PAGE.

2. Which one of the following would best serve as the concluding sentence of the last paragraph?

(A) Close contact allows full benefit from fast-track construction and reduces the likelihood of disputes.
(B) Because no communication is perfect, however, most owners choose conventional construction to avoid disputes.
(C) Unfortunately, owners of multiple projects often cannot maintain such close contact.
(D) Effective communication is ultimately the key to a productive work environment.
(E) Inspection of the building on completion would verify that it continued to adhere to safety regulations.

3. It can be inferred from the passage that contractors find the design-build method advantageous because

(A) it reduces the number of design documents that need to be prepared
(B) design changes are easier to facilitate
(C) owners are less likely to request costly changes in the scope of the project
(D) the financial risks are less than for traditional construction projects
(E) they need hire only one entity

4. Which one of the following best summarizes the main point of the author?

(A) Fast-track programs represent a radical departure from the no-longer-effective traditional method of construction.
(B) Conventional construction and design-build construction are both equally valid methods of construction, though each is best suited to different circumstances.
(C) The combination of design-build and fast-track methods of construction creates financial risks that many landowners find unacceptable.
(D) Contractors have begun to encourage their clients to explore new methods and systems of design and construction.
(E) While the design-build and fast-track methods of construction provide advantages to both landowners and contractors, the fast-track method also carries some risks.

5. In mentioning the "disastrous effects of inflation" (line 33), the author is probably referring to the fact that

(A) delayed completion inhibits renting or selling the building because of higher costs
(B) lengthy construction time can put costs beyond the owner's ability to pay
(C) financiers may, because of inflationary pressures, demand earlier returns
(D) inflation can weaken the link between design-build and fast-track
(E) the contractor may demand higher payment for design changes

6. Based on the information given in the passage, the author would consider each of the following good advice to an owner who has arranged for fast-track construction of a building on his land EXCEPT

(A) after construction is complete, verify that changes have been made according to specifications
(B) reach agreement on the major decisions concerning the project before construction begins
(C) bring problems to the attention of the contractor as soon as they arise
(D) confer with the contractor frequently during construction
(E) prepare a list of important design details before the project begins so that misunderstandings are avoided

GO ON TO THE NEXT PAGE.

Questions 7–14 are based on the following pasage:

In the early 1980s, a number of citizens established organizations devoted to preventing drivers from operating motor vehicles while under the influence of alcohol. These organizations sparked a continuing grassroots social movement that attacks the problem of drunk driving by calling for community awareness and stronger sanctions. Unlike the prohibitionist movements of the late nineteenth and early twentieth centuries, which identified drinking itself as inherently wrong, the anti-drunk-driving movements emphasize the issue of drinking while driving automobiles; the problem is not alcohol use (or abuse), but the irresponsibility of individuals using alcohol. In essence, these organizations have spawned a social movement against the evils caused by personal irresponsibility.

The Progressive reform movements around the turn of the century shared the same moral ethic. As Hofstadter has argued, the Progressive reform movements were strongly based on the "ethos of personal responsibility" and the basic morality of civic consciousness. That approach is reflected in the goals of today's movement and in its views on proposals to solve the drunk-driving problem. The two most important program goals of current-day organizations are public awareness activities, designed to make drinkers understand that it is wrong to drive when under the influence of alcohol, and youth education programs, designed to convey this message to young drivers.

The "ethos of personal responsibility" for one's actions also has an impact in determining what actions are taken to solve the problem. Grassroots organizations call for punitive measures to be taken against drunk drivers. They perceive non-punitive programs—such as the safe-ride program—as ineffective. As one founding member of one organization put it: "Safe ride programs may help temporarily, but they cause people to ignore their part in the problem."

Rehabilitation programs are rejected on the same grounds. In addition to labeling these programs as ineffective, grassroots organizers perceive them as a minor inconvenience to offenders and as a means of avoiding stricter punishment. This punitive approach to "problem drinking" represents a departure from the trend of viewing drinking problems as a disease and thus a medical problem. The movement does not distinguish between the sick alcoholic and the irresponsible "problem drinker" in its desire to enforce sanctions against the drunk driver.

These opinions reflect the basic moral view that citizens should be aware of the dangers of driving while drunk and their individual responsibility to drive sober. As a result of this awareness, those individuals acting irresponsibly should face serious punishment. Society, on the other hand, should not take the responsibility for individual conduct by instituting prohibitionist measures, safe-ride programs, or programs for rehabilitation.

7. The main idea of the passage is that

(A) centuries of anti-alcohol public awareness campaigns reflect the United States' focus on personal responsibility
(B) present-day grassroots anti-drunk-driving organizations emphasize personal responsibility as the key to effecting change
(C) Prohibition failed because it ignored the United States' ethic of responsibility
(D) if non-punitive programs worked, there would be no grassroots anti-drunk-driving movement
(E) no anti-drunk-driving campaign is likely to succeed without punishing the driver

8. According to the passage, the modern grassroots movement designed to prevent drunk driving

(A) is largely unconcerned with the broader issue of alcohol abuse
(B) is more concerned with protecting the lives of sober drivers than of drunk drivers
(C) is less opposed to drunk driving than it is in favor of personal responsibility
(D) is excessively punitive, and, therefore, not likely to be effective
(E) views drunk driving narrowly, and, therefore, promises less success than the prohibition movement

9. The turn-of-the-century Progressive reform movements and the current grassroots movements share all of the following EXCEPT

(A) a belief in personal responsibility
(B) an emphasis on morality
(C) a desire for behavior modification as it relates to civic consciousness
(D) a disapproval of drinking
(E) a commitment to altering certain conduct

GO ON TO THE NEXT PAGE.

10. As used in line 20 of the passage, a person who follows a "basic morality of civic consciousness" probably

(A) abides by community standards for moral behavior
(B) supports the work done by alcoholic-rehabilitation programs
(C) advocates the adoption of severe penalties for driving while intoxicated
(D) proposes that basic rules of moral behavior are essential to a just society
(E) understands that drinking before driving wrongfully endangers the safety and welfare of others

11. According to the passage, grassroots organizations do not believe that prohibition is an effective solution to the drunk-driving problem because prohibition

(A) is too punitive, especially for responsible drinkers
(B) fails to recognize alcoholism as a disease
(C) does not share the aims of the history of Progressive reform movements in the United States
(D) makes society responsible for an individual's problems
(E) does nothing to make citizens aware of the drunk-driving problem

12. In the third paragraph, the author's purpose is to

(A) demonstrate the grassroots rejection of solutions that do not address driver accountability
(B) explain why the safe-ride program is unlikely to eradicate drunk driving
(C) present a view in opposition to that of the Progressive reform movements
(D) support his belief that non-punitive programs are ineffective
(E) distinguish between punitive and non-punitive social reforms, favoring non-punitive reforms

13. Which one of the following best describes the organization of the passage?

(A) A general philosophy of responsibility is presented, and specific approaches that do not adhere to that philosophy are rejected.
(B) An ethos of personal responsibility is described, and then an alternate approach is described.
(C) The history of a movement is outlined in chronological order.
(D) A current political movement is analyzed, and the events that led to its creation are examined.
(E) The historical approaches to a social problem are outlined and comparisons made.

14. The author of the passage would be most likely to agree with which one of the following statements about the "ethos of personal responsibility" and its relationship to grassroots campaigns against drunk driving?

(A) Its impact on the organization of grassroots campaigns has been negligible, because these campaigns favor a more punitive approach.
(B) It causes certain methods for dealing with drunk drivers to be favored over others that are perceived as ineffective or even dangerous.
(C) It has been largely responsible for the introduction of public awareness campaigns involving both adults and teenagers.
(D) It results in the belief that drinking is inherently wrong.
(E) It establishes a general principle that provides a justification for acting irresponsibly while under the influence of alcohol.

GO ON TO THE NEXT PAGE.

Questions 15–20 are based on the following passage:

In a representative democracy, legislatures exist to represent the public and to ensure that public issues are efficiently addressed by a group representative of the population as a whole. It is often written that a legislator confronts a moral dilemma if, on a given issue upon which he must cast a vote, his view is decidedly different from that of the majority of his constituents. In such a circumstance, it is not clear whether voting citizens have chosen the legislator because of their faith in his personal judgment or whether they have elected him in order to give direct effect to their own views.

But this dilemma is more apparent than real. A truly identifiable conflict between the legislator's opinion and that of his constituency is rare, because the legislator is usually better informed than the public on the issue in question and his opinion, therefore, cannot fairly be compared to theirs. Indeed, this fact underscores the legislator's most important function: to gather broad-based information in order to make more considered decisions than each citizen could reach individually and thus to serve the public interest better than the public could do on its own.

Let us suppose that a legislator opposes a very popular proposed public works project because he has studied its financial ramifications and believes, over the long run, it is fiscally unsound. If the legislator's constituents write letters expressing their ardent support for the project, not having studied the relevant financial data, it is entirely too simplistic to view the legislator as having to confront a moral dilemma. The truth is that the legislator does not know how his constituents would view the project if they truly understood its financial consequences. Without such knowledge, the legislator cannot actually conclude that his view differs from that of his constituents. To conclude that their views should dictate his decision might foster his popularity, but would contravene his fundamental legislative responsibility.

The legislator's job is first to study the short-range and long-range goals of the people he represents, without confusing these with his own. Then, using his knowledge and judgment, he is to promote the electorate's goals as he understands them. Consider, for instance, a legislator whose constituents wish to maintain the rural character of their district. If the legislator himself dislikes rural living and would like to see the area undergo industrial development, or if he believes an industrial environment would offer greater benefit to the community than a rural environment, he must separate these viewpoints from his professional judgment. He is not to promote industrialization because he personally favors it.

However, if the legislator's considered opinion is that his district needs to sponsor *some* industrial development in order to maintain its overall agricultural character, it is his duty to promote the industrial development, even if his constituents oppose it. So long as he honestly attempts to serve his electorate's objectives, the legislator should stand firm against the expressed opinions of his own constituents.

15. The author's purpose in the first paragraph is to

(A) explain that many legislative questions require economic as well as political understanding
(B) point out that a possible moral dilemma exists when a legislator disagrees with her constituents
(C) illustrate that the legislator's extra knowledge creates the gap between her views and those of her constituents
(D) argue that legislative decisions should not be made simplistically
(E) encourage the rejection of legislation that runs counter to the public interest

16. According to the passage, the differences between a legislator's view and the views expressed by the legislator's constituents

(A) do not actually create a moral dilemma in most cases
(B) create a moral dilemma only in a democracy
(C) only arise when constituents are ill-informed
(D) require that a legislator gather more information than he would otherwise have done
(E) usually reflect a difference not in opinion, but in long-range goals

GO ON TO THE NEXT PAGE.

17. It can be inferred from the passage that the author believes a legislator should

(A) carry out her constituents' intentions if doing so conforms to her assessment
(B) ignore her constituents' long-range objectives when they are morally incompatible with her own beliefs
(C) take whatever actions her constituents recommend
(D) determine what action will best serve her constituents, regardless of their stated position
(E) put her own assessments aside and embody those of her electorate

18. Which one of the following would the author most likely believe to be true of a legislator who routinely reached legislative decisions by following constituents' instructions?

(A) The legislator would probably not fully understand the public's goals.
(B) The legislator would be acting in a manner contrary to her own interests.
(C) The legislator would probably be unaware of the course of action most favorable to her constituency.
(D) The legislator might not be fulfilling her proper role of defending the best interests of the electorate.
(E) The legislator would be overly concerned with maintaining her own popularity, not carrying out her appropriate duties.

19. Which one of the following, if true, would most weaken the author's contention that a legislator can make "more considered decisions" than can his constituents?

(A) A community should be allowed to make its own decisions, even if these are not the most informed decisions.
(B) Because a legislator does not live in the same circumstances as do his constituents, he is more objective and less emotional in his decision-making.
(C) Some constituents make a great effort to inform themselves on all aspects of proposed legislation.
(D) The information provided to the legislator is occasionally biased or misleading.
(E) Some legislators have difficulty separating their personal views from those of their constituents.

20. According to the author, the introduction of widespread industrialization into the rural community described in lines 42–50 represents

(A) the failure of a legislator to understand the requirements of the region
(B) an example of a legislator advancing his agenda at the expense of that of his constituents
(C) the failure of representative democracy to address the needs of its constituents
(D) the ability of a legislator to ignore the interests of the community he represents
(E) the result of a legislator carrying through on the expressed views of his constituents

GO ON TO THE NEXT PAGE.

Questions 21–27 are based on the following pasage:

The KT boundary, as it is called, marks one of the most violent events ever to befall life on Earth. Sixty-five million years ago, according to current theory, the Cretaceous period was brought to a sudden conclusion by the impact of an asteroid or a comet ten kilometers in diameter. It would be natural to suppose that the KT boundary is a fossil hunter's paradise. But it is nothing of the sort. In fact, no bones have been found at the KT boundary anywhere on earth.

Some paleontologists find the situation frustrating, to put it mildly. Granted, they say, the record of life preserved in sedimentary rocks is far from perfect. But in this case the event of record is a cosmic catastrophe that killed all the dinosaurs in the world. Shouldn't the concentration of bones in the fossil record be, at very least, above average?

In some places the sedimentary rocks preserve detailed temporal signals with near-textbook fidelity, but such detailed windows into the past are relatively rare. More commonly, various natural forces like the wind and rain disrupt the chronological ordering of the fossils-to-be.

The first serious proposal for solving this sedimentary puzzle came in 1940, in a paper by the Soviet paleontologist Ivan A. Efremov. Paleontologists, Efremov said, were too inclined to take the fossil record at face value; instead, he advised, they ought to pay more attention to the processes whereby living organisms become, or fail to become, fossils. A better understanding of burial and fossilization might enable paleontologists to "back calculate" and reclaim lost data from the fossil record.

Paleontologists Alan Cutler and Anna Behrensmeyer have developed just such a model of fossil preservation. Starting with a hypothetical population of dinosaurs, they estimated normal annual mortality rates for dinosaurs from ecological data collected for large mammals in African wildlife preserves. Next, to estimate what fraction of the dinosaurs' bones would end up safely buried, they drew on data from Behrensmeyer's study of the decay of mammal carcasses in Ambesoli National Park, Kenya. Finally, they ran the model to see what sort of bone spike would result if the entire population of dinosaurs suddenly died. The answer, they discovered, was no bone spike at all.

In the mixed, or convoluted, record, spikes in the abundance of species are attenuated and tail off exponentially. The thicker the mixing layer, the greater the smearing. Thus, the sudden extinction of a species shows up not as an abrupt disappearance of fossils, but a gradual petering out.

There is no way of predicting exactly what further research may bring. However promising its results may be, though, one caveat is necessary: It will never be able to work miracles. The most sophisticated mathematics in the world cannot unscramble an egg or resurrect the dinosaurs.

21. Which of the following may be inferred about the KT boundary?

(A) The fossil record it contains is above average in both the quantity of fossils and their degree of preservation.
(B) It was destroyed by a large comet sixty-five million years ago.
(C) The fossil record it contains is, in some ways, inconsistent with the dominant theory of dinosaur extinction.
(D) Its significance was first described by paleontologist Ivan A. Efremov.
(E) Paleontologists consider it to be the single richest source in the fossil record.

22. Which of the following best describes the main idea of the passage?

(A) If paleontologists are to achieve significant results in the future, they must reject their older methods.
(B) Because it cannot be substantiated by the fossil record, the dominant theory of dinosaur extinction should be rejected.
(C) Because of the nature of the process by which bones become fossils, scientists should not be surprised by the relative absence of fossils at the KT boundary.
(D) Back-calculation indicates that the KT boundary should contain more fossils than more recent rock layers.
(E) More recent methods of modeling fossil preservation provide evidence that contradicts earlier findings made by paleontologists.

GO ON TO THE NEXT PAGE.

23. Which one of the following best describes the relationship between the work of Efremov and that of Cutler and Behrensmeyer?

(A) Efremov's work described the need for a significant shift in approach and Cutler and Behrensmeyer carried out research based in part on his approach.
(B) Efremov's work provided the data from which Cutler and Behrensmeyer were able to develop a model of fossil preservation.
(C) Whereas Efremov focused principally on why bones do not become fossils, Cutler and Behrensmeyer focused on why they do.
(D) Efremov's work was theoretically more complex than that carried out by Cutler and Behrensmeyer.
(E) Efremov focused on processes whereas Cutler and Behrensmeyer focused on data collection.

24. Which of the following best describes the organization of the passage?

(A) Data gathered from a broad range of sources is presented, inconsistencies among the data are described, then these inconsistencies are resolved.
(B) Research from two different groups of scientists is presented, a question about the research is posed, and an answer is offered.
(C) A new theoretical model is explained, problems with the model are pointed out, and possible explanations for the problem are suggested.
(D) A paradox is described, and both theoretical and empirical information is presented to help explain the paradox.
(E) A fundamental scientific failure is described, evidence substantiating this failure is presented, then a new approach to the problem is described.

25. The author would be most likely to agree with which of the following statements?

(A) Data from large mammal populations are essential in any attempt to model the process of dinosaur extinction.
(B) Fossil evidence indicates that the dinosaurs probably became extinct over a longer period of time than previously believed.
(C) The KT boundary provides a unique source of information about animal extinction.
(D) In most fossil layers, evidence of extinction trails off exponentially but contains an initial bone spike.
(E) Improvements in paleontological research, while useful, will not provide sufficient answers to all of the questions about dinosaur extinction.

26. The author states that, in their evaluation of the fossil record, Cutler and Behrensmeyer did all of the following EXCEPT

(A) conclude that the data from the fossil record was consistent with a mass extinction of dinosaurs
(B) work with paleontologist Ivan A. Efremov
(C) use data gathered from populations of large animals to estimate characteristics of dinosaur populations
(D) base their work on hypothetical information about dinosaur populations
(E) use data from studies of the decay of mammal carcasses in Africa

27. According to the passage, a segment of the fossil record in which paleontologists would LEAST expect to see a clear record of a period of sudden extinction would be one in which

(A) an abundance of bone spikes exist
(B) an unusually large portion of the bones were safely buried before fossilization
(C) "back calculation" would be difficult, but possible
(D) drought occurred at the time of fossilization
(E) a particularly thick mixing layer was present during fossil formation

S T O P

IF YOU FINISH BEFORE TIME IS CALLED, YOU MAY CHECK YOUR WORK ON THIS SECTION ONLY.
DO NOT WORK ON ANY OTHER SECTION IN THE TEST.

SECTION II

Time—35 Minutes

25 Questions

Directions: The questions in this section are based on the reasoning contained in brief statements or passages. For some questions, more than one of the choices could conceivably answer the question. However, you are to choose the best answer; that is, the response that most accurately and completely answers the question. You should not make assumptions that are by commonsense standards implausible, superfluous, or incompatible with the passage. After you have chosen the best answer, blacken the corresponding space on your answer sheet.

1. The quality of our public schools is more likely to decline if people expect it to. The number of illiterate graduates and the level of administrative incompetence will increase as people's disrespect for public schools discourages more able people from pursuing careers in teaching.

   The logical structure of the above statement is most consistent with which one of the following?

   (A) If people believe that an eagerly anticipated event will take place, then it most likely will.
   (B) When people believe that money grows on trees, then, for all practical purposes, money does grow on trees.
   (C) When people expect the economy to flourish, they become willing to spend and invest more, thus helping the economy to flourish.
   (D) When people expect world affairs to be tragic, they notice tragic events more than they do pleasant ones.
   (E) If people enjoy sporting events, the stadiums and arenas will be full, thus encouraging high attendance at future sporting events.

2. In an experiment, first-year college students were asked to listen to a tape of someone speaking French. When asked to repeat the sounds they had heard, students who had studied French in high school could repeat more of the sounds than could students who had no knowledge of French. When asked to listen to a tape of only meaningless sounds, none of the students were able to repeat more than a few seconds' worth of the sounds made on the tape.

   Which one of the following conclusions is best supported by the information above?

   (A) Knowledge of a foreign language interferes with one's ability to repeat unfamiliar sounds.
   (B) People who have a knowledge of French have better memories than do people who have no knowledge of French.
   (C) The ability to repeat unrelated sounds is not improved by frequent practice.
   (D) The ability to repeat sounds is influenced by one's ability to comprehend the meaning of the sounds.
   (E) Learning a foreign language requires an ability to distinguish unfamiliar sounds from gibberish.

GO ON TO THE NEXT PAGE.

Questions 3–4

Many commercial pesticides, used primarily in indoor atriums, greenhouses, and solariums, release toxic levels of Acephate and other potentially carcinogenic agents hazardous to the health of workers and other individuals who pass through the area. This problem can be avoided by providing adequate ventilation, but this becomes difficult during winter months when the area must maintain sufficient heat to ensure the survival of the plants. A recent study shows that certain tropical grasses will remove some of these toxins from the air, eliminating the danger to humans. In one winter trial, a four-foot-square patch of tropical grass eliminated Acephate in a solarium of average size.

3. Assume that a patch of tropical grass is introduced into a solarium of average size that contains toxic pesticide residue.

Which one of the following can be expected as a result?

(A) Occasional ventilation, even during the summer, will become unnecessary.
(B) The concentration of toxic pesticide residues will remain unchanged.
(C) The solarium will continue to maintain a constant level of toxicity and temperature.
(D) If there are toxic Acephate residues in the solarium, these levels will decrease.
(E) If Acephate and other potentially carcinogenic agents are being released in the solarium, the quantities of each agent will decrease.

4. The passage above is designed to lead to which one of the following conclusions?

(A) Tropical grass removes all carcinogenic agents from the air.
(B) Natural pesticides do not release toxins into greenhouses, solariums, or corporate atriums.
(C) Planting tropical grass is an effective means of maintaining a constant temperature in a greenhouse.
(D) Growing tropical grass can counteract some of the negative effects of a poorly ventilated atrium.
(E) The air in an atrium that contains tropical grass and maintains a constant temperature will contain fewer toxic residues than will the air in a similarly maintained atrium without tropical grass.

5. Medical Researcher: If I don't get another research grant soon, I'll never be able to discover a cure for phlebitis.

Assistant: But that's great. If your grant does come through, that dreaded disease will finally be eradicated.

Which one of the following statements best describes the flaw in the assistant's reasoning?

(A) The assistant believes the researcher will be unable to cure phlebitis unless the grant comes through.
(B) The assistant thinks the researcher will use the grant to find a cure for phlebitis, rather than for some other purpose.
(C) The assistant believes it is more important to cure phlebitis than to eradicate other, more deadly conditions.
(D) The assistant believes that all the researcher needs in order to cure phlebitis is another research grant.
(E) The assistant thinks the researcher will cure phlebitis even if the grant does not come through.

6. Economist: The keys to a growth economy are low interest rates and a high number of investments; because there cannot be investments without low interest rates, it can be concluded that where there are low interest rates there are investments.

Which one of the following, if true, would most weaken the argument above?

(A) Many growth economies with high interest rates have few investments.
(B) Stagnant economies with high interest rates have few investments.
(C) Stagnant economies with low interest rates have few investments.
(D) A high number of investments is adequate to guarantee low interest rates.
(E) Some stagnant economies have low interest rates.

GO ON TO THE NEXT PAGE.

7. A study commissioned by the National Association of Women Professors seems to indicate that women face greater obstacles in becoming tenured professors than do men. Whereas more than 70 percent of the male professors in this country have tenure, fewer than half of the female professors have achieved that rank.

Which one of the following statistics would be most relevant to an assessment of the accuracy of the study mentioned above?

(A) the respective percentages of eligible women and men who have earned tenure in each of the past ten years
(B) the percentage of all tenured positions that have gone to women in each of the past ten years
(C) an analysis of the bias faced by women in other professional fields
(D) the number of men who have been appointed to tenured positions, and the number of women who have not been appointed to tenured positions
(E) the number of professional women who cite the difficulty of achieving tenure when asked to explain why they decided against entering academia

8. Sheet for sheet, Brand A paper towels cost less than Brand B paper towels and are more absorbent. Yet a roll of Brand A paper towels costs more than a roll of Brand B paper towels.

Which one of the following, if true, explains how the statements above can both be true?

(A) Both Brand A and Brand B towels are manufactured by the same company, which often creates artificial competition for its expensive products.
(B) A roll of Brand B paper towels is more absorbent than a roll of Brand A paper towels.
(C) A roll of Brand A paper towels is more absorbent than a roll of Brand B paper towels.
(D) The cost of a roll of Brand A towels has risen every year for the last five years.
(E) A roll of Brand A paper towels has more sheets than a roll of Brand B paper towels.

9. State agricultural officials are hoping to save California's $30 billion-a-year fruit industry from destruction by the Mediterranean fruit fly by releasing nearly one billion sterile female fruit flies throughout the state. This has, in the past, been shown to be the only effective means of limiting the spread of this destructive pest, outside of large-scale pesticide spraying.

Which one of the following best explains the intended effect of the program described above?

(A) To drastically increase the number of potential mates for the male fruit flies, requiring them to devote more of their energies to mating rather than eating fruit.
(B) To saturate a given area with fruit flies, creating greater competition for food and thereby containing the damage done by the fruit fly to a smaller area.
(C) To ensure that a large number of fruit flies in succeeding generations are born infertile.
(D) To limit the growth of the population by reducing the number of successful matings between fruit flies.
(E) To encourage overpopulation of the fruit fly in the hopes that nature will correct the situation itself.

10. A fit, well-tuned body is essential to good health because exercise acts to improve circulation and helps to eliminate toxins from the body. If one is to remain healthy, one must get regular exercise.

Which one of the following conclusions can most logically be drawn from the passage above?

(A) If one exercises, one will be healthy.
(B) Only exercise acts to improve the circulation and eliminate toxins from the body.
(C) A healthy person must have eliminated all toxins from his or her body.
(D) If one does not exercise regularly, one will not remain healthy.
(E) A person who is not healthy must not exercise.

GO ON TO THE NEXT PAGE.

11. Marie: I just found out that it is cheaper for me to heat my home with gas or oil than for me to use any of the alternative methods available. I don't understand why environmentalists insist that the cost of fossil fuels is so high.

Louise: That's because you are confusing the price of fossil fuels with their cost. Gas and oil release tremendous amounts of pollution into the water and air, causing great damage to the environment. Not only does this pose a threat to the ecological balance that will affect the quality of life for future generations, but it also causes health problems that may be related to the consumption of these fuels. Once you add in these factors, it is clear that there are many alternatives that are actually cheaper than gas or oil, and consumers should adopt them.

According to her argument above, if an alternative energy source were to be found, under which one of the following conditions would Louise definitely object to its use?

(A) if its price and cost were equal
(B) if its cost were higher than the price of fossil fuels
(C) if its cost were higher than the cost of fossil fuels
(D) if the price of fossil fuels were to fall
(E) if it were less efficient than fossil fuels

12. An office equipment rental firm made the following claim:

Owning your office equipment is actually more expensive than renting it. Over a three-year period, a mid-sized copier, for example, costs $23,000 per year to own, based on the average purchase price of the machine and the cost of its maintenance. The cost of renting a comparable copier is $22,000 per year.

Which one of the following statements, if true, provides the most effective criticism of the argument above?

(A) The average lifespan of a copier is between five and six years.
(B) The figures cited above remain proportionally the same even when more expensive copiers are considered.
(C) The price of copiers actually has decreased in the last ten years.
(D) The price of copier paper and electricity may soon rise sharply.
(E) Buying used copiers can save money, even though such machines need more maintenance.

GO ON TO THE NEXT PAGE.

Questions 13–14

Despite advances in geothermal technology and equipment, experts rarely agree which method is the best indicator of a likely source of oil. Some believe the cycle of environmental changes determines the primary sources for crude oil, while others look to the evolution of organic matter as the most significant indicator. What they do agree on, however, is where oil won't be found. They agree that in areas that were scraped clean of organic sedimentary deposits by glaciers during the last million years or so, the biological "ingredients" that they believe are necessary for the formation of oil and gas are not present. That is, where glaciers have scoured a landmass, oil and gas will not be found.

13. If all of the information above is true, which one of the following can be reasonably inferred?

(A) Geologists understand some of the physical conditions necessary for the formation of deposits of oil.
(B) Scientists leave open the possibility that oil may have been formed during the last million years in some regions that were covered by glaciers during the same period.
(C) Geologists can, with a fairly high degree of accuracy, predict whether an area that meets the necessary preconditions for the formation of oil will, in fact, yield oil.
(D) Geologists can, with a fairly high degree of accuracy, predict whether oil can be found in a particular landmass that was not scoured by glaciers.
(E) If geologists can determine the biological "ingredients" necessary for the formation of oil, they can determine the locations of the most promising oil fields.

14. Which one of the following, if true, would most seriously weaken the geologists' view?

(A) Relatively little of the earth's surface is known to rest above the sort of organic sedimentary deposits described above.
(B) Despite the existence of permanent glaciers, oil has been found at both the North and South Poles.
(C) There are too many variables involved for experts to be able to identify what does and does not need to be present for the formation of oil.
(D) The glacier theory cannot help locate oil in the ocean because ocean beds went untouched by glaciers.
(E) Oil deposits exist below the crust of the entire Earth, and are brought nearer to the surface by cracks in the crust.

15. Although all societies have some form of class system, there are systems that are based on neither wealth nor power. Still, there is no society that does not divide its population into the privileged and the common.

If the above statements are correct, it can be properly concluded that

(A) making distinctions between haves and have-nots is a part of human nature
(B) there are some people in all cultures who are considered privileged
(C) every society has its own unique hierarchy
(D) privileged people must have money
(E) all societies have a tradition of seeing themselves as either privileged or common

16. One can predict that the number of people in the nation's labor force will diminish in the next 20 years. Population growth in our country reached its apex in 1961, and by the late 1960s there were more employed heads of households in this country than ever before. The growth has slackened significantly, and by 2007 the total number of households will be reduced, thus limiting the number of potential employees in the work force.

Which one of the following, if true, would most seriously damage the conclusion of the above argument?

(A) The urge to acquire wealth contributed to the growth of the labor force in the 1960s.
(B) There will be greater competition among employers to attract employees from a shrinking population base during the next decade.
(C) In the next decade there will be more people who are not the heads of household entering the labor force than there were in the 1960s.
(D) Employers fared well in the 1950s with fewer potential employees than exist today.
(E) By 2007 there will be far more people running their own businesses than there are today.

GO ON TO THE NEXT PAGE.

Questions 17–18

A controversy recently erupted at College X after the student newspaper printed several letters to the editor that attacked the college's affirmative action program in offensive, racially charged language. Two psychologists at the school took advantage of the controversy by conducting an experiment on campus. Psychologist #1, posing as a reporter, stopped a student at random, ostensibly to solicit his or her opinion of the controversy. At the same time, psychologist #2, posing as a student, also stopped, joined the discussion, and made the first reply to the questions of the "reporter." The experiment showed that when psychologist #2 expressed support for the racist sentiments expressed in the letters, 75 percent of the subjects responded similarly. When psychologist #2 expressed strong disapproval of the language and substance of the letters, 90 percent of the subjects responded similarly.

17. Which one of the following represents the most reasonable conclusion that can be drawn from the information in the passage above?

(A) People are more likely to voice their opposition to racism if they hear others doing the same.
(B) People are less likely to hide their sympathy for certain racist attitudes if they feel that others share the same feelings.
(C) People's willingness to voice their racist sentiments is proportional to the percentage of all people who share such sentiments.
(D) People may be influenced by the opinions of others when they express their opinions of racist sentiments.
(E) The extent to which popular opinion molds the opinions of individuals is significant, though not easily quantifiable.

18. If the psychologists described above were to conclude from their data that some people are more willing to speak up against racism if they hear others doing so, their conclusion would depend on the validity of which one of the following assumptions?

(A) The students at College X are no more racist than are students at other colleges.
(B) The students at College X are more likely to have experienced racism personally.
(C) Some of the subjects in the experiment knew that the psychologists were posing as a reporter and a student.
(D) Some of the subjects in their experiment would have changed their response to psychologist #1's questions if psychologist #2 had responded differently.
(E) All of the subjects in the experiment stated their heartfelt, uninfluenced opinion of the incident in question.

19. Evidence seems to indicate that people's faith in some mystical practices increases when these practices offer relief in frightening or challenging situations. One significant piece of evidence is the observation that the use of "healing crystals" is more prevalent among people who suffer from life-threatening diseases such as cancer than it is among people who have minor health problems such as colds or the flu.

Which one of the following, if true, would most seriously weaken the conclusion drawn in the passage above?

(A) Rapid social change has alienated people and has led to an overall increase in people's adoption of mystical practices.
(B) Many mystical practices are never used by more than a small number of extremely ill people.
(C) If someone has a life-threatening disease, he may try nontraditional cures without necessarily believing that they will work.
(D) Psychics and mediums do not experience a surge in business after the occurrence of earthquakes and plane crashes.
(E) The use of crystals is one of the most ancient methods utilized for healing.

GO ON TO THE NEXT PAGE.

20. Lithotripsy is a relatively new procedure for the treatment of kidney stones. The patient is suspended in a tub of water and sound waves are aimed at his kidneys. Upon impact, the waves shatter the stones. Recovery time from this procedure is shorter than that of surgery, which is the conventional method of treatment. Lithotripsy is also less expensive than surgery. Therefore, physicians should stop performing invasive surgery for kidney stones soon.

Which one of the following statements, if true, most seriously weakens the argument in the passage above?

(A) There has been little research done on the effect of lithotripsy on senior citizens.
(B) It will be many years before lithotripsy equipment can be produced in sufficient quantity to meet demand.
(C) Many doctors do not know much about lithotripsy, as it is a relatively new procedure.
(D) Some insurance companies do not cover treatments such as lithotripsy.
(E) Lithotripsy is not an available option for children.

21. The human body changes a great deal over the course of a lifetime. As people enter middle age, for instance, they tend to become overweight, regardless of their body type as young adults. Though this weight gain has long been blamed on the tendency of middle-aged people to consume an excess of calories daily, recent evidence suggests that it is instead attributable to the body's decreased demand for calories. This decreased demand means that a maintenance of prior caloric consumption will provide an excess of calories, most of which will simply be stored as body fat.

A logical critique of the passage above would likely emphasize the fact that the author fails to

(A) establish definitively the connection between caloric intake and weight gain
(B) offer any hard evidence of the percentage of middle-aged people who are actually overweight
(C) give detailed information as to the causes of the body's decreased demand for calories in middle age
(D) offer a consistent definition of the term "excess" as it relates to caloric consumption
(E) discuss the causes of obesity in the population at large

22. If a candidate is to win an election easily, that candidate must respond to the electorate's emotional demands—demands that the opponent either does not see or cannot act upon. Though these emotional demands are often not directly articulated by the electorate or by the candidate responding to them, they are an integral part of any landslide victory.

Which one of the following conclusions can most logically be drawn from the passage above?

(A) If neither candidate responds to the emotional demands of the electorate, either candidate might win in a landslide.
(B) If an election was close, the emotional demands of the electorate were conflicting.
(C) If a candidate responds to the emotional demands of the electorate, that candidate will have a landslide victory.
(D) An election during which neither candidate responds to the emotional demands of the electorate will not result in a landslide.
(E) Emotional demands are the only inarticulated issues in an election.

23. Commodities analysts maintain that if the price of soybeans decreases by more than half, the consumer's purchase price for milk produced by livestock fed these soybeans will also decrease by more than half.

Which one of the following, if true, casts the most doubt on the prediction made by the commodities analysts?

(A) New genetic strains of livestock and improvements in feed lot procedures have enabled some cows to increase their milk output while decreasing their soybean intake.
(B) Dairy farmers cannot expand their profit margins any further without compromising the health of their livestock.
(C) Many different dairy suppliers compete with each other, forcing a consumer-driven market.
(D) Studies in other dairy-producing countries show that the amount of milk purchased by consumers usually rises after an initial decrease in milk prices.
(E) Pasteurization and distribution costs, neither of which varies with the price of soybeans, constitute the major portion of the price of milk.

GO ON TO THE NEXT PAGE.

24. The more dairy products a person consumes, the higher his cholesterol level is. More than half of the people in this country eat in excess of four dairy products each day, whereas in Germany the figure is only 10 percent. Accordingly, more than 65 percent of the people in this country have cholesterol levels that are considered too high and only 2 percent of Germans have similarly excessive levels. Therefore, if the cholesterol levels of Americans are to be brought down, we must eat fewer dairy products.

Which one of the following, if established, could strengthen the author's argument?

(A) Citizens of the United States are less concerned with cholesterol levels than citizens of Germany.
(B) Germans are more disciplined about watching their diets than Americans.
(C) People who are concerned about their cholesterol levels will eat fewer dairy products.
(D) A person's cholesterol level is reduced significantly when he or she consumes fewer than two dairy products per day.
(E) Dairy products, and not any other food items, are the critical factors in determining cholesterol levels.

25. The introduction of new technologies and equipment into the marketplace can significantly alter the quality of life for the members of a society. The automatic dishwasher, for example, eased the housekeeping burdens traditionally borne by women. At the same time, the convenience of an automatic dishwasher has fostered a dependence upon its time-saving qualities. It has become increasingly difficult to find a household with an automatic dishwasher where small numbers of dishes are washed by hand. In the long run, the environmental cost of such behavior is scarcely worth the amount of time saved.

Which one of the following principles is best illustrated by the example presented in the passage?

(A) The significance of a benefit should be weighed in terms of its overall effect.
(B) People should make a unified effort to reduce their negative impact upon the environment.
(C) Some new technologies offer no perceptible benefit to society.
(D) The acquisition of leisure time is not worth the destruction of the biosphere.
(E) Most new machinery makes our lives more streamlined and economical.

STOP

IF YOU FINISH BEFORE TIME IS CALLED, YOU MAY CHECK YOUR WORK ON THIS SECTION ONLY. DO NOT WORK ON ANY OTHER SECTION IN THE TEST.

SECTION III

Time—35 Minutes

25 Questions

Directions: The questions in this section are based on the reasoning contained in brief statements or passages. For some questions, more than one of the choices could conceivably answer the question. However, you are to choose the best answer; that is, the response that most accurately and completely answers the question. You should not make assumptions that are by commonsense standards implausible, superfluous, or incompatible with the passage. After you have chosen the best answer, blacken the corresponding space on your answer sheet.

1. Senator: For economic issues, I base my responses on logic. For political issues, I base my responses either on logic or gut instinct. For moral issues, I never base my responses on logic.

   Which one of the following can be correctly inferred from the statements above?

   (A) If the senator relies on logic, he may be responding to a moral issue.
   (B) If the senator relies on logic, he is not responding to an economic issue.
   (C) If the senator does not rely on logic, he is responding to a political issue.
   (D) If the senator does not rely on logic, he must be responding to an economic issue.
   (E) If the senator does not rely on logic, he might be responding to a political issue.

2. Concern about the environmental and health problems associated with nuclear energy has compelled activist groups to join forces in an attempt to shut down nuclear power plants. However, a survey of nuclear power plants across the United States showed that there have only been two accidents in the past ten years, both minor in nature, and in both cases, the danger was quickly contained. If the United States is to produce enough energy to become completely independent from foreign sources of energy, more nuclear power plants must be built, and the misinformation being distributed by activist groups must be countered by the statistics found in the study.

   All of the following are assumptions of the above argument EXCEPT:

   (A) Using nuclear power is the only way for the United States to produce enough energy that no fuel needs to be imported.
   (B) Some people think nuclear power plants are dangerous.
   (C) The accidents caused little harm.
   (D) Other methods of producing energy are also considered dangerous.
   (E) The United States needs to be completely self-sufficient in the production of energy.

3. Rather than learn about Senate hearings by listening to word-of-mouth accounts or by sitting in on the sessions themselves, people now depend mainly on television and the Internet for information about important investigative and confirmation hearings conducted by Senate committees. Thus, the media serve as a surrogate for the millions of people who care deeply about such proceedings but could never attend them themselves.

   The above passage is most likely part of an argument in favor of

   (A) reserving more seats for ordinary citizens at important Senate hearings
   (B) imposing secrecy rules on the Senate committee hearings not already covered by the media
   (C) expanding media coverage of important Senate hearings
   (D) enacting a law that would prohibit any censorship of press coverage of the Senate
   (E) widening the scope of Senate inquiry of press censorship

GO ON TO THE NEXT PAGE.

4. Advertisement: Professional exterminators will tell you that in order to rid your home of roaches, you must do more than kill all the roaches you see. This is why the system that professional exterminators use most includes a poison that inhibits the development of roach eggs already laid, as well as a chemical that kills all adult roaches. This same combination is now available to the nonprofessional in new Extirm. When you're ready to get rid of roaches once and for all, get Extirm in your corner.

All of the following are implied by the advertisement above EXCEPT:

(A) Professional exterminators asked about roach extermination recommended Extirm.
(B) Extirm contains a chemical that inhibits the development of roach eggs.
(C) More than one chemical is required to rid a home of roaches.
(D) Inhibiting the development of roach eggs may not eliminate roaches from the home.
(E) Roaches reproduce by laying eggs.

5. In congressional hearings the question arises: "Which side knows best the potential benefits and dangers involved in the drilling of new offshore oil wells within U.S. territorial waters?" Oil companies' advice must certainly be taken with a grain of salt, because they are concerned only with profit and will oppose any legislation that would reduce such profit. Environmentalists' dire warnings must also be questioned, because many environmentalists' opposition to such drilling is purely reflexive, and without basis in scientific fact. This is why, in order to understand fully the costs and benefits that must be weighed in deciding whether to drill oil wells in U.S. coastal waters, Congress should rely primarily on the advice of academic research geologists, who are both informed and objective on the issue.

Which one of the following, if true, would most seriously weaken the author's conclusion in the passage above?

(A) Environmentalists are more knowledgeable about the dangers associated with drilling oil wells than is the average congressperson.
(B) Most academic research geologists rely heavily on income earned from consulting fees paid by oil companies.
(C) Oil companies have responded to public outcry over environmental damage caused by offshore oil drilling by developing technology that makes offshore oil drilling much safer than it used to be.
(D) The oil industry lobby is responsible each year for significant campaign contributions to legislators.
(E) Academic research geologists are not unanimous in their support of or opposition to new offshore oil drilling in U.S. coastal waters.

GO ON TO THE NEXT PAGE.

Questions 6–7

Throughout the twentieth century, anthropologists studying the myths and ceremonies of a particular group indigenous to the Amazon rain forest in Brazil have maintained that their presence and the questions they asked were not influencing the group's culture. Researchers now note, however, that the earliest recorded observations, made in 1919, of the group's ceremonies marking the onset of the rainy season made no reference to a creation myth. The first mention of a creation myth's appearance in the ceremony is found in 1933, and by 1986, nearly twenty minutes of the seventy-minute ceremony were devoted to a myth explaining the rains in relation to a "First Great Storm," during which the world was supposed to have been created.

6. Which one of the following is most strongly implied by the argument above?

(A) The observations of the ceremonies in 1919 were either incomplete or inaccurate.
(B) After the anthropologists explained the importance of creation myths to their subjects, the group developed myths of its own.
(C) The anthropologists' interests in particular cultural beliefs, such as creation myths, may have induced a gradual change in the group's ceremonies.
(D) If the anthropologists had been more conscientious, their records would not reflect apparent discrepancies in their accounts of the group's beliefs.
(E) The subjects of study, trying to secure the benefits of the industrial world enjoyed by anthropologists, changed their ceremonies to correspond to the ideas of the anthropologists.

7. Which one of the following represents an illustration of the same phenomenon that the author describes in the passage above?

(A) A sociologist notes that a wave of immigration invariably results in changes in some religious practices of the dominant culture.
(B) A psychologist discovers that patients who originally reported few or no dreams consistently acknowledge frequent and vivid dreams after eight months of dream-analysis therapy.
(C) An economist studying a Third World country finds an increasing reliance on Western technology rather than on indigenous agricultural methods.
(D) An astronomer, using two different telescopes to measure the distance to a nearby star, gets two different results.
(E) A historian of religion finds that the creation myths of several cultures have changed over time.

GO ON TO THE NEXT PAGE.

8. Mayor: An across-the-board increase of just twenty cents on all the city's toll bridges and tunnels would raise close to a hundred thousand dollars a year at the current bridge and tunnel traffic levels. Because a toll increase of three dollars would therefore raise more than a million dollars a year, such an increase seems like the ideal solution to our persistent school-budget shortfalls. The toll increase would offer further savings by lessening the volume of traffic over our bridges and tunnels, which would result in reduced maintenance costs for those structures.

Which one of the following identifies most accurately the error in the mayor's reasoning?

(A) She incorrectly assumes that two different causes are necessarily related.
(B) She bases her argument on erroneous figures for the current traffic flow.
(C) She makes assumptions that are mutually exclusive.
(D) She takes as a given what should instead first be established as evidence.
(E) She bases her argument on political considerations rather than logical analysis.

9. Dale: The city can't possibly have budget problems this quarter because of the heavier than normal snows this winter. A recent article mentioned that Haline, a substance used to de-ice roads and sidewalks, costs three cents a pound, which is quite cheap considering how effective it is.

Glenn: In actuality the cost of Haline is closer to eighty cents a pound. When you factor in the destructive effect of Haline on the infrastructure, and its deleterious effects on ground water and vegetation, the cost of Haline clearly exceeds its price.

If a substance performs as effectively as Haline and has no harmful side effects (but its price is higher than that of Haline), Glenn would be most likely to oppose its use if

(A) its price fluctuates seasonally
(B) its price and its cost are similar
(C) it must be handled in the same manner as Haline
(D) its cost is higher than the price of Haline
(E) its price is higher than the cost of Haline

10. Since mandatory water conservation measures were enacted by the state of California in response to the drought of 1987–1992, water consumption in the state has increased by nearly 10 percent. Clearly, the state's water conservation measures have been counterproductive, and California's water situation is more dire now than it was in 1992, the year of the last drought.

All of the following facts, if true, would be useful in evaluating the validity of the argument above EXCEPT:

(A) The population of California has increased by 15 percent since 1992.
(B) The average California resident now uses less water on an annual basis than he or she did in 1992.
(C) The water conservation measures did not apply to agricultural usage.
(D) In accordance with the conservation measures, nonessential water use in private homes has declined by 50 percent since 1992.
(E) In the years since 1992, water collection technology has developed to such a point that state and municipal water districts have an increased capacity to gather and store water.

GO ON TO THE NEXT PAGE.

11. Netta: A recent study revealed that while the overall crime rate has gone down, crimes committed by youths have increased dramatically. The irony is that our own judicial system is fostering this situation. By treating young people who commit crimes less severely than adults who commit similar crimes, the courts allow these young criminals to go free, and they then commit more crimes. The message that "crime is wrong, but not as bad if you're not of age" is being communicated. A person who is convicted of a crime should be sufficiently punished regardless of age, otherwise the number of crimes committed by youths will continue to increase.

Trey: Netta, you are being extremely shortsighted. The alternative to allowing young criminals to go free is incarcerating them in a youth facility or penitentiary. But sociologists have found that the social environment in such facilities encourages and condones delinquent behavior within the facility, and by extension, outside the facility. When the youth returns to society after having been incarcerated for even a short period, recidivism occurs within three to four weeks.

The point at issue between Netta and Trey is

(A) the extent to which the judicial system is contributing to the increase in the crime rate
(B) whether the leniency shown toward adolescents can be cited as the sole cause of the increase in crimes committed by young people
(C) what types of judicial reform could affect the rise in youth crime
(D) how most effectively to stop the increase in crime by examining which cause is most often to blame
(E) whether incarceration as an alternative to leniency for convicted youths will in fact help to solve the problem

12. Computer Technician: This system has either a software problem or a hardware problem. None of the available diagnostic tests has been able to determine where the problem lies. The software can be replaced, but the hardware cannot be altered in any way, which means that if the problem lies in the hardware, the entire system will have to be scrapped. We must begin work to solve the problem by presupposing that the problem is with the software.

On which one of the following principles could the technician's reasoning be based?

(A) In fixing a problem that has two possible causes, it makes more sense to deal with both causes rather than spend time trying to determine which is the actual cause of the problem.
(B) If events outside one's control bear on a decision, the best course of action is to assume the "worst-case" scenario.
(C) When the soundness of an approach depends on the validity of an assumption, one's first task must be to test that assumption's validity.
(D) When circumstances must be favorable in order for a strategy to succeed, the strategy must be based on the assumption that conditions are indeed favorable until proved otherwise.
(E) When only one strategy can be successful, the circumstances affecting that strategy must be altered so that strategy may be employed.

GO ON TO THE NEXT PAGE.

13. To become a master at chess, a person must play. If a person plays for at least four hours a day, that person will inevitably become a master of the game. Thus, if a person is a master at the game of chess, that person must have played each day for at least four hours.

The error in the logic of the argument above is most accurately described by which one of the following?

(A) The conclusion is inadequate because it fails to acknowledge that people who play for four hours each day might not develop a degree of skill for the game that others view as masterful.
(B) The conclusion is inadequate because it fails to acknowledge that playing one hour a day might be sufficient for some people to become masters.
(C) The conclusion is inadequate because it fails to acknowledge that if a person has not played four hours a day, that person has not become a master.
(D) The conclusion is inadequate because it fails to acknowledge that four hours of playing time each day is not a strategy recommended by any world-champion chess players.
(E) The conclusion is inadequate because it fails to acknowledge that most people are not in a position to devote four hours each day to playing chess.

14. Libraries are eliminating many subscriptions to highly specialized periodicals due to budget cuts. Yet without these reference materials, many subjects cannot be researched effectively. Therefore, efforts must be made to provide better funding so as to ensure the maintenance of at least those periodicals that will be most used by researchers in the future.

Which one of the following can be inferred from the author's argument for the maintenance of funding for the periodicals?

(A) If a periodical is highly specialized, the maintenance of its subscription is more important than any financial considerations.
(B) Research performed with periodicals is not a valid consideration in determining funding.
(C) Research should be the focus of a library's funding.
(D) It can be predicted which periodicals will be of value for researchers in the future.
(E) The elimination of periodicals is simply an inevitable part of library organization.

15. Last year, Marcel enjoyed a high income from exactly two places: his sporting goods store and his stock market investments. Although Marcel earns far more from his store than from his investments, the money he earns from the stock market is an important part of his income. Because of a series of drops in the stock market, Marcel will not earn as much from his investments this year. It follows then that Marcel will make less money this year than he did last year.

Which one of the following is an assumption necessary to the author's argument?

(A) Increased profits at Marcel's sporting goods store will not offset any loss in stock market income.
(B) Sporting goods stores earn lower profits when the stock market drops.
(C) Drops in the stock market do not always affect all of a particular investor's stocks.
(D) Marcel's stock market investments will be subject to increased volatility.
(E) If his income is lower, Marcel will not be able to meet his expenses.

GO ON TO THE NEXT PAGE.

16. Johanna: Quinto admits that because of his governmental post he can select which companies are awarded municipal contracts. He further admits that he awarded a contract to a company owned by a member of the town council who offered to support Quinto in his mayoral bid in exchange for the contract. There is no excuse for this kind of unethical behavior.

Iya: I don't see his actions as unethical. The company awarded the contract is known to produce the highest-quality work at a comparatively competitive price. So in getting support for his mayoral bid, Quinto has ensured the city will get quality work, and thus has saved the taxpayers thousands of dollars.

Iya disagrees with Johanna by

(A) insisting that ethical behavior can only be viewed in the context in which it takes place
(B) countering that the result of Quinto's actions determines whether those activities are ethical
(C) comparing Quinto's actions to the actions of the company and finding both behaviors to be ethical
(D) applying a different definition of the word "ethical" to two situations
(E) defining ethical behavior as being formed by personal, religious, or spiritual philosophies

17. One of the criticisms of recent political campaigns is that the candidate with the greater financial resources usually wins. A long presidential election campaign is more equitable than is the quick and expedient process recommended by some. A longer campaign, however, decreases the likelihood that a candidate with tremendous resources can control the campaign through a barrage of high-priced media campaigns. In a long campaign, a candidate is forced to speak substantively on the issues, and the voters have more complete access to the candidate. Thus, a long campaign creates parity among candidates who may not be equally financed by permitting the less popular, less well-funded candidates to invest time rather than money in their campaigns, thereby gaining recognition for themselves through the use of speeches, debates, and other media-oriented forums.

Which one of the following statements most seriously weakens the argument made above in favor of long presidential campaigns?

(A) Voters who lose interest during a long campaign are less likely to show up at the polls, thus contributing to the already significant problem of voter apathy.
(B) A long campaign requires candidates to divide their attention between public matters and the needs of their parties.
(C) A long campaign weakens the general public's interest in the process of global democracy.
(D) Candidates depend on volunteers, whose sense of commitment is frayed by a long campaign.
(E) A long campaign precludes participation by many able candidates who cannot afford to take time off from their private occupations for extended periods of time.

GO ON TO THE NEXT PAGE.

18. Some botanists have found it extremely difficult to save certain species of elm trees from fungal infection. Even the most potent fungicide has been unsuccessful in preventing its growth on such trees. However, researchers have managed to control the growth and spread of the fungus by spraying the fungus with a 0.2% saline solution.

Which one of the following, if true, offers the strongest explanation as to why the saline spray has been successful?

(A) The cell walls of the fungus cannot filter out the salt compounds, which, once inside the cell, interfere with reproduction.
(B) The presence of salt creates an electrolyte imbalance within living cells, ultimately killing each cell it comes in contact with.
(C) When salt is used in combination with strong fungicide, the fungicide becomes potent enough to kill any fungus.
(D) It has been on record that farmers have used salt to kill destructive plant fungi since the late eighteenth century.
(E) Fungicides have generally been unsuccessful because any fungicide strong enough to destroy a fungus would be strong enough to destroy the roots as well.

19. In concluding that there has been a shift in the sense of parental responsibility in America since the 1960s, researchers point to the increase in the frequency with which fathers tend to the daily needs of their children. However, this increase cannot be attributed exclusively to a shift in parental mores, for during the same period there has been an increase in the percentage of mothers who have jobs. With this in mind, the increased participation of fathers in child-rearing may well be only a symptom of a more fundamental change in society.

The author of the passage criticizes the conclusion of the researchers by

(A) offering a clearer definition of the researchers' premises, thereby compromising their argument
(B) attacking the integrity of the researchers rather than their reasoning
(C) showing that the researchers have reversed cause and effect in making their argument
(D) pointing out that their criteria for "parental responsibility" are not a logical basis for their argument
(E) suggesting an alternative cause for the effect cited by the researchers

GO ON TO THE NEXT PAGE.

Questions 20–21

Upon exiting an exhibit, some visitors to art museums find it difficult to describe what it was that they liked and didn't like about the paintings. Yet because these visitors feel strongly about which art they believed to be good and which art they believed to be bad, appreciating a work of art obviously does not require the ability to articulate what, specifically, was perceived to be good or bad.

20. The argument above assumes which one of the following?

(A) The fact that some people find it difficult to articulate what they like about a work of art does not mean that no one can.
(B) If an individual feels strongly about a work of art, then he or she is capable of appreciating that work of art.
(C) The vocabulary of visual art is not a part of common knowledge, but rather is known only to those who study the arts.
(D) When a person can articulate what he or she likes about a particular painting, he or she is able to appreciate that work of art.
(E) Paintings can be discussed only in general terms of good and bad.

21. According to the passage above, all of the following could be true EXCEPT:

(A) Some museum visitors can explain with great precision what they liked and didn't like about a certain painting.
(B) If a person studies art, then that person will be able to articulate her opinion about paintings.
(C) If a person can't say why she likes a piece of art, it doesn't necessarily mean that she doesn't appreciate that piece.
(D) Some visitors can explain what they liked about a piece, but are unable to explain what they didn't like.
(E) The inability to articulate always indicates the inability to appreciate.

22. Evan: Earlier this year, the *Stockton Free Press* reported that residents consider Mayor Dalton more concerned with his image than with advancing the cause of the less fortunate of Stockton.

Dalia: But the mayor appointed a new director of the public television station, and almost immediately the station began running a documentary series promoting the mayor's antipoverty program.

Evan: Clearly the mayor has, by this appointment, attempted to manipulate public opinion through the media.

Evan's second statement counters Dalia's argument by

(A) disputing the relevancy of her statement
(B) suggesting that Dalia is less informed about the issue than he
(C) confusing the argument she presents with his own
(D) appealing to popular opinion that the mayor should not misuse his access to the media
(E) claiming that Dalia's argument is an example that actually strengthens his own argument

GO ON TO THE NEXT PAGE.

23. Naturalist: Every year, thousands of animals already on the endangered species list are killed for their hides, furs, or horns. These illegal and often cruel deaths serve to push these species further toward the brink of extinction. The products made from these animals, such as articles of clothing and quack medical remedies, are goods no one really needs. What is needed is a large-scale media campaign to make the facts of the killings known and lessen the demand for these animal products. Such a campaign would be a good start in the effort to save endangered species from extinction.

Environmentalist: For the overwhelming majority of currently endangered species, the true threat of extinction comes not from hunting and poaching, but from continually shrinking habitats. Concentrating attention on the dangers of poaching for a very few high-visibility species would be counterproductive, leading people to believe that a boycott of a few frivolous items is enough to protect endangered species, when what is needed is a truly global environmental policy.

The point at issue between the naturalist and the environmentalist is which one of the following?

(A) whether the poaching of some endangered species actually increases that species' chances of becoming extinct
(B) whether a large-scale media campaign can affect the demand for some products
(C) whether more endangered species are threatened by poaching and hunting or shrinking of habitat
(D) whether some species could be saved from extinction by eliminating all commercial demand for that species
(E) whether a large-scale media campaign that lessens the demand for products made from endangered species is a good strategy for saving endangered species

24. Deborah: If one-third of the people who do not recycle would start recycling their paper products, approximately 150,000 fewer trees would be destroyed each year.

Lee: That is unlikely. It would then follow that in the next ten years, the forests will increase by more than 1.5 million trees, more than there is room for.

Which one of the following statements could Deborah offer Lee to clarify her own position and address the point that Lee makes?

(A) It is possible for forests to increase by 150,000 trees per year if the growth rate of the previous year was unusually low.
(B) The 150,000 trees that are saved would still be subject to forest fires and other destructive natural phenomena.
(C) If the number of recyclers was increased by more than a third, the number of trees saved would be more than 150,000.
(D) Any prediction of tree growth always presumes a constant growth and death rate.
(E) For the number of nonrecyclers to be reduced by a third, the number of recycling materials, special recyclable trash bins, for example, would have to be increased by much more than a third.

GO ON TO THE NEXT PAGE.

25. Adoption Agent: Although my view runs counter to the trend in public sentiment, I believe a proposed new law granting adoptive parents access to the birth records of children to be adopted should not be passed. My experience as an adoption agent has supplied me with two reasons for holding this view. First, granting adoptive parents access to the records will result in wasted hours on the part of the adoption agency employees, who will be forced to spend time finding and subsequently returning files, when that time could be better spent out in the field. Second, based upon my agency experience, no adoptive parents are going to request the children's records anyway.

Which one of the following, if true, establishes that the adoption agent's second reason does not negate the first?

(A) The new law would necessitate that adoption agents, when reviewing the adoption agreement with prospective adoptive parents, have at hand the birth record of the child to be adopted, not simply have access to them.

(B) The task of retrieving and explaining birth records would fall to the least experienced member of the adoption agency's staff.

(C) Any children who asked to see their birth records would also insist on having details they did not understand explained to them.

(D) The new law does not exclude adoption agencies from charging adoptive parents for extra expenses incurred in order to comply with the new law.

(E) Some adoption agencies have always had a policy of allowing children access to their birth records, but none of those agencies' children took advantage of that policy.

STOP

IF YOU FINISH BEFORE TIME IS CALLED, YOU MAY CHECK YOUR WORK ON THIS SECTION ONLY. DO NOT WORK ON ANY OTHER SECTION IN THE TEST.

SECTION IV

Time—35 Minutes

23 Questions

Directions: Each group of questions in this section is based on a set of conditions. In answering some of the questions, it may be useful to draw a rough diagram. Choose the response that most accurately and completely answers each question and blacken the corresponding space on your answer sheet.

Questions 1–6

An interior decorator is designing a color scheme using at least one of the following colors: red, orange, yellow, indigo, green, and violet. No other colors will be used. The selection of colors for the scheme is consistent with the following conditions:

If the scheme uses orange, then it does not use indigo.
If the scheme does not use green, then it uses orange.
If the scheme uses yellow, then it uses both indigo and violet.
If the scheme uses violet, then it uses red or green or both.

1. Which one of the following could be a complete and accurate list of the colors the scheme includes?

(A) yellow, indigo
(B) indigo, green
(C) yellow, indigo, violet
(D) yellow, green, violet
(E) orange, yellow, indigo, violet

2. Which one of the following could be the only color the scheme uses?

(A) red
(B) yellow
(C) indigo
(D) green
(E) violet

3. Which one of the following CANNOT be a complete and accurate list of the colors the scheme uses?

(A) orange, green
(B) green, violet
(C) red, orange, violet
(D) yellow, indigo, green, violet
(E) red, orange, yellow, indigo, violet

4. If the scheme doesn't use violet, then which one of the following must be true?

(A) The scheme uses orange.
(B) The scheme uses at least two colors.
(C) The scheme uses at most three colors.
(D) The scheme uses neither yellow nor indigo.
(E) The scheme uses neither yellow nor orange.

5. If the scheme uses violet, then which of the following must be false?

(A) The scheme does not use red.
(B) The scheme does not use green.
(C) The scheme does not use indigo.
(D) The scheme uses indigo but not yellow.
(E) The scheme uses indigo but not green.

6. If the condition that if the scheme doesn't use green then it does use orange is suspended, and all the other conditions remain in effect, then which one of the following CANNOT be a complete and accurate list of the colors the scheme uses?

(A) indigo
(B) red, indigo
(C) yellow, indigo, violet
(D) red, indigo, violet
(E) red, yellow, indigo, violet

GO ON TO THE NEXT PAGE.

Questions 7–13

Five runners—Fanny, Gina, Henrietta, Isabelle, and Mona—are assigned to lanes numbered 1 through 5 on a track. Each runner has the option of wearing a knee brace during the competition. Two of the runners are from Palo Alto, two are from San Jose, and one is from Newcastle. The following conditions must apply:

Isabelle and Mona are assigned to the first two lanes, but not necessarily in that order.
The runner in the third lane is from Newcastle and wears a knee brace.
Neither runner from San Jose wears a knee brace.
Both Gina and Fanny are assigned higher-numbered lanes than that of Henrietta.
Neither Mona nor Fanny comes from San Jose.

7. Which one the following could be an accurate list of the runners, in order from lane 1 to lane 5?

(A) Isabelle, Henrietta, Fanny, Mona, Gina
(B) Isabelle, Mona, Gina, Henrietta, Fanny
(C) Mona, Gina, Henrietta, Isabelle, Fanny
(D) Mona, Isabelle, Gina, Henrietta, Fanny
(E) Mona, Isabelle, Henrietta, Fanny, Gina

8. Which one of the following could be true?

(A) Fanny runs in lane 5.
(B) Gina runs in lane 1.
(C) Henrietta runs in lane 2.
(D) Isabelle runs in lane 3.
(E) Mona runs in lane 5.

9. If the runner in lane 1 is from San Jose, then which one of the following could be true?

(A) Fanny runs in a lane numbered one higher than Isabelle's.
(B) Henrietta runs in a lane numbered one higher than Fanny's.
(C) Henrietta runs in a lane numbered one higher than Mona's.
(D) Henrietta runs in a lane numbered one higher than Isabelle's.
(E) Isabelle runs in a lane numbered one higher than Mona's.

10. If a runner with a knee brace runs in lane 1, then which one of the following CANNOT be true?

(A) Fanny runs in lane 4.
(B) Gina runs in lane 5.
(C) A runner with a knee brace runs in lane 2.
(D) A runner with a knee brace runs in lane 3.
(E) A runner with a knee brace runs in lane 4.

11. Which one of the following must be true?

(A) Gina runs without a knee brace.
(B) Henrietta runs without a knee brace.
(C) Mona runs without a knee brace.
(D) Fanny runs with a knee brace.
(E) Isabelle runs with a knee brace.

12. If runners wearing knee braces do not run in consecutively-numbered lanes, and runners not wearing knee braces do not run in consecutively-numbered lanes, then in exactly how many distinct orders could the runners be assigned to lanes?

(A) one
(B) two
(C) three
(D) four
(E) five

13. If a runner with a knee brace runs in lane 2, then which one of the following CANNOT be true?

(A) The runner in lane 1 is from San Jose.
(B) The runner in lane 1 is from Palo Alto.
(C) The runner in lane 4 is from San Jose.
(D) The runner in lane 5 is from San Jose.
(E) The runner in lane 5 is from Palo Alto.

GO ON TO THE NEXT PAGE.

Questions 14–18

The Paulson, Rideau, Stevenson, Tisch, Van Pelt, and Wong families have each rented a time-share in a 6-unit condominium. The condominium has three floors, labeled first to third from bottom to top. Each floor has an identical layout consisting of two units: a garden view apartment on the west side of the building and an ocean view apartment on the east side of the building. The following conditions must apply:

The Rideaus rent the unit immediately beneath the Paulsons' ocean-view unit.
If the Wongs rent an ocean-view apartment, the Rideaus occupy the same floor as the Van Pelts.
If the Paulsons and the Tisches occupy the same floor, the Wongs rent the unit immediately and directly beneath the Stevensons' unit.
If the Tisches rent a garden-view unit, the Wongs occupy a unit on the first floor.
If the Tisches occupy a first-floor unit, the Stevensons occupy a third-floor unit.

14. Which of the following could be true?

(A) The Stevensons occupy a second-floor unit, whereas the Tisches occupy a first-floor unit.
(B) The Paulsons occupy a unit immediately and directly below the Wongs, and share a floor with the Tisches.
(C) The Paulsons rent a garden-view unit on the same floor as the Van Pelts.
(D) The Wongs rent an ocean-view unit on the same floor as the Van Pelts.
(E) The Tisches and Wongs both occupy the third floor.

15. If the Van Pelts and the Tisches both rent garden-view units, then which of the following could be true?

(A) The Wongs rent the first-floor ocean-view unit.
(B) The Stevensons rent the first-floor garden-view unit.
(C) The Paulsons and the Tisches occupy the same floor.
(D) The Paulsons and the Wongs occupy the same floor.
(E) The Van Pelts and the Wongs occupy the same floor.

16. If the Wongs rent a third-floor unit, then which of the following must be true?

(A) The Rideaus rent a second-floor unit.
(B) The Stevensons rent a second-floor unit.
(C) The Stevensons rent a first-floor unit.
(D) The Tisches rent a third-floor unit.
(E) The Van Pelts rent a first-floor unit.

17. If the Tisches rent the first-floor ocean-view unit, then each of the following must be true EXCEPT:

(A) The Paulsons and the Stevensons occupy the same floor.
(B) The Rideaus and the Van Pelts occupy the same floor.
(C) The Van Pelts rent a garden-view unit.
(D) The Wongs rent a garden-view unit.
(E) The Paulsons rent a third-floor unit.

18. If neither the Paulsons nor the Stevensons rent a third-floor unit, then which one of the following could be true?

(A) The Rideaus rent a second-floor unit.
(B) The Tisches rent a second-floor unit.
(C) The Wongs rent a second-floor unit.
(D) The Stevensons rent an ocean-view unit.
(E) The Wongs rent an ocean-view unit.

GO ON TO THE NEXT PAGE.

Questions 19–23

Four racehorses and their four jockeys are assigned to consecutive tracks at a racetrack—tracks 1, 2, 3, and 4. Each horse has exactly one jockey, and each pair is assigned to exactly one track. The horses are Ficklehoof, Galloper, Knackerbound, and Lackluster; the jockeys are Ramos, Simon, Tonka, and Urbach. The following conditions apply:

Ficklehoof is assigned to a lower-numbered track than is Galloper, and at least one track separates the two.
Knackerbound is assigned to track 2.
Lackluster's jockey is Urbach.

19. Which one of the following horse and jockey teams could be assigned to track 1?

(A) Ficklehoof and Ramos
(B) Ficklehoof and Urbach
(C) Galloper and Ramos
(D) Galloper and Urbach
(E) Lackluster and Tonka

20. If Ramos is assigned to a higher-numbered track than is Urbach, which one of the following statements cannot be true?

(A) Ficklehoof is assigned to a lower-numbered track than is Simon.
(B) Knackerbound is assigned to a lower-numbered track than is Ramos.
(C) Knackerbound is assigned to a lower-numbered track than is Tonka.
(D) Simon is assigned to a lower-numbered track than is Ramos.
(E) Tonka is assigned to a lower-numbered track than is Knackerbound.

21. If Lackluster is assigned to a lower-numbered track than is Galloper, which one of the following statements could be false?

(A) Ficklehoof is assigned to a lower-numbered track than is Urbach.
(B) Galloper is assigned to track 4.
(C) Either Ramos or Tonka is assigned to a lower-numbered track than is Urbach.
(D) Simon is assigned to a lower-numbered track than is Urbach.
(E) Urbach is assigned to track 3.

22. What is the maximum possible number of different horse and jockey teams, any one of which could be assigned to track 4?

(A) 2
(B) 3
(C) 4
(D) 5
(E) 6

23. If Simon is assigned to a higher-numbered track than is Lackluster, then which one of the following statements could be false?

(A) Galloper is assigned to a higher-numbered track than is Ramos.
(B) Galloper is assigned to a higher-numbered track than is Tonka.
(C) Lackluster is assigned to a higher-numbered track than is Tonka.
(D) Tonka is assigned to a higher-numbered track than is Ramos.
(E) Urbach is assigned to a higher-numbered track than is Ramos.

STOP

IF YOU FINISH BEFORE TIME IS CALLED, YOU MAY CHECK YOUR WORK ON THIS SECTION ONLY. DO NOT WORK ON ANY OTHER SECTION IN THE TEST.

The Princeton Review

Completely darken bubbles with a No. 2 pencil. If you make a mistake, be sure to erase mark completely.

1. YOUR NAME: ______ (Print) Last First M.I.

SIGNATURE: ______ DATE: __/__/__

HOME ADDRESS: ______ (Print) Number

______ City State Zip Code

PHONE NO.: ______ (Print)

IMPORTANT: Please fill in these boxes exactly as shown on the back cover of your test book.

2. TEST FORM

3. TEST CODE

4. REGISTRATION NUMBER

5. YOUR NAME

First 4 letters of last name | FIRST INIT | MID INIT

6. DATE OF BIRTH

Month | Day | Year

JAN FEB MAR APR MAY JUN JUL AUG SEP OCT NOV DEC

7. SEX

MALE

FEMALE

The Princeton Review

FORM NO. 00001-PR

Test 2 Start with number 1 for each new section.
If a section has fewer questions than answer spaces, leave the extra answer spaces blank.

Section 1: 1–27 (A) (B) (C) (D) (E)

Section 2: 1–25 (A) (B) (C) (D) (E)

Section 3: 1–25 (A) (B) (C) (D) (E)

Section 4: 1–24 (A) (B) (C) (D) (E)

COMPUTING YOUR SCORE

Directions

1. Use the Answer Key on the next page to check your answers.
2. Use the Scoring Worksheet below to compute your raw score.
3. Use the Score Conversion Chart to convert your raw score into the 120–180 LSAT scale.

Your scaled score on this virtual test is for general guidance only.

Scores obtained by using the Score Conversion Chart can only approximate the score you would receive if this virtual test were an actual LSAT. Your score on an actual LSAT may differ from the score obtained on this virtual test.

In an actual test, final scores are computed using an equating method that makes scores earned on different editions of the LSAT comparable to one another. This virtual test has been constructed to reflect an actual LSAT as closely as possible, and the conversion of raw scores to the LSAT scale has been approximated.

What this means is that the Conversion Chart reflects only an estimate of how raw scores would translate into final LSAT scores.

Scoring Worksheet

1. Enter the number of questions you answered correctly in each section.

	Number Correct
Section I	______
Section II..........	______
Section III	______
Section IV	______

2. Enter the sum here: ______

This is your raw score.

SCORE CONVERSION CHART

For Converting Raw Scores to the 120–180 LSAT Scaled Score

Reported Score	Raw Score Lowest	Raw Score Highest
180	99	100
179	—*	—*
178	98	98
177	97	97
176	96	96
175	95	95
174	94	94
173	93	93
172	92	92
171	91	91
170	90	90
169	89	89
168	88	88
167	86	87
166	85	85
165	84	84
164	82	83
163	81	81
162	79	80
161	77	78
160	76	76
159	74	75
158	72	73
157	71	71
156	69	70
155	67	68
154	65	66
153	63	64
152	61	62
151	59	60
150	58	58
149	56	57
148	54	55
147	52	53
146	50	51
145	48	49
144	46	47
143	44	45
142	43	43
141	41	42
140	39	40
139	37	38
138	36	36
137	34	35
136	32	33
135	30	31
134	29	29
133	27	28
132	26	26
131	24	25
130	23	23
129	22	22
128	20	21
127	19	19
126	18	18
125	17	17
124	16	16
123	15	15
122	14	14
121	13	13
120	0	12

*There is no raw score that will produce this scaled score for this form.

SECTION I

1.	A	8.	A	15.	B	22.	C
2.	A	9.	D	16.	A	23.	A
3.	D	10.	E	17.	D	24.	D
4.	E	11.	D	18.	D	25.	E
5.	B	12.	A	19.	D	26.	B
6.	A	13.	E	20.	B	27.	E
7.	B	14.	C	21.	C		

SECTION II

1.	C	8.	E	15.	B	22.	D
2.	D	9.	D	16.	C	23.	E
3.	D	10.	D	17.	D	24.	E
4.	D	11.	C	18.	D	25.	A
5.	D	12.	A	19.	C		
6.	C	13.	A	20.	B		
7.	A	14.	E	21.	D		

SECTION III

1.	E	8.	C	15.	A	22.	E
2.	D	9.	E	16.	B	23.	E
3.	C	10.	E	17.	E	24.	B
4.	A	11.	E	18.	A	25.	A
5.	B	12.	D	19.	E		
6.	C	13.	B	20.	B		
7.	B	14.	D	21.	E		

SECTION IV

1.	B	7.	E	13.	B	19.	A
2.	D	8.	A	14.	E	20.	C
3.	E	9.	C	15.	A	21.	D
4.	C	10.	C	16.	D	22.	C
5.	E	11.	A	17.	B	23.	D
6.	C	12.	A	18.	C		

11

Answers and Explanations to Practice Test 2

SECTION I

Questions 1–6 are based on the following passage:

Conventionally, the landowner wishing to build on his land has the structure designed by one entity and then built by another; the design and build functions are viewed as separate. With the innovative "design-build" construction arrangement, however, a single entity performs both the design and construction functions. That single entity may be a joint venture between an architect or engineer and general contractor, a design-build firm that employs both professionals and contractors, or a general contracting firm subcontracting with an architectural or engineering firm. Design-build contracts appeal to owners because they require only one entity for performance; if a problem arises, the owner does not have to decide whether the architect or the contractor is the culprit. From the standpoint of the contractor, design-build contracts are advantageous because they secure both design fees and construction profits. In addition, many design-build contracts are calculated on a cost-plus basis and are therefore less risky than fixed-price work.

A design-build job may be carried out like a traditional project, in which the contractor prepares design documents and obtains owner approval before construction commences, or as a series of tasks entailing the preparation of design documents in phases, with construction beginning as each phase of the design is completed. The process of starting construction before the overall design is complete is known as the "fast-track" construction plan. Often, the design-build and fast-track concepts are employed together.

Fast-track construction appeals to owners because it reduces the time between a project's conception and its completion, thus minimizing finance costs and the often disastrous effects of inflation and increasing the likelihood that the budget will be adequate to complete the project. On the other hand, the fast-track approach presents problems to owners seeking construction changes. Normally, a builder is obliged to conform to designs and, with compensation for extra expense, to owner-requested changes when such changes are within the "scope of the project"; while in the traditional format, determining whether or not a change is within the scope of the project is relatively simple.

On a fast-track job, however, the finishing details of the job are defined after construction begins. Thus, there is more room for misunderstanding between the owner and the contractor as to whether design changes are within the scope of the project.

In this regard, a contractor should define the parameters of his obligations as early as possible. For example, the parties should be able to agree on the type and function of the structure, the number of stories, and the approximate area before any construction commences. Once building has begun, the keys to minimizing disputes are constant communication with the owner regarding what the contractor deems the scope of his work, and prompt notice if the contractor perceives that these bounds are being overstepped.

SECTION I

QUESTIONS

1. According to the passage, the design-build method of construction is attractive to a landowner who wishes to build on her land because

    (A) she no longer needs to work with two separate entities
    (B) it allows earlier marketing, thereby reducing finance costs
    (C) its speed of construction protects her against inflation
    (D) when problems develop, she has financial recourse
    (E) it enables her to make changes even after the building has begun

2. Which one of the following would best serve as the concluding sentence of the last paragraph?

    (A) Close contact allows full benefit from fast-track construction and reduces the likelihood of disputes.
    (B) Because no communication is perfect, however, most owners choose conventional construction to avoid disputes.
    (C) Unfortunately, owners of multiple projects often cannot maintain such close contact.
    (D) Effective communication is ultimately the key to a productive work environment.
    (E) Inspection of the building on completion would verify that it continued to adhere to safety regulations.

EXPLANATIONS

1. This is a SPECIFIC question. Find the part of the passage that talks about the benefits for landowners.

    (A) Yes, take a look at lines 11–12.
    (B) Marketing isn't mentioned in the passage.
    (C) Inflation is an issue for fast-track construction, not design-build.
    (D) The passage does not mention financial recourse.
    (E) This is a fast-track construction issue.

2. This is a MAIN IDEA question. Come up with what you think is the main point of the last paragraph before you go to the answer choices.

    (A) Yes, the paragraph is talking about how close contact between the owner and contractor during fast-track construction is necessary. This choice summarizes that thought.
    (B) We don't know the percentages of conventional vs. design-build construction projects.
    (C) The passage never mentions owners of multiple projects.
    (D) This is too general an answer choice—we're talking construction projects in the passage, and this choice merely says "a productive work environment."
    (E) Safety regulations were never mentioned in the passage—it's out of scope.

SECTION I

QUESTIONS

3. It can be inferred from the passage that contractors find the design-build method advantageous because

(A) it reduces the number of design documents that need to be prepared
(B) design changes are easier to facilitate
(C) owners are less likely to request costly changes in the scope of the project
(D) the financial risks are less than for traditional construction projects
(E) they need hire only one entity

4. Which one of the following best summarizes the main point of the author?

(A) Fast-track programs represent a radical departure from the no-longer-effective traditional method of construction.
(B) Conventional construction and design-build construction are both equally valid methods of construction, though each is best suited to different circumstances.
(C) The combination of design-build and fast-track methods of construction creates financial risks that many landowners find unacceptable.
(D) Contractors have begun to encourage their clients to explore new methods and systems of design and construction.
(E) While the design-build and fast-track methods of construction provide advantages to both landowners and contractors, the fast-track method also carries some risks.

EXPLANATIONS

3. This is a SPECIFIC question. Find the part of the passage that talks about the benefits for design-build contractors.

(A) The number of design documents was never mentioned in the passage.
(B) Easier to facilitate than what? Design changes are talked about later in the passage.
(C) This has the same problem as (B). This is talked about later in the passage.
(D) See line 19. This is the answer.
(E) No, this is a benefit for landowners.

4. This is a MAIN IDEA question. Come up with your own main idea before you go to the answer choices.

(A) This doesn't talk about the design-build arrangement, which is also a key element of the passage. Eliminate it.
(B) The author seems to like design-build better, and this choice doesn't talk about fast-track construction, which is also a key element of the passage.
(C) No, the only financial risks that are talked about in the passage are those of the fast-track method.
(D) This isn't specific enough—what are the new methods?
(E) Bingo, it mentions both things and even says that there are both advantages and disadvantages to fast-track.

SECTION I

QUESTIONS	EXPLANATIONS

5. In mentioning the "disastrous effects of inflation" (line 33), the author is probably referring to the fact that

   (A) delayed completion inhibits renting or selling the building because of higher costs
   (B) lengthy construction time can put costs beyond the owner's ability to pay
   (C) financiers may, because of inflationary pressures, demand earlier returns
   (D) inflation can weaken the link between design-build and fast-track
   (E) the contractor may demand higher payment for design changes

6. Based on the information given in the passage, the author would consider each of the following good advice to an owner who has arranged for fast-track construction of a building on his land EXCEPT

   (A) after construction is complete, verify that changes have been made according to specifications
   (B) reach agreement on the major decisions concerning the project before construction begins
   (C) bring problems to the attention of the contractor as soon as they arise
   (D) confer with the contractor frequently during construction
   (E) prepare a list of important design details before the project begins so that misunderstandings are avoided

5. This is a LINE REFERENCE question. Read five lines above and five lines below the line reference.

   (A) The renting or selling of the building is never mentioned in the passage.
   (B) This is the answer—see line 34, which mentions concerns about the adequacy of the budget.
   (C) Earlier returns were never mentioned in the passage.
   (D) The passage never says this. This portion of the passage is not really concerned with the design-build approach, either.
   (E) Design changes are an issue of fast-track building, just not an inflationary one.

6. This is a SPECIFIC question. Find out what the important issues are surrounding fast-track building. Remember that this is an EXCEPT question, so we're looking for the one thing not mentioned in the passage.

   (A) We don't know anything about what happens after the building is completed—there is no mention of this in the passage. It's the answer.
   (B) No, because this is mentioned in lines 50–52.
   (C) No, because this is mentioned in lines 55–57.
   (D) No, because this is mentioned in lines 54–55.
   (E) No, because this is mentioned in lines 43–45.

Questions 7–14 are based on the following passage:

In the early 1980s, a number of citizens established organizations devoted to preventing drivers from operating motor vehicles while under the influence of alcohol. These organizations sparked a continuing grassroots social movement that attacks the problem of drunk driving by calling for community awareness and stronger sanctions. Unlike the prohibitionist movements of the late nineteenth and early twentieth centuries, which identified drinking itself as inherently wrong, the anti-drunk-driving movements emphasize the issue of drinking while driving automobiles; the problem is not alcohol use (or abuse), but the irresponsibility of individuals using alcohol. In essence, these organizations have spawned a social movement against the evils caused by personal irresponsibility.

The Progressive reform movements around the turn of the century shared the same moral ethic. As Hofstadter has argued, the Progressive reform movements were strongly based on the "ethos of personal responsibility" and the basic morality of civic consciousness. That approach is reflected in the goals of today's movement and in its views on proposals to solve the drunk-driving problem. The two most important program goals of current-day organizations are public awareness activities, designed to make drinkers understand that it is wrong to drive when under the influence of alcohol, and youth education programs, designed to convey this message to young drivers.

The "ethos of personal responsibility" for one's actions also has an impact in determining what actions are taken to solve the problem. Grassroots organizations call for punitive measures to be taken against drunk drivers. They perceive non-punitive programs—such as the safe-ride program—as ineffective. As one founding member of one organization put it: "Safe-ride programs may help temporarily, but they cause people to ignore their part in the problem."

Rehabilitation programs are rejected on the same grounds. In addition to labeling these programs as ineffective, grassroots organizers perceive them as a minor inconvenience to offenders and as a means of avoiding stricter punishment. This punitive approach to "problem drinking" represents a departure from the trend of viewing drinking problems as a disease and thus a medical problem. The movement does not distinguish between the sick alcoholic and the irresponsible "problem drinker" in its desire to enforce sanctions against the drunk driver.

These opinions reflect the basic moral view that citizens should be aware of the dangers of driving while drunk and their individual responsibility to drive sober. As a result of this awareness, those individuals acting irresponsibly should face serious punishment. Society, on the other hand, should not take the responsibility for individual conduct by instituting prohibitionist measures, safe-ride programs, or programs for rehabilitation.

SECTION I

QUESTIONS

7. The main idea of the passage is that
   (A) centuries of anti-alcohol public awareness campaigns reflect the United States' focus on personal responsibility
   (B) present-day grassroots anti-drunk-driving organizations emphasize personal responsibility as the key to effecting change
   (C) Prohibition failed because it ignored the United States' ethic of responsibility
   (D) if non-punitive programs worked, there would be no grassroots anti-drunk-driving movement
   (E) no anti-drunk-driving campaign is likely to succeed without punishing the driver

8. According to the passage, the modern grassroots movement designed to prevent drunk driving
   (A) is largely unconcerned with the broader issue of alcohol abuse
   (B) is more concerned with protecting the lives of sober drivers than of drunk drivers
   (C) is less opposed to drunk driving than it is in favor of personal responsibility
   (D) is excessively punitive, and, therefore, not likely to be effective
   (E) views drunk driving narrowly, and, therefore, promises less success than the prohibition movement

9. The turn-of-the-century Progressive reform movements and the current grassroots movements share all of the following EXCEPT
   (A) a belief in personal responsibility
   (B) an emphasis on morality
   (C) a desire for behavior modification as it relates to civic consciousness
   (D) a disapproval of drinking
   (E) a commitment to altering certain conduct

EXPLANATIONS

7. This is a MAIN IDEA question. Come up with your own main idea before you go to the answer choices.
   (A) This is too broad—we're talking about grassroots organizations of the present day for most of the passage. Eliminate it.
   (B) Bingo. It mentions the new grassroots organizations and what their philosophy is based on.
   (C) Doesn't mention the all-important grassroots folks.
   (D) We have no idea whether this is true and this is not what the author is interested in talking about.
   (E) Possibly true, but this is too specific an issue for it to be the main idea of the whole passage.

8. This is a SPECIFIC question. Find the part of the passage that talks about the grassroots folks.
   (A) This looks pretty good. Take a look at lines 9–12.
   (B) No, they care about all drivers. Eliminate it.
   (C) No, they really hate drunk driving. Eliminate it.
   (D) The movement isn't punitive; their recommendations are. Eliminate it.
   (E) No, the author thinks that they've got a good idea here and will be more successful than the prohibition movements. Eliminate it.

9. This is a SPECIFIC question. Find the part of the passage that talks about the grassroots folks AND the prohibition folks. This is an EXCEPT question, too.
   (A) They both believe in this. See lines 16–19.
   (B) They both believe in this. See line 17.
   (C) They both believe in this. See line 20.
   (D) Here's the answer—see lines 7–9. The grassroots people of today don't condemn drinking altogether.
   (E) They both tried to do this with various initiatives.

QUESTIONS	EXPLANATIONS

10. As used in line 20 of the passage, a person who follows a "basic morality of civic consciousness" probably

(A) abides by community standards for moral behavior
(B) supports the work done by alcoholic rehabilitation programs
(C) advocates the adoption of severe penalties for driving while intoxicated
(D) proposes that basic rules of moral behavior are essential to a just society
(E) understands that drinking before driving wrongfully endangers the safety and welfare of others

10. This is a LINE REFERENCE question. Read five lines above and five lines below the line reference.

(A) This is a bit general because we're talking about drinking and driving in the passage. Moral behavior is a pretty big topic.
(B) We don't like rehab programs. This answer choice is crossing its signals. Eliminate it.
(C) This is what the grassroots people think should happen, but we don't know about the community at large. Let's see if there is anything better than this.
(D) As in answer choice (A), this is too general. We're talking about drinking and driving.
(E) Bingo. Grassroots people see civic consciousness and education as going hand-in-hand. See lines 23–28.

11. According to the passage, grassroots organizations do not believe that prohibition is an effective solution to the drunk-driving problem because prohibition

(A) is too punitive, especially for responsible drinkers
(B) fails to recognize alcoholism as a disease
(C) does not share the aims of the history of Progressive reform movements in the United States
(D) makes society responsible for an individual's problems
(E) does nothing to make citizens aware of the drunk-driving problem

11. This is a SPECIFIC question. Find the part of the passage that talks about the grassroots and prohibition.

(A) Not that it's too punitive, just that it's not the point. Eliminate it.
(B) Not the point here. Eliminate it.
(C) No, that's what the old Progressive reforms were pushing for.
(D) This looks good, because the grassroots people think it's about each person individually. It's the answer.
(E) That's not why they think it's a bad idea. They can still educate people.

12. In the third paragraph, the author's purpose is to

(A) demonstrate the grassroots rejection of solutions that do not address driver accountability
(B) explain why the safe-ride program is unlikely to eradicate drunk driving
(C) present a view in opposition to that of the Progressive reform movements
(D) support his belief that non-punitive programs are ineffective
(E) distinguish between punitive and non-punitive social reforms, favoring non-punitive reforms

12. This is a PARAGRAPH REFERENCE question. Reread the third paragraph to see what its purpose was.

(A) Yes, this paragraph's purpose is to show how non-punitive solutions aren't very good. It's the answer.
(B) This is something that the paragraph does, but it's not the overall goal of the paragraph. Too specific.
(C) No, we don't even know what those people thought about rehab or safe-ride programs. Eliminate it.
(D) No, we don't know what the author thinks about these programs yet. The author is telling us what the grassroots people think.
(E) No, we don't learn this until the following paragraph.

SECTION I

QUESTIONS

13. Which one of the following best describes the organization of the passage?

    (A) A general philosophy of responsibility is presented, and specific approaches that do not adhere to that philosophy are rejected.
    (B) An ethos of personal responsibility is described, and then an alternate approach is described.
    (C) The history of a movement is outlined in chronological order.
    (D) A current political movement is analyzed, and the events that led to its creation are examined.
    (E) The historical approaches to a social problem are outlined and comparisons made.

14. The author of the passage would be most likely to agree with which one of the following statements about the "ethos of personal responsibility" and its relationship to grassroots campaigns against drunk driving?

    (A) Its impact on the organization of grassroots campaigns has been negligible, because these campaigns favor a more punitive approach.
    (B) It causes certain methods for dealing with drunk drivers to be favored over others that are perceived as ineffective or even dangerous.
    (C) It has been largely responsible for the introduction of public awareness campaigns involving both adults and teenagers.
    (D) It results in the belief that drinking is inherently wrong.
    (E) It establishes a general principle that provides a justification for acting irresponsibly while under the influence of alcohol.

EXPLANATIONS

13. This is a STRUCTURE question. Go back to the passage and find out how the passage flowed from paragraph to paragraph.

    (A) No, the passage starts off talking historically, not philosophically. Eliminate it.
    (B) Same problem as (A). We don't get this personal responsibility stuff until later.
    (C) No, because the author mentions the old Progressive people throughout the passage.
    (D) Is it a political movement? Not really.
    (E) The social problem is drinking, and the approaches between the old and the new are indeed contrasted. This is our answer.

14. This is a SPECIFIC question. Find the part of the passage that talks about the ethos of personal responsibility.

    (A) Negligible impact? Hardly. It's one of their basic tenets. Eliminate it.
    (B) Dangerous methods? Never mentioned in the passage.
    (C) Bingo—it's a basic part of their philosophy. This is our answer.
    (D) No, because then the grassroots people would have contradicted themselves.
    (E) Acting *irresponsibly*? It's the opposite of what we want here. Eliminate it.

SECTION I

Questions 15–20 are based on the following passage:

In a representative democracy, legislatures exist to represent the public and to ensure that public issues are efficiently addressed by a group representative of the population as a whole. It is often written that a legislator confronts a moral dilemma if, on a given issue upon which he must cast a vote, his view is decidedly different from that of the majority of his constituents. In such a circumstance, it is not clear whether voting citizens have chosen the legislator because of their faith in his personal judgment or whether they have elected him in order to give direct effect to their own views.

But this dilemma is more apparent than real. A truly identifiable conflict between the legislator's opinion and that of his constituency is rare, because the legislator is usually better informed than the public on the issue in question and his opinion, therefore, cannot fairly be compared to theirs. Indeed, this fact underscores the legislator's most important function: to gather broad-based information in order to make more considered decisions than each citizen could reach individually and thus to serve the public interest better than the public could do on its own.

Let us suppose that a legislator opposes a very popular proposed public works project because he has studied its financial ramifications and believes, over the long run, it is fiscally unsound. If the legislator's constituents write letters expressing their ardent support for the project, not having studied the relevant financial data, it is entirely too simplistic to view the legislator as having to confront a moral dilemma. The truth is that the legislator does not know how his constituents would view the project if they truly understood its financial consequences. Without such knowledge, the legislator cannot actually conclude that his view differs from that of his constituents. To conclude that their views should dictate his decision might foster his popularity, but would contravene his fundamental legislative responsibility.

The legislator's job is first to study the short-range and long-range goals of the people he represents, without confusing these with his own. Then, using his knowledge and judgment, he is to promote the electorate's goals as he understands them. Consider, for instance, a legislator whose constituents wish to maintain the rural character of their district. If the legislator himself dislikes rural living and would like to see the area undergo industrial development, or if he believes an industrial environment would offer greater benefit to the community than a rural environment, he must separate these viewpoints from his professional judgment. He is not to promote industrialization because he personally favors it.

However, if the legislator's considered opinion is that his district needs to sponsor *some* industrial development in order to maintain its overall agricultural character, it is his duty to promote the industrial development, even if his constituents oppose it. So long as he honestly attempts to serve his electorate's objectives, the legislator should stand firm against the expressed opinions of his own constituents.

SECTION I

QUESTIONS	EXPLANATIONS

15. The author's purpose in the first paragraph is to

(A) explain that many legislative questions require economic as well as political understanding
(B) point out that a possible moral dilemma exists when a legislator disagrees with her constituents
(C) illustrate that the legislator's extra knowledge creates the gap between her views and those of her constituents
(D) argue that legislative decisions should not be made simplistically
(E) encourage the rejection of legislation that runs counter to the public interest

15. This is a PARAGRAPH REFERENCE question. Reread the first paragraph and see what its purpose was.

(A) Economic issues weren't mentioned in paragraph one. Eliminate it.
(B) Looks pretty good. See lines 4–11. This is the answer.
(C) This isn't mentioned until later in the passage. Eliminate it.
(D) This is true but this isn't the purpose of the first paragraph. The first paragraph is talking about a dilemma.
(E) The author is not talking about rejection of legislation here.

16. According to the passage, the differences between a legislator's view and the views expressed by the legislator's constituents

(A) do not actually create a moral dilemma in most cases
(B) create a moral dilemma only in a democracy
(C) only arise when constituents are ill-informed
(D) require that a legislator gather more information than he would otherwise have done
(E) usually reflect a difference not in opinion, but in long-range goals

16. This is a SPECIFIC question. Find the part of the passage that talks about the two views.

(A) Yep. See line 12. It doesn't really exist.
(B) The passage isn't talking about any specific types of government.
(C) No, they can still disagree even when everyone has the same information.
(D) The differences don't require this—his job does.
(E) No, the passage says they should have the same goals.

17. It can be inferred from the passage that the author believes a legislator should

(A) carry out her constituents' intentions if doing so conforms to her assessment
(B) ignore her constituents' long-range objectives when they are morally incompatible with her own beliefs
(C) take whatever actions her constituents recommend
(D) determine what action will best serve her constituents, regardless of their stated position
(E) put her own assessments aside and embody those of her electorate

17. This is a SPECIFIC question. Find the part of the passage that talks about legislators.

(A) This isn't specific enough. Only if their intentions are also in line with the short- and long-range goals of the community.
(B) No, the community's goals need to drive the process. See lines 38–40.
(C) No, it's bad for the legislator to just be a rubber stamp. See lines 34–38.
(D) Bingo. See lines 17–22.
(E) No, she needs to do both.

SECTION I

QUESTIONS

18. Which one of the following would the author most likely believe to be true of a legislator who routinely reached legislative decisions by following constituents' instructions?

    (A) The legislator would probably not fully understand the public's goals.
    (B) The legislator would be acting in a manner contrary to her own interests.
    (C) The legislator would probably be unaware of the course of action most favorable to her constituency.
    (D) The legislator might not be fulfilling her proper role of defending the best interests of the electorate.
    (E) The legislator would be overly concerned with maintaining her own popularity, not carrying out her appropriate duties.

19. Which one of the following, if true, would most weaken the author's contention that a legislator can make "more considered decisions" than can his constituents?

    (A) A community should be allowed to make its own decisions, even if these are not the most informed decisions.
    (B) Because a legislator does not live in the same circumstances as do his constituents, he is more objective and less emotional in his decision-making.
    (C) Some constituents make a great effort to inform themselves on all aspects of proposed legislation.
    (D) The information provided to the legislator is occasionally biased or misleading.
    (E) Some legislators have difficulty separating their personal views from those of their constituents.

EXPLANATIONS

18. This is a SPECIFIC question. Find the part of the passage that talks about a legislator merely following instructions.

    (A) Maybe she would, maybe she wouldn't. We don't know. Eliminate it.
    (B) Same problem as (A). We don't know.
    (C) She might know but just want to be more popular than honest. Eliminate it.
    (D) Exactly. The passage states that the legislator has to look further than the wishes of her electorate.
    (E) Maybe, or maybe she can't think for herself. We don't know either way. Eliminate it.

19. This is a WEAKEN question. See which choice will weaken the author's point that a legislator is in a better position to make decisions.

    (A) Permission isn't the issue—ability is.
    (B) This would strengthen the author's point, not weaken it.
    (C) This looks pretty good, but "some" constituents isn't very strong. "Some" could be two, or five. Let's look for something stronger.
    (D) This is it. If the legislator's information is bad, he won't make better decisions. (D) is better than (C).
    (E) Same problem as (C). Not strong enough. (D) is the best choice here.

QUESTIONS

20. According to the author, the introduction of widespread industrialization into the rural community described in lines 42–50 represents

(A) the failure of a legislator to understand the requirements of the region
(B) an example of a legislator advancing his agenda at the expense of that of his constituents
(C) the failure of representative democracy to address the needs of its constituents
(D) the ability of a legislator to ignore the interests of the community he represents
(E) the result of a legislator carrying through on the expressed views of his constituents

EXPLANATIONS

20. This is a LINE REFERENCE question. Read five lines above and five lines below the line reference.

(A) No, because he might have understood them but just blew them off.
(B) Bingo—he knows what they want but because he has the power, he can do what he thinks is best.
(C) Way out of the scope of the passage here.
(D) This sounds okay, but compare it to (B). The lines are more about advancing his own position than ignoring others.
(E) Nope—they wanted to remain as rural as possible.

Questions 21–27 are based on the following passage:

The KT boundary, as it is called, marks one of the most violent events ever to befall life on earth. Sixty-five million years ago, according to current theory, the Cretaceous period was brought to a sudden conclusion by the impact of an asteroid or a comet ten kilometers in diameter. It would be natural to suppose that the KT boundary is a fossil hunter's paradise. But it is nothing of the sort. In fact, no bones have been found at the KT boundary anywhere on earth.

Some paleontologists find the situation frustrating, to put it mildly. Granted, they say, the record of life preserved in sedimentary rocks is far from perfect. But in this case the event of record is a cosmic catastrophe that killed all the dinosaurs in the world. Shouldn't the concentration of bones in the fossil record be, at very least, above average?

In some places the sedimentary rocks preserve detailed temporal signals with near-textbook fidelity, but such detailed windows into the past are relatively rare. More commonly, various natural forces like the wind and rain disrupt the chronological ordering of the fossils-to-be.

The first serious proposal for solving this sedimentary puzzle came in 1940, in a paper by the Soviet paleontologist Ivan A. Efremov. Paleontologists, Efremov said, were too inclined to take the fossil record at face value; instead, he advised, they ought to pay more attention to the processes whereby living organisms become, or fail to become, fossils. A better understanding of burial and fossilization might enable paleontologists to "back calculate" and reclaim lost data from the fossil record.

Paleontologists Alan Cutler and Anna Behrensmeyer have developed just such a model of fossil preservation. Starting with a hypothetical population of dinosaurs, they estimated normal annual mortality rates for dinosaurs from ecological data collected for large mammals in African wildlife preserves. Next, to estimate what fraction of the dinosaurs' bones would end up safely buried, they drew on data from Behrensmeyer's study of the decay of mammal carcasses in Ambesoli National Park, Kenya. Finally, they ran the model to see what sort of bone spike would result if the entire population of dinosaurs suddenly died. The answer, they discovered, was no bone spike at all.

In the mixed, or convoluted, record, spikes in the abundance of species are attenuated and tail off exponentially. The thicker the mixing layer, the greater the smearing. Thus, the sudden extinction of a species shows up not as an abrupt disappearance of fossils, but a gradual petering out.

There is no way of predicting exactly what further research may bring. However promising its results may be, though, one caveat is necessary: It will never be able to work miracles. The most sophisticated mathematics in the world cannot unscramble an egg or resurrect the dinosaurs.

SECTION I

QUESTIONS

21. Which of the following may be inferred about the KT boundary?

 (A) The fossil record it contains is above average in both the quantity of fossils and their degree of preservation.
 (B) It was destroyed by a large comet sixty-five million years ago.
 (C) The fossil record it contains is, in some ways, inconsistent with the dominant theory of dinosaur extinction.
 (D) Its significance was first described by paleontologist Ivan A. Efremov.
 (E) Paleontologists consider it to be the single richest source in the fossil record.

22. Which of the following best describes the main idea of the passage?

 (A) If paleontologists are to achieve significant results in the future, they must reject their older methods.
 (B) Because it cannot be substantiated by the fossil record, the dominant theory of dinosaur extinction should be rejected.
 (C) Because of the nature of the process by which bones become fossils, scientists should not be surprised by the relative absence of fossils at the KT boundary.
 (D) Back-calculation indicates that the KT boundary should contain more fossils than more recent rock layers.
 (E) More recent methods of modeling fossil preservation provide evidence that contradicts earlier findings made by paleontologists.

EXPLANATIONS

21. This is a SPECIFIC question. Find the part of the passage that first talks about the KT boundary.

 (A) No, it's the opposite. There should be more fossils, but there aren't. Eliminate it.
 (B) The boundary wasn't destroyed; the dinosaurs were.
 (C) Yep—we've got a bunch of dead dinosaurs but no fossils showing that.
 (D) Wrong part of the passage on this one.
 (E) No, it's got few fossils considering what happened.

22. This is a MAIN IDEA question. Come up with your own main idea before you go to the answer choices.

 (A) This is way too general—we're talking about this one specific event, the KT thing.
 (B) Too extreme! We don't know enough about this stuff to pass a judgment like this.
 (C) Yes—we've got some inconsistencies, but there seems to be an explanation for them. Bingo.
 (D) Too specific, way too specific. This was only mentioned once.
 (E) No, there still aren't a lot of fossils, no matter how you slice it.

SECTION I

QUESTIONS	EXPLANATIONS

23. Which one of the following best describes the relationship between the work of Efremov and that of Cutler and Behrensmeyer?

(A) Efremov's work described the need for a significant shift in approach and Cutler and Behrensmeyer carried out research based in part on his approach.
(B) Efremov's work provided the data from which Cutler and Behrensmeyer were able to develop a model of fossil preservation.
(C) Whereas Efremov focused principally on why bones do not become fossils, Cutler and Behrensmeyer focused on why they do.
(D) Efremov's work was theoretically more complex than that carried out by Cutler and Behrensmeyer.
(E) Efremov focused on processes whereas Cutler and Behrensmeyer focused on data collection.

23. This is a SPECIFIC question. Find the part of the passage that talks about these folks.

(A) Yup. He had the idea, and they proved it was pretty accurate.
(B) Nope, this has the facts switched. Efremov came up with the idea, not the data.
(C) No, they worked around the same ideas.
(D) We have no idea whether Efremov was more complex.
(E) Close, but not as good as (A). This just talks about how they're different from each other. (A) is a better description of how they both fit into the KT discussion.

24. Which of the following best describes the organization of the passage?

(A) Data gathered from a broad range of sources is presented, inconsistencies among the data are described, then these inconsistencies are resolved.
(B) Research from two different groups of scientists is presented, a question about the research is posed, and an answer is offered.
(C) A new theoretical model is explained, problems with the model are pointed out, and possible explanations for the problem are suggested.
(D) A paradox is described, and both theoretical and empirical information is presented to help explain the paradox.
(E) A fundamental scientific failure is described, evidence substantiating this failure is presented, then a new approach to the problem is described.

24. This is a STRUCTURE question. Go back to the passage and find out how the passage flowed from paragraph to paragraph.

(A) Broad range of sources? Where? We're only talking about the KT boundary.
(B) No, we only get research from one group.
(C) No, the new theory is pretty good.
(D) Yes—the fact that we have lots of dead dinosaurs but no evidence. That's the paradox. This is the answer.
(E) Is this a failure of science? It's just a failure to obtain evidence.

SECTION I

QUESTIONS	EXPLANATIONS

25. The author would be most likely to agree with which of the following statements?

(A) Data from large mammal populations are essential in any attempt to model the process of dinosaur extinction.
(B) Fossil evidence indicates that the dinosaurs probably became extinct over a longer period of time than previously believed.
(C) The KT boundary provides a unique source of information about animal extinction.
(D) In most fossil layers, evidence of extinction trails off exponentially but contains an initial bone spike.
(E) Improvements in paleontological research, while useful, will not provide sufficient answers to all of the questions about dinosaur extinction.

25. This is a GENERAL INFERENCE question. Go to the answer choices and see which statement must be true given the information in the passage.

(A) Data are useful, but "essential" may be a bit too strong here. Let's look for something more wishy-washy.
(B) We have no idea. We've got no evidence. We're clueless.
(C) No, it doesn't provide enough information. That's the problem with it—it should, but it doesn't. Also, we don't know that it is unique.
(D) We have no idea about this.
(E) Nice and wishy-washy—we'll find out some answers, but just not all of them. That's what lines 56–58 are implicating.

26. The author states that, in their evaluation of the fossil record, Cutler and Behrensmeyer did all of the following EXCEPT

(A) conclude that the data from the fossil record was consistent with a mass extinction of dinosaurs
(B) work with paleontologist Ivan A. Efremov
(C) use data gathered from populations of large animals to estimate characteristics of dinosaur populations
(D) base their work on hypothetical information about dinosaur populations
(E) use data from studies of the decay of mammal carcasses in Africa

26. This is a SPECIFIC question. Find the part of the passage that talks about these folks. Remember that it's an EXCEPT question.

(A) Yes, see lines 44–45. No bone spike occurred. Eliminate it.
(B) No, they just used his idea. This is the answer.
(C) Yes, see lines 37–38. Eliminate it.
(D) Yes, see lines 35–36. Eliminate it.
(E) Yes, see lines 41–42. Eliminate it.

27. According to the passage, a segment of the fossil record in which paleontologists would LEAST expect to see a clear record of a period of sudden extinction would be one in which

(A) an abundance of bone spikes exist
(B) an unusually large portion of the bones were safely buried before fossilization
(C) "back calculation" would be difficult, but possible
(D) drought occurred at the time of fossilization
(E) a particularly thick mixing layer was present during fossil formation

27. This is a SPECIFIC question. But make sure you're looking for the thing we'd LEAST expect to see.

(A) We'd expect this, because where there is mass extinction, there are no spikes.
(B) We'd expect this, because we haven't found a lot of fossilized bones.
(C) We'd expect this, because there isn't all that much information with which to calculate.
(D) We'd expect this, since there would be more evidence.
(E) We wouldn't expect this, because it would indicate a gradual extinction, not a sudden one. This is the answer.

SECTION II

QUESTIONS

1. The quality of our public schools is more likely to decline if people expect it to. The number of illiterate graduates and the level of administrative incompetence will increase as people's disrespect for public schools discourages more able people from pursuing careers in teaching.

   The logical structure of the above statement is most consistent with which one of the following?

   (A) If people believe that an eagerly anticipated event will take place, then it most likely will.
   (B) When people believe that money grows on trees, then, for all practical purposes, money does grow on trees.
   (C) When people expect the economy to flourish, they become willing to spend and invest more, thus helping the economy to flourish.
   (D) When people expect world affairs to be tragic, they notice tragic events more than they do pleasant ones.
   (E) If people enjoy sporting events, the stadiums and arenas will be full, thus encouraging high attendance at future sporting events.

2. In an experiment, first-year college students were asked to listen to a tape of someone speaking French. When asked to repeat the sounds they had heard, students who had studied French in high school could repeat more of the sounds than could students who had no knowledge of French. When asked to listen to a tape of only meaningless sounds, none of the students were able to repeat more than a few seconds' worth of the sounds made on the tape.

   Which one of the following conclusions is best supported by the information above?

   (A) Knowledge of a foreign language interferes with one's ability to repeat unfamiliar sounds.
   (B) People who have a knowledge of French have better memories than do people who have no knowledge of French.
   (C) The ability to repeat unrelated sounds is not improved by frequent practice.
   (D) The ability to repeat sounds is influenced by one's ability to comprehend the meaning of the sounds.
   (E) Learning a foreign language requires an ability to distinguish unfamiliar sounds from gibberish.

EXPLANATIONS

1. This is a PARALLEL-THE-REASONING question. Try to get the theme or diagram of the logic and then match it to each answer choice.

   (A) No, we're looking for something in which people have an expectation, and then the expected result occurs. This leaves out the middle step.
   (B) This is silly. It's expectation, not belief.
   (C) Yep. We need that middle step that they are "willing to spend and invest more." This is the same construction as the argument, i.e., having an expectation, an action, and a result.
   (D) It's not noticing what meets expectations. It's that the expectation causes the action.
   (E) There is no expectation here.

2. This is an INFERENCE question. Your goal is to find the one choice that must be true based on the information in the passage.

   (A) No, because none of the students was able to repeat the sounds for more than a few seconds.
   (B) General memory is not related to an ability to speak French.
   (C) Maybe, but we don't know about practice.
   (D) Do we have proof of this? Yes—the French-speaking students remembered more of the sounds that were the French language than they did of the gibberish language. Plus, it's nice and wishy-washy—"is influenced by." This is the answer.
   (E) Maybe, but we don't know about learning a foreign language.

SECTION II

QUESTIONS	EXPLANATIONS

Questions 3–4

Many commercial pesticides, used primarily in indoor atriums, greenhouses, and solariums, release toxic levels of Acephate and other potentially carcinogenic agents hazardous to the health of workers and other individuals who pass through the area. This problem can be avoided by providing adequate ventilation, but this becomes difficult during winter months when the area must maintain sufficient heat to ensure the survival of the plants. A recent study shows that certain tropical grasses will remove some of these toxins from the air, eliminating the danger to humans. In one winter trial, a four-foot-square patch of tropical grass eliminated the Acephate in a solarium of average size.

3. Assume that a patch of tropical grass is introduced into a solarium of average size that contains toxic pesticide residue.

   Which one of the following can be expected as a result?

   (A) Occasional ventilation, even during the summer, will become unnecessary.
   (B) The concentration of toxic pesticide residues will remain unchanged.
   (C) The solarium will continue to maintain a constant level of toxicity and temperature.
   (D) If there are toxic Acephate residues in the solarium, these levels will decrease.
   (E) If Acephate and other potentially carcinogenic agents are being released in the solarium, the quantities of each agent will decrease.

3. This is an INFERENCE question. Your goal is to find the one choice that must be true based on the information in the passage.

   (A) "Unnecessary" is too extreme.
   (B) We don't know—is there Acephate in this residue or not? If so, they should decrease.
   (C) No, the grass should reduce toxic Acephate.
   (D) This is extreme, but it's the right answer. We know that the grass reduces the level of Acephate, so this is our answer.
   (E) Too far out there—we know about the Acephate, but "each agent" is too extreme.

4. The passage above is designed to lead to which one of the following conclusions?

   (A) Tropical grass removes all carcinogenic agents from the air.
   (B) Natural pesticides do not release toxins into greenhouses, solariums, or corporate atriums.
   (C) Planting tropical grass is an effective means of maintaining a constant temperature in a greenhouse.
   (D) Growing tropical grass can counteract some of the negative effects of a poorly ventilated atrium.
   (E) The air in an atrium that contains tropical grass and maintains a constant temperature will contain fewer toxic residues than will the air in a similarly maintained atrium without tropical grass.

4. This is an INFERENCE question. Your goal is to find the one choice that must be true based on the information in the passage.

   (A) "All" is too extreme. We only know that the grass removes the Acephate.
   (B) We have no idea about natural pesticides. Eliminate it.
   (C) No, the grass is there to counteract pesticides, not regulate temperature. Eliminate it.
   (D) Nice and wishy-washy. "Some" negative effects (i.e., Acephate) can be counteracted. This is our answer.
   (E) "Will" is too extreme here. And we don't know this—unless the atrium definitively contained Acephate, the residues might not decrease.

SECTION II

QUESTIONS

5. Medical Researcher: If I don't get another research grant soon, I'll never be able to discover a cure for phlebitis.

Assistant: But that's great. If your grant does come through, that dreaded disease will finally be eradicated.

Which one of the following statements best describes the flaw in the assistant's reasoning?

(A) The assistant believes the researcher will be unable to cure phlebitis unless the grant comes through.
(B) The assistant thinks the researcher will use the grant to find a cure for phlebitis, rather than for some other purpose.
(C) The assistant believes it is more important to cure phlebitis than to eradicate other, more deadly conditions.
(D) The assistant believes that all the researcher needs in order to cure phlebitis is another research grant.
(E) The assistant thinks the researcher will cure phlebitis even if the grant does not come through.

6. Economist: The keys to a growth economy are low interest rates and a high number of investments; because there cannot be investments without low interest rates, it can be concluded that where there are low interest rates there are investments.

Which one of the following, if true, would most weaken the argument above?

(A) Many growth economies with high interest rates have few investments.
(B) Stagnant economies with high interest rates have few investments.
(C) Stagnant economies with low interest rates have few investments.
(D) A high number of investments is adequate to guarantee low interest rates.
(E) Some stagnant economies have low interest rates.

EXPLANATIONS

5. **Conclusion:** If the researcher gets the grant, the disease will be eradicated.

Premise: If the researcher doesn't get the grant, she'll never discover a cure.

Assumption: There's no other factor preventing her from discovering a cure.

This is a FLAW question. Come up with your own description of how the assistant made a mistake before you go to the answer choices, and then match your description to the choices.

(A) No, this is what the medical researcher said. Look for something that mentions how the assistant thinks the researcher said that the grant was sufficient to ensure success.
(B) This isn't a flaw in the argument—it's accurate.
(C) Other diseases weren't mentioned by anyone.
(D) Yes, he confused *necessary* with *sufficient* in this case—the researcher said it was necessary for her to get the grant, the assistant assumed that the grant will be sufficient to effect the cure.
(E) No, neither person said this.

6. **Conclusion:** Where there are low interest rates, there are investments.

Premise: There cannot be investments without low interest rates.

Assumption: Because investments can exist, they will exist.

This is a WEAKEN question. Figure out which answer choice has the most negative impact on the conclusion of the argument. Remember to assume the hypothetical truth of each choice and apply it to the argument.

(A) This would strengthen the argument.
(B) This would strengthen the argument.
(C) Here's a situation where low interest rates have NOT produced investments, which is what the argument said would happen. This is the answer.
(D) This is saying the causality can flow the other way, but it doesn't preclude it from happening in the way the argument says it does. (C) is a better answer.
(E) What about the number of investments?

SECTION II

QUESTIONS	EXPLANATIONS

7. A study commissioned by the National Association of Women Professors seems to indicate that women face greater obstacles in becoming tenured professors than do men. Whereas more than 70 percent of the male professors in this country have tenure, fewer than half of the female professors have achieved that rank.

Which one of the following statistics would be most relevant to an assessment of the accuracy of the study mentioned above?

(A) the respective percentages of eligible women and men who have earned tenure in each of the past ten years
(B) the percentage of all tenured positions that have gone to women in each of the past ten years
(C) an analysis of the bias faced by women in other professional fields
(D) the number of men who have been appointed to tenured positions, and the number of women who have not been appointed to tenured positions
(E) the number of professional women who cite the difficulty of achieving tenure when asked to explain why they decided against entering academia

7. **Conclusion:** Women face greater obstacles to becoming tenured than do men.

Premise: More than 70 percent of male professors are tenured, where fewer than half of all female professors are.

Assumption: The proportions of male and female professors who have been teaching long enough to be eligible for tenure are roughly equivalent.

This is most like an ASSUMPTION question because you are looking for a fact that will help you to evaluate the validity of the assumption.

(A) This would definitely have an impact. If the percentages were equal, the argument would be weakened. This is our answer.
(B) What about men? This doesn't help as much as (A).
(C) What about men? This doesn't help as much as (A).
(D) Without the overall percentages, the numbers themselves are useless.
(E) What about men? This doesn't help as much as (A).

8. Sheet for sheet, Brand A paper towels cost less than Brand B paper towels and are more absorbent. Yet a roll of Brand A paper towels costs more than a roll of Brand B paper towels.

Which one of the following, if true, explains how the statements above can both be true?

(A) Both Brand A and Brand B towels are manufactured by the same company, which often creates artificial competition for its expensive products.
(B) A roll of Brand B paper towels is more absorbent than a roll of Brand A paper towels.
(C) A roll of Brand A paper towels is more absorbent than a roll of Brand B paper towels.
(D) The cost of a roll of Brand A towels has risen every year for the last five years.
(E) A roll of Brand A paper towels has more sheets than a roll of Brand B paper towels.

8. This is a PARADOX question. Look for an answer choice that allows both parts of the argument to be true, and remember to assume the hypothetical truth of each of the answer choices.

(A) This doesn't explain the discrepancy in the per sheet vs. overall price issue.
(B) Absorbency is totally out of the scope here. Eliminate it.
(C) Same problem as (B). Eliminate it.
(D) What about Brand B? Without anything to compare this information to, it's useless. Eliminate it.
(E) Can this explain why the overall price is higher? Yes—there are more sheets on Brand A. It's the answer.

SECTION II

QUESTIONS

9. State agricultural officials are hoping to save California's $30 billion-a-year fruit industry from destruction by the Mediterranean fruit fly by releasing nearly one billion sterile female fruit flies throughout the state. This has, in the past, been shown to be the only effective means of limiting the spread of this destructive pest, outside of large-scale pesticide spraying.

   Which one of the following best explains the intended effect of the program described above?

   (A) To drastically increase the number of potential mates for the male fruit flies, requiring them to devote more of their energies to mating rather than eating fruit.
   (B) To saturate a given area with fruit flies, creating greater competition for food and thereby containing the damage done by the fruit fly to a smaller area.
   (C) To ensure that a large number of fruit flies in succeeding generations are born infertile.
   (D) To limit the growth of the population by reducing the number of successful matings between fruit flies.
   (E) To encourage overpopulation of the fruit fly in the hopes that nature will correct the situation itself.

10. A fit, well-tuned body is essential to good health because exercise acts to improve circulation and helps to eliminate toxins from the body. If one is to remain healthy, one must get regular exercise.

   Which one of the following conclusions can most logically be drawn from the passage above?

   (A) If one exercises, one will be healthy.
   (B) Only exercise acts to improve the circulation and eliminate toxins from the body.
   (C) A healthy person must have eliminated all toxins from his or her body.
   (D) If one does not exercise regularly, one will not remain healthy.
   (E) A person who is not healthy must not exercise.

EXPLANATIONS

9. This is a CONCLUSION question. Look for the answer that is the goal of the agricultural officials. What are they trying to do here?

   (A) This looks okay, but they're still going to eat some fruit. Let's see if there is something better.
   (B) Still not all that great, is it? At least part of the state isn't going to have any fruit left at all. Let's keep looking.
   (C) But if we're releasing sterile flies, there won't be succeeding generations. Eliminate it.
   (D) This looks really good. By releasing sterile flies, we should be able to reduce the population of fruit flies. It's the answer.
   (E) Overpopulation is the opposite of what we want here. Eliminate it.

10. This is an INFERENCE question. Your goal is to find the one choice that must be true based on the information in the passage.

   (A) This does not necessarily have to be true—it's an invalid contrapositive of what is in the argument.
   (B) We don't know this to be true—exercise is necessary, but is it the only thing that is necessary?
   (C) "All" is too extreme here. Eliminate it.
   (D) Bingo! This is the contrapositive of the last sentence of the argument.
   (E) This is another invalid contrapositive. You could exercise but still have some unhealthy genetic defect. Eliminate it.

SECTION II

QUESTIONS

11. Marie: I just found out that it is cheaper for me to heat my home with gas or oil than for me to use any of the alternative methods available. I don't understand why environmentalists insist that the cost of fossil fuels is so high.

Louise: That's because you are confusing the price of fossil fuels with their cost. Gas and oil release tremendous amounts of pollution into the water and air, causing great damage to the environment. Not only does this pose a threat to the ecological balance that will affect the quality of life for future generations, but it also causes health problems that may be related to the consumption of these fuels. Once you add in these factors, it is clear that there are many alternatives that are actually cheaper than gas or oil, and consumers should adopt them.

According to her argument above, if an alternative energy source were to be found, under which one of the following conditions would Louise definitely object to its use?

(A) if its price and cost were equal
(B) if its cost were higher than the price of fossil fuels
(C) if its cost were higher than the cost of fossil fuels
(D) if the price of fossil fuels were to fall
(E) if it were less efficient than fossil fuels

12. An office equipment rental firm made the following claim:

Owning your office equipment is actually more expensive than renting it. Over a three-year period, a mid-sized copier, for example, costs $23,000 per year to own, based on the average purchase price of the machine and the cost of its maintenance. The cost of renting a comparable copier is $22,000 per year.

Which one of the following statements, if true, provides the most effective criticism of the argument above?

(A) The average lifespan of a copier is between five and six years.
(B) The figures cited above remain proportionally the same even when more expensive copiers are considered.
(C) The price of copiers actually has decreased in the last ten years.
(D) The price of copier paper and electricity may soon rise sharply.
(E) Buying used copiers can save money, even though such machines need more maintenance.

EXPLANATIONS

11. This is most like a WEAKEN or STRENGTHEN or PARADOX question, because you're looking for the one thing in the answer choices that, if known, will have the most IMPACT on the argument. So let's go looking for that.

(A) It depends. If they were equal at current cost levels? No. At current price levels? Maybe. Eliminate it.
(B) This confuses "cost" and "price." Eliminate it.
(C) Yep. We know she doesn't like the current situation, and this would make it worse. She would object to this.
(D) This would have no impact on the argument either way. Eliminate it.
(E) Efficiency is not the issue—cost is.

12. **Conclusion:** Owning office equipment is more expensive than is renting it.

Premise: Over a three-year period, owning a copier would cost $23,000, whereas renting it would cost only $22,000.

Assumptions: Copiers are like all office equipment; owning a copier does not become more cost-efficient over longer periods of time.

This is a WEAKEN question. Figure out which answer choice has the most negative impact on the conclusion of the argument. Remember to assume the hypothetical truth of each choice and apply it to the argument.

(A) So if this were true, it would be better to buy because the price would be lower than $23,000 because we're now spreading it out over five or six years rather than just three. It's the answer.
(B) This would strengthen the argument.
(C) This has no relevance to the argument because it affects renting and leasing equally.
(D) Same problem as (C)—there is no relevance.
(E) This just says that it can save money, not that it will—so it doesn't have as much impact as (A).

SECTION II

QUESTIONS

Questions 13–14

Despite advances in geothermal technology and equipment, experts rarely agree which method is the best indicator of a likely source of oil. Some believe the cycle of environmental changes determines the primary sources for crude oil, while others look to the evolution of organic matter as the most significant indicator. What they do agree on, however, is where oil won't be found. They agree that in areas that were scraped clean of organic sedimentary deposits by glaciers during the last million years or so, the biological "ingredients" that they believe are necessary for the formation of oil and gas are not present. That is, where glaciers have scoured a landmass, oil and gas will not be found.

13. If all of the information above is true, which one of the following can be reasonably inferred?

(A) Geologists understand some of the physical conditions necessary for the formation of deposits of oil.
(B) Scientists leave open the possibility that oil may have been formed during the last million years in some regions that were covered by glaciers during the same period.
(C) Geologists can, with a fairly high degree of accuracy, predict whether an area that meets the necessary preconditions for the formation of oil will, in fact, yield oil.
(D) Geologists can, with a fairly high degree of accuracy, predict whether oil can be found in a particular landmass that was not scoured by glaciers.
(E) If geologists can determine the biological "ingredients" necessary for the formation of oil, they can determine the locations of the most promising oil fields.

14. Which one of the following, if true, would most seriously weaken the geologists' view?

(A) Relatively little of the earth's surface is known to rest above the sort of organic sedimentary deposits described above.
(B) Despite the existence of permanent glaciers, oil has been found at both the North and South Poles.
(C) There are too many variables involved for experts to be able to identify what does and does not need to be present for the formation of oil.
(D) The glacier theory cannot help locate oil in the ocean because ocean beds went untouched by glaciers.
(E) Oil deposits exist below the crust of the entire Earth, and are brought nearer to the surface by cracks in the crust.

EXPLANATIONS

13. This is an INFERENCE question. Your goal is to find the one choice that must be true based on the information in the passage.

(A) This is nice and wishy-washy—they understand "some" of the conditions. Let's leave it.
(B) No, they said that there shouldn't be any. Eliminate it.
(C) We have no idea about their accuracy. They're still arguing methodology. Eliminate it.
(D) Same problem as (C). Eliminate it.
(E) We don't know this for sure. (A) is by far our safest choice here.

14. **Conclusion:** Where glaciers have scoured a landmass, there will be no oil.

Premise: Geologists agree that in areas scraped clean of organic sedimentary deposits by glaciers, the 'ingredients' necessary to form oil do not exist.

Assumption: Geologists are correct.

This is a WEAKEN question. Try to see which answer choice has the most negative impact on the conclusion of the argument. Remember to assume the hypothetical truth of each choice and apply it to the argument.

(A) This has no impact on the argument.
(B) This choice doesn't say whether the glaciers have actually scoured the landmasses in these places. Let's see if there is anything better.
(C) Remember, the geologists are trying to say what the conditions are for it not happening, not the other way around. This has no impact.
(D) This also has no impact on the argument.
(E) Oops—the geologists are boneheads because oil exists below the "entire earth." Thus, there are no places it doesn't exist, which totally destroys their argument. It's the answer.

SECTION II

QUESTIONS

15. Although all societies have some form of class system, there are systems that are based on neither wealth nor power. Still, there is no society that does not divide its population into the privileged and the common.

If the above statements are correct, it can be properly concluded that

(A) making distinctions between haves and have-nots is a part of human nature
(B) there are some people in all cultures who are considered privileged
(C) every society has its own unique hierarchy
(D) privileged people must have money
(E) all societies have a tradition of seeing themselves as either privileged or common

16. One can predict that the number of people in the nation's labor force will diminish in the next 20 years. Population growth in our country reached its apex in 1961, and by the late 1960s there were more employed heads of households in this country than ever before. The growth has slackened significantly, and by 2007 the total number of households will be reduced, thus limiting the number of potential employees in the work force.

Which one of the following, if true, would most seriously damage the conclusion of the above argument?

(A) The urge to acquire wealth contributed to the growth of the labor force in the 1960s.
(B) There will be greater competition among employers to attract employees from a shrinking population base during the next decade.
(C) In the next decade there will be more people who are not the heads of household entering the labor force than there were in the 1960s.
(D) Employers fared well in the 1950s with fewer potential employees than exist today.
(E) By 2007 there will be far more people running their own businesses than there are today.

EXPLANATIONS

15. This is an INFERENCE question. Your goal is to find the one choice that must be true based on the information in the passage.

(A) "Human nature" is a little too general here. Eliminate it.
(B) "Some" is nice and wishy-washy. Let's leave it.
(C) It doesn't have to be true that every society's hierarchy is "unique." Eliminate it.
(D) Money is out of the scope of the argument. Eliminate it.
(E) Each society has BOTH privileged and common categories. (B) is our best answer here.

16. **Conclusion:** The number of people in the labor force will drop over the next 20 years.

Premise: Population growth reached its peak in 1961.

Assumption: The proportion of people working has not grown; people are not waiting longer to retire.

This is a WEAKEN question. Figure out which answer choice has the most negative impact on the conclusion of the argument. Remember to assume the hypothetical truth of each choice and apply it to the argument.

(A) This has no impact—we're looking to weaken the conclusion that there will be fewer people in the workforce.
(B) This would strengthen the argument that there will be fewer people.
(C) So we've got this second whole group of people—this would weaken the argument. It's the answer.
(D) The 1950s are totally out of the scope here.
(E) Running your own business is out of scope.

SECTION II

QUESTIONS

Questions 17–18

A controversy recently erupted at College X after the student newspaper printed several letters to the editor that attacked the college's affirmative action program in offensive, racially charged language. Two psychologists at the school took advantage of the controversy by conducting an experiment on campus. Psychologist #1, posing as a reporter, stopped students at random, ostensibly to solicit his or her opinion of the controversy. At the same time, psychologist #2, posing as a student, also stopped, joined the discussion, and made the first reply to the questions of the "reporter." The experiment showed that when psychologist #2 expressed support for the racist sentiments expressed in the letters, 75 percent of the subjects responded similarly. When psychologist #2 expressed strong disapproval of the language and substance of the letters, 90 percent of the subjects responded similarly.

17. Which one of the following represents the most reasonable conclusion that can be drawn from the information in the passage above?

(A) People are more likely to voice their opposition to racism if they hear others doing the same.
(B) People are less likely to hide their sympathy for certain racist attitudes if they feel that others share the same feelings.
(C) People's willingness to voice their racist sentiments is proportional to the percentage of all people who share such sentiments.
(D) People may be influenced by the opinions of others when they express their opinions of racist sentiments.
(E) The extent to which popular opinion molds the opinions of individuals is significant, though not easily quantifiable.

18. If the psychologists described above were to conclude from their data that some people are more willing to speak up against racism if they hear others doing so, their conclusion would depend on the validity of which one of the following assumptions?

(A) The students at College X are no more racist than are students at other colleges.
(B) The students at College X are more likely to have experienced racism personally.
(C) Some of the subjects in the experiment knew that the psychologists were posing as a reporter and a student.
(D) Some of the subjects in their experiment would have changed their response to psychologist #1's questions if psychologist #2 had responded differently.
(E) All of the subjects in the experiment stated their heartfelt, uninfluenced opinion of the incident in question.

EXPLANATIONS

17. This is an INFERENCE question. Your goal is to find the one choice that must be true based on the information in the passage.

(A) This just focuses on the opponents of racism, and the argument is about both opponents and supporters.
(B) Same problem as (A), so they are both wrong.
(C) Same problem as (A)—we're only focusing on half of the people.
(D) Nice and wishy-washy, and this is talking about both groups of people.
(E) "Popular opinion" is too general a term here. (D) is the best answer.

18. This is an ASSUMPTION question. The correct answer will be something necessary for the conclusion to be true, and, if made false, will make the argument fall apart.

(A) Racism per se is not the issue. The issue is students' willingness to express an opinion on racism.
(B) Personal experiences are outside the scope of the argument.
(C) If this were true, it would probably destroy the argument. Eliminate it.
(D) Otherwise, the whole experiment would have had no impact—this is the answer.
(E) We're interested in the willingness of people to express themselves, not in whether their opinions were heartfelt or uninfluenced.

SECTION II

QUESTIONS	EXPLANATIONS

19. Evidence seems to indicate that people's faith in some mystical practices increases when these practices offer relief in frightening or challenging situations. One significant piece of evidence is the observation that the use of "healing crystals" is more prevalent among people who suffer from life-threatening diseases such as cancer than it is among people who have minor health problems such as colds or the flu.

    Which one of the following, if true, would most seriously weaken the conclusion drawn in the passage above?

    (A) Rapid social change has alienated people and has led to an overall increase in people's adoption of mystical practices.
    (B) Many mystical practices are never used by more than a small number of extremely ill people.
    (C) If someone has a life-threatening disease, he may try nontraditional cures without necessarily believing that they will work.
    (D) Psychics and mediums do not experience a surge in business after the occurrence of earthquakes and plane crashes.
    (E) The use of crystals is one of the most ancient methods utilized for healing.

19. **Conclusion:** Faith in mystical practices increases in life-threatening situations.

    Premise: People are more likely to use healing crystals for cancer than for a cold or flu.

    Assumption: The people who use healing crystals actually believe they will work.

    This is a WEAKEN question. Figure out which answer choice has the most negative impact on the conclusion of the argument. Remember to assume the hypothetical truth of each choice and apply it to the argument.

    (A) We're concerned more with crystals and specific diseases—this is a little too general.
    (B) Mystical practices that are not used are not the issue.
    (C) Ah, so while they are trying these cures, their faith in them hasn't necessarily increased—this would weaken the argument. This is the answer.
    (D) None of this is talking about anything in the argument. Eliminate it.
    (E) The ancientness of crystals has no impact on the argument. Eliminate it.

20. Lithotripsy is a relatively new procedure for the treatment of kidney stones. The patient is suspended in a tub of water and sound waves are aimed at his kidneys. Upon impact, the waves shatter the stones. Recovery time from this procedure is shorter than that of surgery, which is the conventional method of treatment. Lithotripsy is also less expensive than surgery. Therefore, physicians should stop performing invasive surgery for kidney stones soon.

    Which one of the following statements, if true, most seriously weakens the argument in the passage above?

    (A) There has been little research done on the effect of lithotripsy on senior citizens.
    (B) It will be many years before lithotripsy equipment can be produced in sufficient quantity to meet demand.
    (C) Many doctors do not know much about lithotripsy, as it is a relatively new procedure.
    (D) Some insurance companies do not cover treatments such as lithotripsy.
    (E) Lithotripsy is not an available option for children.

20. **Conclusion:** Physicians should stop invasive surgery for kidney stones.

    Premise: Lithotripsy is less expensive and easier to recover from.

    Assumption: Invasive surgery has no advantage over lithotripsy; lithotripsy is available to everyone.

    This is a WEAKEN question. Figure out which answer choice has the most negative impact on the conclusion of the argument. Remember to assume the hypothetical truth of each choice and apply it to the argument.

    (A) Bummer, but we don't know if kidney stone operations are performed on senior citizens to begin with. Eliminate it.
    (B) So the fact that surgery will stop "soon" is not going to happen. This is the answer.
    (C) The fact that they don't know doesn't mean that they can't find out quickly. Eliminate it.
    (D) Bummer, but maybe they will soon.
    (E) Same problem as (A)—we don't know if children ever need kidney stone operations.

SECTION II

QUESTIONS

21. The human body changes a great deal over the course of a lifetime. As people enter middle age, for instance, they tend to become overweight, regardless of their body type as young adults. Though this weight gain has long been blamed on the tendency of middle-aged people to consume an excess of calories daily, recent evidence suggests that it is instead attributable to the body's decreased demand for calories. This decreased demand means that a maintenance of prior caloric consumption will provide an excess of calories, most of which will simply be stored as body fat.

    A logical critique of the passage above would likely emphasize the fact that the author fails to

    (A) establish definitively the connection between caloric intake and weight gain
    (B) offer any hard evidence of the percentage of middle-aged people who are actually overweight
    (C) give detailed information as to the causes of the body's decreased demand for calories in middle age
    (D) offer a consistent definition of the term "excess" as it relates to caloric consumption
    (E) discuss the causes of obesity in the population at large

22. If a candidate is to win an election easily, that candidate must respond to the electorate's emotional demands—demands that the opponent either does not see or cannot act upon. Though these emotional demands are often not directly articulated by the electorate or by the candidate responding to them, they are an integral part of any landslide victory.

    Which one of the following conclusions can most logically be drawn from the passage above?

    (A) If neither candidate responds to the emotional demands of the electorate, either candidate might win in a landslide.
    (B) If an election was close, the emotional demands of the electorate were conflicting.
    (C) If a candidate responds to the emotional demands of the electorate, that candidate will have a landslide victory.
    (D) An election during which neither candidate responds to the emotional demands of the electorate will not result in a landslide.
    (E) Emotional demands are the only inarticulated issues in an election.

EXPLANATIONS

21. This is a FLAW question. Come up with your own description of why the author's conclusion is flawed before you go to the answer choices, and then match your description to the choices.

    (A) No, the author does establish the connection, just not exactly how it works.
    (B) Lack of hard evidence is almost never the correct answer. Just because the author doesn't provide statistics is not why the argument is internally bad. Eliminate it.
    (C) Same problem as (B).
    (D) This is the biggest problem here. The author never tells us that a certain amount isn't in excess when you're younger but then is later on—that's why the argument is bad. This is the answer.
    (E) Obesity was never mentioned. (D) is the best answer here.

22. This is an INFERENCE question. Your goal is to find the one choice that must be true based on the information in the passage.

    (A) No, because if candidates don't respond, there can't be a landslide.
    (B) We have no idea what would happen if the election were close. Eliminate it.
    (C) This is the invalid contrapositive of the first sentence. Eliminate it.
    (D) Bingo—it's the contrapositive of the first sentence—that if you don't respond, you can't have a landslide.
    (E) "Only" is too extreme here. Eliminate it.

SECTION II

QUESTIONS

23. Commodities analysts maintain that if the price of soybeans decreases by more than half, the consumer's purchase price for milk produced by livestock fed these soybeans will also decrease by more than half.

Which one of the following, if true, casts the most doubt on the prediction made by the commodities analysts?

(A) New genetic strains of livestock and improvements in feed lot procedures have enabled some cows to increase their milk output while decreasing their soybean intake.
(B) Dairy farmers cannot expand their profit margins any further without compromising the health of their livestock.
(C) Many different dairy suppliers compete with each other, forcing a consumer-driven market.
(D) Studies in other dairy-producing countries show that the amount of milk purchased by consumers usually rises after an initial decrease in milk prices.
(E) Pasteurization and distribution costs, neither of which varies with the price of soybeans, constitute the major portion of the price of milk.

24. The more dairy products a person consumes, the higher his cholesterol level is. More than half of the people in this country eat in excess of four dairy products each day, whereas in Germany the figure is only 10 percent. Accordingly, more than 65 percent of the people in this country have cholesterol levels that are considered too high and only 2 percent of Germans have similarly excessive levels. Therefore, if the cholesterol levels of Americans are to be brought down, we must eat fewer dairy products.

Which one of the following, if established, could strengthen the author's argument?

(A) Citizens of the United States are less concerned with cholesterol levels than citizens of Germany.
(B) Germans are more disciplined about watching their diets than Americans.
(C) People who are concerned about their cholesterol levels will eat fewer dairy products.
(D) A person's cholesterol level is reduced significantly when he or she consumes fewer than two dairy products per day.
(E) Dairy products, and not any other food items, are the critical factors in determining cholesterol levels.

EXPLANATIONS

23. **Conclusion:** If soybean prices decrease by more than half, the cost of milk from livestock fed by soybeans will decrease by more than half.

Assumption: There is no other factor in the cost of milk besides the cost to feed livestock.

This is a WEAKEN question. Figure out which answer choice has the most negative impact on the conclusion of the argument. Remember to assume the hypothetical truth of each choice and apply it to the argument.

(A) Great! Unfortunately, we're interested in the price of milk. No impact here.
(B) Bummer for them. However, no impact on the argument again.
(C) One would assume that people in the same business compete with each other. No impact.
(D) Other countries really won't help us here. No impact.
(E) Yes—this would show that the price of milk won't change because the soybean component of it is small. It's the answer.

24. **Conclusion:** We must eat fewer dairy products to lower our cholesterol levels.

Premises: We eat lots of dairy and have high cholesterol; Germans eat less dairy and don't have high cholesterol.

Assumption: Decreasing dairy alone will be sufficient to lower our cholesterol.

This is a STRENGTHEN question. Figure out which answer choice has the most positive impact on the conclusion of the argument. Remember to assume the hypothetical truth of each choice and apply it to the argument.

(A) We need something about dairy products here—level of concern has no impact.
(B) Discipline has no impact—we're looking for dairy products.
(C) This is the same problem as (A). Eliminate it.
(D) This looks pretty good, but we don't know exactly how many dairy products the Germans consume, just that they don't consume "in excess of four." Let's see if there is something better.
(E) Bingo—this shows a necessary causality, because the author's conclusion doesn't allow for any other explanations. Therefore, dairy has to be the critical factor.

QUESTIONS

25. The introduction of new technologies and equipment into the marketplace can significantly alter the quality of life for the members of a society. The automatic dishwasher, for example, eased the housekeeping burdens traditionally borne by women. At the same time, the convenience of an automatic dishwasher has fostered a dependence upon its time-saving qualities. It has become increasingly difficult to find a household with an automatic dishwasher where small numbers of dishes are washed by hand. In the long run, the environmental cost of such behavior is scarcely worth the amount of time saved.

Which one of the following principles is best illustrated by the example presented in the passage?

(A) The significance of a benefit should be weighed in terms of its overall effect.
(B) People should make a unified effort to reduce their negative impact upon the environment.
(C) Some new technologies offer no perceptible benefit to society.
(D) The acquisition of leisure time is not worth the destruction of the biosphere.
(E) Most new machinery makes our lives more streamlined and economical.

EXPLANATIONS

25. This is a PRINCIPLE question. We are given five principles in the answer choices for this specific question, so we should come up with our own principle for the actions in the argument and match it to the answer choices.

(A) This looks good. Even though dishwashers are cool, their overall impact is negative. Let's leave this one.
(B) The argument is about dishwashers, not people.
(C) But dishwashers do—it's just that they also offer a perceptible downside, too.
(D) This is good, but it is a bit extreme—will dishwashers really destroy the biosphere? (A) is a more balanced response here.
(E) True, but this doesn't talk about the downside at all—(A) is the answer.

SECTION III

QUESTIONS

1. Senator: For economic issues, I base my responses on logic. For political issues, I base my responses either on logic or gut instinct. For moral issues, I never base my responses on logic.

   Which one of the following can be correctly inferred from the statements above?

   (A) If the senator relies on logic, he may be responding to a moral issue.
   (B) If the senator relies on logic, he is not responding to an economic issue.
   (C) If the senator does not rely on logic, he is responding to a political issue.
   (D) If the senator does not rely on logic, he must be responding to an economic issue.
   (E) If the senator does not rely on logic, he might be responding to a political issue.

2. Concern about the environmental and health problems associated with nuclear energy has compelled activist groups to join forces in an attempt to shut down nuclear power plants. However, a survey of nuclear power plants across the United States showed that there have only been two accidents in the past ten years, both minor in nature, and in both cases, the danger was quickly contained. If the United States is to produce enough energy to become completely independent from foreign sources of energy, more nuclear power plants must be built, and the misinformation being distributed by activist groups must be countered by the statistics found in the study.

   All of the following are assumptions of the above argument EXCEPT:

   (A) Using nuclear power is the only way for the United States to produce enough energy that no fuel needs to be imported.
   (B) Some people think nuclear power plants are dangerous.
   (C) The accidents caused little harm.
   (D) Other methods of producing energy are also considered dangerous.
   (E) The United States needs to be completely self-sufficient in the production of energy.

EXPLANATIONS

1. This is an INFERENCE question. Your goal is to find the one choice that must be true based on the information in the passage.

   (A) No, the senator never bases moral issue responses on logic. Eliminate it.
   (B) No, the senator may very well be responding to an economic issue. Eliminate it.
   (C) No, the senator could be responding to a moral issue. Eliminate it.
   (D) No, the senator always uses logic to respond to economic issues. Eliminate it.
   (E) Bingo. Nice and wishy-washy, and accurate. With political issues, the senator might respond with a gut instinct. This is the answer.

2. **Conclusion:** If the U.S. is going to become independent from foreign energy sources, more nuclear power plants must be built, and the misinformation spread by activists must be countered.

   Premise: Nuclear power isn't really unsafe— there have only been two minor accidents in the past ten years.

   Assumptions: The U.S. needs to be independent from foreign energy sources; just because there have been no major accidents in the past ten years means nuclear power is safe.

   This is an ASSUMPTION question. Because this is an EXCEPT question, the correct answer will be the one thing that is NOT necessary for the conclusion to be true, and, if made false, will NOT make the argument fall apart.

   (A) If there were another method, the argument would fall apart. This is a necessary assumption—eliminate it.
   (B) If no one thought they were dangerous, then what are they worrying about? Eliminate it.
   (C) If they caused a lot of harm, it would weaken the argument. Eliminate it.
   (D) Bummer, but it isn't necessary for the conclusion to be true that nuclear power is the ONLY way. Let's leave it.
   (E) If we didn't need to be self-sufficient, then why bother with building more nuclear power plants? This is also necessary, so the answer here is (D).

SECTION III

QUESTIONS	EXPLANATIONS

3. Rather than learn about Senate hearings by listening to word-of-mouth accounts or by sitting in on the sessions themselves, people now depend mainly on television and the Internet for information about important investigative and confirmation hearings conducted by Senate committees. Thus, the media serve as a surrogate for the millions of people who care deeply about such proceedings but could never attend them themselves.

   The above passage is most likely part of an argument in favor of

   (A) reserving more seats for ordinary citizens at important Senate hearings
   (B) imposing secrecy rules on the Senate committee hearings not already covered by the media
   (C) expanding media coverage of important Senate hearings
   (D) enacting a law that would prohibit any censorship of press coverage of the Senate
   (E) widening the scope of Senate inquiry of press censorship

3. This is a CONCLUSION question. Look for the answer that is the goal of the passage. What is it trying to do here?

   (A) No, we want to look for something about how the media is so good for us.
   (B) This would go against what the argument is saying—we want more, not less, coverage.
   (C) Bingo—they're doing such a great job, let's expand their coverage. This is the answer.
   (D) We're not concerned in the argument with anyone taking away the media's power or coverage rights. Eliminate it.
   (E) We don't care about Senate inquiries. We like the press. Eliminate it.

4. Advertisement: Professional exterminators will tell you that in order to rid your home of roaches, you must do more than kill all the roaches you see. This is why the system that professional exterminators use most includes a poison that inhibits the development of roach eggs already laid, as well as a chemical that kills all adult roaches. This same combination is now available to the nonprofessional in new Extirm. When you're ready to get rid of roaches once and for all, get Extirm in your corner.

   All of the following are implied by the advertisement above EXCEPT:

   (A) Professional exterminators asked about roach extermination recommended Extirm.
   (B) Extirm contains a chemical that inhibits the development of roach eggs.
   (C) More than one chemical is required to rid a home of roaches.
   (D) Inhibiting the development of roach eggs may not eliminate roaches from the home.
   (E) Roaches reproduce by laying eggs.

4. This is an INFERENCE question. It is also an EXCEPT question, so your goal is to find the one choice that doesn't have to be true based on the information in the passage.

   (A) We have no idea what they recommend. It's never mentioned in the passage. This is the answer.
   (B) Yes, this is mentioned in the second sentence. Eliminate it.
   (C) Yes, this is mentioned in the second sentence. One for eggs, one for adults. Eliminate it.
   (D) Which is why we need two chemicals—see the second sentence again.
   (E) This is a major part of sentence two. Eliminate it.

QUESTIONS	EXPLANATIONS

5. In congressional hearings the question arises: "Which side knows best the potential benefits and dangers involved in the drilling of new offshore oil wells within U.S. territorial waters?" Oil companies' advice must certainly be taken with a grain of salt, because they are concerned only with profit and will oppose any legislation that would reduce such profit. Environmentalists' dire warnings must also be questioned, because many environmentalists' opposition to such drilling is purely reflexive, and without basis in scientific fact. This is why, in order to understand fully the costs and benefits that must be weighed in deciding whether to drill oil wells in U.S. coastal waters, Congress should rely primarily on the advice of academic research geologists, who are both informed and objective on the issue.

Which one of the following, if true, would most seriously weaken the author's conclusion in the passage above?

(A) Environmentalists are more knowledgeable about the dangers associated with drilling oil wells than is the average congressperson.
(B) Most academic research geologists rely heavily on income earned from consulting fees paid by oil companies.
(C) Oil companies have responded to public outcry over environmental damage caused by offshore oil drilling by developing technology that makes offshore oil drilling much safer than it used to be.
(D) The oil industry lobby is responsible each year for significant campaign contributions to legislators.
(E) Academic research geologists are not unanimous in their support of or opposition to new offshore oil drilling in U.S. coastal waters.

5. **Conclusion:** Congress should rely on academic geologists when deciding whether to drill for oil offshore.

Premises: Academic geologists are both informed and objective; oil companies and environmental groups are not objective.

Assumption: Academic geologists are not actually allied with either oil companies or environmental groups.

This is a WEAKEN question. Figure out which answer choice has the most negative impact on the conclusion of the argument. Remember to assume the hypothetical truth of each choice and apply it to the argument.

(A) We want something that shows how the geologists are biased. This doesn't do that. Eliminate it.
(B) Oops! So the geologists may not be objective. This is the answer.
(C) It's nice that it's safer than it used to be, but this doesn't call into question the geologists' suitability.
(D) Doesn't say anything about how the geologists would be biased. Eliminate it.
(E) This would strengthen the argument that the geologists would be unbiased. Eliminate it.

SECTION III

QUESTIONS

Questions 6–7

Throughout the twentieth century, anthropologists studying the myths and ceremonies of a particular group indigenous to the Amazon rain forest in Brazil have maintained that their presence and the questions they asked were not influencing the group's culture. Researchers now note, however, that the earliest recorded observations, made in 1919, of the group's ceremonies marking the onset of the rainy season made no reference to a creation myth. The first mention of a creation myth's appearance in the ceremony is found in 1933, and by 1986, nearly twenty minutes of the seventy-minute ceremony were devoted to a myth explaining the rains in relation to a "First Great Storm," during which the world was supposed to have been created.

6. Which one of the following is most strongly implied by the argument above?

   (A) The observations of the ceremonies in 1919 were either incomplete or inaccurate.
   (B) After the anthropologists explained the importance of creation myths to their subjects, the group developed myths of its own.
   (C) The anthropologists' interests in particular cultural beliefs, such as creation myths, may have induced a gradual change in the group's ceremonies.
   (D) If the anthropologists had been more conscientious, their records would not reflect apparent discrepancies in their accounts of the group's beliefs.
   (E) The subjects of study, trying to secure the benefits of the industrial world enjoyed by anthropologists, changed their ceremonies to correspond to the ideas of the anthropologists.

7. Which one of the following represents an illustration of the same phenomenon that the author describes in the passage above?

   (A) A sociologist notes that a wave of immigration invariably results in changes in some religious practices of the dominant culture.
   (B) A psychologist discovers that patients who originally reported few or no dreams consistently acknowledge frequent and vivid dreams after eight months of dream-analysis therapy.
   (C) An economist studying a Third World country finds an increasing reliance on Western technology rather than on indigenous agricultural methods.
   (D) An astronomer, using two different telescopes to measure the distance to a nearby star, gets two different results.
   (E) A historian of religion finds that the creation myths of several cultures have changed over time.

EXPLANATIONS

6. This is an INFERENCE question. Your goal is to find the one choice that must be true based on the information in the passage.

   (A) We have no evidence for this. Eliminate it.
   (B) We have no evidence that they explained anything, just that they asked questions. Eliminate it.
   (C) The anthropologists asked questions. That could have been how they showed their interest in the creation myths. Let's leave this in.
   (D) We have no evidence that they weren't conscientious. Eliminate it.
   (E) We have no evidence that the subjects had any knowledge of the benefits of the industrial world. Eliminate it. (C) is the best answer here.

7. This is a PARALLEL-THE-REASONING question. Try to get the theme or diagram of the logic and then match it to each answer choice.

   (A) They didn't add people to the group in the passage—they just observed them. Eliminate it.
   (B) This looks pretty good. The argument had people starting out without finding anything they were looking for, and then later on, what they were looking for developed. This is the answer.
   (C) The people in the passage weren't relying on anything. Eliminate it.
   (D) Two telescopes? Two results? Huh?
   (E) Yes, but was there any observation or questioning of these cultures along the way? We have no idea. Eliminate it.

SECTION III

QUESTIONS

8. Mayor: An across-the-board increase of just twenty cents on all the city's toll bridges and tunnels would raise close to a hundred thousand dollars a year at the current bridge and tunnel traffic levels. Because a toll increase of three dollars would therefore raise more than a million dollars a year, such an increase seems like the ideal solution to our persistent school budget shortfalls. The toll increase would offer further savings by lessening the volume of traffic over our bridges and tunnels, which would result in reduced maintenance costs for those structures.

Which one of the following identifies most accurately the error in the mayor's reasoning?

(A) She incorrectly assumes that two different causes are necessarily related.
(B) She bases her argument on erroneous figures for the current traffic flow.
(C) She makes assumptions that are mutually exclusive.
(D) She takes as a given what should instead first be established as evidence.
(E) She bases her argument on political considerations rather than logical analysis.

9. Dale: The city can't possibly have budget problems this quarter because of the heavier than normal snows this winter. A recent article mentioned that Haline, a substance used to de-ice roads and sidewalks, costs three cents a pound, which is quite cheap considering how effective it is.

Glenn: In actuality the cost of Haline is closer to eighty cents a pound. When you factor in the destructive effect of Haline on the infrastructure, and its deleterious effects on ground water and vegetation, the cost of Haline clearly exceeds its price.

If a substance performs as effectively as Haline and has no harmful side effects (but its price is higher than that of Haline), Glenn would be most likely to oppose its use if

(A) its price fluctuates seasonally
(B) its price and its cost are similar
(C) it must be handled in the same manner as Haline
(D) its cost is higher than the price of Haline
(E) its price is higher than the cost of Haline

EXPLANATIONS

8. This is a FLAW question. Come up with your own description of why the author's conclusion is flawed before you go to the answer choices, and then match your description to the choices.

(A) No, we're looking for some sort of contradiction here. This doesn't say that. Eliminate it.
(B) We have no idea whether or not the figures are erroneous. Eliminate it.
(C) Bingo. If both assumptions are true, the argument makes no sense. You can't simultaneously generate the same sort of money and have fewer people paying the tolls.
(D) Same problem as (A). Eliminate it.
(E) There is no mention of political considerations. Eliminate it.

9. This is most like a WEAKEN or STRENGTHEN or PARADOX question, because you're looking for the one thing in the answer choices that, if known, will have the most IMPACT on the argument. So let's go looking for that.

(A) By how much? Eliminate it.
(B) Similar to what? Each other or to Haline? Eliminate it.
(C) We're more interested in cost and price, not handling. Eliminate it.
(D) Close, but actually we want the opposite of this.
(E) Bingo. If this were the case, the new substance would be even worse than Haline, so Glenn would oppose it. This is the answer.

QUESTIONS

10. Since mandatory water conservation measures were enacted by the state of California in response to the drought of 1987–1992, water consumption in the state has increased by nearly 10 percent. Clearly, the state's water conservation measures have been counterproductive, and California's water situation is more dire now than it was in 1992, the year of the last drought.

All of the following facts, if true, would be useful in evaluating the validity of the argument above EXCEPT:

(A) The population of California has increased by 15 percent since 1992.
(B) The average California resident now uses less water on an annual basis than he or she did in 1992.
(C) The water conservation measures did not apply to agricultural usage.
(D) In accordance with the conservation measures, nonessential water use in private homes has declined by 50 percent since 1992.
(E) In the years since 1992, water collection technology has developed to such a point that state and municipal water districts have an increased capacity to gather and store water.

EXPLANATIONS

10. **Conclusion:** California's water conservation measures have been counterproductive.

Premise: Since the measures were enacted, water consumption has increased by 10 percent.

Assumptions: Water consumption would not have increased even more in the absence of the conservation measures; population has not increased by 10 percent or more.

This is most like an ASSUMPTION question because you are looking for a fact that will help you to evaluate the validity of the assumption.

(A) This would be useful because, if true, it would tell us that the conservation measures actually are working. Eliminate it.
(B) This would also tell us that the conservation measures are working, so eliminate this too.
(C) So maybe there is more agriculture happening, so this information would be useful too. Eliminate it.
(D) Same thing as in (A), (B), and (C). It would tell us that the conservation is actually working. Eliminate it.
(E) This is nice, but it doesn't let us know whether or not the conservation measures are working or not—it tells us that we won't have to worry about it, which isn't the point of the argument. So this is the answer.

SECTION III

QUESTIONS

11. Netta: A recent study revealed that while the overall crime rate has gone down, crimes committed by youths have increased dramatically. The irony is that our own judicial system is fostering this situation. By treating young people who commit crimes less severely than adults who commit similar crimes, the courts allow these young criminals to go free, and they then commit more crimes. The message that "crime is wrong, but not as bad if you're not of age" is being communicated. A person who is convicted of a crime should be sufficiently punished regardless of age, otherwise the number of crimes committed by youths will continue to increase.

Trey: Netta, you are being extremely shortsighted. The alternative to allowing young criminals to go free is incarcerating them in a youth facility or penitentiary. But sociologists have found that the social environment in such facilities encourages and condones delinquent behavior within the facility, and by extension, outside the facility. When the youth returns to society after having been incarcerated for even a short period, recidivism occurs within three to four weeks.

The point at issue between Netta and Trey is

(A) the extent to which the judicial system is contributing to the increase in the crime rate
(B) whether the leniency shown toward adolescents can be cited as the sole cause of the increase in crimes committed by young people
(C) what types of judicial reform could affect the rise in youth crime
(D) how most effectively to stop the increase in crime by examining which cause is most often to blame
(E) whether incarceration as an alternative to leniency for convicted youths will in fact help to solve the problem

EXPLANATIONS

11. This is a REASONING question. Come up with your own description of what they're arguing about, and then match your description to the choices.

(A) No, because it just says "crime rate," which is too general. We're talking juvenile crimes here. Eliminate it.
(B) "Sole cause" is a bit extreme here. They're not arguing absolutes. Eliminate it.
(C) We're arguing about what would cause decreases, not increases. Eliminate it.
(D) Same problem as (A). It only talks about crime generally. Eliminate it.
(E) Bingo—Netta thinks incarceration would be a deterrent; Trey thinks it would cause even greater recidivism. This is the answer.

QUESTIONS

12. Computer Technician: This system has either a software problem or a hardware problem. None of the available diagnostic tests has been able to determine where the problem lies. The software can be replaced, but the hardware cannot be altered in any way, which means that if the problem lies in the hardware, the entire system will have to be scrapped. We must begin work to solve the problem by presupposing that the problem is with the software.

On which one of the following principles could the technician's reasoning be based?

(A) In fixing a problem that has two possible causes, it makes more sense to deal with both causes rather than spend time trying to determine which is the actual cause of the problem.

(B) If events outside one's control bear on a decision, the best course of action is to assume the "worst-case" scenario.

(C) When the soundness of an approach depends on the validity of an assumption, one's first task must be to test that assumption's validity.

(D) When circumstances must be favorable in order for a strategy to succeed, the strategy must be based on the assumption that conditions are indeed favorable until proved otherwise.

(E) When only one strategy can be successful, the circumstances affecting that strategy must be altered so that strategy may be employed.

EXPLANATIONS

12. This is a PRINCIPLE question. We are given five principles in the answer choices for this specific question, so we should come up with our own principle for the actions in the argument and match it to the answer choices.

(A) But they're not dealing with both causes—only the software cause. Eliminate it.

(B) They're not assuming that—if they were, they'd go out and replace the hardware. Eliminate it.

(C) They're not testing assumptions; they can't test anything. They just have to hope it's the problem that's cheaper to fix. Eliminate it.

(D) They're hoping that it's the software until it's really obvious it's not. This is the answer.

(E) They're not altering any strategy in the argument. Eliminate it.

SECTION III

QUESTIONS	EXPLANATIONS

13. To become a master at chess, a person must play. If a person plays for at least four hours a day, that person will inevitably become a master of the game. Thus, if a person is a master at the game of chess, that person must have played each day for at least four hours.

The error in the logic of the argument above is most accurately described by which one of the following?

(A) The conclusion is inadequate because it fails to acknowledge that people who play for four hours each day might not develop a degree of skill for the game that others view as masterful.
(B) The conclusion is inadequate because it fails to acknowledge that playing one hour a day might be sufficient for some people to become masters.
(C) The conclusion is inadequate because it fails to acknowledge that if a person has not played four hours a day, that person has not become a master.
(D) The conclusion is inadequate because it fails to acknowledge that four hours of playing time each day is not a strategy recommended by any world-champion chess players.
(E) The conclusion is inadequate because it fails to acknowledge that most people are not in a position to devote four hours each day to playing chess.

13. **Conclusion:** If a person is a master, she must have played chess at least four hours each day.

Premise: If a person plays four hours each day, she will become a master.

Assumption: Playing four hours each day is the only way to become a master.

This is a FLAW question. Try to come up with your own description of why the author's conclusion is flawed before you go to the answer choices, and then match your description to the choices.

(A) Whether other people think the player is a master is irrevelant. According to the argument, anyone who plays at least four hours a day "will inevitably become a master."
(B) Bingo. The author makes an invalid contrapositive in the argument. This is the answer.
(C) We have no idea whether this is true. Eliminate it.
(D) We don't care about chess champion recommendations. Eliminate it.
(E) We don't care about most people. The argument doesn't say everyone. Eliminate it.

14. Libraries are eliminating many subscriptions to highly specialized periodicals due to budget cuts. Yet without these reference materials, many subjects cannot be researched effectively. Therefore, efforts must be made to provide better funding so as to ensure the maintenance of at least those periodicals that will be most used by researchers in the future.

Which one of the following can be inferred from the author's argument for the maintenance of funding for the periodicals?

(A) If a periodical is highly specialized, the maintenance of its subscription is more important than any financial considerations.
(B) Research performed with periodicals is not a valid consideration in determining funding.
(C) Research should be the focus of a library's funding.
(D) It can be predicted which periodicals will be of value for researchers in the future.
(E) The elimination of periodicals is simply an inevitable part of library organization.

14. This is an INFERENCE question. Your goal is to find the one choice that must be true based on the information in the passage.

(A) This is a little too extreme. What if the periodical cost more than the library itself? Eliminate it.
(B) The argument says it is. Eliminate it.
(C) Should it be the focus of their funding or of their subscription policies? Eliminate it.
(D) See the last sentence of the passage. If we can't predict this, the argument falls apart. This is the answer.
(E) We have no idea whether or not this is true. Eliminate it.

SECTION III

QUESTIONS

15. Last year, Marcel enjoyed a high income from exactly two places: his sporting goods store and his stock market investments. Although Marcel earns far more from his store than from his investments, the money he earns from the stock market is an important part of his income. Because of a series of drops in the stock market, Marcel will not earn as much from his investments this year. It follows then that Marcel will make less money this year than he did last year.

Which one of the following is an assumption necessary to the author's argument?

(A) Increased profits at Marcel's sporting goods store will not offset any loss in stock market income.
(B) Sporting goods stores earn lower profits when the stock market drops.
(C) Drops in the stock market do not always affect all of a particular investor's stocks.
(D) Marcel's stock market investments will be subject to increased volatility.
(E) If his income is lower, Marcel will not be able to meet his expenses.

EXPLANATIONS

15. **Conclusion:** Marcel will make less money this year than last year.

Premise: He made less from his investments.

Assumption: His other sources of income did not increase by enough to offset the decrease in profit from investments.

This is an ASSUMPTION question. The correct answer will be something necessary for the conclusion to be true, and, if made false, will make the argument fall apart.

(A) If they did offset, then Marcel could make just as much, which would make the argument fall apart. This is the answer.
(B) There is no connection between these two things except for the fact that Marcel is interested in both of them. Eliminate it.
(C) But we are specifically told in the argument that his portfolio WILL be affected. Eliminate it.
(D) Bummer, but we already know he's not going to make as much. Eliminate it.
(E) Bummer, but the argument never mentions his expenses. This is out of scope.

SECTION III

QUESTIONS

16. Johanna: Quinto admits that because of his governmental post he can select which companies are awarded municipal contracts. He further admits that he awarded a contract to a company owned by a member of the town council who offered to support Quinto in his mayoral bid in exchange for the contract. There is no excuse for this kind of unethical behavior.

Iya: I don't see his actions as unethical. The company awarded the contract is known to produce the highest-quality work at a comparatively competitive price. So in getting support for his mayoral bid, Quinto has ensured the city will get quality work, and thus has saved the taxpayers thousands of dollars.

Iya disagrees with Johanna by

(A) insisting that ethical behavior can only be viewed in the context in which it takes place
(B) countering that the result of Quinto's actions determines whether those activities are ethical
(C) comparing Quinto's actions to the actions of the company and finding both behaviors to be ethical
(D) applying a different definition of the word "ethical" to two situations
(E) defining ethical behavior as being formed by personal, religious, or spiritual philosophies

EXPLANATIONS

16. This is a REASONING question. Come up with your own description of how Iya disagrees with Johanna, and then match your description to the choices.

(A) This choice is too general; she's talking about one instance, not ethical behavior in general.
(B) Iya claims that everything's all right because the results will all be good. This is the answer.
(C) Iya is not comparing actions; she's commenting on the actions of the mayor.
(D) The definition remains the same—Iya just thinks everything is cool and Johanna doesn't.
(E) This is all out of the scope of the argument. Eliminate it.

SECTION III

QUESTIONS	EXPLANATIONS

17. One of the criticisms of recent political campaigns is that the candidate with the greater financial resources usually wins. A long presidential election campaign is more equitable than is the quick and expedient process recommended by some. A longer campaign, however, decreases the likelihood that a candidate with tremendous resources can control the campaign through a barrage of high-priced media campaigns. In a long campaign, a candidate is forced to speak substantively on the issues, and the voters have more complete access to the candidate. Thus, a long campaign creates parity among candidates who may not be equally financed by permitting the less popular, less well-funded candidates to invest time rather than money in their campaigns, thereby gaining recognition for themselves through the use of speeches, debates, and other media-oriented forums.

Which one of the following statements most seriously weakens the argument made above in favor of long presidential campaigns?

(A) Voters who lose interest during a long campaign are less likely to show up at the polls, thus contributing to the already significant problem of voter apathy.
(B) A long campaign requires candidates to divide their attention between public matters and the needs of their parties.
(C) A long campaign weakens the general public's interest in the process of global democracy.
(D) Candidates depend on volunteers, whose sense of commitment is frayed by a long campaign.
(E) A long campaign precludes participation by many able candidates who cannot afford to take time off from their private occupations for extended periods of time.

17. **Conclusion:** Long campaigns are more equitable than are short campaigns.

Premise: Long campaigns force candidates to address issues, not just advertise.

Assumption: There is not some other reason that more financially well-off candidates have an advantage in political campaigns besides being able to buy advertising.

This is a WEAKEN question. Figure out which answer choice has the most negative impact on the conclusion of the argument. Remember to assume the hypothetical truth of each choice and apply it to the argument.

(A) We don't care about the percentage of people voting. We're talking candidates here, not voter turnout. No impact.
(B) This would have impact on both the well-funded and nonfunded people equally, so eliminate it.
(C) Global democracy isn't the point here. Eliminate it.
(D) This looks good, but it actually has the same problem as (B)—it would affect both groups equally.
(E) Yes. So a long campaign isn't going to create parity, because the people with money will be able to stick with it longer. This is the answer.

SECTION III

QUESTIONS	EXPLANATIONS

18. Some botanists have found it extremely difficult to save certain species of elm trees from fungal infection. Even the most potent fungicide has been unsuccessful in preventing its growth on such trees. However, researchers have managed to control the growth and spread of the fungus by spraying the fungus with a 0.2% saline solution.

Which one of the following, if true, offers the strongest explanation as to why the saline spray has been successful?

(A) The cell walls of the fungus cannot filter out the salt compounds, which, once inside the cell, interfere with reproduction.
(B) The presence of salt creates an electrolyte imbalance within living cells, ultimately killing each cell it comes in contact with.
(C) When salt is used in combination with strong fungicide, the fungicide becomes potent enough to kill any fungus.
(D) It has been on record that farmers have used salt to kill destructive plant fungi since the late eighteenth century.
(E) Fungicides have generally been unsuccessful because any fungicide strong enough to destroy a fungus would be strong enough to destroy the roots as well.

18. This is a PARADOX question. Look for an answer choice that allows both parts of the argument to be true, and remember to assume the hypothetical truth of each of the answer choices.

Figure out which answer choice has the most positive impact on the conclusion of the argument. Remember to assume the hypothetical truth of each choice and apply it to they argument.

(A) This would explain why the growth and spread of the fungus would be stopped—it couldn't reproduce. This is the answer.
(B) If this were true, the saline would actually kill the fungus—but the argument says it controls the fungus. Eliminate it.
(C) The argument doesn't say we're using the saline in conjunction with the fungicide. Eliminate it.
(D) This is a nice bit of history, but it doesn't explain WHY the salt is effective—just that it was effective in the past. Eliminate it.
(E) Right. Which is why we're using the saline. But this doesn't explain why the saline works. Eliminate it.

19. In concluding that there has been a shift in the sense of parental responsibility in America since the 1960s, researchers point to the increase in the frequency with which fathers tend to the daily needs of their children. However, this increase cannot be attributed exclusively to a shift in parental mores, for during the same period there has been an increase in the percentage of mothers who have jobs. With this in mind, the increased participation of fathers in child-rearing may well be only a symptom of a more fundamental change in society.

The author of the passage criticizes the conclusion of the researchers by

(A) offering a clearer definition of the researchers' premises, thereby compromising their argument
(B) attacking the integrity of the researchers rather than their reasoning
(C) showing that the researchers have reversed cause and effect in making their argument
(D) pointing out that their criteria for "parental responsibility" are not a logical basis for their argument
(E) suggesting an alternative cause for the effect cited by the researchers

19. This is a REASONING question. Come up with your own description of how the author makes the argument and then match your description to the choices.

(A) Their argument is clear; it's their conclusion that stinks. Eliminate it.
(B) The author doesn't say that they are liars, just that their conclusion is wrong.
(C) No, the author is saying that there is a different cause. Eliminate it.
(D) Their criteria and premises are fine; it's their conclusion that is bad. Eliminate it.
(E) Yes—that it's not that fathers care more, it's just that they are exposed more to their children because mothers now work. This is the answer.

QUESTIONS | EXPLANATIONS

Questions 20–21

Upon exiting an exhibit, some visitors to art museums find it difficult to describe what it was that they liked and didn't like about the paintings. Yet because these visitors feel strongly about which art they believed to be good and which art they believed to be bad, appreciating a work of art obviously does not require the ability to articulate what, specifically, was perceived to be good or bad.

20. The argument above assumes which one of the following?

(A) The fact that some people find it difficult to articulate what they like about a work of art does not mean that no one can.
(B) If an individual feels strongly about a work of art, then he or she is capable of appreciating that work of art.
(C) The vocabulary of visual art is not a part of common knowledge, but rather is known only to those who study the arts.
(D) When a person can articulate what he or she likes about a particular painting, he or she is able to appreciate that work of art.
(E) Paintings can be discussed only in general terms of good and bad.

20. **Conclusion:** Appreciating art does not depend on your ability to say what was good or bad.

Premise: Many visitors can't say what they liked or didn't like about art, yet they feel strongly about it.

Assumption: Strong feelings about art are the same as appreciating art.

This is an ASSUMPTION question. The correct answer will be something necessary for the conclusion to be true, and, if made false, will make the argument fall apart.

(A) We're looking for a connection between articulation and appreciation. This isn't it.
(B) Bingo. If it were not true that strong feelings can lead to appreciation, the argument would totally fall apart. This is the answer.
(C) This is classic LSAT babble. Vocabulary of visual art? Eliminate it.
(D) Always? What if the person hates it? Is that appreciation?
(E) We're not talking specific or general here; we're more concerned with whether or not we merely can or can't say anything at all. (B) is the best choice.

21. According to the passage above, all of the following could be true EXCEPT:

(A) Some museum visitors can explain with great precision what they liked and didn't like about a certain painting.
(B) If a person studies art, then that person will be able to articulate her opinion about paintings.
(C) If a person can't say why she likes a piece of art, it doesn't necessarily mean that she doesn't appreciate that piece.
(D) Some visitors can explain what they liked about a piece, but are unable to explain what they didn't like.
(E) The inability to articulate always indicates the inability to appreciate.

21. This is an INFERENCE question. Because it is also an EXCEPT question, your goal is to find the one choice that can't be true based on the information in the passage.

(A) This can be true—the argument only says that some can't. Eliminate it.
(B) This can be true—there could be some people who can do this. Eliminate it.
(C) Yes—as long as they feel strongly about it, they can still appreciate it. Articulation isn't necessary.
(D) This can be true also—there is no contradiction in the argument.
(E) This is the opposite of the argument, which says you can feel strongly and appreciate. This is the answer.

SECTION III

QUESTIONS	EXPLANATIONS

22. Evan: Earlier this year, the *Stockton Free Press* reported that residents consider Mayor Dalton more concerned with his image than with advancing the cause of the less fortunate of Stockton.

Dalia: But the mayor appointed a new director of the public television station, and almost immediately the station began running a documentary series promoting the mayor's antipoverty program.

Evan: Clearly the mayor has, by this appointment, attempted to manipulate public opinion through the media.

Evan's second statement counters Dalia's argument by

(A) disputing the relevancy of her statement
(B) suggesting that Dalia is less informed about the issue than he
(C) confusing the argument she presents with his own
(D) appealing to popular opinion that the mayor should not misuse his access to the media
(E) claiming that Dalia's argument is an example that actually strengthens his own argument

22. This is a REASONING question. Come up with your own description of how Evan's second statement counters Dalia, and then match your description to the choices.

(A) No, he attacks it directly, so he does think it's relevant. Eliminate it.
(B) He doesn't call into question the amount of information she possesses, but rather her interpretation of that information. Eliminate it.
(C) No, he's not confused at all. He's actually saying that her argument supports his argument.
(D) He doesn't appeal to anyone. Eliminate it.
(E) Bingo. He twists it around so it supports his argument. This is the answer.

SECTION III

QUESTIONS

23. Naturalist: Every year, thousands of animals already on the endangered species list are killed for their hides, furs, or horns. These illegal and often cruel deaths serve to push these species further toward the brink of extinction. The products made from these animals, such as articles of clothing and quack medical remedies, are goods no one really needs. What is needed is a large-scale media campaign to make the facts of the killings known and lessen the demand for these animal products. Such a campaign would be a good start in the effort to save endangered species from extinction.

Environmentalist: For the overwhelming majority of currently endangered species, the true threat of extinction comes not from hunting and poaching, but from continually shrinking habitats. Concentrating attention on the dangers of poaching for a very few high-visibility species would be counterproductive, leading people to believe that a boycott of a few frivolous items is enough to protect endangered species, when what is needed is a truly global environmental policy.

The point at issue between the naturalist and the environmentalist is which one of the following?

(A) whether the poaching of some endangered species actually increases that species' chances of becoming extinct
(B) whether a large-scale media campaign can affect the demand for some products
(C) whether more endangered species are threatened by poaching and hunting or shrinking of habitat
(D) whether some species could be saved from extinction by eliminating all commercial demand for that species
(E) whether a large-scale media campaign that lessens the demand for products made from endangered species is a good strategy for saving endangered species

EXPLANATIONS

23. This is a REASONING question. Come up with your own description of what they're arguing about, and then match your description to the choices.

(A) They both agree poaching is bad; they're arguing about whether or not it's the primary cause of extinction.
(B) Not whether this campaign will affect the demand, but whether it will affect extinction.
(C) We don't know the numbers. Eliminate it.
(D) They're arguing over the best method for saving as many species as possible.
(E) Yes—the environmentalist thinks that the strategy of saving habitats is more important than the naturalist's strategy of a media campaign. This is the answer.

QUESTIONS

24. Deborah: If one-third of the people who do not recycle would start recycling their paper products, approximately 150,000 fewer trees would be destroyed each year.

Lee: That is unlikely. It would then follow that in the next ten years, the forests will increase by more than 1.5 million trees, more than there is room for.

Which one of the following statements could Deborah offer Lee to clarify her own position and address the point that Lee makes?

(A) It is possible for forests to increase by 150,000 trees per year if the growth rate of the previous year was unusually low.
(B) The 150,000 trees that are saved would still be subject to forest fires and other destructive natural phenomena.
(C) If the number of recyclers was increased by more than a third, the number of trees saved would be more than 150,000.
(D) Any prediction of tree growth always presumes a constant growth and death rate.
(E) For the number of nonrecyclers to be reduced by a third, the number of recycling materials, special recyclable trash bins, for example, would have to be increased by much more than a third.

EXPLANATIONS

24. This is a STRENGTHEN question. Figure out which answer choice has the most positive impact on the conclusion of Deborah's argument. Remember to assume the hypothetical truth of each choice and apply it to the argument.

(A) We're not talking about increasing trees, just saving already existing ones. This has no impact. Eliminate it.
(B) So the forest wouldn't really expand more than there is room for, since natural phenomena will regulate it. This is the answer.
(C) We've already scared Lee enough. This wouldn't answer her issue at all. Eliminate it.
(D) There is no prediction of tree growth in Deborah's argument.
(E) The discussion about recycling bins, while fascinating, is outside the scope of the argument. Eliminate it.

QUESTIONS

25. Adoption Agent: Although my view runs counter to the trend in public sentiment, I believe a proposed new law granting adoptive parents access to the birth records of children to be adopted should not be passed. My experience as an adoption agent has supplied me with two reasons for holding this view. First, granting adoptive parents access to the records will result in wasted hours on the part of the adoption agency employees, who will be forced to spend time finding and subsequently returning files, when that time could be better spent out in the field. Second, based upon my agency experience, no adoptive parents are going to request the children's records anyway.

Which one of the following, if true, establishes that the adoption agent's second reason does not negate the first?

(A) The new law would necessitate that adoption agents, when reviewing the adoption agreement with prospective adoptive parents, have at hand the birth record of the child to be adopted, not simply have access to them.
(B) The task of retrieving and explaining birth records would fall to the least experienced member of the adoption agency's staff.
(C) Any children who asked to see their birth records would also insist on having details they did not understand explained to them.
(D) The new law does not exclude adoption agencies from charging adoptive parents for extra expenses incurred in order to comply with the new law.
(E) Some adoption agencies have always had a policy of allowing children access to their birth records, but none of those agencies' children took advantage of that policy.

EXPLANATIONS

25. This is a PARADOX question. Look for an answer choice that allows both parts of the argument to be true, and remember to assume the hypothetical truth of each of the answer choices.

(A) Bingo. So we're going to spend the time of the employees anyway, whether or not anyone walks in the door and actually asks for the records. This is the answer.
(B) If no one asks for the records, it doesn't matter.
(C) Children requesting records is out of the scope of the argument.
(D) Money isn't the issue—time is the issue.
(E) This is the same problem as (C). Eliminate it.

SECTION IV

QUESTIONS

Questions 1–6

An interior decorator is designing a color scheme using at least one of the following colors: red, orange, yellow, indigo, green, and violet. No other colors will be used. The selection of colors for the scheme is consistent with the following conditions:

If the scheme uses orange, then it does not use indigo.
If the scheme does not use green, then it uses orange.
If the scheme uses yellow, then it uses both indigo and violet.
If the scheme uses violet, then it uses red or green or both.

1. Which one of the following could be a complete and accurate list of the colors the scheme includes?

   (A) yellow, indigo
   (B) indigo, green
   (C) yellow, indigo, violet
   (D) yellow, green, violet
   (E) orange, yellow, indigo, violet

2. Which one of the following could be the only color the scheme uses?

   (A) red
   (B) yellow
   (C) indigo
   (D) green
   (E) violet

3. Which one of the following CANNOT be a complete and accurate list of the colors the scheme uses?

   (A) orange, green
   (B) green, violet
   (C) red, orange, violet
   (D) yellow, indigo, green, violet
   (E) red, orange, yellow, indigo, violet

4. If the scheme doesn't use violet, then which one of the following must be true?

   (A) The scheme uses orange.
   (B) The scheme uses at least two colors.
   (C) The scheme uses at most three colors.
   (D) The scheme uses neither yellow nor indigo.
   (E) The scheme uses neither yellow nor orange.

EXPLANATIONS

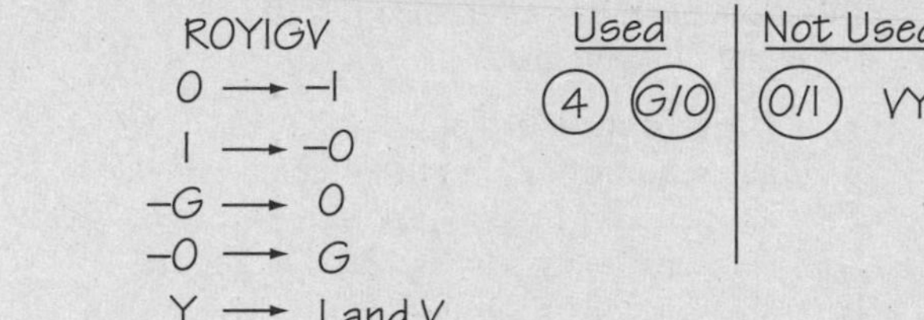

1. (A) No. If Y is in, V has to be in.
   (B) Yes.
   (C) No. If V is in, R or G has to be in.
   (D) No. If Y is in, I has to be in.
   (E) No. If orange is in, I has to be out.

2. (A) No. The scheme must use G or O.
   (B) No. If Y is in, I and V have to be in.
   (C) No. The scheme must use G or O.
   (D) Yes.
   (E) No. If V is in, R or G has to be in.

3. (A) This is possible.
   (B) This is possible.
   (C) This could happen.
   (D) This is possible. Y, I, and V are all there, and either G or O is used.
   (E) No. Both O or I cannot be used.

4. (A) Not necessarily. Watch your contrapositives.
   (B) Not necessarily. Orange could be used alone.
   (C) Right. There are at least three colors that have to be unused—V, Y, and either I or O—so at most three can be used.
   (D) Not necessarily. It might use indigo.
   (E) Not necessarily. It might use orange.

SECTION IV

QUESTIONS	EXPLANATIONS

5. If the scheme uses violet, then which of the following must be false?

    (A) The scheme does not use red.
    (B) The scheme does not use green.
    (C) The scheme does not use indigo.
    (D) The scheme uses indigo but not yellow.
    (E) The scheme uses indigo but not green.

5. (A) This is possible.
    (B) This could happen.
    (C) This is true, when Y is also not used.
    (D) This is also possible if Y is out of the picture.
    (E) Right. This is impossible. If the scheme uses I, then O can't be used. If O isn't used, then G must also be used. So (E) must be false.

6. If the condition that if the scheme doesn't use green then it does use orange is suspended, and all the other conditions remain in effect, then which one of the following CANNOT be a complete and accurate list of the colors the scheme uses?

    (A) indigo
    (B) red, indigo
    (C) yellow, indigo, violet
    (D) red, indigo, violet
    (E) red, yellow, indigo, violet

6. (A) This is possible.
    (B) This is possible.
    (C) No. If V is in, R or G must be in, too.
    (D) This is possible.
    (E) This is possible.

QUESTIONS

EXPLANATIONS

Questions 7–13

Five runners—Fanny, Gina, Henrietta, Isabelle, and Mona—are assigned to lanes numbered 1 through 5 on a track. Each runner has the option of wearing a knee brace during the competition. Two of the runners are from Palo Alto, two are from San Jose, and one is from Newcastle. The following conditions must apply:

Isabelle and Mona are assigned to the first two lanes, but not necessarily in that order.
The runner in the third lane is from Newcastle and wears a knee brace.
Neither runner from San Jose wears a knee brace.
Both Gina and Fanny are assigned higher-numbered lanes than that of Henrietta.
Neither Mona nor Fanny comes from San Jose.

FGHIM

S/K

H—G
H—F

M/S F/S

	1	2	3	4	5
Runner:	I/M	M/I	(H)	G/F	F/G
SSPPN:	S/P	P/S	N	S/P	P/S
Y/N Knee:	N/	/N	Y	N/	/N

(12)

M	I	H	G	F
P	S	N	S	P
Y	N	Y	N	Y

(13)

I	M	H	G/F	F/G
S	P	N	S/P	P/S
N	Y	Y	N/	/N

You can deduce that H must be third, because two runners come before and two come after her. Because M and F can't be from San Jose, they must be from Palo Alto, and therefore I and G must be from San Jose and don't wear

7. Which one the following could be an accurate list of the runners, in order from lane 1 to lane 5?

(A) Isabelle, Henrietta, Fanny, Mona, Gina
(B) Isabelle, Mona, Gina, Henrietta, Fanny
(C) Mona, Gina, Henrietta, Isabelle, Fanny
(D) Mona, Isabelle, Gina, Henrietta, Fanny
(E) Mona, Isabelle, Henrietta, Fanny, Gina

7. (A) No. H must be third.
(B) No. H must be third.
(C) No. I and M must be first and second.
(D) No. H must be third.
(E) Yes. This is possible.

8. Which one of the following could be true?

(A) Fanny runs in lane 5.
(B) Gina runs in lane 1.
(C) Henrietta runs in lane 2.
(D) Isabelle runs in lane 3.
(E) Mona runs in lane 5.

8. (A) Yes. See deductions above. Fanny can be in lane 4 or 5.
(B) No. Gina's in 4 or 5.
(C) No. H is in 3.
(D) No. H is in 3.
(E) No. M is in 1 or 2.

9. If the runner in lane 1 is from San Jose, then which one of the following could be true?

(A) Fanny runs in a lane numbered one higher than Isabelle's.
(B) Henrietta runs in a lane numbered one higher than Fanny's.
(C) Henrietta runs in a lane numbered one higher than Mona's.
(D) Henrietta runs in a lane numbered one higher than Isabelle's.
(E) Isabelle runs in a lane numbered one higher than Mona's.

9. (A) No. At least H is in between them.
(B) No. F comes after H.
(C) Right. M could be second.
(D) No. Isabelle is from San Jose, and is therefore in lane 1.
(E) No. Isabelle is from San Jose, and is therefore in lane 1.

SECTION IV

QUESTIONS | **EXPLANATIONS**

10. If a runner with a knee brace runs in lane 1, then which one of the following CANNOT be true?

(A) Fanny runs in lane 4.
(B) Gina runs in lane 5.
(C) A runner with a knee brace runs in lane 2.
(D) A runner with a knee brace runs in lane 3.
(E) A runner with a knee brace runs in lane 4.

10. (A) This could be true.
(B) This could be true.
(C) Right. It must be M in lane 1, so it must be I in lane 2, and I can't wear a knee brace.
(D) This is definitely true.
(E) This could be true.

11. Which one of the following must be true?

(A) Gina runs without a knee brace.
(B) Henrietta runs without a knee brace.
(C) Mona runs without a knee brace.
(D) Fanny runs with a knee brace.
(E) Isabelle runs with a knee brace.

11. Which one of the following must be true?

(A) Right. G must be from San Jose, and therefore can't wear a brace.
(B) This must be false.
(C) This could be true, but doesn't have to be.
(D) This could be true, but doesn't have to be.
(E) This must be false.

12. If runners wearing knee braces do not run in consecutively-numbered lanes, and runners not wearing knee braces do not run in consecutively-numbered lanes, then in exactly how many distinct orders could the runner be assigned to lanes?

(A) one
(B) two
(C) three
(D) four
(E) five

12. (A) Right. We can fill in the whole diagram.
(B) No. We can fill in the whole diagram.
(C) No. We can fill in the whole diagram.
(D) No. We can fill in the whole diagram.
(E) No. We can fill in the whole diagram.

13. If a runner with a knee brace runs in lane 2, then which one of the following CANNOT be true?

(A) The runner in lane 1 is from San Jose.
(B) The runner in lane 1 is from Palo Alto.
(C) The runner in lane 4 is from San Jose.
(D) The runner in lane 5 is from San Jose.
(E) The runner in lane 5 is from Palo Alto.

13. If a runner with a knee brace runs in lane 2, then which one of the following CANNOT be true?

(A) This must be true.
(B) Right. The runner in lane 1 must be from San Jose.
(C) This might be true.
(D) This might be true.
(E) This might be true.

SECTION IV

QUESTIONS | EXPLANATIONS

<u>Questions 14–18</u>

The Paulson, Rideau, Stevenson, Tisch, Van Pelt, and Wong families have each rented a time-share in a 6-unit condominium. The condominium has three floors, labeled first to third from bottom to top. Each floor has an identical layout consisting of two units: a garden view apartment on the west side of the building and an ocean view apartment on the east side of the building. The following conditions must apply:

The Rideaus rent the unit immediately beneath the Paulsons' ocean-view unit.
If the Wongs rent an ocean-view apartment, the Rideaus occupy the same floor as the Van Pelts.
If the Paulsons and the Tisches occupy the same floor, the Wongs rent the unit immediately and directly beneath the Stevensons' unit.
If the Tisches rent a garden-view unit, the Wongs occupy a unit on the first floor.
If the Tisches occupy a first-floor unit, the Stevensons occupy a third-floor unit.

PRSTVW

P_o / R_o

$W_o \rightarrow$ RV

PT $\rightarrow$ S / W

$T_G \rightarrow W_1$

$T_1 \rightarrow S_3$

		Garden	Ocean
–R	3		
	2		
–P	1		

14. Which of the following could be true?
    (A) The Stevensons occupy a second-floor unit, whereas the Tisches occupy a first-floor unit.
    (B) The Paulsons occupy a unit immediately and directly below the Wongs, and share a floor with the Tisches.
    (C) The Paulsons rent a garden-view unit on the same floor as the Van Pelts.
    (D) The Wongs rent an ocean-view unit on the same floor as the Van Pelts.
    (E) The Tisches and Wongs both occupy the third floor.

14. (A) No. Try it.
    (B) No. Try it.
    (C) No. The Paulsons can never rent a garden-view unit.
    (D) No. Try it.
    (E) Right. See your diagram from question 18.

15. If the Van Pelts and the Tisches both rent garden-view units, then which of the following could be true?
    (A) The Wongs rent the first-floor ocean-view unit.
    (B) The Stevensons rent the first-floor garden-view unit.
    (C) The Paulsons and the Tisches occupy the same floor.
    (D) The Paulsons and the Wongs occupy the same floor.
    (E) The Van Pelts and the Wongs occupy the same floor.

15. (A) Yes. This is possible.
    (B) This isn't possible. Try it.
    (C) This isn't possible. Try it.
    (D) No. The Paulsons can never be on the first floor.
    (E) This isn't possible. Try it.

SECTION IV

QUESTIONS	EXPLANATIONS

16. If the Wongs rent a third-floor unit, then which of the following must be true?

(A) The Rideaus rent a second-floor unit.
(B) The Stevensons rent a second-floor unit.
(C) The Stevensons rent a first-floor unit.
(D) The Tisches rent a third-floor unit.
(E) The Van Pelts rent a first-floor unit.

16. (A) No. The Rideaus would have to be in a first-floor unit.
(B) Not necessarily. They could be on the second floor, too.
(C) Not necessarily. They could be on the second floor, too.
(D) Right.
(E) Not necessarily. They could be on the second floor, too.

17. If the Tisches rent the first-floor ocean-view unit, then each of the following must be true EXCEPT:

(A) The Paulsons and the Stevensons occupy the same floor.
(B) The Rideaus and the Van Pelts occupy the same floor.
(C) The Van Pelts rent a garden-view unit.
(D) The Wongs rent a garden-view unit.
(E) The Paulsons rent a third-floor unit.

17. (A) This must be true. They're both on the third floor.
(B) Right. They could be on the same floor, but they don't have to be.
(C) This must be true.
(D) This must be true.
(E) This must be true.

18. If neither the Paulsons nor the Stevensons rent a third-floor unit, then which one of the following could be true?

(A) The Rideaus rent a second-floor unit.
(B) The Tisches rent a second-floor unit.
(C) The Wongs rent a second-floor unit.
(D) The Stevensons rent an ocean-view unit.
(E) The Wongs rent an ocean-view unit.

18. (A) No. They must be on the first floor.
(B) No. They must be on the third floor.
(C) Yes. This is possible.
(D) No. They must have a garden view.
(E) No. They must have a garden view.

SECTION IV

QUESTIONS / EXPLANATIONS

Questions 19–23

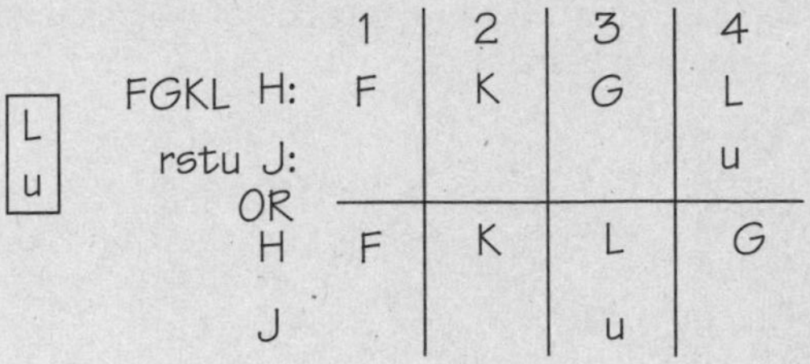

Four racehorses and their four jockeys are assigned to consecutive tracks at a racetrack—tracks 1, 2, 3, and 4. Each horse has exactly one jockey, and each pair is assigned to exactly one track. The horses are Ficklehoof, Galloper, Knackerbound, and Lackluster; the jockeys are Ramos, Simon, Tonka, and Urbach. The following conditions apply:

Ficklehoof is assigned to a lower-numbered track than is Galloper, and at least one track separates the two.
Knackerbound is assigned to track 2.
Lackluster's jockey is Urbach.

L / u (box)

	1	2	3	4
FGKL H:	F	K	G	L
rstu J:				u
OR				
H	F	K	L	G
J			u	

19. Which one of the following horse and jockey teams could be assigned to track 1?

(A) Ficklehoof and Ramos
(B) Ficklehoof and Urbach
(C) Galloper and Ramos
(D) Galloper and Urbach
(E) Lackluster and Tonka

19. (A) Right.
(B) No. Urbach must be paired with Lackluster.
(C) No. Ficklehoof must be in track 1.
(D) No. Ficklehoof must be in track 1.
(E) No. Ficklehoof must be in track 1.

20. If Ramos is assigned to a higher-numbered track than is Urbach, which one of the following statements cannot be true?

(A) Ficklehoof is assigned to a lower-numbered track than is Simon.
(B) Knackerbound is assigned to a lower-numbered track than is Ramos.
(C) Knackerbound is assigned to a lower-numbered track than is Tonka.
(D) Simon is assigned to a lower-numbered track than is Ramos.
(E) Tonka is assigned to a lower-numbered track than is Knackerbound.

20. (A) This could be true. If R is higher than U, then R would be in 4 and L/U would be in 3.
(B) This must be true.
(C) Right. This can't be true. Tonka must be in track 1 or 2.
(D) This must be true, because R is in track 4.
(E) This could be true, because T must be in 1 or 2.

21. If Lackluster is assigned to a lower-numbered track than is Galloper, which one of the following statements could be false?

(A) Ficklehoof is assigned to a lower-numbered track than is Urbach.
(B) Galloper is assigned to track 4.
(C) Either Ramos or Tonka is assigned to a lower-numbered track than is Urbach.
(D) Simon is assigned to a lower-numbered track than is Urbach.
(E) Urbach is assigned to track 3.

21. (A) No. This must be true. F must be in track 1.
(B) No. This must be true. L and G must be in tracks 3 and 4.
(C) No. This must be true. Only one track is higher than U, so one of them must be in a lower track.
(D) Right. Simon could be on track 4.
(E) No. This must be true. Same as (B).

SECTION IV

QUESTIONS

22. What is the maximum possible number of different horse and jockey teams, any one of which could be assigned to track 4?

    (A) 2
    (B) 3
    (C) 4
    (D) 5
    (E) 6

23. If Simon is assigned to a higher-numbered track than is Lackluster, then which one of the following statements could be false?

    (A) Galloper is assigned to a higher-numbered track than is Ramos.
    (B) Galloper is assigned to a higher-numbered track than is Tonka.
    (C) Lackluster is assigned to a higher-numbered track than is Tonka.
    (D) Tonka is assigned to a higher-numbered track than is Ramos.
    (E) Urbach is assigned to a higher-numbered track than is Ramos.

EXPLANATIONS

22. (A) No.
    (B) No.
    (C) Right. L and U, G and R, G and S, or G and T.
    (D) No.
    (E) No.

23. (A) No. Galloper has to be in track 4.
    (B) No. Galloper has to be in track 4 with Simon.
    (C) No. Lackluster is in track 3, and Tonka is in either 1 or 2.
    (D) Right. They could each be in either track 1 or 2.
    (E) No. Urbach is in track 3, and Ramos is in either 1 or 2.

AFTERWORD

The Princeton Review was founded in New York City in 1981 to prepare students for the SAT. Our SAT students improved their scores by an average of 150 points, so in a few years we became the largest SAT course in the country. In 1985 we started our courses for the graduate exams.

The Princeton Review's LSAT course consists of four to eight weeks of instruction. To ensure plenty of individual attention, class size is strictly limited—never more than eight students. Because the best approach to the LSAT depends so much on individual strengths and weaknesses, we create a setting in which instructors can tailor their advice specifically to you, and make further refinements in one-on-one sessions outside schedule classtimes at *no additional cost*. For students who want the utmost in personal attention, we also offer full tutoring in preparation for the LSAT.

Each student begins the class by taking the first of our four diagnostic LSATs. These diagnostic tests are actual LSATs to give students accurate feedback about their performance and improvement. Within a few days of each test, we'll provide you with a detailed computerized analysis of your responses. This personalized assessment will pinpoint your test-taking strengths and weaknesses. Armed with this evaluation, you will be able to study with maximum efficiency.

All the practice tests used by The Princeton Review are actual LSATs. The materials you will use throughout the course have been prepared by our research staff to reflect the most up-to-date techniques we have developed to crack the LSAT. For example, when the LSAC contracted with new test developers in 1986 (and again in 1989, and again in 1991), Princeton Review students were prepared for the subtle changes in test design.

If you'd like more information about The Princeton Review and its courses, you can reach us at our toll-free number, 800-2Review, or on the web at www.PrincetonReview.com.

LSAT Practice Test System Software

ABOUT THE SOFTWARE

The Practice Test System on the CD-ROM was designed to be as much like a real LSAT as possible. However, since at this time the real test can only be taken using pencil and paper, we also recommend practicing with written tests (such as those included in your *Cracking the LSAT* book) and previously administered LSATs (available through www.lsac.org).

Of course we know you got the book with the CD inside so you could benefit from its obvious advantages like offline testing and easy review of answer explanations, so you definitely want to use it!

Don't forget to have scratch paper handy. Just because you are taking a test on the computer doesn't mean you can't write things down.

Although the software does have a feature that lets you suspend the test in the middle and finish it later, we recommend trying to take an entire test in one sitting. We also advise making good use of the review features—look at the explanations for questions you missed, and see what types of problems you are having the most trouble with.

SYSTEM REQUIREMENTS

WINDOWS™	MACINTOSH®
600-MHz or higher Pentium-based processor	600-MHz or faster G3 processor
Windows 98, 2000, ME, XP only (does not include NT)	Macintosh OS 9.0.1 or higher (including all versions of OS 10)
32 MB RAM (64 MB RAM recommended)	32 MB RAM (64 MB RAM recommended)
40 MB hard disk space	40 MB hard disk space
800 x 600-pixel monitor (capable of displaying at least thousands of colors)	800 x 600-pixel monitor (capable of displaying at least thousands of colors)
Keyboard	Keyboard
Mouse	Mouse
8X or faster CD-ROM drive	8X or faster CD-ROM drive
Internet connection recommended, but not required for basic use	Internet connection recommended, but not required for basic use

INSTALLATION AND START-UP

IMPORTANT: Your Practice Test System software will expire one year after the first use. During that year, the software's **Update** feature will automatically check for newer versions. You may manually check for updates by launching the Updater for your test type and following the instructions. If you have access to the Internet, you should log on to your Internet Service Provider before you launch. This will enable the Update software to operate and download any updates that may be available.

WINDOWS

Make sure that no other applications are running before installing the software.

1. Insert the CD in your CD-ROM drive. The CD will automatically launch the Setup program. **Note:** You will need to have your book handy for the setup process!

2. Follow the instructions in the installer.

3. At the end of the setup, you may select the option to run the Practice Test System software after exiting the setup.

To run the Practice Test System software any time after you have installed it, select it from The Princeton Review folder in the Start menu.

MACINTOSH

1. Insert the CD in your CD-ROM drive.

2. Double-click the LSAT Practice Test Installer icon.

3. Follow the onscreen instructions until installation is complete.

USING LSAT PRACTICE TESTS

Logging In

You will be prompted to create an account before using the Practice Test System software for the first time, and you'll be prompted before you sign in each time. The log-in information enables the program to distinguish your history and answer choices from those of anyone else who may also be using the Practice Test System on the same computer.

If you have already registered at PrincetonReview.com, simply enter the same username and password to access your Practice Test System. (This requires Internet access.) If you have forgotten your username or password, you can retrieve it from the Forgot Password button or through PrincetonReview.com.

If you do not have an account with PrincetonReview.com, then you will need to create a new username just for the Practice Test System. When you create your account, you will also be asked to enter some additional information that will let you retrieve your password later if you forget it.

If you want more detailed score reports, you'll want to upload your tests from the Practice Test System to the website. To do this, you need to register online. Go to PrincetonReview.com/cracking and sign up for the online tools that go along with your book. Then update your Practice Test System information so you can successfully upload your tests.

Be sure to have your book handy before you take your first test, since you will be prompted to enter a code from the book in order to use the program.

The Main Menu

Each time you launch the Practice Test System, you will begin with the main menu screen. Any **Completed** or **Suspended** tests will be marked as such. From the main menu screen, you can either **Take a Test**—one of four LSAT practice exercises—or you can **Review a Test** you've already taken. You can also exit the software by clicking **Quit** on the lower left-hand corner.

Taking a Test

To start a test, select one from the list and click **Start Test**. You will be asked to type in a word from your copy of the book, and then you will then go directly to the first question of your selected test. (Note: These tests do not include an experimental section or a Writing section.) If you need to review the functions of any of the buttons on your screen, simply click them. Also, you can click the **?** button at the bottom of any active screen to access the Help section.

To select an answer, click on the oval next to the answer or the answer itself. You can change an answer as many times as you want by clicking on a new selection.

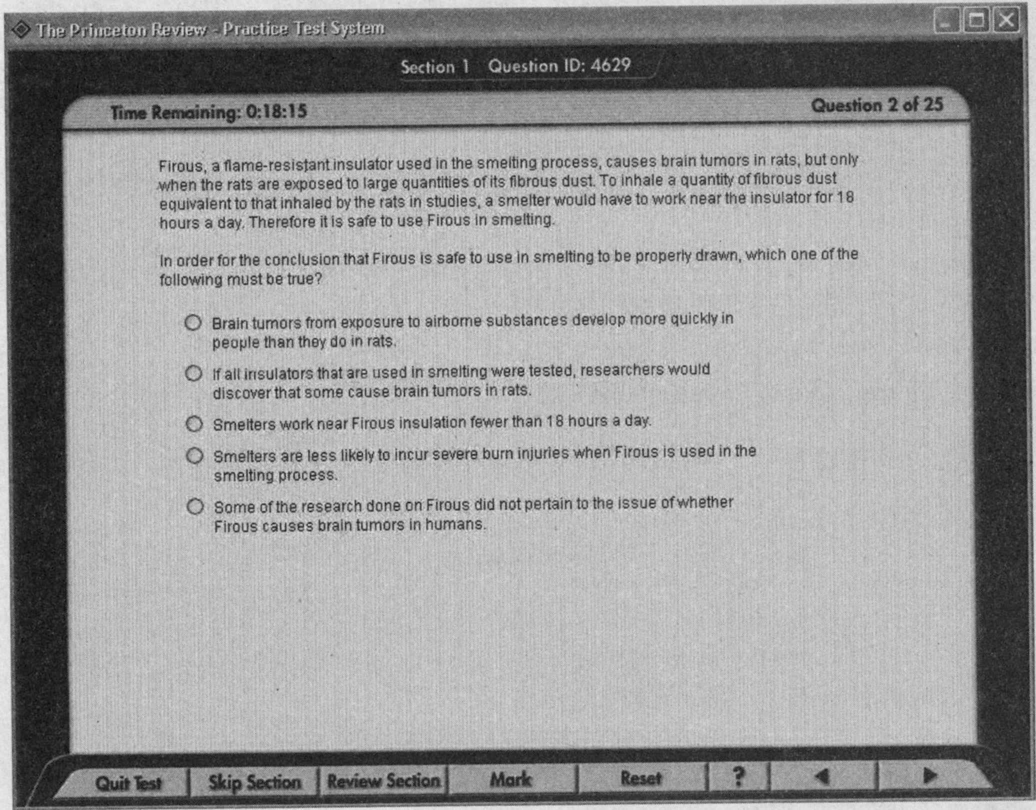
The Princeton Review - Practice Test System
Section 1 Question ID: 4629
Time Remaining: 0:18:15
Question 2 of 25
Firous, a flame-resistant insulator used in the smelting process, causes brain tumors in rats, but only when the rats are exposed to large quantities of its fibrous dust. To inhale a quantity of fibrous dust equivalent to that inhaled by the rats in studies, a smelter would have to work near the insulator for 18 hours a day. Therefore it is safe to use Firous in smelting.
In order for the conclusion that Firous is safe to use in smelting to be properly drawn, which one of the following must be true?
Brain tumors from exposure to airborne substances develop more quickly in people than they do in rats.
If all insulators that are used in smelting were tested, researchers would discover that some cause brain tumors in rats.
Smelters work near Firous insulation fewer than 18 hours a day.
Smelters are less likely to incur severe burn injuries when Firous is used in the smelting process.
Some of the research done on Firous did not pertain to the issue of whether Firous causes brain tumors in humans.
Quit Test
Skip Section
Review Section
Mark
Reset
?

THE TOOLBAR

Once you begin your practice session, you will see various buttons on the screen. These buttons are **Quit Test, Skip Section, Review Section, Mark, Reset, ? (Help), ◀ (Left Arrow), and ▶ (Right Arrow)**. These buttons allow you to navigate through your tests.

Quit Test — Clicking **Quit Test** will give you the following warning:

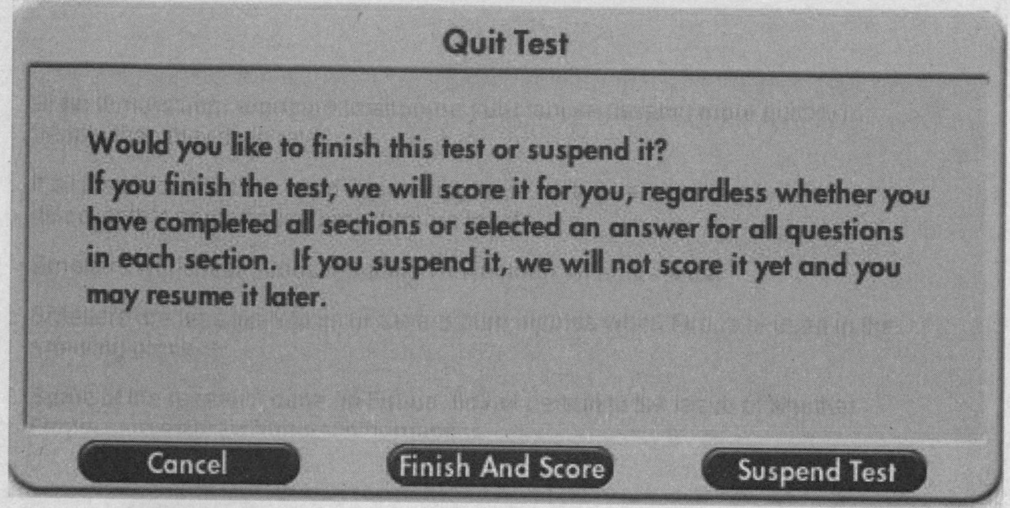

If you click **Finish and Score**, the test will end, regardless of whether you have completed all sections or selected an answer for all questions in each section.

If you **Suspend** it, you may resume it later.

If you choose **Cancel**, you will return to the test.

Skip Section — Clicking **Skip Section** will allow you to move to the next section.

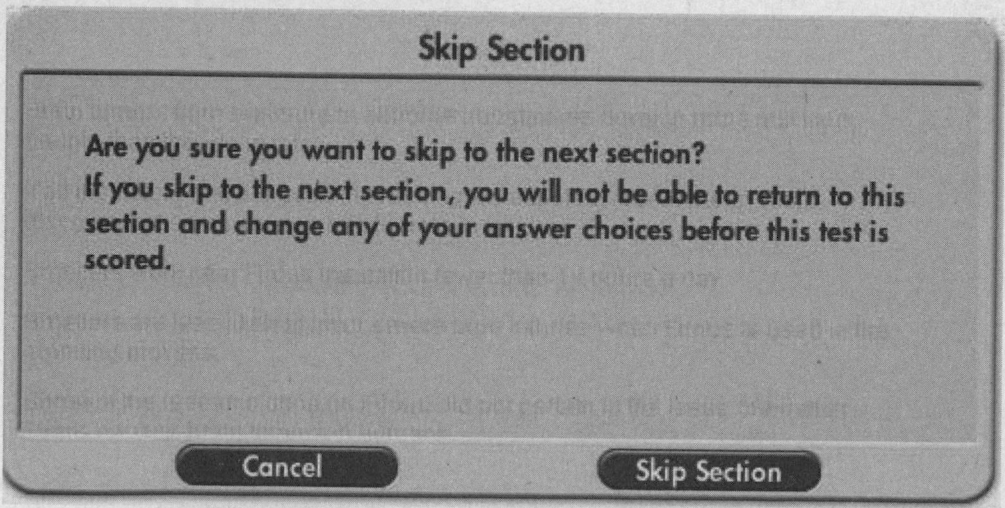

However, you will not be able to return to the section you are leaving, nor will you be able to make any changes to your answers in this section before scoring.

Review Section Clicking **Review Section** will allow you to see a chart of every question in the section.

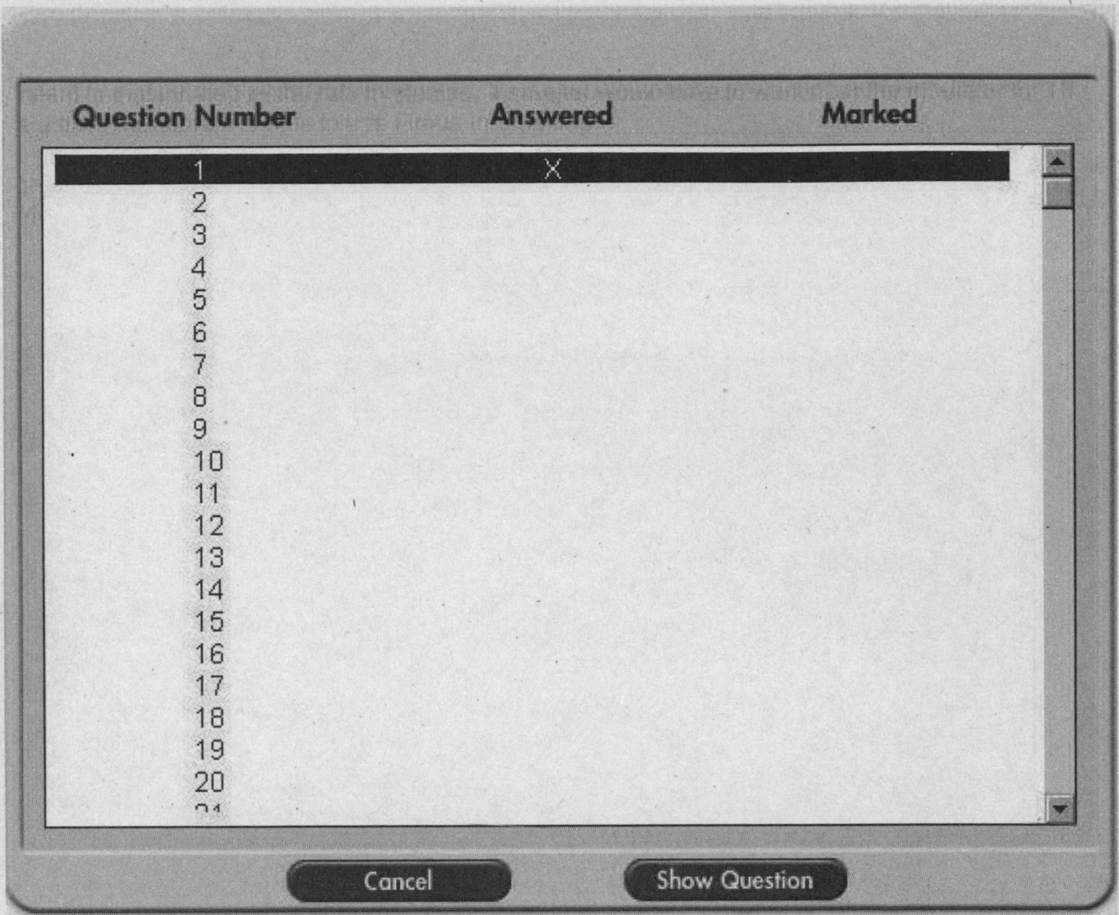

The chart lets you see which questions you have answered and which you have not. Any question that you marked earlier using the **Mark** tool will be checked. To return to one of these questions, select it with the mouse and click **Show Question**.

To return to the place in the test where you were when you clicked **Review Section**, click on **Cancel**.

Mark

Clicking **Mark** will flag the question on the screen to remind you that it requires further attention.

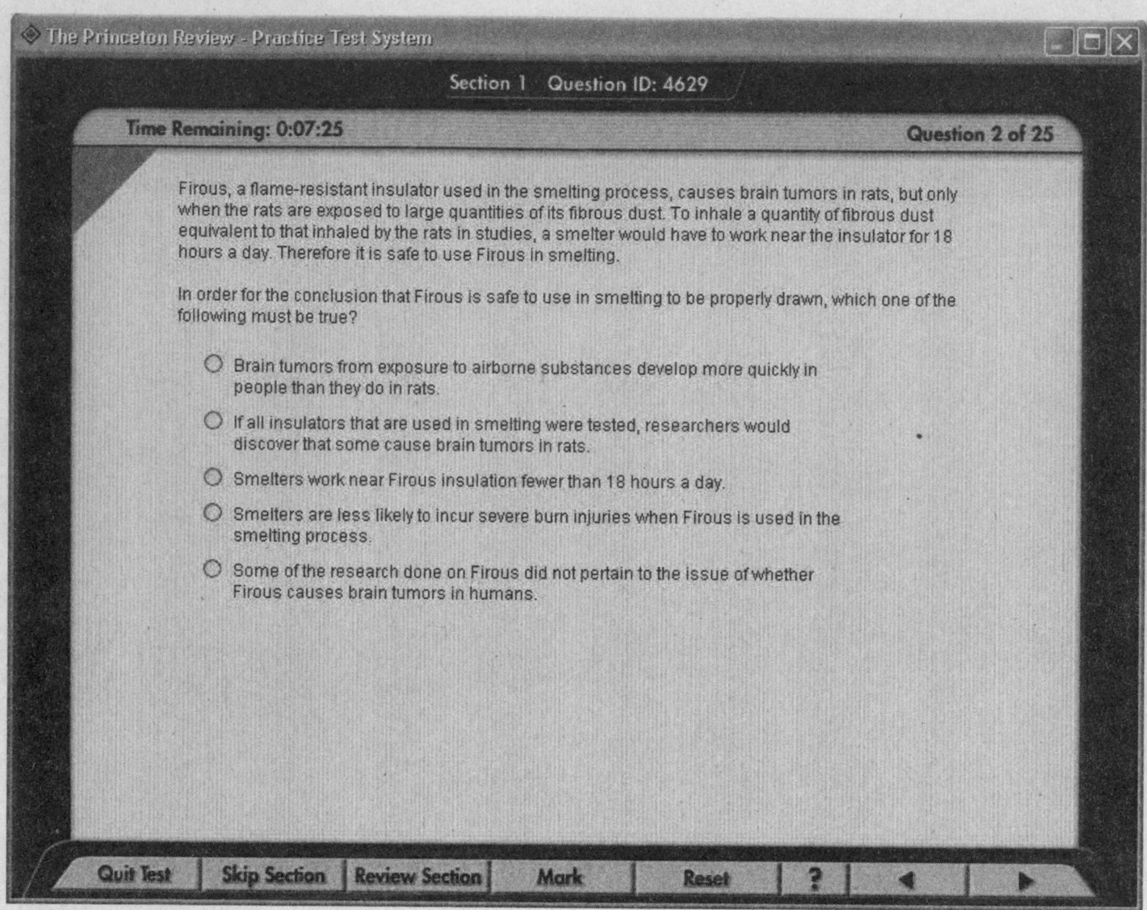

The Princeton Review - Practice Test System
Section 1 Question ID: 4629
Time Remaining: 0:07:25
Question 2 of 25
Firous, a flame-resistant insulator used in the smelting process, causes brain tumors in rats, but only when the rats are exposed to large quantities of its fibrous dust. To inhale a quantity of fibrous dust equivalent to that inhaled by the rats in studies, a smelter would have to work near the insulator for 18 hours a day. Therefore it is safe to use Firous in smelting.
In order for the conclusion that Firous is safe to use in smelting to be properly drawn, which one of the following must be true?
Brain tumors from exposure to airborne substances develop more quickly in people than they do in rats.
If all insulators that are used in smelting were tested, researchers would discover that some cause brain tumors in rats.
Smelters work near Firous insulation fewer than 18 hours a day.
Smelters are less likely to incur severe burn injuries when Firous is used in the smelting process.
Some of the research done on Firous did not pertain to the issue of whether Firous causes brain tumors in humans.
Quit Test
Skip Section
Review Section
Mark
Reset
?

Marking a question is not the same as answering it, and has no effect on your score. Unmark a question by clicking the **Mark** button a second time. Unmarking a question does not erase your answer.

Clicking **Reset** clears your answer to a question, if you wanted to erase your answer before moving onto the next question.

Clicking **? (Help)** reviews directions, lists the tools, and explains their functions.

Left Arrow will take you to the preceding question.

Right Arrow will take you to the very next question in that section, or, if you are on the last question in a section, it will bring you to the first question in the next section. Once you click the **Right Arrow** on the last question in a section, all of the answers you selected in that section will be recorded as your choices. Once you click the **Right Arrow** on the last question of the last section, your entire test will be recorded.

To Uninstall

Windows

1. Select Control Panel from your Start Menu.
2. Click on "Add/Remove Programs."
3. Locate the test that you want to uninstall.
4. Click on the Add/Remove option.

Macintosh

1. Select the Practice Test System folder from your hard drive.
2. Click and drag to the Trash. (Please note that this will uninstall the Practice Test System for all users.)

If you have any questions, please e-mail our Technical Support Center at: techsupport.online@mail.review.com.

ABOUT THE AUTHORS

Adam Robinson was born in 1955. He lives in New York City.

Kevin Blemel started working with The Princeton Review in 1994. Over the years, he has served as a teacher, tutor, and Master Trainer throughout the United States as well as in Bangkok, Thailand. In addition to creating written materials, Kevin has developed educational content for a Distance Learning program that provides web-based instruction. He makes his home in Austin, TX, but can often be seen traveling here and abroad to feed his addictions to taking risks outdoors and to eating anything strange he can get his hands on.

The Princeton Review Admissions Services

At The Princeton Review, we care about your ability to get accepted to the best school for you. But, we all know getting accepted involves much more than just doing well on standardized tests. That's why, in addition to our test preparation services, we also offer free admissions services to students looking to enter college or graduate school. You can find these services on our website, *www.PrincetonReview.com*, the best online resource for researching, applying to, and learning how to pay for the right school for you.

No matter what type of program you're applying to—undergraduate, graduate, law, business, or medical—**PrincetonReview.com has the free tools, services, and advice you need to navigate the admissions process.** Read on to learn more about the services we offer.

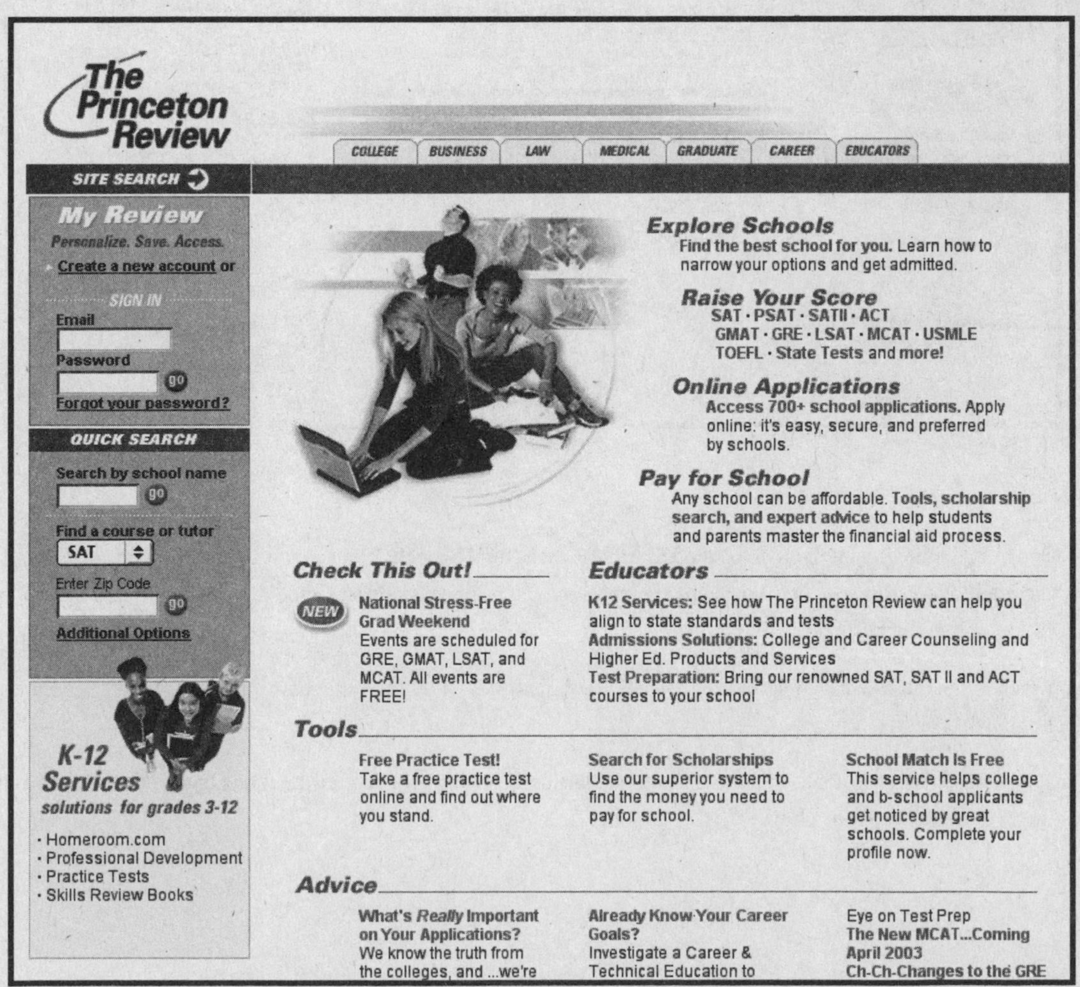

Research Schools
www.PrincetonReview.com/Research

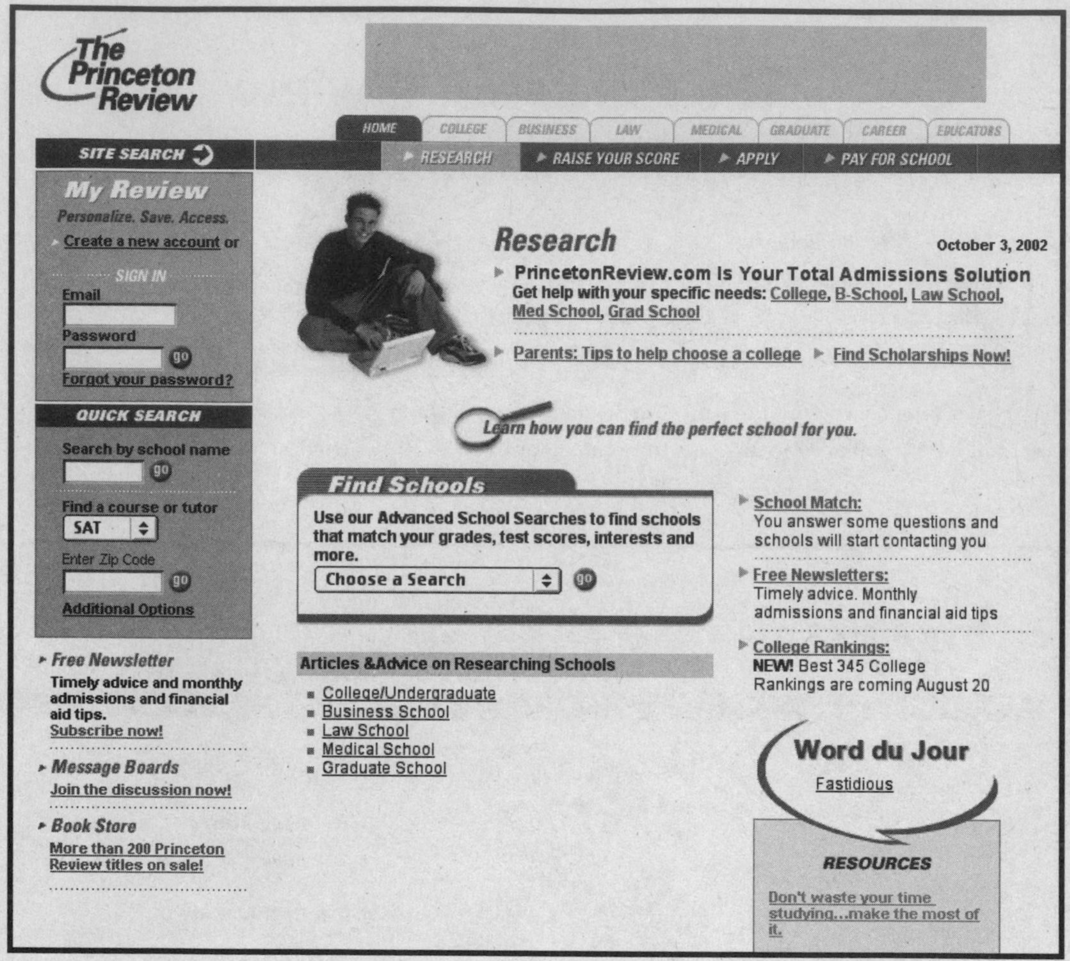

PrincetonReview.com features an interactive tool called **Advanced School Search.** When you use this tool, you enter stats and information about yourself to find a list of schools that fit your needs. From there, you can read statistical and editorial information about every accredited business school, law school, medical school, and graduate school.

If you are applying to business school, make sure to use **School Match**. You tell us your scores, interests, and preferences and Princeton Review partner schools will contact you.

No matter what type of school or specialized program you are considering, **PrincetonReview.com has free articles and advice, in addition to our tools, to help you make the right choice.**

Apply to School
www.PrincetonReview.com/Apply

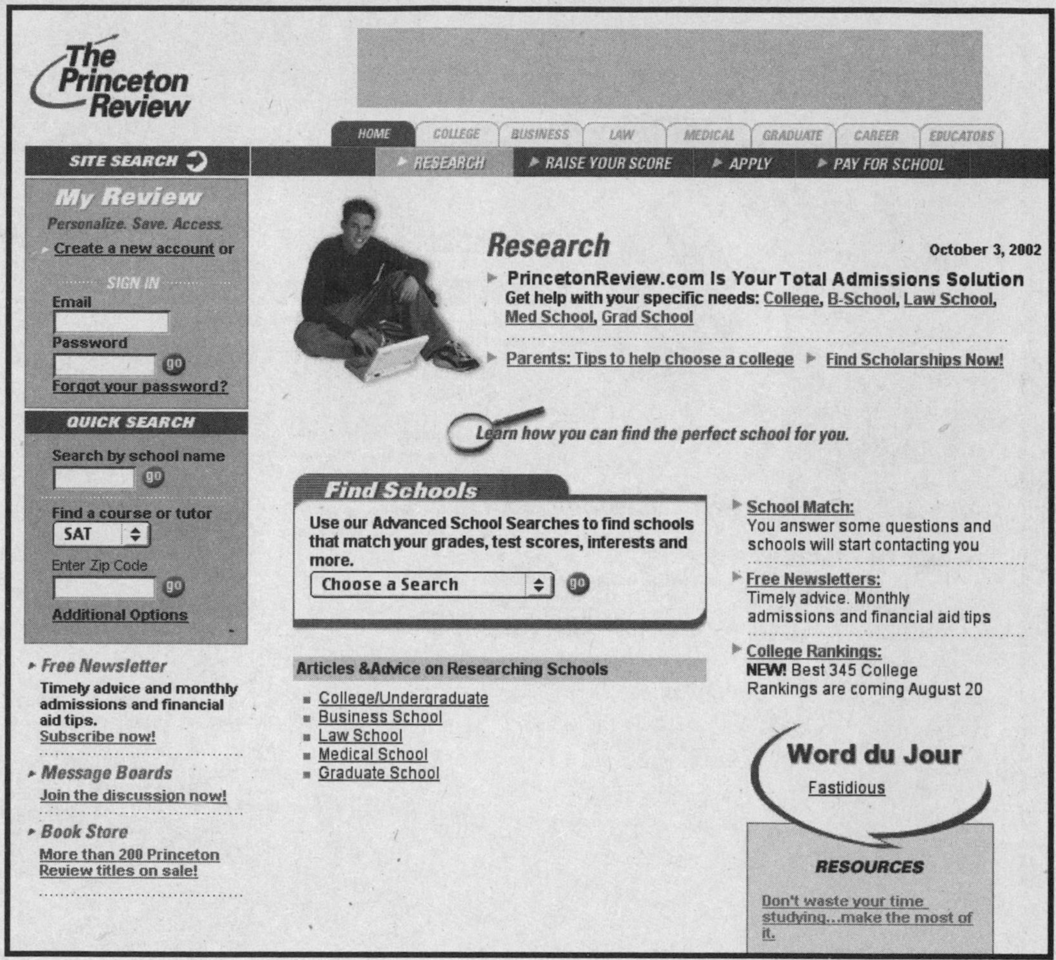

For most students, completing the school application is the most stressful part of the admissions process. PrincetonReview.com's powerful **Online School Application Engine** makes it easy to apply.

Paper applications are mostly a thing of the past. And, our hundreds of partner schools tell us they prefer to receive your applications online.

Using our online application service is simple:

- Enter information once and the common data automatically transfers onto each application.
- Save your applications and access them at any time to edit and perfect.
- Submit electronically or print and mail in.
- Pay your application fee online, using an e-check, or mail the school a check.

Our powerful application engine is built to accommodate all your needs.

Be a Part of the PrincetonReview.com Community

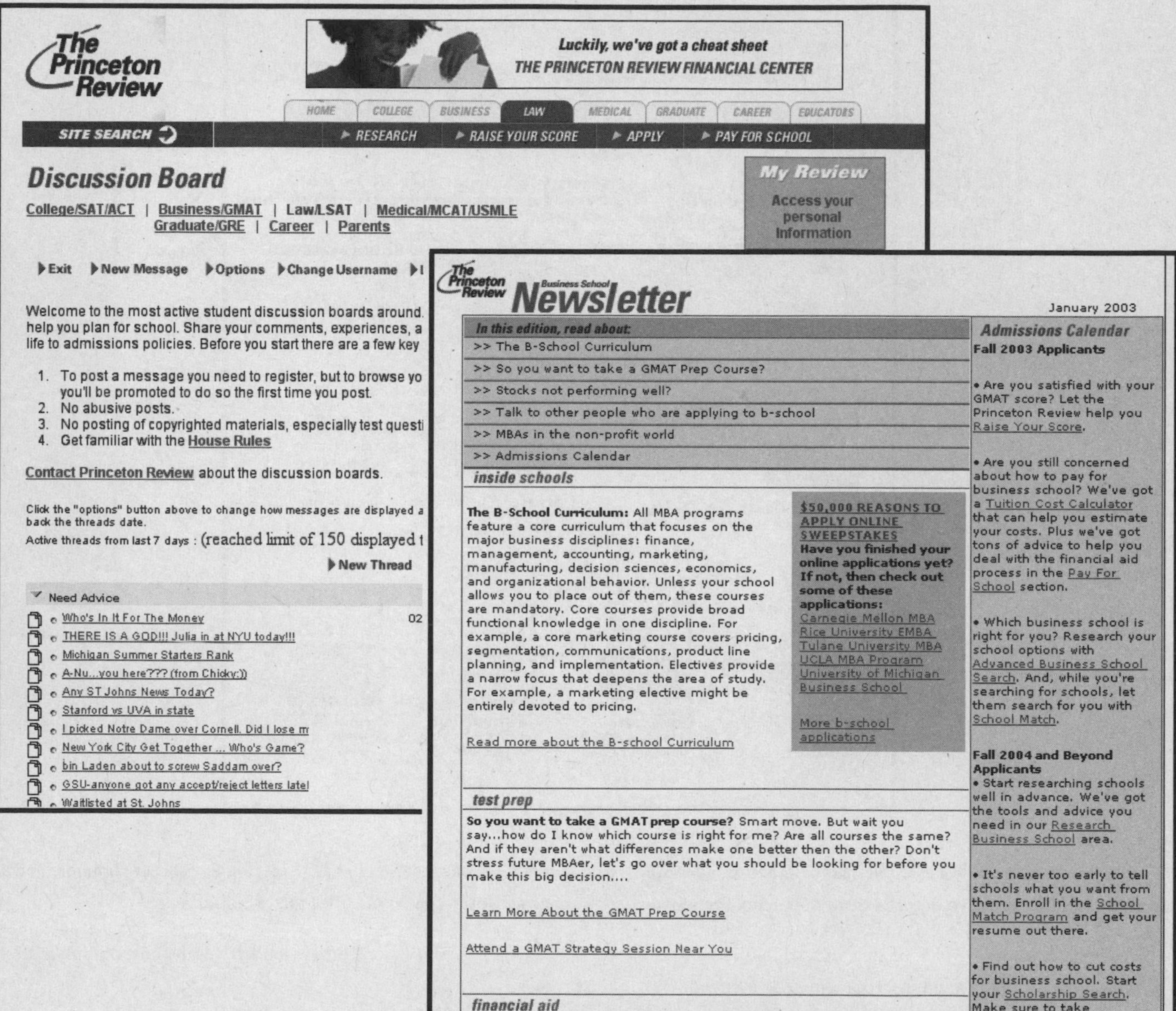

PrincetonReview.com's **Discussion Boards** and **Free Newsletters** are additional services to help you to get information about the admissions process from your peers and from The Princeton Review experts.

Book Store
www.PrincetonReview.com/college/Bookstore.asp

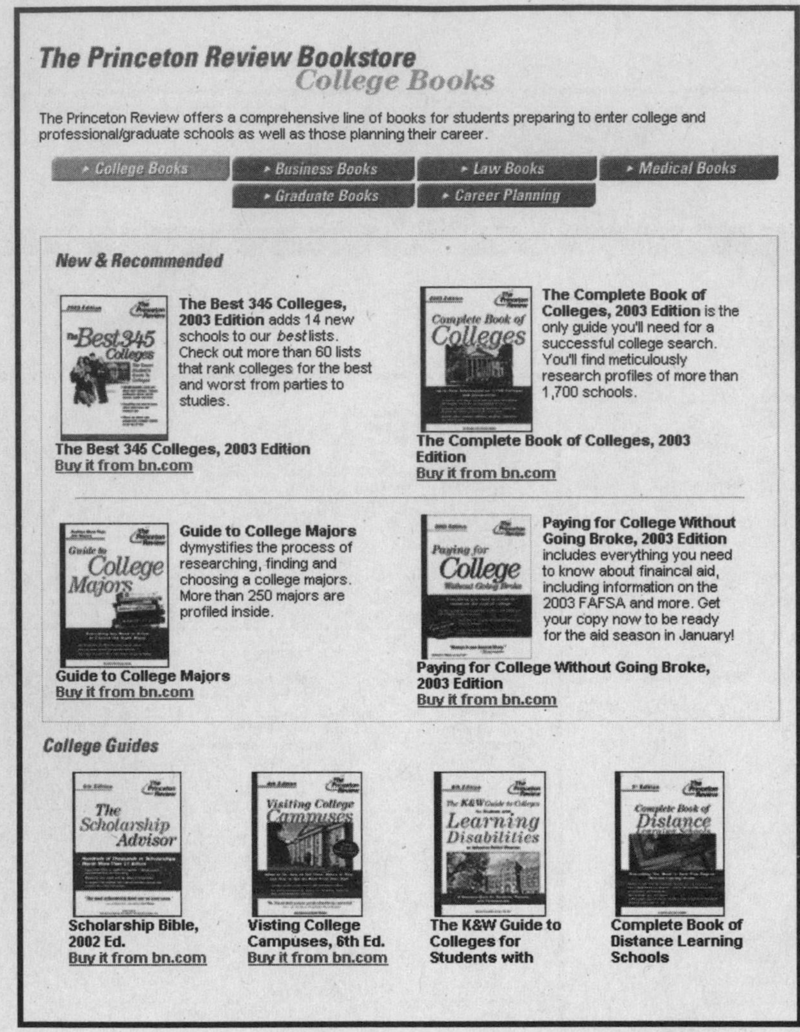
The Princeton Review Bookstore
College Books

The Princeton Review offers a comprehensive line of books for students preparing to enter college and professional/graduate schools as well as those planning their career.

College Books | Business Books | Law Books | Medical Books | Graduate Books | Career Planning

New & Recommended

The Best 345 Colleges, 2003 Edition adds 14 new schools to our *best* lists. Check out more than 60 lists that rank colleges for the best and worst from parties to studies.

The Best 345 Colleges, 2003 Edition
Buy it from bn.com

The Complete Book of Colleges, 2003 Edition is the only guide you'll need for a successful college search. You'll find meticulously research profiles of more than 1,700 schools.

The Complete Book of Colleges, 2003 Edition
Buy it from bn.com

Guide to College Majors dymystifies the process of researching, finding and choosing a college majors. More than 250 majors are profiled inside.

Guide to College Majors
Buy it from bn.com

Paying for College Without Going Broke, 2003 Edition includes everything you need to know about finaincal aid, including information on the 2003 FAFSA and more. Get your copy now to be ready for the aid season in January!

Paying for College Without Going Broke, 2003 Edition
Buy it from bn.com

College Guides

Scholarship Bible, 2002 Ed.
Buy it from bn.com

Visting College Campuses, 6th Ed.
Buy it from bn.com

The K&W Guide to Colleges for Students with

Complete Book of Distance Learning Schools

In addition to this book, we publish hundreds of other titles, including guidebooks that highlight life on campus, student opinion, and all the statistical data that you need to know about any school you are considering. Just a few of the titles that we offer are:

- Complete Book of Business Schools
- Complete Book of Law Schools
- Complete Book of Medical Schools
- The Best 345 Colleges
- The K&W Guide to Colleges for Students with Learning Disabilities or Attention Deficit Disorder
- Guide to College Majors
- Paying for College Without Going Broke

For a complete listing of all of our titles, visit our **online book store**:

ttp://www.princetonreview.com/college/bookstore.asp

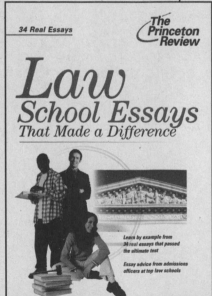